## Books by JAY ROBERT NASH

*Fiction*

ON ALL FRONTS

*Nonfiction*

DILLINGER: DEAD OR ALIVE?
CITIZEN HOOVER, *A Critical Study of the Life and Times*
  *of J. Edgar Hoover and His F.B.I.*
BLOODLETTERS AND BADMEN, *A Narrative Encyclopedia of American*
  *Criminals from the Pilgrims to the Present*
HUSTLERS AND CON MEN, *An Anecdotal History*
  *of the Confidence Man and His Games*
DARKEST HOURS, *A Narrative Encyclopedia of Worldwide Disasters*
  *from Ancient Times to the Present*

*Poetry*

LOST NATIVES & EXPATRIATES

*Theater*

THE WAY BACK
OUTSIDE THE GATES
1947

# AMONG THE MISSING

*An Anecdotal History of Missing Persons*
*from 1800 to the Present*

## by JAY ROBERT NASH

SIMON AND SCHUSTER · NEW YORK

Designed by Irving Perkins
Manufactured in the United States of America


1   2   3   4   5   6   7   8   9   10


Library of Congress Cataloging in Publication Data
Nash, Jay Robert.
    Among the missing.

    Bibliography: p.
    Includes index.
    1. Missing persons—United States—History.
2. Missing persons—History.   I. Title.
HV6762.U5N37        920'.00904        78–540
ISBN  0-671-24005-6

My deepest gratitude goes to James Patrick Agnew, grand friend and *Acknowledgments* tireless coresearcher, who haunted libraries, archives, police stations, and the dark alleyways of the vanished on this book's behalf. My sincere thanks to my loyal friend and typist Carolyn Zozak. To my staff members, Julia Carol Milliken, Nora Forker and Elizabeth Winefield, who labored with additional research, proofreading, indexing, graphics and endless phone work, goes my sincere appreciation. Demanding photographic work was marvelously completed by John Agnew, Jr., and Thomas Buckley; certain investigations conducted for me in Europe by Patrick Agnew and Richard Fuchs were more than helpful. Rare books, memorabilia, broadsheets and fruitful "leads" were generously supplied by James Elkins, John Agnew, Sr., Neil H. Nash, Jack Jules Klein, Jr., Art Kluge, Jim Small, Hank Oettinger, Leonard Des Jardins, Jack Lane, P. Michael O'Sullivan, Sydney Harris, Arnold L. Kaye, Ed and Barbara Kita, Ken Petchenik, Jerry Wall, Edgar Krebs, Phil Krapp, Bob Howe and Larry Goldberg.

A phalanx of reporters, news-service people and professional writers provided much-needed help, and those include Chester Clayton Long, Curt Johnson, Bruce Spivey, Dan McConnell, Bob Abel, Jack Conroy, Ray Peekner, James and Edie McCormick, Jeff Kamen, Raymond Friday Locke, Jay Odell, Neal and Joan Amidei, Marc Davis, Bob Connelly, Catherine Winham, Joseph Longmeyer of *Police Podium,* Jerry Goldberg of the *Orange County* (Calif.) *City News,* John Cannon, *Gallatin* (Tenn.) *Examiner,* Nicki Davis Maude, *Selma* (Ala.) *Times Journal,* Robert D. McFadden, Michael T. Kaufmann, and Tom Wicker of *The New York Times;* Clarence Page, Mike LaVelle, Dick Griffin, Phillip Watley, Anne Keegan of the *Chicago Tribune;* Charles Nicodemus, Barry Felcher, Henry Kisor, Larry S. Finley, Robert Herguth, Mike Royko of the *Chicago Daily News;* Herman Kogan, Philip Nobile, Paul McGrath, Jerry Demuth, Bill Granger, Roger Ebert, Paul Galloway, Tom Fitzpatrick, and Lynn Sweet of the *Chicago Sun-Times;* Jack Lazar, Dave Smothers, Al Wolff, Lou Tempke and Hank Scheafer of *United Press International;* William Kelly, Joe Sherman and Strat Douthat of the *Associated Press* (Wide World).

Many thanks go to the many librarians and archivists who spent time and effort in providing information, chiefly the New York Public Library; Joseph C. Lutz of the Chicago Public Library; Peter Weil, microfilm, and the staff of the Newberry Library of Chicago; Robert C. Miller, assistant director for general services and the reference department at the Joseph Regenstein Library of the University of Chicago; the staff of the microfilm department at Northwestern University; the staff of the John Crerar Library at IIT; the Chicago Historical Society; the New-York Historical Society; the San Francisco Historical Society.

The missing-persons bureaus of many police departments across the

*Acknowledgments*

country were consulted for hard data and I am particularly indebted to Detective John Griffin of the Missing Persons Bureau of the New York Police Department and Lieutenants Bill Bodner, John Doyle and Bill Frost of the Missing Persons Bureau of the Chicago Police Department. Private detectives specializing in missing persons—such as Robert Eisenberg, Director of Investigations for Tracer Company of America, Inc., of New York, and Tony Pellicano of Chicago—were very helpful. Other social agencies checking on missing persons provided wonderful cooperation. These include Mrs. (Colonel) Lloyd Robb, of the Salvation Army, Chicago; Miss Margaret O'Connor, of the American Red Cross, Washington, D.C.; Mrs. Barbara Clauson, of the Seaman's Institute of New York City. Military personnel providing information of great use include Major James Badmai, Department of Defense, Washington, D.C.; Lieutenant Ray Priest, U.S. Marine Corps; Major David Gardiner, U.S. Army; Captain Peter Hefler, U.S. Air Force; Lieutenant John Shackleford, U.S. Navy; Lieutenant Robert O'Brien, U.S. Coast Guard, all with the Department of Public Affairs in Washington, D.C.

Court officials, law and business officers throughout the United States were exceedingly helpful in dealing with missing persons. These include: Tom Bigbee, Record Planning Commission, Canton, Ala.; Irene Thuringer, Deputy Clerk, Probate Dept., Pima County, Tucson, Ariz.; San Mateo County Sheriff's Office, Hall of Justice, Redwood City, Calif.; Carl M. Olsen, Deputy Clerk, San Francisco, Calif.; Susan Cottrell, Deputy, R. D. Zumwalt, County Clerk, San Diego, Calif.; John M. Walker, Chief of Public Services, John J. Corcoran, Acting County Clerk, Los Angeles, Calif.; Nell E. Anderson, Clerk of the District Court, Teller County, Cripple Creek, Col.; Richard P. Brinker, Clerk, probate division of Circuit Court of Miami, Fla.; Harriet L. Gosnell, Trust Officer, Peoples Bank of Bloomington, Ill.; John T. Curry, Circuit Clerk, Probate Division, Macon County, Ill.; Leland Larrison, Clerk, Probate Court, Terre Haute, Ind.; St. Joseph County Health Department, South Bend, Ind.; Mildred Gonder, Deputy Clerk, Probate Court, New Albany, Ind.; Sarah Montjoy, Deputy Clerk, Bremer Ehrler, Clerk, Jefferson County Court, Probate Division, Louisville, Ky.; Elisabeth F. Sachse, Deputy Clerk of court, Baton Rouge, La.; James B. Kelley, Jr., Register, Probate Court, Taunton, Mass.; Mrs. Lana J. Olson, Register of Probate, Luce County, Newberry, Mich.; County Court, Probate Division, Olmsted County, Minn.; Jean Smith, Deputy Clerk of court, Watonwan County, St. James, Minn.; Carole J. Hals, Deputy Clerk, County Court, Probate Division, Stark, Minn.; Director of Licensing, Public Service Level, Minneapolis, Minn.; Lorna Pierce, secretary to Judge Donald Gunn, Probate Court of St. Louis, Mo.; Probate Clerk, Storey County, Nevada; C. Edward Bourassa, Register of Probate, Hillsborough County Probate Court, Nashua, N.H.;

Virginia Crane, Deputy Court Clerk, Neptune, N.J.; Surrogates Court of Essex, N.J.; Nancy M. Spaulding, Chief Clerk, Schoharie, N.Y.; Madelina S. Marting, Deputy Clerk, Putnam County, N.Y.; C. Fatni, Record Clerk, Surrogate's court, Kings County, N.Y.; William J. Regan, Judge of the Surrogates Court, Buffalo, N.Y.; Julia Kowrak, Register of Wills, City Hall, Philadelphia, Pa.; Probate Court, City Hall, Providence, R.I.; B. J. Dunavant, Clerk of the Probate Court, Shelby County, Memphis, Tenn.; Jackie Griffin, Chief Deputy, Ellis County, Tex.; David M. Warren, Assistant Chief Deputy, Probate Courts Department, Harris County, Houston, Tex.; Probate Court, Port Arthur, Tex.; Mildred Fulton, County Clerk, Cherokee County, Rusk, Tex.; Joan R. Saunder, Deputy Register of Wills, Clerk of the Probate Division, Washington, D.C.; Arlene D. Connors, Deputy Register in Probate, Milwaukee County, Milwaukee, Wisc.

7

# Contents

Since childhood, when I discovered that my own Aunt Florence had disappeared following a notification from the Red Cross of her existence in war-torn Bucharest, Rumania, the chasm of the missing has held great interest for me. Among my special collections of books, memorabilia and documents, the files of the missing grew to bloated proportions each year.

With the documentation grew the wonder of how and why those fabulous disappearances occurred—an obsession with discovery, as it were, beyond the love of the mystery surrounding any missing person, celebrated or obscure. To be sure, the famous in their absences embraced most of the headlines: the odd "literary" disappearances of Agatha Christie and Sherwood Anderson; the devastating "political" vanishing acts of Judge Joseph Force Crater and President Grover Cleveland; the lost adventurers Colonel Percy Fawcett, Richard Halliburton, and George Leigh-Mallory; the mysteries of Amelia Earhart and Lionel Crabb; the vacuums into which Aimee Semple McPherson and others abruptly stepped.

Yet there were others, thousands of them, whose names are little remembered but whose disappearances are marked by unforgettable, bizzare circumstances—persons who vanished inside ship staterooms; while swimming underwater; while walking around the corner, through a doorway, into a fog. Many were victims—abducted for sexual purposes, kidnapped for profit, murdered out of revenge or to keep them from revealing explosive knowledge. Others slipped away of their own accord, forsaking family, friends, and the security of an established life for the love of another. Scores were drawn into oblivion by their own minds' turning blank, or by following the siren calls of adventure and treasure. Then there were those whose crimes—from white collar embezzlement to dark-hooded murder—pushed them into the world of the lost, and many more who heartlessly arranged their own disappearances for money or for obscure reasons known only to the heart. And there were the rogues who stepped forward as outrageous impostors to collect what wealth awaited those who had disappeared, and even more sinister, the scabrous crooks who bilked the relatives of the missing with fraudulent promises.

Early in my research into this field, it became obvious that to chronicle every disappearance on record would be impossible, although I closely inspected many thousands of cases. I selected those that seemed the most dramatic and informative, the most entertaining and arcane; there were innumerable cases, like those occurring in the Bermuda Triangle, that do not and never will have logical solutions. Those hundreds of cases related herein are, I hope, a representative cross-section of the great number of disappearances that have been recorded in the last two centuries, or even much earlier.

Documenting in detail the hordes of persons missing as a result of modern warfare was impossible. The available statistics in this category of the lost, released to the author by Washington officials, will give the reader some idea of the staggering numbers involved: World War I, 4,500; World War II, 139,709; Korea, 4,753; Vietnam, 733. In addition to these figures there are overwhelming numbers of persons—many millions each year—from runaway children to wandering adults, who take a brief respite from their everyday lives but who return in a matter of days, most within hours.

Whenever possible, the reasons for the disappearances described here are explained, but many remain enigmatic and puzzling. The puzzle is the goad, because there is in most of us a wide-eyed fascination with the baffling world of the vanished. Theory is easy when a fate fashioned by the subject's fear befalls another, even one very close in friendship or family. But beyond our unsubstantiated theories, we are mostly left with the haunting fact of the disappearance, a brief ending that gnaws for explanation; and for those whose lives are touched and changed by the disappearance, there are undying memories and unrelenting apprehension.

Hopefully, this book will illuminate the world of the missing and in many respects portray the story of the common man, the very person whose predictable, planned life is so drastically altered. Moreover, these documented tales should remind us that any one of us can vanish—businessman or homemaker, prisoner or king—though comforted by the misleading thought that we are fixed in our time, rooted on our earth, and in utter possession of our separate futures.

JAY ROBERT NASH
Chicago, 1977

# AMONG THE MISSING

*Escape*

*to*

*Love*

Of those who step into oblivion, missing persons who become part of a terrible unknown, none appeals to our sense of romance more than those who slip away for reasons of the heart. Unlike the dark and sinister characters portrayed elsewhere in these pages, those who disappear out of love are generally driven by hot emotion, totally unaware that blind affection has taken them into the realms of the ridiculous, the bizarre, and sometimes the tragically fatal.

Such was the case in the classic vanishing act of Austrian Crown Prince Rudolf and his mistress, Baroness Maria Vetsera, who disappeared in 1889. They were discovered later at Mayerling, the royal hunting lodge, dead of a double suicide. No less spectacular was the violent end of chemical genius Dr. Ernest Watzl and his gorgeous lover, model Mary Horvath MacGranahan.

### Beau Geste of a Lost Husband

Viennese-born Dr. Ernest Watzl was one of the most respected residents of Cleveland, Ohio, a chemical wizard who had worked for the Austrian government in American chemical factories to learn about new inventions and devices employed in modern warfare. Watzl arrived in Cleveland in 1912, a dapper, monocled twenty-two-year-old whose volatile temper had already involved him in a number of sword and pistol duels. He married an American girl and returned to Austria with her at the outbreak of World War I. Watzl fought on the Italian front as captain of a liquid-fire division. The horrible mass deaths he wreaked upon the enemy gave him nightmares for years.

He returned with his wife and two small children to the United States following the war. His marriage seemed solid, and there was no indication that this devoted forty-year-old family man with an international reputation in chemistry was about to forsake all for the charms of a woman twenty years his junior. But Mrs. Mary Horvath MacGranahan, a secretary-model whom Watzl employed in late 1929, was a devastating redhead of curvaceous form and lusty appetite. Watzl found her irresistible, and they plunged into a love affair, with meetings in small hotel rooms or traumatic trysts in his office.

*Dr. Ernest Watzl, gallant missing husband, 1929.* (UPI)

The proper Austrian, however, felt that such a clandestine affair lacked grace and style. Watzl concluded that it was time to disappear with his tempestuous lover. But he was still a family man at heart and could not bear to think of his wife, Marie, and his two children, Herta and Jane, left without funds. A good, clean death was the answer, at least a death that the world, his wife, and the insurance company (with which he had taken out a $60,000 policy) would accept without suspicion.

Watzl and Mary packed and left their families as they slept on a dark night in late October 1929. They drove east in Watzl's car until they reached the Schuylkill River outside the hamlet of Ryersford, Pennsylvania. Watzl removed their bags from the car and, using a chemical he had specially prepared for the occasion, ignited the car; then, with Mary's help, he pushed the blazing auto into the rushing river.

"We are now dead," Watzl told his lover as they walked along the night-enshrouded road gripping their luggage.

"And free," Mary whispered.

After Watzl's disappearance there was a great alarm. City and state police, plus the entire diplomatic contingent of the Austrian government, searched for him in a dozen states. (His father was one of the largest manufacturers in Austria; his mother and brother-in-law held high offices in the Austrian government.) The burned-out car was quickly found and it was speculated that Watzl had been murdered for his chemical-warfare secrets. But there was no body. The search went on, week after week, month after month, until authorities on four continents were frantically looking for the absent chemist, a new theory being that Watzl had been abducted by a foreign power, and its sinister agents were holding him until they could extract his chemical formulas. The chemist's faked death had exploded in his face, and instead of being allowed to slip quietly into anonymity, he was now hunted worldwide.

Four months later, on March 24, two shots rang out in a Viennese hotel. Employees of the Hotel Sacher ran into a small room and found a beautiful red-headed woman shot through the heart, her companion dead alongside her in the bed, both neatly dressed down to polished shoes. The man had a bullet wound in his head.

Registered in the hotel as Johann Flassak and Josefa Kropej, the couple were subsequently identified as Dr. Ernest Watzl and Mary MacGranahan. They had left notes; they had also mailed letters to the United States on the last day of their lives. Not only were they tired of running but, as Watzl explained in one note, he was so penniless that he could not afford to pay the next premium on the insurance policy for his family's support. He told Mary when the insurance premium came due. They had sat together the night before, sipping wine. He killed her and then himself only a few minutes before midnight. (Watzl had prepared well, paying exorbitant premiums for a policy that, indeed, covered suicide.)

Some time after the double suicide, Marie Watzl received a letter from Vienna in which Watzl told her: "I want to thank you for all kindness, love, and patience, and loyalty you have shown me for so many years. Forgive me if you can. I thought honestly that you and the children would be happier with me gone and some safe income." Marie Watzl was a forgiving wife, writing to authorities in Austria that her husband and Mrs. MacGranahan should be cremated and their mingled ashes be placed in a common urn, as was their last request. Watzl, however, was buried quietly outside Vienna by his high-born family, and Mary's body was returned to the United States, where her husband, who had filed suit for divorce shortly after her disappearance, reluctantly buried her in a Cleveland cemetery.

Watzl's last letter to a friend revealed him to be a man of old-world honor, capable beyond his obsessive love affair of a grand gesture, that of taking his life for his family's sake. "My wife will be robbed unless I die today," he had written. He then related his nomadic odyssey. Following the fake accident, he explained, "I first went to New York, where I bought a fake passport in the name of Flassak and secretly married Mary MacGranahan. Fearing recognition, we determined to quit New York, which we did, and went to Canada.

"In Canada we were nearly caught, so we decided to go to the Coast and take a steamer across the Pacific. We did so, sailing to Tokyo, where I hoped to find a job, but quickly realized there was no chance, so we went to India. Here we bought jewelry and trinkets, which will be found in our luggage. Leaving India, we went to London, but stopped there only a short time, pushing on to Vienna.

"But the $5,000 I took from my bank at Philadelphia after my automobile escapade was soon eaten up. We were faced with two alternatives: Either to go to my parents and relatives and ask assistance and confess my misdemeanors, or to commit suicide. I preferred the latter."

Another posthumous letter arrived in Cleveland, addressed to Mrs. MacGranahan's mother. The love-infected artist's model told her mother that Watzl, just before he shot himself with his army revolver, had asked her to return to Cleveland—"but I love Ernest more than my life and I want to die with him. Do not worry about me dying. . . . It is really nothing. Everyone has to die." It was all ordained, Mary wrote, and she added the postscript: "We went to Japan, China, Sumatra, India, Arabia, Egypt, Africa, France, Italy and Austria. I had a delightful time."

### A Legion of Missing Lovers

No matter how tragic the cases of lost lovers might appear to be, they still contain moments of absurd macabre humor. In 1898 a New England heiress named Grace Marian Perkins disappeared without a trace. Her parents initiated a nationwide search for her. Months later the parents positively identified the body of a murder victim as that of their daughter, and preparations were made for an elaborate funeral. In the middle of the ceremony, the real Grace Perkins burst into the chapel and angrily denounced her startled parents for making a laughingstock of her. She had run away to get married, she shouted to those assembled, and now her honeymoon had been ruined.

Often, parental objections to a daughter's choice of fiance have precipitated a defiant marriage and have led to many a missing person. Such was the case of Mary Hortense Smith, daughter of a New Orleans real-estate magnate. She vanished after her father voiced his disapproval of her fiance in 1882 and waited forty-eight years before contacting her brother in 1930, to inform him that she was residing in Denver, Colorado—happily married to the man she had run off with five decades earlier.

A year after Mary Smith announced her existence, a wealthy

young socialite in Nashville, Tennessee, Thomas Craighead Buntin, disappeared, leaving a wife and three small sons. Six weeks after Buntin was declared missing in November 1931, his former secretary, Betty McCuddy, also vanished. Buntin had been drinking heavily and was deep in debt, squandering the $300-a-month salary he received from his millionaire grandfather's insurance firm as well as a $200-a-month allowance from his widowed mother.

What elevated the Buntin case above the myriad disappearances, particularly in that dark year of the depression, was that considerable money was involved, including a $50,000 life-insurance policy on Buntin, an amount his wife demanded after waiting seven years and then moving to have her husband legally declared dead. Relatives of the twenty-four-year-old Betty McCuddy asked that she, too, be declared dead; they insisted that she had lost the right to a fifth interest in her wealthy uncle's estate. In 1937 Betty's share of the estate, more than $125,000, was awarded to relatives.

The New York Life Insurance Company was reluctant to settle Buntin's $50,000 insurance case, but the Tennessee Supreme Court ruled that the alcoholic Buntin would not have had the physical strength or the mental ability to survive.

It was revealed how Buntin, a man with a dazzling future, had seemed to go to pieces at the age of twenty-eight. He was already the general manager of his grandfather's lucrative insurance company. He owned two cars and a luxurious home and was loved by an attractive wife. Yet the tall, handsome executive sank into moody depressions. He drank himself into stupors and at such times talked wildly about committing suicide, just as his father had done. His wife wakened one night to find Buntin sitting on the edge of their bed with a pistol held to his head; she knocked it out of his hand. One September afternoon in 1931 the fitful executive inexplicably broke down the door of two terrified spinsters and began to wreck their home before police hauled him screaming to a lockup. Two days later he disappeared, and Buntin's Nashville friends immediately concluded that he had moved off like some wounded animal to perform the suicide he had so earnestly vowed to commit.

The insurance was finally paid, and the money was placed in a trust fund for Buntin's three sons, along with an impressive inheritance from Buntin's mother.

*"We were in love," said Betty McCuddy, when explaining why she and her playboy boss, Thomas Craighead Buntin, had vanished twenty-two years earlier.* (UPI)

Then in 1953—twenty-two years after the disappearances—Inspector Wallace Murray, insurance sleuth for New York Life, discovered that Buntin, using an alias, was alive somewhere in Texas, in a citrus-growing area. How Murray came by these peculiar facts was never explained, but the aroused *Nashville Tennesseean* determined to find the missing Buntin.

This impossible task fell to one of its young reporters, John Seigenthaler, who was simply told to scour Texas looking for a thin man with a protruding left ear, an unnatural defect of Buntin's. Seigenthaler began his strange quest by moving through one Texas town after another, haunting the police stations, hotels, and credit bureaus. He fell asleep in bus stations eyeing the passengers. Just as the young reporter was about to wire his paper that the effort was useless, he spotted a tall, gray-haired man with spectacles limping from a bus in Orange, Texas. The elderly man had an oddly-shaped left ear.

Seigenthaler followed the limping man to a suburb and watched him enter a small one-story house. The reporter learned that the man's name was Thomas D. Palmer, a television salesman. His motherly-looking wife was named Betty. Seigenthaler confronted them with his suspicions. The couple hesitated for a moment and then admitted that they were Thomas Buntin and Betty McCuddy. The reporter hastily offered them a thousand dollars for their exclusive story.

"If money had meant anything to us," Betty McCuddy replied, "we wouldn't have done what we did. We were in love."

They told their tale of life together after leaving Nashville, a course of love that, for years, was as hardscrabble as any back road they traveled. The road first led to Brownsville, where Buntin continued to drink, losing one service-man or car-salesman job after another. One night he fell from a curb in a drunken haze and broke his hip so severely that he was compelled to use crutches for years. Slowly, he sobered, Betty staying at his side, working to support him and their growing family.

The man the court had declared hopeless, a man who could not survive without the cozy insulation of his family's wealth, began to drink less and to hold onto jobs. By the time the runaway lovers were found they had two married daughters, a son in the Marine

Corps, a crippled fourteen-year-old boy named Duncan, and two younger girls. The Palmers had built a fortress out of their family. The story of their elopement and conjugal life abroad was an old one to them, but it enthralled newspaper readers throughout the nation.

Buntin's bigamous marriage was ignored; his first wife had remarried in 1944 to Louie Phillips, one of Nashville's leading lawyers. When the story broke, Thomas Craighead Buntin talked with his aged mother by phone for the first time in twenty-two years. Betty McCuddy also called home and discovered that her mother and only brother had died during her absence. Her seventy-six-year-old father was alive and delighted. "I have a family again," he said. Days after the couple were exposed, their Orange, Texas, neighbors sent them flowers.

## The Irreverent Reverend

Neighbors, relatives and the world in general were less forgiving with the Reverend Cornelius Densel, who disappeared from his pastorship in Passaic, New Jersey, in 1920, forsaking his family for a pretty member of his flock, one Trina Hannenberg.

A steady man and an unchipped pillar of the Netherlands Reform Church of Passaic, Reverend Mr. Densel had been pastor for eleven years without the slightest suggestion that his was a double life. Before the other side of his character was discovered by his loyal flock, the Reverend Densel had quietly disappeared. On November 12, 1920, he appeared shivering outside the home of his married daughter, Mrs. William Donkersloot, murmuring to her at the front door that he "was going on a trip, that's all, going on a long trip." An hour later, Densel slipped into his church and left his letter of resignation on the first pew. That afternoon he vanished, leaving a wife and eight children and the congregation flabbergasted.

One dedicated member of Densel's church was not astounded. The day following the pastor's disappearance, Trina Hannenberg, twenty-six-year-old choir singer and daughter of one of the church's leading elders, picked up her purse and left home. Her little sister

*Trina Hannenberg fled with her married pastor, the Reverend Cornelius Densel, in 1921.*
(UPI)

accompanied her to the end of the block. Trina's last words to her were: "I don't think I shall ever return."

Police investigated, and Passaic buzzed with the twin disappearances. Carl Tilton, the stationmaster of the Erie Railroad, reported that the Reverend Mr. Densel had purchased two single tickets to New York.

Mrs. Densel and her eight children attended church every day the Reverend was missing. Next to them sat the Hannenberg family. All prayed fervently for the safe return of the parson and the choir singer. From the pulpit Cornelius Vander Hoven, an elder who had temporarily assumed Densel's spiritual chores, boomed: "I urge you fellow churchgoers, do not prejudge the pastor's actions."

Almost a month passed and it came time for the church elders to choose another pastor. A meeting was held at which time the elders not only made their replacement suggestions but argued as to the religious significance of not expelling the entire Hannenberg family from their midst. Just as the elders fell to arguing over their highly publicized scandals, Reverend Cornelius Densel burst through the door. Accompanied by two of his sons, Densel, his face running rivers of tears, moved slowly about the Sunday-school room, reaching for the hands of the elders and begging the forgiveness of each.

But the world of the Reverend Densel would not permit it. His disappearance with Trina was damning enough, but to return and ask that he be reinstated was unthinkable. Densel was ousted, and to show that the church members were not gullible dupes, the elders also expelled Trina and her parents. Said one elder: "They were missing and we prayed for them. They fooled us. They lived . . . and together. It would be better if they never came back."

## The Girl in the Baker Chapeau

Countless missing lovers never came back. The most celebrated of these cases, a stupefying mystery, was the unknown fate that befell Dorothy Harriet Camille Arnold, the niece of United States Supreme Court Justice Rufus Peckham and an heiress to one of the more bloated Manhattan fortunes. There was never any doubt that the twenty-five-year-old heiress was desperately in love with a forty-two-year-old ne'er-do-well. The Bryn Mawr graduate, class of 1905, whose life was outwardly as conservative and proper as that of the Reverend Densel, had taken several secret trips with one George Griscom, Jr., from New York to various trysting places in Boston. Though Griscom was the scion of a wealthy family himself, Dorothy always paid the way. On one occasion the couple spent the heiress' money so freely that Dorothy was compelled to pawn some of her jewelry to pay the staggering hotel bill.

Dorothy, however, always returned home to resume the rigid Edwardian style of living expected of a rich girl of her social position, her parents and friends none the wiser about her clandestine affair. Her daily routine was one of casual shopping through the better stores along Fifth Avenue, quiet tearoom luncheons with other single girls of her stratum, and special debutante balls and fetes. December 12, 1910, was not unlike any other day in Dorothy Arnold's life, except that toward the close of that day she vanished forever.

Leaving her stately home at 108 East 79th Street, Dorothy ventured forth to buy a dress to wear at her younger sister's upcoming debut. It was 11 A.M. She was attired in handsome, expensive clothes: a hip-length coat over a dress that went to her high-buttoned suede shoes, flimsy fringe jiggling at the bottom. One hand was tucked into a silver-fox muff, and the other clutched a satin handbag containing thirty-six dollars, which she had recently withdrawn from her bank account. On her head rested an enormous monstrosity, a "Baker" hat, the most desired chapeau of the day, its black velvet brim and crown bedecked with artificial roses.

On her walk into oblivion, Dorothy met and talked with many friends. The plumpish, somewhat square-faced Dorothy walked almost two miles to Park & Tilford's at 59th Street, where she charged a box of chocolates to the family account. Cold as the day was, Dorothy set out on an even longer trek that brought her to the 27th Street Brentano's bookstore; such distances were not unusual for Dorothy, whose solid, almost hefty body was equal to the strain. As she emerged from the bookstore, Dorothy ran into another society girl, Gladys King, who noticed that she was carrying a copy of Emily Calvin Blake's *An Engaged Girl's Sketches*. They chatted briefly about attending the debut of Dorothy's sister. Then, waving goodbye, the girls parted, Dorothy walking across Fifth Avenue and into the dense afternoon crowds. It was the last time that anyone was known to have seen her.

When Dorothy failed to arrive at home that night the Arnolds quietly phoned friends, but no one had seen her that evening. Days passed, and the Arnold family, disdaining to call in the police, as was the custom of the rich in such indelicate matters, quietly employed a number of private detectives. They turned up nothing.

Six weeks after their daughter's disappearance, the Arnolds finally called the police and held a formal press conference. No, Dorothy was not in the habit of disappearing. She led a restricted, controlled life, Mrs. Arnold crisply told reporters, with no men in it. (She was unaware of George Griscom's involvement at this point.)

One brash newsman leaned forward and stared into the scowling face of Dorothy's father, the venerable Francis R. Arnold, the martinet boss of F. R. Arnold & Company, importers, a seventy-three-year-old merchant whose ancestors went back to the *Mayflower*. "Do you object to your daughter keeping company with men?" inquired the reporter.

Arnold exploded. "It is not true that I objected to her having men call at the house! I would have been glad to see her associate more with young men than she did, especially some young men of brains and position, one whose profession or business would keep him occupied. I don't approve of young men who have nothing to do."

The last line of Arnold's hortatory speech, newsmen later discovered, was a direct reference to the playboy Griscom. (Arnold, by that time, had learned that Griscom had secretly visited Dorothy.) Dorothy's father plunged on, embarrassed to admit that his daughter had romantic notions about writing and that he had found some of the short stories she had penned hidden in her room. (Dorothy had written two stories, "Poinsettia Flames" and "Lotus Leaves," both of which had been rejected by *McClure's Magazine;* her family had teased her unmercifully about her literary ambitions, and when she casually mentioned to her father that she might move to Greenwich Village to continue her writing career, he had shouted: "A good writer can write anywhere," and he forbade her to leave home.)

"Were the stories any good?".

Arnold shook his head and told the reporters, "Drivel, that's all!" Naturally, he had burned them.

One of Dorothy's memos to herself, it was later discovered, struck a despondent note concerning her literary efforts. *"McClure's* has turned me down. Failure stares me in the face. All I can see ahead is a long road with no turning." The blue-eyed heiress added a cryptic line that has haunted police and historians ever after: "Mother will always think it was an accident."

Scandal-scenting reporters soon discovered the existence of George Griscom, and the details of his secret affair with Dorothy Arnold burst into the press, rocking New York society. The playboy was conveniently in Florence, Italy, at the time the story broke; he insisted by cable that he knew nothing of Dorothy's vanishing act. Although Mr. Arnold told reporters that his wife had retired to a

*One of the many thousands of posters issued by the family of heiress Dorothy Arnold through the New York Police Department in their search for their missing daughter.*

country estate to relieve her apprehensions about her daughter, Mrs. Arnold was, at the time, on a secret mission. She and her son had sailed to Italy in search of the missing Dorothy. All they found was George Griscom, a stereotypical "mama's boy" who insisted that all his friends call him "Junior," seemingly perplexed by the whole affair. Dorothy's brother John angrily throttled the rich bachelor and threatened to "soundly thrash" him unless he provided information as to Dorothy's whereabouts. The terrified Griscom cowered as he turned over the love letters he had received from the missing girl over the two-year period before she vanished. None of them gave the meagerest hint as to what might have happened to the heiress.

When Griscom did return to the United States, he took great pains to appear desperate to locate Dorothy, placing "Come Home" ads in all the newspapers. They were never answered. Police were stymied. There were no clues, no trails to follow. The missing heiress was reported as having been seen in more than a hundred cities, "recognized" by newspaper readers. All of these identifications proved false. Francis Arnold spent more than $100,000 to recover his daughter. Private detectives, including the much-vaunted Pinkertons, turned up nothing. Thousands of letters from crackpots flooded the Arnold family. One writer doggedly claimed that he had seen the heiress in a small Mexican town, drugged and compelled by white slavers to perform lewd acts in a bordello. Another letter-writer talked of seeing Dorothy in Honolulu, strolling on the beach with a handsome young man. The wackiest correspondent, a crackpot supernaturalist, wrote that on the day Dorothy disappeared a beautiful white swan was seen to appear out of nowhere in the Central Park lagoon. The heiress, he pointed out with scientific mumbojumbo, had been transformed. (Francis Arnold to the end of his life must have been moved by this particular "vision," for he insisted on his deathbed that his daughter had been murdered in Central Park.)

Francis Arnold died in 1922, his wife in 1928. Their wills were identical in their references to the missing heiress: "I have made no provision for my beloved daughter, Dorothy H. C. Arnold, as I am satisfied that she is not alive."

Six years after the girl's disappearance, a Rhode Island convict released a story to the press in which he claimed that he had been paid $150 to dig a grave for the heiress. He was paid, he stated, by a young man of great wealth. His description of the man was strikingly similar to that of George Griscom, Jr. The convict stated that Dorothy had died following a "secret operation" and was buried at night in the cellar of a house near West Point. Police dug up scores of cellars in West Point and unearthed nothing.

Police Captain John H. Ayers, newly appointed head of New York City's Missing Persons Bureau, did little more than confuse matters in April 1921, when he told a group of high-school students in a lecture that the police had known for years the exact and terrible fate of the missing Dorothy Arnold. Ayers was grilled about his off-hand comments but steadfastly refused to impart any information (the Arnold file in the Missing Persons Bureau in New York is open as of this writing). The captain obviously had been seeking to impress the students and never possessed any pertinent information on the case.

John S. Keith, lawyer for the Arnold family, didn't believe any of it. It was he who often had escorted Dorothy to social functions and who, at the request of the Arnolds, was the first to act as sleuth in the disappearance before the Pinkertons and police were called into the case. For weeks Keith searched morgues, hospitals, and jails in Philadelphia, Boston and New York, inspecting corpses, prisoners and patients before giving up.

It was later said that Dorothy Arnold had committed suicide over Griscom's refusal to marry her, jumping from a Fall River ferryboat one night. Others gossiped that the wealthy girl had become pregnant and was living in a remote chalet in Switzerland, that her publicity-conscious parents had sent her away to live out her life in seclusion for her sins. The most persistent theory of the heiress' disappearance was that she had gone to an abortionist on the day she vanished and had died on the operating table, the quack who performed the highly illegal operation later disposing of her body. But in the end it was only theory. The girl in the Baker hat was never found.

### A Sister Snatched from Glory

She was not a sign of the times. She *was* the times—all the neurotic, ebullient desires for spree and pleasure pent up in the nation before the 1920s, the Jazz Age, the era of the flapper, exploded in a universal adoration of trivia and nonsense. The rise of Aimee Semple McPherson, "the world's most pulchritudinous evangelist," as she billed herself, was ordained not in heaven but through muted saxophones, short skirts, bad booze and a worse law that suppressed it. She was the product, spanking new and hollering for Jesus, of a national mental relapse.

The religious stodginess of the past coupled with America's first modern war of attrition had produced a cross-country listlessness that every citizen was desperate to discard. City and farm folk alike bellied up to speakeasy bars, and others, tens of thousands knowing they were surrounded by bathtub sin, poured into the tents and makeshift churches of revivalists and religious "healers," eager for a new kind of religion that would truly redeem without the traditional fire and brimstone, salvation without condemnation. These sought a sinless avenue to the pastures of God. A bosomy husky-voiced blonde showed many the way and rose to a kind of religious stardom not seen before or since, only to have her mighty spiritual ambitions dashed on the reefs of her love for a married man and an odd disappearance that is a hallmark in the annals of the vanished.

More than a million and a half persons leaving the tired lands of the East during the early 1920s, filtered into California, chiefly Los Angeles, seeking sunshine and a new and easier way of life. Sister Aimee was there to greet them for God. She too had left the farm, a small plot of land outside Ingersoll, Ontario, where she was born on October 9, 1890. Early in life, Aimee came under the Bible-quoting sway of her mother, Minnie "Ma" Kennedy, who had once labored for souls in the Salvation Army before marrying a farmer and settling down to harvests of wheat and beans.

While the impressionistic Aimee was still in her teens, a towering religious orator, Robert Semple, appeared at a revival meeting in Ingersoll. The apprentice evangelist was immediately smitten. Aimee was to describe Semple's Bible-swollen speech as sinking "into my heart like a swift-flung arrow." The preacher proposed and took Aimee's hand as they knelt in prayer. Sister later gushingly added: "As we prayed . . . my girlish heart suddenly began to pound against my ribs—like a caged, tropical bird beating its wings against the bars that kept it from the golden, mellow sunlight of a South Sea Island paradise. Love, triumphant, powerful and elemental, was surging and taking possession of me like a giant set free."

Following their marriage, the couple quickly left for China to convert souls to Christianity. Semple took sick and died in Hong Kong. Sister Aimee, age nineteen, was left stranded with a child. Penniless, Aimee earned passage home by conducting frenetic religious services aboard the *Empress of China*. She was rewarded when wealthy passengers forked over more than she needed, an experience that led her to believe that she was one of God's chosen, a person to lead and to be favored. After another marriage (to grocery clerk Harold McPherson), another child, and a quick divorce, Aimee received "the clarion call that brooks no denial" and in 1917 embarked on the zealous road of evangelism; she called it the Foursquare Gospel evangelism. "For the next two years," Aimee was to write, "in summer and in winter, north or south, I worked by day and dreamed by night in the shadow of a tent."

What Sister was dreaming of was her own temple. She had crossed the continent four times, holding revival meetings all the way; saving souls, she had toured New Zealand, Australia and Canada. Yet, by the time she reached Los Angeles in 1921, Sister Aimee had only a broken-down car and a hundred dollars in her purse. Her turnabout success in the next two years was based largely on "healing sessions" at which a few "incurables" seemed to get well by merely touching the glistening hem of Sister Aimee's flowing dress. "Those healings were the one topic of conversation on the streets, in hotel lobbies, even in the theaters," commented Sister Aimee. The miracle woman later guardedly added: "I am not a healer. Jesus is the healer. I am only the little office girl who opens the door and says, 'Come in.'"

The tremendous outpourings of new believers allowed Sister to open her long-dreamed-of Angelus Temple in Echo Park on January 1, 1923, at a cost of $1,500,000. An auditorium with a seating capacity of five thousand and a $75,000 radio station that broadcast daily Sister Aimee's Foursquare Gospel were quickly added to the miracle woman's spreading realm. (There was also a Cradle Room

*Sister Aimee Semple McPherson clutching flowers and leading her fanatical flock inside the Angelus Temple during her heyday.* (UPI)

Chapel for babies, and a Miracle Room patterned after the alcove at Lourdes, where discarded crutches, braces and wheelchairs were stacked to the ceiling.) Sister's spiritual kingdom blossomed, with more than 400 branch churches in the United States and 178 missionary stations. During its peak period the Angelus Temple employee payroll soared beyond $7,000 each month. Sister Aimee had made religion into a big-time business. And what kept that business booming was her technique, evangelism that did not cry out for the eternal hell-fire for sinners but, in the words of one scribe, called for "flowers, music, golden trumpets, red robes, angels, incense, nonsense, and sex appeal."

The sex appeal was all Aimee's, and she enhanced it with long silken gowns of many hues that clung to her more than ample figure as she cavorted across the stage and shouted to her fanatical congregation, money clutched in hand for the inevitable collection pails: "What makes people jump out of their seats? If there's fire under you, you just can't stand still. Did you ever try sitting on a hot stove?"

Sister's presence was unique and inspiring. Carey McWilliams, who often saw her perform wrote:

> She suggested sex without being sexually attractive. The suggestion was to be found, perhaps, in some quality of the voice; some radiation of that astonishing physical vitality. While constantly emanating sex, she lacked the graceful presence, the subtlety of manner, the mysterious reticence of a real siren. There was about her a trifle too much masculine vigor; the hips were too wide; the shoulders too broad; the neck too thick; the wrists and ankles too large. But wherever she moved or stirred, sex was present, at least in its public aspects, its gross implications; sex in headlines, sex emblazoned in marquee lights.

Said author Paul Sann:

> Sister Aimee was hefty without being fat and made a vibrant exciting appearance on the pulpit in her flowing white satin gowns. She had special colored lights play over her during her sermons and this Hollywood effect set off her blond locks nicely.

For all her success, by 1926 Sister was moaning the blues. (Whenever she was depressed, Aimee would sing a line from a hymn—"....

33

sunlight, sunlight in my soul today.") She had the adoration of tens of thousands of converts to her brand of happy religion, but she had no man of her own. She yearned for privacy and physical attention. "Sometimes," she told a confidant, "I wish I didn't have to carry on the Lord's work in such a conspicuous capacity."

What happened next had nothing to do with the Lord and turned out to be the most conspicuous event in Sister Aimee's meteoric career. The miracle woman disappeared.

One of Sister's few diversions was swimming in the Pacific; she preferred the beaches around Carmel, but on May 18, 1926, in company with her stoic secretary, Emma Schaeffer, Aimee drove in her Kissel car to Venice. She took a room in the Ocean View Hotel and squeezed into a green bathing suit. That afternoon she sat in a tent on the beach and prepared her notes for her next sermon, one entitled "Lightness and Darkness." Suddenly she looked up at Emma Schaeffer and sent her on a petty errand. When Emma returned she found the tent empty. The secretary peered toward the lapping waves but did not see a head bobbing in the surf. She waited. Aimee was a strong swimmer of great distances. After an hour, Emma Schaeffer began to get worried, then hysterical.

When "Ma" Kennedy received word that her evangelist daughter had disappeared at the seaside, she screamed: "Drowned!" The search was on. Thousands of Aimee's dedicated followers swarmed onto the beaches in Venice. Rumors flew hot and heavy. Some said Sister had been killed by gangsters after her alleged statement that she "would rather see my children in their graves than in a Venice dance hall." Police combed the area on tips that Mrs. McPherson had been kidnapped. (A card was later found, the work of a prankster, which read: "Help! They took me to a cabin in Bouquet.")

Crowds of Sister Aimee's flock became frantic in their daily vigil by the sea. The search took on circus proportions. One on-the-spot news account had it that "airplanes zoomed down to the wave tops, their pilots peering into the depths. Grapplers in boats raked the ocean floor." Meanwhile the sensation hunters milled up and down the waterfront. They poured in by automobile and train every minute to add to the dense crowds that waited for

something to happen. . . . Throughout the day the dance halls of Venice, the Sunday dance halls which the evangelist fought so vigorously, beat out their syncopated strains of ceaseless jazz as an obbligato to the voices of the temple worshippers which from time to time rose in the melody of old-fashioned hymns.

The religious were beside themselves as they fruitlessly watched the placid ocean. As the days passed, impatience turned to lunacy. One young man stepped from the crowd, his entire body shaking as if with palsy, and staggered toward the water, screaming at the top of his lungs: "I see her! I see her! She is there . . . walking on the water!" He was dragged off to an asylum. Three days later, another McPherson devotee, Robert Browning, age twenty-six, burst from the crowd and yelled, "I'm going after her!" He raced to the sea and began a mad swim that took him out too far. He drowned. A young girl committed suicide. One of the scores of deep-sea divers searching for the body was found dead of exposure.

The armies of searchers did not quiet. Ma Kennedy, from the stage of the Angelus Temple, demanded of her packed audience that a special collection be taken to mount a $25,000 reward for Aimee, dead or alive. Ardent followers immediately dumped $4,690.56 into the milk pails used for such special collections and pledged another $29,500 to be paid within the year. After the collection, a resigned Ma Kennedy said, "We do not believe Sister's body will ever be recovered. Her young body was too precious to Jesus." Minnie Kennedy then chartered an airplane to scatter lilies over the spot where Sister was thought to have drowned.

Hand-wrenching days passed. Then the nation's press burst forth with yet another spectacular wrinkle to Sister's disappearance. She had been kidnapped, absolutely. A blind attorney in Long Beach, R. A. McKinley, appeared at a police station and told of a visit by two men named Miller and Wilson, who came unannounced into his office and stated that they had kidnapped Sister Aimee Semple McPherson and would release her alive only after they received $25,000 in ransom.

Police could make nothing more of the blind lawyer's story. Three days later, on June 4, 1926, Sheriff William I. Traeger received an anonymous letter stating,

Dear Bill: It might happen to interest you to know that Aimee Semple McPherson was kidnapped and is being held either willingly or unwillingly. I know all about it, but I am afraid to peep. So be careful not to involve me. I am not revealing my identity as the gang will croak me if I squeal. You may find her in the mountains back of Santa Barbara or held in some lonely spot along the Santa Ynez River. Do not pay these crooks any jack, as they double-crossed me once and will do the same with anyone else. [Signed] Willow of the Wisp.

There would be many such letters in the following weeks, sending police in a dozen states on wild and useless hunts. As far away as Edmonton, Alberta, Canada, police broke into a room at the Corona Hotel on a tip that Sister was being held captive inside. They surprised one astonished couple who had taken separate autos from Spokane to "get away from it all." The police backed out apologizing while the lovers hurriedly packed and prepared explanations for their spouses.

On June 19, with Sister Aimee gone more than a month, Ma Kennedy received a letter that demanded $500,000 in ransom for the return of her daughter. It was signed "Avengers." According to writer Lately Thomas, "Minnie placed this letter on the pillow beside her head" and tried to figure its meaning. Others were to say that Minnie already knew the significance of the letter, since she had it mailed special delivery to herself!

The mysterious disappearance of the evangelist came to an end on the morning of June 23, 1926. Getting into his taxi in Agua Prieta,

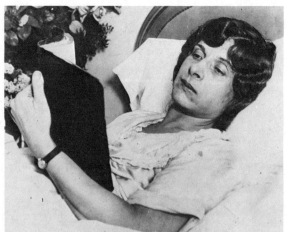

*The evangelist in a Douglas, Ariz., hospital bed on June 23, 1926; the ordeal of her disappearance was far from over.* (UPI)

Mexico, just across the border from Douglas, Arizona, an American named John Anderson spotted a figure curled up on the porch of a house. Anderson approached and stood above a sleeping woman with golden hair. "She had a pillow under her head," he later told authorities, "and a quilt had been thrown over her. Her face was lined as though from fatigue and her hair was disheveled, although her dress was not torn. I placed her in my car and took her to the American side." Sister Aimee had been resurrected and her thousands of followers went delirious with joy.

As Minnie Kennedy and Sister's two children, Roberta and Rolf, immediately took the train to Douglas to retrieve the precious religious leader, Aimee told her story to American officials from a hospital bed. She had been kidnapped at Venice, she said convincingly. A woman had come to her just as she was about to run into the surf and asked her to bless her sick baby in a nearby car. Aimee went to the car and was suddenly grabbed by two powerful men and thrown inside, where she was drugged. The woman was named "Rose," the men were "Steve" and "Jake," she remembered.

Aimee told of being driven wildly through the desert, stopping at several remote spots and finally arriving in a miserable shack somewhere across the border. "From what I overheard my abductors saying," she said, "I was being held at some place in Mexicali, if there is a place by that name. The woman, Rose, treated me very nicely, and the men did not molest me with any undue attention. I prayed constantly and talked to them of God. I'll bet they were tired of hearing my preaching. From certain parts of the conversation I overheard while they had me in their power, I believe that they were to make a final appeal to my mother for ransom money Friday."

The indomitable Aimee waited for her moment, she explained. On the night of June 22, with the kidnappers momentarily gone, in the shack where she was being held prisoner she managed to wedge a jagged tin can between her hands and saw through the ropes that bound her. Once free, Sister stealthily let herself outside and ran across the desert for miles under the starsmeared night, she said.

The moment taxi driver Anderson deposited his startling find in Douglas, Sister went to a phone and called Ma Kennedy. Only two words came from the Los Angeles end of the call: "Don't talk!"

Posses of armed men rode furiously into Mexico seeking the kidnappers. Mexican and American diplomats began to argue. The disappearance had all the makings of an international incident. Meanwhile, the much-put-upon Sister Aimee made her way back to Los Angeles, to be received by tens of thousands of well-wishers. The doubters received her later. One of these was District Attorney Asa Keyes of Los Angeles, who asked, "How was a woman like Mrs. McPherson, known almost all over the civilized world, kidnapped in broad daylight from a crowded beach?"

Indignant, Aimee shot back: "Every word I have uttered about my kidnapping and escape is true! If I have been unable to answer any questions propounded by a score of newspaper men, detectives, attorneys, friends, even my own mother, I have told them. 'I do not know,' or 'I do not remember.' My story is true." She went on to explain how the kidnapper named Steve had held a cigar to her hand, torturing her, and threatened to give her to a sex-crazed Mexican named Felipe unless she cooperated. She displayed burns on her fingers, bruised ankles from the cord shackles and blisters on her feet from her long run to freedom. Her shoes were hardly scuffed, one reporter pointed out. Her dress was barely wrinkled another put in.

Sister leapfrogged to another point. "I was wondering," she said dramatically, for she was an excellent actress, "if that house into which my captors last took me could have been a camping outfit of canvas or light wood."

A reporter provided a piece of burlap. "No," Sister remarked, "it could not have been made of that for I can see through that. I could not see through the walls of the house I was in, and there was a wooden floor in the shack."

"Forgive me, Mrs. McPherson," a reporter said, "but didn't you really have a reason to vanish?"

Sister bristled. "Why should I disappear? To rest? I was not tired. Amnesia? I never suffered that. Publicity? That is absurd. Love?" At the last word Mrs. McPherson began to laugh long and loud, but she was unconvincing, especially when someone brought up the name of Kenneth G. Ormiston, which promptly ended the interview.

Ormiston had been the shadowy figure hovering over the fantastic disappearance of Aimee Semple McPherson. A man known to some of Sister's followers and a few newsmen, Ormiston was now a man on the run. He had been Sister's radio operator since 1925, a sophisticated, intelligent man, whose marriage to another woman did not prevent him from comforting Aimee after her exhausting programs. His soothing voice from the control room would coo: "You have done splendidly tonight," or "You sound as though you were tired tonight, Mrs. McPherson." Soon, the two were meeting in hotel rooms all over Los Angeles, both using a string of aliases, driving unmarked cars, and wearing disguises, Kenneth Ormiston certainly was not the kind of man Sister had told her congregation she would look for as a new life-mate. "The man I marry has not appeared on the scene yet," she said. "He must be good-looking. He must be six feet tall or more. He must be a preacher. He must have certain rigid standards. He must play the trombone and be a good singer, and he must be a good and holy man." Yet Kenneth Ormiston was attentive, responsive, and always willing.

Ormiston had vanished on the same day as Sister, reporters discovered. They learned of the many roadhouses, hotels, motels, and

*The only photograph ever taken of Sister Aimee and her radio operator, Kenneth G. Ormiston. (UPI)*

cottages Ormiston and a mystery woman—not his wife, who sued for divorce some months later—had stayed at in California and Arizona during the evangelist's disappearance.

District Attorney Keyes gathered more evidence and concluded that the vanishing act was a cover-up for Mrs. McPherson's going away with her lover, that being the star of the revivalist world she could not flaunt lust for a married man. She had concocted the bizarre disappearance story, Keyes insisted, when it became apparent that she was too well-known to disappear permanently with the man of her heart. Keyes brought an indictment against Aimee and her mother for obstructing justice during the "disappearance" and, in the case of the so-called "Avengers" ransom note, using the mails to defraud.

Damning evidence mounted. A blue trunk that Ormiston had shipped from California to New York (where he was living incognito) was discovered, and inside were found sexy nightgowns, panties and hosiery that were traced to Sister. Keyes's investigation bogged down a bit when a Mrs. Lorraine Wiseman came forth and insisted that *she* was the mystery woman Ormiston had driven from bedroom to bedroom during Aimee's absence. But Mrs. Wiseman later further undermined Sister's case by admitting that Ma Kennedy and Aimee had paid her a large sum of money to make her false statements.

Aimee Semple McPherson would not succumb, however, to such indictments. She fought back with fiery oratory. One spell-binding speech, shouted from the stage of the Angelus Temple and beamed by her radio station across the country, was entitled "Saint or Sinner? Did I go from Pulpit to Paramour?" Roared Sister Aimee: "I have waged unrelenting battle with the batlike demons from hell and they fear me and revile me as the Devil hates holy water. What brought about District Attorney Keyes's change of belief? (Keyes had first seemed to accept the kidnapping story before unearthing the Ormiston trail.)

"Did the overlords of the underworld who are fighting me and who are heavily interested in Los Angeles have anything to do with it? I am being crucified by the very bats of hell, who have gone the limit in perfidy; brutal, conscienceless, hardly human. They have

*Sister Aimee and her mother, Minnie "Ma" Kennedy, on trial for fraud, a stigma that wrecked the evangelist's career.* (UPI)

gone to the extent of the mummer's art in 'making up' women to look like me and pose them in questionable places as Sister Aimee!"

The trial dragged on, with Mrs. McPherson making much of her persecution. Not until January 10, 1927, did Keyes ask the court to dismiss all charges on the grounds that it would be impossible to obtain a conviction. Upon hearing the news, Sister, as usual, fainted. The next day, she embarked upon a "Vindication Tour" of the country. A month later Mrs. Ormiston was granted an uncontested divorce on the grounds of desertion.

Aimee's tour was an utter failure; no one believed her kidnapping story, and many of those who sat smirking in the half-empty audiences were more interested in hearing about her lover, hooting obscenities from the darkness. It was too much for the miracle woman, and her star faded. In September 1944, she was found in her ornate bedroom, dead of what appeared to be an overdose of sleeping pills.

In the years when her fame had become threadbare and shabby, Sister Aimee often recalled the greatest highlight of her life, when tens of thousands greeted her in Los Angeles after her fabulous 1926 disappearance ended. More and more she heard the echo of thirty thousand throats cheering her as she was carried in a wicker chair from her private train car, with flowers adorning her, carried above the heads of the multitude to an auto completely coated with roses. More and more, Sister Aimee remembered how 100,000 citizens of Los Angeles roared their approval as she was driven down the main streets, a white-robed Temple band going before her. It was a more tumultuous reception than Woodrow Wilson and the King of Belgium received when they entered the city. Until the end, Sister Aimee remembered how—in the brief period after she reappeared and before the gathering scandal crushed her—the deafening chant of thousands drifted up to her as she stepped onto the stairs of her temple, smiled and waved to her admirers—

"Coming back, back, back,
Coming back, back, back,
Our sister in the Lord is coming back.
There is shouting all around
For our sister has been found;
There is nothing now of joy or peace we lack."

Psychiatrists and other medical messiahs argue to this day about amnesia; many hold that it is nothing more than a convenient excuse for countless harassed souls to escape their all-too-worldly problems, while others insist that such a state of mind is real, dangerous and inexplicable. (*Aphasia,* once used as a catch-all for loss of memory, really means the inability to communicate, whereas the word *amnesia* stems from the Greek prefix *a,* meaning "not," and the verb *mnasthai,* meaning "to remember." Amnesia is medically broken down into two categories. Organic amnesia involves a physical disorder of the neuron memory cells; it often results from a blow on the head, a deficiency in the diet, or simply senescence. Psychogenic amnesia is created by a psychological need to inhibit the memory, to escape reality.)

Loss of memory, whatever its source, is captivating—the strange and compelling ability of humans to move completely from one identity to another without ever knowing why, pushed, as it were, by an unknown force from a familiar life style into a born-again existence. Such was the case of Thomas O'Grady, owner of a successful grocery store on White Street in Williamsburg, Virginia. One morning in 1847 he kissed his wife and son goodbye and started for market with $400 in his pocket. He never returned. O'Grady had a happy home life; a devoted husband and doting father, he was debt-free, and a rock-bottom citizen. After O'Grady's disappearance, his wife endeavored to run his store; but, according to a news account of the day, "her grief over his loss was excessive and she died within a few months, leaving the property in the possession of a son, age fifteen years." O'Grady's son sold the store and moved to Alabama, where he grew wealthy as the owner of a great plantation, forgetting about the father who walked out of his life.

The O'Grady disappearance would have been just another absence had it not been for a sailor from Williamsburg, Bernard Grenner, who visited the Sandwich Islands thirty years later, in 1877. There he met a "half-demented, gray-haired old man whom he recognized, after some difficulty, as an old friend." The elderly man was the merchant O'Grady, and, as Grenner quizzed him about his disappearance, the old man's "manner and talk seemed wild and incoherent, as though the powers of concentration and memory had forsaken him. He remembered nothing about home save his own name, and references to former associations amazed him."

When the sailor asked O'Grady how he had come to dwell in the islands, the lost merchant replied: "I do not know. I cannot recall. But I am here and I am comfortable and I have made money."

"You have a son living in Alabama," Grenner said in an attempt to induce the old man to return to the United States. "Perhaps you should visit him."

"I have no memory of a son," O'Grady replied without emotion. "I cannot leave here. It is my home. I know no other."

Grenner wrote to O'Grady's son in Alabama, recounting his experience. The son responded in kind with his father: "I shall not seek him out. He is of another world now. We are strangers."

## *People of Distinction*

Loss of memory appears to be a recurrent plague of persons of repute and great responsibility, an historic symptom of many who can no longer bear the obligations of their own personalities, and who suddenly exchange one identity for another, one defined and one blank. Intellectuals have also proved to be likely amnesia prospects. For instance, there is the case of Luther Maynard Jones.

Jones was a member of Yale's class of 1860, a brilliant orator who won the most coveted debating prize in the country, the De Forest Award. His graduating classmates had voted him "the most versatile" and "most promising" of their ranks. Born the son of a Congregational minister, the Reverend Levi Jones, in Marlboro, New Hampshire, on April 21, 1837, Jones moved to New York following his graduation and plunged into law studies at Columbia, taking a Master's degree in 1868. His star in the legal profession skyrocketed and he was soon a man of wealth and renown.

A dedicated bachelor, Jones spent most of his adult life collecting books and antiques, walling himself in, so to speak, against a world he more and more thought of as "crass and thoughtless." His knowledge of rare antiques and paintings became so vast that authorities at the Metropolitan Museum of Art in New York tried to induce him to become a ranking staff member. He declined. Less and less of his time was spent on his law practice; at age sixty, Jones handled very little business. His law partner, the distinguished William C. Whitney, thought a trip to Europe would refresh Jones's outlook and sent him on a legal errand to England in 1897. Jones promptly disappeared.

Yale graduates and businessmen from New York who had known Jones and who traveled extensively in Europe made futile efforts to find him. Then, in 1909, a classmate bumped into Jones on a London street. He was no longer the same man; in fact, he stated his name was Luther Maynard, period, and who was this Jones anyway? Not until June 20, 1912, was the pride of Yale heard from again. This time the seventy-three-year-old scholar was found penniless in London's Streatham Hill Workhouse. He had no memory of his life in America and was startled to hear that he had once been a man of prestige in New York society. Friends set up a pension fund for him, but before Luther Maynard Jones could be convinced that he was someone other than the one he thought himself to be, he died, slipping into death with a terrible uncertainty. His last words were: "Who am I then, please? Who?"

That was the same question that Dr. William Horatio Bates, a celebrated eye specialist in New York, asked himself in 1902 when he vanished. A report in *The New York Times* stated that "medical men have regarded the case of Dr. Bates as one of the most remarkable having to do with the disease of aphasia, or loss of memory." What was remarkable was that the forty-two-year-old Bates suddenly abandoned his lucrative practice and his wife on August 30, 1902, to become a one-man clinic, or so he informed his wife in a letter that arrived some days after his departure—"My Dear Wife: I am called out of town to do some major operations. I go with Dr. Forche, an old student . . . and do a mastoid, some cataracts, and other operations. He promises me a bonanza! Too bad to miss the Horse Show, but I am glad to get so much money for us all. I am in such a flurry! Do not worry. I will write details later. Yours lovingly, Willie."

Willie never wrote again, and he did not return. Six weeks later Mrs. Bates received an anonymous letter informing her that her husband was studying medicine in a London hospital. The startled woman went to England and found her spouse in the Charing Cross

Hospital. Bates did not recognize her, insisting that he had never heard of a Dr. William Horatio Bates, celebrated eye specialist. The doctor recalled nothing of their marriage or his famous background, and constantly murmured "I don't know why you bother, madam. We are strangers." Two days later, Dr. Bates disappeared again, and his wife returned to New York, where she died in bed three years later, while embracing the portrait of her husband.

Nine years passed. Suddenly in 1911, at age fifty-one, Dr. Bates showed up in New York and resumed his practice as if nothing unusual had occurred. When reporters attempted to get his strange story, they were turned away, learning only that Bates had wandered throughout Europe as an amnesia victim, operating as a ghost doctor. Dr. Bates's practice again grew large and successful. He remained one of the most distinguished men in his profession until his death a decade later. He never explained what happened to nine years of his life, but in the words of one of his associates: "That was impossible. It was as if he had had a chunk of his mind removed, like a slice of watermelon chopped away and eaten by an invisible monster."

The monster, which claims an average of 20,000 victims each year, was once described by Dr. Noland Lewis of the New York Psychiatric Institute: "Amnesia is like the shutting off of a light in one room in the house of memory. While the rest of the mind is bright, that which has to do with one's name, address and friends is in total darkness." In endless cases of missing businessmen—professionals and generally those who rely upon their minds to provide a living— excruciating mental stress and anxiety have been offered as explanations for temporary amnesia, which usually lasts no more than a few days or, at the most, a few weeks. Freud gave other causes, such as conflict, repression, automatic censorship, unconscious activities and wish fulfillment, of amnesia. In the annals of the missing, of course, there has been deliberate deceit practiced by those claiming amnesia for a plethora of reasons, from illicit sexual activities to participation in serious crime.

In a University of Pennsylvania study that encompassed eight years and dozens of amnesia patients, three eminent neurologists reached the conclusion that fifty percent of all victims were faking. "By feigning amnesia," the experts stated, "the forgetter gained sympathy, shelter or personal oblivion at a moment when maintenance of identity would have meant unpleasant or serious consequences." Yet the archives contain thousands of cases of authentic Rip Van Winkles whose stories are too believable to ignore. The most convincing are about those who disappear with nothing to gain and who, like Seward Heidelbach, eventually lose everything.

One day in August 1907, Heidelbach, a wealthy Cincinnati banker, was having lunch with his brother at the Café Savarin in New York City. Suddenly, the businessman remembered that he had to obtain an express money order for his firm, Heidelbach, Ickelheimer & Company. He excused himself and went across the street. When Seward Heidelbach failed to return, his brother notified the authorities. Heidelbach's brother told police that the banker had been carrying on his person at least five thousand dollars and that he might have been the "victim of foul play."

Seward, however, was the victim of his own mind. It was many months later when the banker awoke in a Liverpool, England, hospital, vaguely remembering leaving his brother in the New York café. His mind, it was later theorized, had gone blank from the moment he stepped across the street to get his money order. That little stroll took the banker to Philadelphia, Boston, and then by boat to England, wanderings even expert detectives the bank later hired could not detail.

The banker's amnesia not only caused him to lose a large chunk of his known life but most of his personal fortune. In his abscence, Heidelbach's family, thinking him dead, sold off all his interests in his bank.

Gustav Stern, another millionaire, disappeared just as abruptly as Heidelbach, eight years later. One day in May 1915, Stern left his Manhattan office and failed to return. Some weeks later, a reporter named Robert Simmons was walking through the elegant lobby of the United States Hotel in Paterson, New Jersey, when he noticed solid-gold cuff links worn by a man lounging nearby. The unusual cuff links had been part of the description sent out on Stern. Simmons immediately notified the local police. Captain John Tracey appeared at the hotel and interviewed the suspect who was registered under the name of Howard Ellis.

"What's your business?" Tracy asked Ellis.

"I'm a manufacturer," the man replied in a monotone. "I have a factory on the outskirts of Trenton."

"What is your telephone number?"

"I haven't any telephone."

"What street is your factory on?"

"It is just on the outskirts of Trenton," the man replied lamely. "I can't tell you any more than that."

"Isn't your name Gustav Stern, the industrialist?"

"Gustav who?"

Tracey turned to one of his men and ordered "Ellis" to be kept under surveillance until Stern's brother, who had spent a fortune looking for the absent tycoon, could travel from Manhattan to Paterson. Upon his arrival, the brother threw his arms around the man in the hotel room.

"Say," shouted the man, yanking his brother's arms from about his neck. "What do you think you're doing?"

It took several hours for his brother to convince Gustav Stern, amnesia victim, that he, indeed, was a real business magnate whose interests were not "on the outskirts of Trenton" but all over the world.

The transition from lofty position to mere survival status is common among respectable amnesia victims, Dr. Edward E. Rowell, Jr., of Stamford, Connecticut, who disappeared May 25, 1915, came to his senses six weeks later when he looked down at his blistered, bleeding hands; he was working as a digger in a gravel pit in Judson, Indiana. Dr. John L. Brand, who had a history of vanishing for short periods, left his Boston home in 1917 and was not found until December 22, 1920, when a kindly minister took him into his Lambertville, New Jersey, rectory. Brand, one of the nation's leading scholars, had been living like a tramp and had been jailed dozens of times as a vagrant.

A year after Dr. Brand was located, insurance executive James H. Epworth disappeared without a trace from his home in Nutley, New Jersey. Some weeks later, Epworth discovered that he had suffered an attack of amnesia and that he had traveled from one end of the country to the other, despite a cross-country search for him. He was working as a busboy when his true identity flashed before him and he raced to a Western Union office to wire his wife: "Memory returning. Will come East as soon as possible. Will be glad to see you all. How are you? How are the children? How is Mother? Suppose all Nutley is worked up." When Epworth did return home he was forever incapable of relating what had occurred between the time he disappeared and the time "he realized that he was collecting dishes in a Pacific Coast restaurant."

Unlike the Epworths who vanish in a shroud of amnesia and eventually regain memory, there are those who never fully realize who they are long after they are found and identified. Such was the case of Benjamin Levy, a baker from Brooklyn, who was absent for two years and then, quite by accident, was recognized by an old friend who entered the offices of an auto agency on September 25, 1926.

"Hello, Ben," the friend said, "where have you been for the past two years?"

Levy looked up at the young man, putting up the broom he had been using to sweep out a hallway. "Huh? You mean me?"

"You're Ben Levy. You've been missing for more than two years."

"You're nuts, buddy. Beat it."

The acquaintance called the police and Levy was taken to the station. His wife, daughter, and family physician arrived and identified the baker.

"I think you're all crazy," Levy protested. "My name is Frank Lloyd. I'm no Jew, I'm a Roman Catholic. I ain't married and never have been."

"You own a bakery in Brooklyn," Levy's daughter Esther said.

Levy laughed. "I work as a day laborer. I wouldn't know a baker's oven if I saw it!"

Mrs. Levy produced a letter Levy had reportedly written during his absence. "It says here," the frustrated wife said, "in your own handwriting that you were a prisoner on a rum-running ship in New York harbor. Don't you remember writing this?"

"Some joke."

"It's no joke, Levy," a police sergeant interrupted. He snatched the letter from Mrs. Levy. "Here's what you wrote two years ago: 'I am in a ship's hold and I can see a large bridge through the port hole!' We also found another note in a bottle that washed ashore that said you were still a prisoner. Half the force was out searching every ship in the harbor at the time."

"I don't know anything about such letters," said Levy. "I'm not Levy! My name is Lloyd!"

"You're Levy all right and we'll prove it to you," the sergeant said. Levy's fingerprints were taken and compared to those the police had on file, obtained years earlier. They were identical.

"Come back to the bakery and home," pleaded Esther Levy.

"Look, missy," Levy said, getting angry, "I work as a porter. I been sweeping out saloons and offices for years. Ask anyone on the Bowery; they know me."

Mrs. Levy too got angry. "You are Benjamin Levy and you are my husband. I want you to come home this instant!"

"Lady, I don't doubt you think I'm Mr. Levy, but I'm not."

"Don't call me 'Lady.' I'm Helen, I'm your wife!"

"Maybe you are my wife but I don't remember a thing about it."

At that moment Levy's seventeen-year-old nephew walked into the room and said casually: "Oh, hi, Uncle Benny!"

The amnesia victim squinted and then clucked his tongue. "Well, if even the kid is calling me uncle, maybe there's something to it, but I certainly don't ever remember being this guy Levy." Unconvinced, Benjamin Levy went back to Brooklyn and his bakery to learn his life all over again.

In the enigmatic case of Colonel Raymond Robins, a wealthy social worker and Prohibitionist crusader, the old life was completely discarded in the haze of amnesia, and a new one, drastically different, was embraced just as fanatically as Robins had once attempted to destroy all the booze in America.

On the night of September 3, 1932, Colonel Robins devoured a large meal at the City Club at 55 West Forty-fourth Street in Manhattan. His dinner companion was New York's most fiery Prohibitionist crusader, Dr. Daniel A. Poling. Robins left the club at 7 P.M. and was not seen or heard from again for two and a half months. He was scheduled to appear at the White House for a special conference with President Herbert Hoover the following Tuesday to outline his plans for a nationwide speaking tour that would emphasize the President's support of the losing battle against John Barleycorn. When Robins failed to appear, the President himself ordered a search for the missing crusader.

Reports of Robins' being seen throughout the country at the same time filled endless columns of the nation's press. He was reportedly seen walking the streets of Chicago a few days after his disappearance. Russian imperialists had murdered him, one account had it, because of Robins' enthusiastic support of the new Soviet regime. Rumrunners, incensed at Robins' attacks on their activities, had reportedly kidnapped him and killed him by throwing him into the Atlantic forty miles off Montauk Point, Long Island. Another account had it that bootleggers in Florida, against whom Robins had been particularly active, snatched the Prohibitionist first and murdered him in a Miami warehouse, jamming a shotgun down his throat and pulling both triggers.

None of this rumored gore could be substantiated as investigators and reporters raced about in their frenetic search for the missing Robins. While the manhunt took place, a man calling himself Reynolds Rogers, wearing a brand-new pair of overalls, heavy shoes and a hunting cap, tramped up to the boardinghouse of Mrs. W. E. Bryson in Balsam, North Carolina, a remote mountain hamlet between Whittier and Asheville. Rogers told Mrs. Bryson that he was a miner from Harlan, Kentucky, and that he intended to prospect for gold in the hills of North Carolina, which struck Mrs. Bryson as curious since there was no gold in those hills. He paid his rent a week in advance and began his gold-hunting early the next morning. When Rogers returned that night he learned that a man named Howd from Miami was staying at the same boardinghouse. He became nervous and avoided Howd. Two days later, Rogers moved to Whittier, staying at a rooming house run by a Mrs. McHan. He was careful to determine that there was no one from Miami staying at the Whittier boarding house.

For more than two months, Rogers comfortably worked himself into the life of the little community, strolling through the mountain hollows. He became so familiar that normally apprehensive still operators grew friendly toward him. Rogers sat in the shadows of their stills and even sipped some of the raw moonshine while he regaled his rapt listeners with stories of his "friends," Presidents Theodore Roosevelt and Herbert Hoover. When pressed to explain how he had come to meet these giants, Rogers merely shook his head and mumbled: "I can't recall that."

The prospector entered the councils of the Cherokee Indians,

*Colonel Raymond Robins as mighty crusader against Demon Rum, and in a more leisurely pose as an amnesia victim in North Carolina, where he was known as Reynolds Rogers.* (UPI)

who lived in the nearby hills, and delivered talks to schoolchildren. Most of the hill people thought of him as a gifted back country prophet until thirteen-year-old Carl Byrd Fisher, who lived in the McHan boardinghouse, spotted a newspaper photo of the missing Colonel Robins and compared it to that of the bearded Reynolds Rogers. The Fisher boy contacted authorities, and overnight a host of newsmen, psychologists (then commonly called "alienists") and detectives descended upon sleepy Whittier.

Rogers was held virtually prisoner in his room while doctors and police examined him. "I don't know why these people are trying to make me into somebody else," complained Rogers to the local press. "All I want is to be let alone."

Robins' wife arrived and confronted Rogers, escorted into the room by psychiatrist M. A. Griffin. The psychiatrist introduced the woman, who was weeping.

"Do you say this is my wife?" Rogers said to Dr. Griffin.

"Yes, this is Mrs. Robins."

Even through his heavy beard, the workings of Rogers' face were visible as he silently struggled to remember. After several minutes, Rogers turned to the psychiatrist and said quietly: "Doctor, I am Raymond Robins, and this is my wife, Margaret Dreier Robins."

Mrs. Robins told reporters minutes after the moving scene that "slowly but steadily the change came in him. It was not all of a sudden, and was visibly a severe strain on the colonel. But there came into his face a completely new look. He looked into my face and called me Margaret."

Colonel Robins had suffered one of the most talked-about amnesia disappearances in this country, reverting back to the time when he had been a successful gold prospector in the Klondike at the turn of the century and blotting out his role as the nation's leading Prohibitionist. Many said he did it intentionally because he knew the cause of President Hoover and Prohibition was doomed in the next election (which it was, when Franklin Delano Roosevelt and the "wets" won the presidency in an overwhelming victory in November).

Rogers' avoidance of the man from Miami was due to instinct, explained the alienists, since he knew Miami bootleggers had sworn to kill him after his crusade in Florida to wipe out the rumrunners. Thomas R. Henry, writing in the *Washington Evening Star*, likened Robins' state of mind to a "prolonged waking phenomenon somewhat allied to sleepwalking." Robert J. Casey, staff correspondent of the *Chicago Daily News* and one of the first reporters to cover the case, poetically described the end of that "sleep" the day after Robins slipped back inside his real identity: "Mr. Robins arose this morning bright and refreshed—obviously cheered at remembering his name and antecedents. He looked out across a frosty valley swimming in haze, at the edge of which is the cemetery where lies buried O. Henry, one of whose principal works was a sprightly bit entitled 'Adventures in Aphasia.'"

The fate of Dr. George H. Bigelow, director of the Massachusetts General Hospital in Boston, was considerably less inspiring than the happy return experienced by Colonel Robins. Bigelow, forty-four years old and one of the nation's leading experts on respiratory diseases, wandered away from his office December 3, 1934, suffering from exhaustion, officials later stated. Reservoir employees of the Metropolitan District Commission near Framingham, Massachusetts, encountered a tall man with a crew cut a day after Bigelow's

*Dr. George H. Bigelow, director of the Massachusetts General Hospital in Boston, shortly before his 1934 disappearance.* (WIDE WORLD)

disappearance. The man stated that he could not "remember my name, where I live or where I am supposed to go." The workers merely shrugged, and the man in the expensive suit trudged off through the snow.

Not until March 23, 1935, was the famous physician found, ironically by a man, H. Hervey Frost, with whom Bigelow attended school as a child. Frost, strolling along a path near the Framingham reservoir, saw the body of a man floating beneath the ice. With the help of a reservoir employee, Frost chopped a hole in the ice and pulled up the head of the corpse, which he instantly recognized as his boyhood pal Bigelow. Said one of the reservoir employees with whom the doctor had talked as he aimlessly drifted in amnesia: "I guess we should have listened to the guy and done something for him. What's this amnesia stuff anyway?"

Although he insisted that he was not a victim of amnesia during his six-year absence, scientist Albert Clark Reed was unable to explain why he disappeared on July 7, 1952. After six years, Reed, an aeronautical specialist who had been working on a top-secret project for the Defense Department at the California Institute of Technology, was found working as a groom at the Hollywood Park Race Track and was known as Alfred C. Reese.

Reed remembered having drifted into Arizona, where he worked as a teamster's helper shortly after his disappearance. His lifelong love of horses led him, he said, quite naturally to stable work. Said

*Aeronautical research scientist Albert Clark Reed, before he vanished from his top secret post in 1952, and in his new identity as a California stable hand six years later.*

the scientist to reporters: "Thank God I've been found; now I can see my boy again!"

Another scientist, an internationally famous cellulose chemist, Professor Carl Vernon Holmberg, very much in the pattern of Albert Clark Reed, walked out of his office at Syracuse University on May 11, 1955, and vanished. Holmberg drove to a nearby intersection, abandoned his car and walked on foot out of his academic life and away from his wife and three sons.

Holmberg appeared months later in Rockford, Illinois, as Verne Hansen, a common laborer who had worked as a shipping clerk and later a pigment grinder in a paint firm. He told his employers that he had only a high-school education. In 1959 Hansen married a divorced woman who had two daughters.

Hansen displayed such superior intelligence in the paint factory that it was a plant joke that a man of his intellectual ability associated with semi-illiterates. This may have been the reason why Hansen began to drink, a problem that led to his separation from his wife. On February 4, 1961, Hansen was picked up by Rockford police for drunken driving, and a routine fingerprint check was made. The F.B.I. channeled the prints to Syracuse authorities who contacted officials in Rockford.

*Carl Vernon Holmberg as New York college professor in 1955 and as day laborer Verne Hansen, amnesia victim, in 1962. (UPI)*

A reporter from the Rockford *Register-Republic* was the first to tell Hansen that he was a famous scientist and educator. "It seems rather incredible to me," Hansen responded. "I suppose I will have to go check up to see if the story is true, but I don't see how a man could break off one life and start another." That, however, is exactly what Professor Holmberg had done. The forty-five-year-old educator could recall nothing of his former life. "My mind was a complete blank when I came to Rockford," he tried to explain. "My suit had a New York label and I seem to recall the hills of New York. I recalled some other places, too, mostly landscapes. When I got to Rockford I tossed lumber in the yard and picked up a few other odd jobs. I don't know what I'm going to do now."

Holmberg-Hansen did not have to think about returning to his first wife; she had divorced him in 1960 and remarried. Upon hearing the news of his discovery, she said, "I have no further interest in Dr. Holmberg, other than satisfying my curiosity. We have no connection with him, either legally or emotionally anymore."

This feeling toward the vanished professor was shared by the amnesia victim himself, who stayed on in Rockford, apparently content to spend the rest of his days as a pigment grinder. To Hansen, "reading and hearing the story about Dr. Holmberg is to me just as though I were reading the biography of a strange man, a man I do not know."

That same strange feeling, but in reverse, overcame John R. Cross, a retired contractor in his late eighties, who was recovering from a stroke in Joplin, Missouri, on September 26, 1973. Cross began to babble from his sickbed to one of his two daughters, Martha Jane Barker, a nurse who was looking after him. "We need to get something straightened out here," Cross shouted desperately at his startled daughter. "I'm not Cross . . . my name is . . . my name is Crosswhite, John R. Crosswhite. Call my folks, the Crosswhites in Enid, Oklahoma. They will tell you."

At first the daughter thought her father was merely raving, but he persisted in calling himself Crosswhite, and Mrs. Barker finally called Enid. The seemingly incoherent babble of her father was true, she learned. John R. Crosswhite had been missing for thirty-seven years, a record for an amnesia victim.

Crosswhite had left his Cape Girardeau, Missouri, home in 1936 on a business trip to St. Louis. His wrecked car was found sometime later, but no body was recovered. His first wife had him legally declared dead in 1940. In 1941 a man calling himself John R. Cross appeared in Joplin, Missouri. He married the following year. From that period to the time of his stroke, Cross, who never spoke of his past, remembered nothing. Experts concluded that he had struck his head in the car accident and that produced a loss of memory, a memory that was rekindled by a massive stroke thirty-seven years later. Crosswhite's first wife who was eighty-three when he came to his senses, was never told that her husband was alive, for fear of upsetting her.

A tale of two wives half a continent apart was told in the bizarre case of Lawrence Joseph Bader, a kitchenware salesman from Akron, Ohio, who, as John Francis "Fritz" Johnson, became the pride of Omaha, Nebraska. Bader-Johnson presented one of the most baffling amnesia disappearances on record, a weird story forever unanswered.

May 15, 1957, was a balmy day in Akron, Ohio, a day so sweet with spring that Lawrence Joseph Bader completely ignored the business of selling kitchenware for the Reynolds Metals Corporation. He packed his fishing gear in his car and told his wife, Mary Lou, that he was going to try for bass in Lake Erie. He waved goodbye to his four children and drove away.

That afternoon Bader rented a fourteen-foot boat from Lawrence Cotleur on the Rocky River, which fed into Lake Erie. Oddly, Bader insisted that Cotleur install running lights on the boat even though he emphasized that he would return before dark. Cotleur pointed to a blue-black sky in the horizon and warned of heavy weather, but the salesman only laughed and shoved off. After sunset, a Coast Guard launch spotted Bader in his boat and he was asked if he needed help. The salesman waved them off with a smile. Then Larry Bader, whose financial difficulties had been deepening, disappeared. (Personal debts and a mortgage on Bader's home amounted to almost $20,000 and were rising against an annual income of $10,000. On the day of his disappearance, Bader cashed a $400 check and thoughtfully sent off a check for $45.85 to cover the premium of his $7,000 life-insurance policy.)

The storm that night on Lake Erie was certainly not the most severe in its history, but it was considered dangerous enough for anyone so foolish as to be on the water. Bader was one of these; his somewhat damaged boat was found, minus one oar and a small suitcase that Bader had been carrying. A frantic search went on, but officials were not optimistic; Lake Erie is one of the most treacherous of the Great Lakes.

When police came up empty-handed, the Akron *Beacon-Journal* gave up on Bader, its headline proclaiming "Little Hope for Survival." Mary Lou Bader held out much longer, telling the *Beacon-Journal* eight years later, when she learned that her husband was alive in Omaha, Nebraska, "I felt that it had been a disappearance, rather than drowning, that it would have to have been something that was out of his control, definitely."

What was out of control was Bader's memory; it no longer existed, most experts later agreed, by the time he, with a whole new personality, stepped off a bus in Omaha, Nebraska, in May 1957. He was suddenly John Francis "Fritz" Johnson, orphan. He told everyone

that he had been horribly wounded in the United States Navy during the war. Johnson, a free-and-easy going extrovert, became a flamboyant bartender in one of the "in" lounges and then moved on to become one of Omaha's most popular disc jockeys for station KBON.

"Fritz," as Johnson religiously insisted he be called, was never quite the ordinary fellow; his eccentricities, if they had not worked to his benefit as a colorful show business personality, would have caused suspicion. Johnson could not recall much of his past, except that he was raised in a Brookline, Massachusetts, orphanage. He explained away thirteen years previous to his moving to Omaha by telling of his glorious years in the U.S. Navy. Johnson's incredible ability as an archer, he explained, was a result of "being blown off a destroyer by an attacking submarine in the English Channel" during World War II. At that traumatic time, Fritz said, he suffered a terrible back injury ("my back was loaded with shrapnel"). He was invalided to the United States and hospitalized for more than three years. To strengthen his back he took up archery. Johnson entered city and state archery competitions, sweeping away all challengers. In 1962, Fritz married a beautiful divorcée, Nancy Zimmer. His star rose the following year, when he became the sports director for TV station KETV in Omaha.

*Salesman Lawrence Joseph Bader as he looked in 1957 when he vanished on a fishing trip, and as champion archer John F. "Fritz" Johnson in 1965. (UPI)*

Fritz's family grew; Nancy had had a daughter by a former marriage and in 1963 a son was born to the Johnsons. The local press lavished praise upon Fritz, who was profiled several times as one of Omaha's most talented, albeit controversial, characters. Fritz raised tropical fish by the hundreds. No promotion stunt was too zany for him. He once sat atop a flagpole for three days drinking martinis to publicize his station's fund-raising to fight polio. When ordering in restaurants, Fritz would tell waitresses to "bring me a couple dollars worth of food." He dated his checks by the season and, when he worked as a bartender, he would deposit his tips in the bank with a slip marked: "One quart, money."

In March 1964 a malignant tumor was detected in the back wall of Fritz Johnson's left eye. The cancer, as well as the eye, was cut out. Johnson cavalierly donned a black eye patch, which made him all the more colorful.

Fritz added a pencil-thin mustache and went on to win several championships in archery. He became so proficient that the Sanders Archery Company of Columbus, Nebraska, asked him to represent their firm at the National Sporting Goods Show at McCormick Place in Chicago in February 1965. Fritz happily took a vacation from KETV-TV and traveled to Chicago. It was here, at 10 A.M. on February 2, 1965, that John F. "Fritz" Johnson began to fall apart from the shock of recognition.

Fritz stood behind a booth, his black eye patch and easy manner attracting a crowd as he demonstrated archery equipment. A man from Akron, Ohio, moved closer, staring. John "Fritz" Johnson, the man knew, was Lawrence Bader, an old school classmate. The Akron man, who was careful to remain anonymous, called the Bader family in Akron. John Bader, Larry's brother, was skeptical. He telephoned Mrs. Suzanne Peika, his twenty-one-year-old niece, who lived in Chicago, and asked her to go to McCormick Place and look over the Doppelgänger.

"Pardon me," Mrs. Peika blurted out days later as she stood looking at Fritz, "but aren't you my uncle, Larry Bader?"

An innocent laugh greeted her inquiry, but the niece persisted and asked that Fritz talk with Larry's brothers John and Richard in Akron. Fritz made the call and the Bader brothers were convinced that he and their supposedly drowned brother were one. The Baders flew to Chicago and positively identified him as Lawrence Bader. The group adjourned to a police station. Fritz shrugged off the identification as a look-alike fluke, a mistaken identity by a family desperate to have their loved one back among the living.

When the Baders became adamant that Johnson was Bader, the archer turned to Lieutenant Emil Giese, suggesting a way to clear up the puzzle. Why not take my fingerprints and check them with the F.B.I., Fritz volunteered. Giese informed Johnson that he was not compelled to do such a thing. Johnson smilingly insisted, confident that the check would disprove the Bader claim. The Baders returned to Akron and Johnson to his wife and children in Omaha.

A day later Lieutenant Giese called Omaha and reported that his prints had been checked by the F.B.I. against Lawrence Bader's Navy records. (Bader had served as a corpsman in a stateside hospital, never having seen action.) The two sets of prints were identical, Giese told Johnson.

"Now what do I do?"

"Get a lawyer," Giese counseled Bader-Johnson.

The following months consisted of one prolonged nightmare for John "Fritz" Johnson. The question asked nationwide was reflected in the headline, "Man With Two Wives—Amnesia or Hoax?" It was a question that Fritz tried to answer the rest of his days, as he faced charges of bigamy, fraud and desertion. "Up to that moment," Bader said, referring to his call from Lieutenant Giese, "I had no doubt that I was *not* Larry Bader. But when I heard that, it was like a door had slammed and somebody had hit me right in the face."

At his own insistence, Bader-Johnson underwent exhaustive psychological testing, including hypnosis. A team of specialists were convinced that Bader had been an amnesiac for eight years. Mary Lou Bader told the press: "I know I have been wronged." Bader's second wife, Mrs. Fritz Johnson, decided with her husband that a legal separation was imperative "until this matter is resolved." (Nancy Johnson later moved to obtain an annulment.)

The matter was resolved to everyone's everlasting confusion. The malignant cancer once thought to have been removed from Bader-Johnson's head flared up and on September 16, 1966, the celebrated amnesia victim died at St. Joseph's Hospital in Omaha. He left the living to decide whether or not he was one of the truly great amnesiacs of the century or, as one medical expert put it, a startling "modern-day schizophrenic."

### Women in the Unknown

Crammed archives shed much more light on missing male amnesiacs than on female, no doubt due to the status of males as breadwinners and to the fact that women in the past were rooted to the chores of household and the chains of family and were seldom permitted to stray beyond the hearth for any reason. When amnesia was mere speculation in the minds of a few doctors, females who disappeared, such as the Chicago pianist Grace Stewart Potter, were judged to be insane and were sent to an asylum. This was Miss Potter's fate in 1915, when she vanished for almost a week and returned to her

Lake Bluff, Illinois, residence not able to remember where she had been or why she had disappeared.

A month after a tattered Miss Potter reappeared, Mrs. John Sinclair, the wife of a wealthy, socially prominent Philadelphia doctor, was found dead in a broken-down Negro tenement in Atlantic City, New Jersey. Mrs. Sinclair had been missing for several weeks and had had a long history of what was then termed "mental trouble." She would forget completely who she was on occasions and simply wander off, assuming different identities until she remembered her own and somehow returned to Philadelphia.

During her last absence, her husband alerted the police in several Eastern cities and statewide searches were conducted. Mrs. Sinclair's body might never have been identified had not Atlantic City police become suspicious of a Negro undertaker who applied for permission to bury the body of "a mulatto woman" known as "Martha Conday." Officers rushed to the tenement where the body lay in rags and identified it as that of Dr. Sinclair's amnesiac wife. How this once beautiful butterfly of Philadelphia society came to such a dark end remained as unanswered as the causes of the mental malady that hooded her life.

For Joan Ross-Dilley, British tennis star, a blow to her head in early 1954 apparently caused amnesia and her subsequent disappearance. Miss Ross-Dilley had written to her twin sister from Brook-

*Joan Ross-Dilley (left), shown with her twin sister, Jean, was a British tennis star until a blow to her head in 1954 caused a complete loss of memory. (UPI)*

line, Massachusetts, in early August that she was suffering terrific headaches as a result of a fall. Days later the tennis champion vanished. A week passed and a twenty-four-year-old woman got off a bus from Albany and went to the local police station in Burlington, Vermont. "All I can remember," she told a squinting desk sergeant, "is that my name is Suzanne."

Astute officers, who had been alerted to Ross-Dilley's disappearance, compared the amnesia victim with photos of the tennis player and identified her, helped by the fact that the tennis star's middle name was Suzanne. The tennis champion recovered.

Another woman got off a bus with no idea how she arrived in downtown Milwaukee in May 1976. She walked through the busy depot and collapsed before she reached the entrance door. She woke up in the locked ward of Milwaukee County Hospital, telling doctors that she thought her name was Kay Johnson, that she had given birth to at least four children, and that her husband was an "aviator in some branch of military service."

She vaguely recalled that her travels to Milwaukee had brought her through Anchorage, Alaska; Chicago; Salt Lake City; and Oshkosh, Wisconsin. *The Chicago Tribune* sent reporter Jim Gallagher to Milwaukee to interview the mystery woman, and through the *Tribune*'s investigative efforts it was learned that Kay Johnson was, indeed, in Salt Lake City on April 24. In Salt Lake's bus terminal Gary Williams, a youth en route to a school in Arizona, bummed a cigarette from Kay and the two walked across the street to Fred's Restaurant to get a cup of coffee. "She looked weak as all hell," Williams said later, "like she hadn't eaten for days. She told me she had been waiting for some money to be wired."

No sooner were the two inside the restaurant than a man burst through the front door and shot one of the restaurant employees. At the first shot, both Williams and Kay flattened themselves on the floor and then ran out a back door. One policeman who interviewed Kay after the shooting remembered that "she was walking around in a daze." The bewildered woman gave her name and address as "Kay Kathleen, 696 Grand, Grand Rapids, Michigan," an identity and residence that never existed. Four days later the proprietor of the Little America Restaurant asked Kay to leave. Said one waitress, "It looked like she hadn't had a bath for a hundred years and acted so dopey."

That night Kay was arrested for not being able to pay for a $3.13 dinner in the same restaurant and was taken to jail, where she spent the night.

The plight of this amnesia victim was eased for a few days by Travelers Aid, who put her up in an inexpensive hotel. Eloise Thomson, a generous Samaritan, then took the woman into her home. Kay spent most of her time thumbing through the phone book, which she would abruptly close and put aside whenever anyone approached. In late May the withdrawn woman told Mrs. Thomson that she "had to get to Milwaukee because a woman there could help her find her children." Mrs. Thomson responded with typical kindness and not only gave Kay $70 for her fare and food but drove her to Omaha, where Kay boarded a bus.

In Milwaukee Kay waited in the hospital, waited for someone to find her. "If I do have a family somewhere," she asked, "how are they managing without me, and why aren't they looking for me? I don't think I'd just go off and leave them. I don't think I'm that kind of person. Do I look like that kind of person?"

The answer came on September 13, 1976. Milwaukee officials had made contact with a St. Paul family named Heaton and had received a photo album full of wedding pictures. These were shown to Kay and she picked herself out of the photos as the bride and identified her husband, Ed Heaton. She was forty-three-year-old Rita Heaton, who had given birth to five children, ages nine to eighteen and who had been divorced since 1971. She had left St. Paul in March 1976, after telling her relatives that "she was taking a trip." The family never filed a missing-persons report, but luckily for them, Kay Johnson began to vanish when Rita Heaton recognized her own wedding photo.

### The "Sliding Ghost" & Company

Amnesia has caused many a combat soldier to disappear, vanishing into a void that the normal chaos of battle might explain. In this century, the strange story of Harry Miller of Salt Lake City proved that one only had to get near to a war to be declared missing in action.

Miller had enlisted in the Army and was waiting to report to boot camp. On his way to a training center in 1917 Miller was waylaid by a gang of ruffians and knocked unconscious. Miller remembered waking in a cell, having been jailed for fighting. He stood up and moved slowly to the cell door. As he shuffled forward he rubbed the large bump on his head.

"Hey," Miller shouted to a guard. "Did you get those guys who beat me up and stole my wallet?"

The guard said, smirking, "That's a good one, Mac. You know why you're in there."

"Huh? Whaddya talkin' about?"

"You mean you don't remember? Last night they pulled you from a freight car and you tried to fight a cop, old-timer. He tapped you with his night stick and you went out like a light. A man your age shouldn't be on the bum, dad."

"You must be drunk!" thundered Miller. "I got hit by clubs. Some guys were after my money." Miller spotted a newspaper in the guard's hand. "Let me see that." The guard slipped the paper through the cell bars. Miller's eyes popped. He stared at the date— 1937. *"But . . . but this is 1917!"* he screamed in terror. "Is everybody crazy here?"

Miller moved to a cracked mirror in the corner of his cell and fell back in shock. Instead of the clean-shaven healthy young man of twenty-six Harry Miller thought himself to be, the image in the mirror was that of an old man with white hair, unshaven, filthy, the face of a total stranger. Twenty years, the best years of Harry Miller's life, had vanished.

In the same year that Miller was clubbed out of twenty years, a British soldier, C. H. Peachey, was wounded in the head on the Western Front. Following an operation, Peachey, his memory lost, sailed for America, where he remained for ten years, wandering from one mental hospital to another. A surgeon performed another operation and Peachey recalled his entire past. He returned to England in 1927 to find that his wife had remarried and his children were adopted. But a miracle was produced by Peachey's reappearance. His deaf-mute brother was so startled by Peachey's return that, according to author Arthur Grahame, "he regained his hearing and power of speech!"

For the sheer bizarre, nothing approaches the experience of one Captain de Montalt, who was seated with a dozen other officers in a dugout on New Year's Eve of 1916–17 when he heard the whine of a shell about to explode directly above. De Montalt grabbed his coat and thrust one arm into a sleeve just as the dugout was blown to pieces by a direct hit. The captain could remember nothing when he awoke in an army hospital. A doctor handed him a letter which he said had been found in the coat he was partly wearing when he was picked up by stretcher-bearers. He was a Canadian named de Montalt. Without names and addresses of relatives and friends and no evidence to the contrary, de Montalt did not argue with his identity.

Recovering from his wounds, de Montalt joined the R.A.F. During a raid on his airfield, a young British officer had his legs blown away and died in de Montalt's arms, begging the Canadian officer to visit his sister in London. De Montalt promised to do so. Days later he was shot down, so terribly wounded that he was mustered out of the service with one-hundred-percent disability.

Once out of the service the captain made good his promise to visit his dead friend's sister. He fell in love with her and they were married within months. Their marriage was a happy one for seven years, punctured only by brief moments when de Montalt brooded about his identity. One day he overheard Swedish being spoken in a London restaurant and to his astonishment, de Montalt understood every word. From that point de Montalt doubted his nationality. Some weeks later de Montalt was waiting in a government office to discuss his pension with an official. Casually, he picked up a copy of the Swedish *Statskalendern*, a military publication listing all important officials and army officers of Sweden. As he glanced through the lists, de Montalt was suddenly attracted to the name Gustaf Duner, a name oddly familiar to him.

The captain wrote down the address given after the name and sent a letter of inquiry off to Sweden. He received a quick reply, stating that "Herr Gustaf Duner was unfortunately killed on the Western Front at the end of 1916. I am his brother." It was then that de Montalt realized that he was Gustaf Duner. He took the next plane to Sweden, where he visited with his overjoyed brother and mother. He also learned how he came to vanish by assuming another man's identity while suffering from what has been termed epochal amnesia, loss of memory over prolonged periods.

Duner discovered that he had been born in 1880, the son of a professor at Uppsala University. He had earned his commission in the Swedish army but had resigned to serve with the British in the Boer War in 1902, where he learned English fluently and identified himself with the British military personality, a trait expanded into his own personality when he took on de Montalt's identity. Duner remained a soldier of fortune, involving himself in many of the British colonial wars until World War I, which brought him to the dugout where he inadvertently grabbed the wrong man's coat and identity just before the shell landed. The real de Montalt was killed in the explosion.

America's "Sliding Ghost" was another story, one that did not end with a spark of recollection like Montalt-Duner's. Jerry Tarbot was the name given to the first living unknown soldier by a judge after Tarbot had been released from an insane asylum, had been gassed, shot and bayonetted on the French front during World War I. He was also a man who remembered nothing of his life before the war.

Tarbot had been sent to the California Insane Asylum from San Francisco in 1922. He had no idea why he was sent there, and upon his release he could remember only that he had once served with valor on the Western Front in World War I. He wandered about seeking his identity, haunting hospitals and military installations. In Los Angeles a Dr. Samuel Marcus took an interest in Tarbot's case and hypnotized him in the presence of Senator Samuel M. Shortridge of California and playwright and novelist Rupert Hughes. According to one report, Tarbot "in the hypnotic trance tried to dig holes in the carpet and went 'over the top.'"

Dr. Marcus' experiment with Tarbot was highly publicized and several veterans who remembered him stepped forward. One, William R. Beach of San Diego, who had served in the Marines on the Verdun sector, swore out an affidavit that "he saw Tarbot at Verdun in the uniform of a Marine and talked with him." Said Beach: "They used to call him 'The Sliding Ghost' because of his ability to get through difficult territory." Tarbot did not remember Beach or ever having been at Verdun.

Marcus determined from his examination of the amnesia victim that his origins were in New York. Tarbot sought out Marine Corps General W. C. Neville, who thought the missing man served "with the Marine brigade at Belleau Wood." The general arranged for Tarbot to work his way East on a tramp steamer sailing through the Panama Canal. He arrived in Washington so sick that he was hospitalized for seven months in Mount Alto Hospital.

While there he underwent several head operations, and on one occasion Tarbot found himself studying a case of surgical instruments. He suddenly remembered a Brooklyn, New York, shop where he had helped to make just such instruments. He caught a train to New York and found the J. Sklar Manufacturing Company. Several workers in the shop recognized him, but none could recall his name. He was told that he resembled a man who worked there between 1912 and 1914 but records for that period had been destroyed.

Next Tarbot recalled having served Mass in the chapel at Fordham University when he was a youth. He went to the university and spoke to Father Henry McGarvey, who concluded that Tarbot had indeed been a student there. New York's Missing Persons Bureau assigned several men to help Tarbot identify himself, but they turned up nothing. Neville G. Hall of the Veteran's Bureau contacted all branches of the armed services, but records in Washington yielded nothing. Tarbot's fingerprints were not on file. (Only those who had been part of the regular army before the outbreak of the war had their fingerprints on file; draftees and volunteers who poured into enlistment offices so overwhelmed government employees that fingerprints were recorded haphazardly or not at all.)

It was thought that Tarbot may have belonged to either the French or the Canadian army. No records could be found on their muster rolls. Desperately, Jerry Tarbot went to Philadelphia on October 14 , 1923, to stand before thousands of Legionnaires who had gathered for their annual convention and ask from a barren stage while colored lights played upon him: "Please, does anyone here know me? I served in Europe . . . I was wounded in the head in France. Does anyone know me?"

Thousands of veterans glanced about uneasily. Tarbot, his head bowed in discouragement, was about to step off stage when a voice rang out: "I know that man!" A uniformed Legionnaire ran down the aisle and up the steps to the stage. He was Benjamin J. Sprang, of

Philadelphia, who had served in the Forty-seventh Company of the Fifth Regiment.

Overcome by emotion, Tarbot locked his arms around Sprang as the Legionnaire half-shouted: "I know you. I remember your face well. I used to go over to your company often. I used to box a good deal with a man named Sullivan, and you used to watch us."

"What is my name?" Tarbot asked, his anxiety causing him to tremble.

"I don't know, old man," Sprang said. "If I ever did know I have forgotten it. I do remember seeing you at Colombo and Nevars, and again at Belleau Wood."

In front of ten thousand paralyzed veterans the drama played itself out, Tarbot's body shaking, his face twitching as he visibly struggled to recall his past. "Yes . . . yes . . . I remember going into action with twenty-four men led by Lieutenant Robinson."

"That was his name, old boy, Robinson—Lieutenant Robinson—he was killed in the war."

"We hiked into the town of Moulanville and Merines," stammered Tarbot. "I remember stuffing my bag with provisions . . . I think I remember Belleau Wood . . . I think I was wounded there . . . we were running, all of us running. Then the Germans threw grenades and my head opened up . . ." Tarbot's words trailed off, and the two men stood silent in the lights. Then two mothers who had had sons in the war who were still missing stepped forward to scrutinize Tarbot, hoping that he might be the lost loved one.

The gold-star mothers began to cry. Mrs. Bryson Clark, of Clementon, New Jersey, whose son disappeared while he was serving with the 166th Division as a machine-gunner, shook her head. Tarbot was not the man. Mrs. Hugh De Haven, of West Conshohocken, Pennsylvania, moved closer to Tarbot. She, too, burst into tears. "I'm sorry, young man," she sobbed. "I wish you were my son, but you're not."

"I'm sorry, too," Tarbot half-moaned. "You seem like a kind woman . . . I wish, God knows how I wish, I were someone's son!"

As the months went by there were more "positive" identifications of Tarbot. Claude Neil, a New York elevator operator, stated emphatically that Tarbot was really one James Talbot, whom he recognized from a newspaper photo. Talbot, insisted Neil, had worked with him in Havana, Cuba; the war hero had worked his way on a boat to Cuba, landed penniless and subsequently became the manager of the British Club there. Israel Greenberg in Baltimore, Maryland, once a sergeant in the Marines, was just as insistent that Tarbot, whose picture he saw in a newspaper, was a French-Canadian named George Beaupré.

"The last time I saw Beaupré," Greenberg told reporters, "was at Chateau Thierry, when he went into action in 'No-Man's-Land' with a detail of men. He came back badly injured and was sent to a hospital . . . He never rejoined the Sixteenth Company."

Another "informant" identified Tarbot as Bruce Harpin, a Brooklyn lunch-counter owner. None of these identifications could be supported, and Jerry Tarbot drifted, trying to remember his history. He disappeared again and permanently in Akron, Ohio; he was seen wandering through the Goodyear Tire and Rubber plant, where more than fifty workers "recognized" him, but no one knew his name. Jerry Tarbot's past eluded him.

The number of missing men during World War II, Korea and Vietnam soared into the thousands. "Missing in action" became an all too familiar phrase. One spectacular "missing-in-action" case, rivaling that of Tarbot, involved a man named Charles A. Jameson, another living unknown soldier, who was stricken by amnesia and groped for identity for a decade in a Boston hospital.

Jameson was delivered to the hospital as part of the great glut of wounded that poured into the Eastern seaports in early 1945. Records were understandably spotty, since medical staffs busied themselves with saving lives and identifying the injured later. Jameson was unconscious, and a tag tied to him read "Charles A. Jameson, forty-nine, religion—Catholic; citizenship—American, Cutty Sark." That was all.

The patient's back was studded with infected shrapnel wounds, and, through apparent neglect before he reached the States, Jameson had contracted a severe bone disease known as osteomyelitis. An ugly head wound had apparently affected the patient's memory; the shrapnel wounds took three years to finally heal, and during that time Jameson would repeat only one line when identifying himself: "My name is Charles A. Jameson, forty-nine, Catholic, American, the Cutty Sark."

*World War II amnesia victim Charles A. Jameson, a living unknown soldier. (*UPI*)*

Authorities and newsmen tried to identify Jameson. The U.S. Navy had no record of him; neither did the Merchant Marine. The Red Cross searched exhaustively through medical archives and turned up nothing. Frank Castelnovo, an investigator for the U.S. Immigration and Naturalization Service, spent years checking on the man called Jameson. Whatever clues turned up were the result of the investigator asking Jameson to write down his name in order to check his handwriting. It was then officials learned that Jameson had been deaf for years.

Through Jameson's writing it was learned that the patient had an astonishing knowledge of military strategy, particularly the campaigns of Napoleon. "He knew all the maneuvers and deployment of troops at Napoleon's Battle of Austerlitz," said writer Don Hogan. He was able to name every major steamship company in the world, and he recognized from photos—and described in detail—the gunnery school for British sailors at Gosport, England. That, coupled with his distinct British accent, compelled Maxwell Plowman, British vice-consul in Boston, to ask the British Maritime Registry and the Admiralty to conduct a record search on Jameson. Nothing was discovered.

In October 1954, the indefatigable Castelnovo dug up a manifest of the Navy transport, the U.S.S. *LeJeune*, which had delivered Jameson to Boston on February 9, 1945. Jameson, this record showed, had arrived with a cargo of wounded men from Southampton, England. At the bottom of the manifest was written: "Charles W. [*sic*] Jameson, July 17, 1895, Boston, Mass., Catholic, from the ship *Cutty Sark*, documents lost . . . Four years in Belgium . . . a prisoner of war . . . by the Germans."

The merchant ship *Cutty Sark* was a myth, the last vessel so named being stricken from the register in 1900. Jameson wrote on his pad that he thought he had been on the merchant ship *Hinemoa*: "She was a sailing vessel and I was mate. We were carrying nitrates from Chile to England and met with a German cruiser in the Atlantic. We were sunk." A check revealed that just such a vessel had been recorded as sunk by the Germans in the English Channel. The *Hinemoa's* surviving crew members were interviewed. None of them recalled Jameson or could identify his photo—which certainly would not have been the case had Jameson been first mate. In 1956, the search for Jameson's true identity was abandoned. The old man said of his fate: "Sometimes I think I must be like Ulysses when he met the Cyclops—nobody."

## Literary Lights Turned Off

Writers, especially those creating fiction, have an obsession with missing persons. Nathaniel Hawthorne found delicious perversity in one of his own characters, a wealthy, intellectual Londoner named Wakefield, after Hawthorne's story of the same name, who contrived to vanish, abandoning his wife and continuing to live only a few blocks from her in disguise for the next twenty years. Hawthorne's "Outcast of the Universe," as he divined him, "had happened to dissever himself from the world—to vanish—to give up his place and privilege with living men, without being admitted among the dead."

One of America's most colorful writers, Sherwood Anderson, not only disappeared in 1912, leaving his wife and three children in Elyria, Ohio, but to the day he died as a result of swallowing a toothpick in an hors d'oeuvre sausage, the author insisted that he had been a victim of total amnesia.

The thirty-six-year-old Anderson, who had lived in poverty as a boy in Clyde, Ohio, found the going almost as rough following his marriage and the birth of three children. He struggled for five years to support a failing paint-manufacturing company in Elyria. He began to daydream his way out of his troubles, retreating to his office to write short stories when the bills and the pressures became unbearable. Yet the burden of plant and family continued to plague him.

The strain became too excruciating on the afternoon of November 27, 1912. He was dictating a letter to one of his customers when something snapped. "The goods about which you have inquired are the best of their kind made in the—" dictated Anderson.

The secretary waited for words that did not come. "What's the matter?" she asked.

Anderson, his face a blank, replied in a monotone: "My feet are cold and wet. I have been walking too long on the bed of a river." A man with what seemed to be an entirely different personality suddenly buttoned his coat and strode from the office, out the front door, and down the road. Sherwood Anderson, who, in later years, would author such minor masterpieces as *Winesburg, Ohio* and *Windy McPherson's Son,* vanished. For ninety-six hours, employees, family and police searched frantically for him. It was a period of time about which the prolific Anderson would never write an authentic word.

The *Cleveland Leader* was the first to announce the news of Anderson's travels:

> Wandering gypsy-like about the countryside after disappearing from his home in Elyria four days ago, walking almost incessantly save for a few hours of sleep snatched in thickets and all the while unconscious of his identity, Sherwood Anderson . . . was discovered late yesterday afternoon in a drug store at E. 152 St [in Cleveland] . . . Anderson was found by a physician to be suffering from the effects of some severe mental strain and was taken by friends to Huron Road hospital.

Most experts agreed that Anderson was a victim of amnesia. He never told the story, or at least the beginning of his disappearance, the same way twice and he told it often. Quite simply, he could not remember. That he had thought for a long time of leaving his school-teacher wife, Cornelia, there was no doubt. But he was too practical a man to set out on foot across frozen, barren countryside with only three dollars in his pocket. His friend, author Ben Hecht, thought Anderson's excursion into the unknown humorous and wrote sardonically in his *A Child of the Century* that when Anderson was found in Cleveland, he borrowed money from a friend (Edwin Baxter, a Cleveland banker) and then set off "a victim of amnesia. He had arrived on foot in Chicago wearing a shaggy beard and still uncertain of his identity, but nevertheless landed a job immediately as a copy writer for Taylor-Critchfield & Co., where his inability to remember his name or where he came from stamped him as a genius in his employer's mind and resulted in his getting a bigger salary than anybody else writing copy for the firm."

The disappearance had many tales in it for Anderson and he later exaggerated and fabricated its beginnings, implying that he was fully aware of his actions, though the facts insist he was in a state of amnesia. Years later Anderson impishly wrote that he purposely said to his secretary "a final confusing sentence to the woman who now stared at me in speechless amazement: 'My feet are cold, wet, and heavy from long wading in a river [reconstructed from his original statement, which he could not remember]. Now I shall go walk on dry land,' I said, and as I passed out of the door a delicious thought came. 'Oh, you little tricky words, you are my brothers. It is you, not myself, who have lifted me over this threshold. It is you who have dared give me a hand. For the rest of my life I will be a servant to you,' I whispered to myself as I went along a spur of railroad track, over a bridge, out of a town, and out of that phase of my life."

No one ever believed that Anderson had devised his own disappearance or that his amnesia was feigned. The most cynical of scrutinizers, the newsmen, were convinced of his loss of memory, but then Anderson's hometown never took his literary ambitions seriously. When he died in 1941, the *Elyria Chronicle-Telegram* ignored the many books Anderson had written and the literary stature he had attained. Its headline read: "Sherwood Anderson, Former Elyria Manufacturer, Dies."

There were more headlines in late 1926, when Agatha Clarissa Christie vanished, a disappearance that had all the quiet, calculating terror of any of her best murder mysteries. Appropriately, it was a dark, stormy night, December 3, 1926, when Mrs. Christie packed an attaché case with clothing and walked out of her impressive country home at Sunningdale in Berkshire, England. She went to a two-seater sports car, got in, and drove away.

The next morning more than a hundred policemen were combing the countryside for the author, called out by an apprehensive Colonel Archibald Christie, her husband. At 8 A.M. on that Saturday morning, constables were stunned when they found Mrs. Christie's sports car abandoned near Guildford. Their report read that the car was "on the edge of a chalkpit, the front wheels actually overhanging the edge. The car evidently had run away, and only a thick hedge growth prevented it from plunging into the pit." In the car police found Mrs. Christie's attaché case open, and the clothes the writer had packed were scattered about as if someone had conducted a desperate search.

Colonel Christie could offer little help to police; he suggested that his wife had overworked herself to the point of exhaustion and that

*Mystery writer Agatha Christie at the time of her famous disappearance in 1926.* (UPI)

her many book projects might have brought her to a nervous break-down. It was rumored that Mrs. Christie's secretary, Miss Fisher, had received a note from her employer which was sent on the night she disappeared. It allegedly read: "If I don't leave Sunningdale soon Sunningdale will be the end of me." The house, many of the writer's friends pointed out, was "getting on her nerves." Sunningdale, appropriate to the mystery writer's grist, stood in a lonely lane, unlighted and eerie at night. A woman had been murdered not far from the Christie estate, and a man had committed suicide almost on the doorstep of the manor house.

Moreover, Mrs. Christie had been obsessed for more than a decade with the 1910 disappearance of Dorothy Arnold. Mrs. Christie was twenty at the time of that disappearance and empathized deeply with twenty-five-year-old Dorothy Arnold and her speculated fate; the future novelist devoured every word printed about the case, and it was this disappearance, a London reporter said, that had caused Mrs. Christie "to adopt her career of writing mystery fiction."

Rumors were passed onto investigators from Scotland Yard as facts. Mrs. Christie had committed suicide, one account related, despondent over not being able to finish her most recent work, "The Blue Train." For a while police accepted this theory. Another rumor maintained that she had been murdered by an upper-crust Englishman who thought she had wrongly profiled him in one of her stories. (Mrs. Christie, in a 1974 interview published in *Parade,* illustrated how she never drew her material from flesh and blood, albeit her style was as eccentric as her disappearance: "I got some of my plots just sitting in the bathtub, undisturbed, and lining the rim of the tub with apple cores.") Another claim, plausible to the suspicious, was that Mrs. Christie had arranged her own disappearance to promote her new novel, *The Mystery of the Downs,* which was soon to be serialized in several newspapers. Mrs. Christie's literary agent and publishers vehemently denied it. The most absurd rumor had it that the writer had been abducted and was being held for ransom, the payment to come from her considerable royalties.

Scotland Yard, the police and thousands of motorists and tourists intrigued by the disappearance ignored the rumors and met at Newlands' Corner in Surrey, where Mrs. Christie had reportedly been seen last. On foot, pedaling bicycles and driving autos, they fanned out across the countryside, searching every hedgerow and gulley. Not a trace of Mrs. Christie was found. In the following days, thousands more joined the search, until the horde swelled to more than 15,000, "the biggest search ever undertaken in this country for a missing person," according to the London correspondent of *The New York Times*. Even Mrs. Christie's pet terrier was put into the hunt, given the scent from one of her gloves; the dog sniffed the same spot of ground for three hours and then went to sleep. But boxloads of Airedales, bloodhounds, Alsatian police dogs and retrievers were sent barking and sniffing across the downs in Surrey. Hours later a sweating and exhausted Deputy Chief Constable Kenward huffed: "We've covered the ground as completely as it is humanly possible and we've drawn a blank."

Police received information that a mysterious letter, written by Mrs. Christie on the night of her disappearance, had been given to her secretary and was to be opened in the event her body was found; if she reappeared alive, the letter was to be returned to her unopened. There was no such letter.

A furtive woman was supposedly seen darting in and out of a deserted bungalow at night near Sussex Downs, not far from where Mrs. Christie's car had been discovered. Inside the bungalow, owned by one Major Williams-Ellis, was found a bottle labeled "poison lead and opium," pieces of a torn-up postcard, a woman's fur-lined coat, a box of face powder, and the end of a loaf of bread. The night visitor, villagers insisted, was identified as Mrs. Christie. Police put the bungalow under surveillance but no one appeared.

One London newspaper offered a five-hundred-dollar reward to anyone who might supply information leading to the discovery of the missing novelist. This spurred thousands of amateur sleuths to scour the dark lanes and byways of Sussex Downs, which considerably hampered the police. On one occasion, two men wearing Sherlock Holmes caps were almost run over by a police car while they were on their hands and knees in the dark, trying to examine footprints in the road with magnifying glasses.

The resolution of the mystery was as tidy as those ending Mrs. Christie's novels. Her sensational disappearance ended when a guest at the Hydro Harrowgate, a spa in Yorkshire, recognized Mrs. Christie from a newspaper photo as a fellow visitor to the health resort. Stunned officials there learned that the writer did not know who she was, having arrived dazed at the spa on foot on the night of her disappearance and having registered under a different name; she said that she had "come from the Cape of Good Hope."

Her amnesia was apparently complete during her stay at the resort, where she sang, attended dances, and played billiards with other female guests. Along with the other guests she took an avid interest in the disappearance of Agatha Christie, following developments in the papers with the concern of an interested stranger.

Colonel Christie was the first to confront his wife. He entered the spa's main receiving room and sat on a couch. Within minutes his wife walked down the stairs on her way to the dining room but strolled past him without even glancing in his direction.

"Don't you know me?" asked the colonel as he gently grabbed his wife by the arm. "Surely you recognize me?"

Mrs. Christie stared blankly at him. "No," she replied slowly, "I have never met you before."

Mrs. Christie was taken to London, where she slowly regained her memory, first thinking her husband to be her brother. She had no idea how she got to the Hydro Harrowgate, but thought she might have been on a train.

Agatha Christie's loss of memory proved to be her financial gain. As a result of the international publicity connected with her disappearance, newspapers went berserk with bids to serialize her work, and all her old, out-of-print books were reissued. She was now world famous, and she would remain so until her death on January 12, 1976. Fifty years later Mrs. Christie's books were estimated to have sold two hundred million copies in the United States alone. She never mentioned her disappearance directly, but obliquely insisted again and again that she was incapable of feigning such an event for publicity. "A writer must have genuine respect for the reader," she said at age eighty-four. "I myself never cheat."

Since the first explorers bullied their way across uncharted seas and forbidding new continents, the list of missing adventurers has soared, until legions of wanderers have been entered on that list. Men like Richard Halliburton, Percy Fawcett and George Leigh-Mallory, who ventured into unfamiliar terrain, seemed to step into a void just waiting to swallow them. Sometimes their disappearances were as spectacular as the goals they sought. David Livingstone, British explorer and discoverer of Victoria Falls, was one of the most celebrated missing adventurers of the nineteenth century. His discovery in a remote African village by American newsman H. M. Stanley provided the classic understatement, "Dr. Livingstone, I presume."

Perhaps the eeriest disappearance in that century was that of Sir John Franklin's heavily equipped polar expedition that was last heard from in 1845. The black, almost intact hulls of Franklin's ships, the *Erebus* and the aptly named *Terror*, were sighted off Newfoundland on April 6, 1851. Incredibly, they were mounted atop an iceberg.

The captain of the Canadian brig who identified the ships reported no trace of the explorer Franklin or any of his crew members. To the Canadian fishermen the strange, ghostly vision of the two ships was a fitting, if not predictable, end for the adventuresome Franklin. In the words of sea historian Robert de la Croix:

> The history of the sea contains no stranger mystery than the apparition of the two black phantom ships, mounted on their icy thrones and gliding slowly over the waters, as if in defiance of the powers that sought to destroy them. They made their last voyage openly and calmly, before sinking with their secrets to the ocean bed.

Wanderlust often means looking back to a homeland long gone. This nostalgia sometimes leads to inexplicable disappearances, such as the 1898 vanishing act of John O'Brien, a wealthy Brooklyn merchant. O'Brien was calmly sitting on the front porch of his house one summer evening with his wife and children when he decided to "go down to Casey's and get a drink." He strolled away hatless and in shirtsleeves. In the words of *The New York Times:* "From that day he was never seen alive by anybody in America."

For a month police searched for O'Brien. Then came a cable from Ireland that he was dying in the small village of his birth. He had,

*Missing explorer David Livingstone, the most famous of lost adventurers.* (W. H. GROVE & SON)

that fateful night, simply gotten drunk with a friend and, mooning over his hometown across the ocean, climbed aboard a steamship and returned to Ireland.

### *"Bitter" Bierce's "Journey of Death"*

Of all the people who deserved to disappear, many thought, no one was more qualified than the acerbic author Ambrose Gwinnett Bierce. The man who was to become the leading West Coast writer during the 1890s was born in Meigs County, Ohio, on June 24, 1842. As a youth, Bierce became an ardent Abolitionist, working for an antislavery newspaper in northern Indiana. He briefly attended the Kentucky Military Institute in 1859, but left without a degree; his lack of education was to haunt him all his life. This was apparent in his later books, when, as a self-taught scribe, "his tardy discovery of good English rather went to his head," in the words of Van Wyck Brooks, writing in *Our Literary Heritage*. Yet Bierce was considered a master storyteller, and his *Tales of Soldiers and Civilians* and *In the Midst of Life* are considered minor American classics.

Cynical, aloof and moribund, Bierce reveled in the unknown; his life was pockmarked with adventure. He had enlisted three times during the Civil War, rising from the ranks to officer status and participating in such momentous battles as Shiloh, Chickamauga, Lookout Mountain, Missionary Ridge, and Sherman's march to the sea. Following the war, Bierce joined a military expedition that fought its way through hordes of Indians in 1866 to the Pacific. He settled in wild San Francisco, rubbing elbows with miners, thieves, gamblers and prostitutes.

Ambrose Bierce was as unpredictable and peculiar as the denizens of the West he wrote about. A handsome, vain man, Bierce's tall, soldierly bearing, his pink, fair complexion, blue eyes, golden hair and luxuriant mustache attracted almost every woman who glanced in his direction. His first mistress was seventy years old; he was fifteen. Subsequent companions were hardly beauties, as one of his biographers, Walter Neale, pointed out: "All those among Bierce's *chères amies* whom I met personally were ugly, even repulsively so, and in every way unattractive."

*Writer and critic Ambrose Bierce, who disappeared in Mexico in 1914.*

Young men in San Francisco with literary ambitions, however, were as loyal to their mentor Bierce as his mistresses were faithless, for his mixture of romantic melodrama, skepticism and sense of irony held them spellbound. Bierce's awe and obsession with death permeated his fiction, touched his family and seemingly directed his disciples. (His most enthusiastic followers ended in violence—author George Sterling committed suicide and writer Herman Scheffauer killed his wife and then himself.) Bierce related a dream he had at age sixteen, a dream in which he wandered over a "blasted and forbidding plain," to find an enormous building with "columns of cyclopean masonry" inside a nightmare room. He viewed on a bed a "dreadfully decomposed" corpse with black face and grinning lips which slowly opened its eyes. "Imagine my horror . . . the eyes were my own!"

Throughout his life Bierce was conscious and contemptuous of death. He would not allow tombstones to be put above the graves of his wife Mollie or his two sons, Day and Leigh. Day Bierce discovered his girl friend with a rival in 1889, shot both of them and then blew out his own brains. Only the girl recovered. When viewing his son's body upon a marble slab, Bierce half-shouted: "You're a noble soul, Day—you did just right." The other son, Leigh, married a girl of whom Ambrose did not approve. Feeling the disgrace, Leigh went on a devastating bender that resulted in death by pneumonia on March 31, 1901. Ambrose refused to talk to Leigh's wife at the funeral and promptly had his son's body cremated. Bierce kept the ashes in a cigar box on his writing desk, adding the ashes of his own burning cigars to the remains from time to time.

Bierce became one of the star writers in the spreading editorial empire of William Randolph Hearst, his pungent prose appearing in the *New York Journal,* the *New York American,* and the *San Francisco Chronicle,* as well as Hearst's magazine *Cosmopolitan.* His name became a household word, and the stories he told were bizarre, macabre, often frightening, accumulating in curious collections such as *Fantastic Fables* and *Can Such Things Be?* These were stories, based upon real-life happenings, that sought to answer the riddles of life. Many times Bierce wrote of strange disappearances, which obsessed him almost as much as did death. On several occasions, he conducted interviews at the sites where people had vanished. Although his lengthy pieces were full of scoff, they drew attention to these disappearances. He began to joke about the possibility of his own disappearance.

The jest became a reality in January 1914. In the previous year Bierce had decided to visit the battlefields of the Civil War, journey to Mexico, and then to South America, a last long adventure before death closed around him. He wrote to his daughter, Helen, that he was transferring his cemetery lot to her because he did "not wish to lie there. That matter is all arranged, and you will not be bothered about the mortal part of Your Daddy." He wrote to a friend a month later: "Bah! I'd hate to die between sheets, and, God willing, I won't."

Bierce carefully planned his end, as was evident from his farewell letters. All were full of a jocular fatalism. One said: "My plan, so far as I have one, is to go through Mexico to one of the Pacific ports, if I can *get* through without being stood up against a wall and being shot as an American. Thence I hope to sail for some port in South

America. Thence go across the Andes and perhaps across the continent . . . Naturally, it is possible—even probable—that I shall not return. These be 'strange countries,' in which things happen; that is why I am going. And I am seventy-one!"

Getting through Mexico, which was then in a chaotic state, concerned Bierce most. Pancho Villa, the onetime bandit, was leading a popular revolt against the dictator Victoriano Huerta. Bierce confided that he was "dressed for death," and "sleepy for death." He concluded that "my work is finished and so am I. If you hear of my being stood up against a Mexican stone wall and shot to rags, please know that I think that a pretty good way to depart this life. It beats old age, disease and falling down the cellar stairs." Bierce referred to his final adventure as his "*Jornada de Muerte*," a journey of death that would logically be ended by the revolutionaries. "To be a Gringo in Mexico, that is indeed euthanasia."

Bierce did make his sojourn to the battlefields of his youth, leaving his Washington home on October 2, 1913. He visited New Orleans, then Texas. From El Paso, Bierce crossed the border into Juarez, which had recently been liberated by Villa. The bandit-turned-general issued Bierce credentials that allowed him to accompany Villa's army. Bierce did so, an incredible feat for a man of Bierce's age, a man suffering from acute asthmatic seizures, and one who had not been on a horse for thirty years. His last letter, dated December 26, 1913, was sent from Chihuahua, Mexico, to his secretary Carrie Christiansen. He said that he had ridden four miles to mail the letter and that he had been given a sombrero as a present for "picking off" one of the enemy with a rifle at long range. He reported that the following day he would leave with the army for Ojinaga, a city under siege. Here the recorded story ends, and the many legends of Bierce's disappearance begin.

There were endless rumors and explanations. It was said that Bierce was killed during the siege of Ojinaga on January 11, 1914, his death reported in Mexican army dispatches under the name "A Pierce." Bierce is alleged to have argued with Villa, roaring, "You're nothing but a bandit!" at the volatile Pancho and then declaring that he was going over to the enemy. Pancho reportedly smiled, sighed, and ordered Bierce's execution, which was carried out by Rudolfo Fierro, Villa's personal executioner. It was said that Bierce was executed by General Tómas Urbina, Villa's right-hand man, as he and three Mexicans were attempting to run machine guns to the enemy. It was said that Bierce merely collapsed during the Ojinaga siege and died in the dust of Mexico from hardship and exposure.

None of these explanations was ever substantiated, and through the years dozens of more exotic answers to Bierce's adventuresome disappearance were put forward. Bierce either was poisoned or poisoned himself in his own back yard and was secretly buried, said one El Paso citizen. Washington friends insisted that he had blown his brains out on the highest ledge of the Grand Canyon, his body tumbling into the abyss to be forever lost. (Bierce had mentioned the Canyon as an appropriate tombstone to his gigantic ego.) The most incredible of all theories has it that the American author had wandered away from Villa's army, became lost in the wild regions of southern Mexico, and was captured by a tribe of primitive Indians, who boiled him alive and then shrunk his remains so that they would fit into a large bottle, which they proceeded to worship.

The disappearance of Bierce is a mystery to this day and will, no doubt, remain so forever. Bierce would have liked it that way; perhaps he planned the mystery to perpetuate his own memory and to confound death's bookkeeping. In the words of Edmund Wilson writing in *The New Yorker,* "like the man in his famous story who was hanged on the Owl Creek Bridge, he had had only, between war and war, a desperate dream of escape from an immutable doom of death."

### Vanishing at the Top of the World

All roads for the great British climber George Leigh-Mallory led to the top of Mount Everest. Conquering that highest of all mountains was the supreme adventure of his life. And it was on that mountain, perhaps only 800 feet from its summit, that Mallory and his climbing companion A. C. Irvine disappeared forever on June 8, 1924.

The British Alpine Club and the Royal Geographical Society had banded together in 1920 to form the Everest Committee. The sole function of that erstwhile group was to mount expeditions intent upon conquering the "Goddess, Mother of the Snows," as the Sherpa mountain men referred to the monster that reared its beautiful head between Nepal and Tibet in what can still be considered the most remote, inaccessible part of the world. Mallory was with the first contingent of climbers that assaulted Everest from May to June 1921, under the command of Colonel C. K. Howard-Bury. The group was driven back by snowstorms with winds up to 100 m.p.h., but one of Mallory's closest friends, Captain Geoffrey Bruce, vowed revenge, shaking his fist at Everest and shouting: "Just you wait, old thing! We'll get you yet!"

Mallory was on the 1922 expedition that attacked the 29,141-foot mountain with even more vigor, but fell short of its goal by 1,800 feet. Tragedy struck this group, an omen, it seemed to many later, of what was to befall Mallory. A member of the 1922 group recorded how "the whole climbing party was snatched by an avalanche of snow from the mountainside and swept down for hundreds of feet toward the cliff of a glacier; and seven of the cheerful courageous porters with the party were swept to instant death over its brink. The others saved themselves by swimming the breast stroke in the snow and came to a halt only on the very edge of the five-hundred-foot drop over the glacier's perpendicular side."

The 1924 expedition was spearheaded by Mallory, who was obsessed with conquering Everest. The commander of this assault, Colonel E. F. Norton, later described Mallory as one who was "the living soul of the offensive; the thing had become a personal matter with him, and was ultimately somewhat different from what it was to the rest of us." To reporters who asked the great mountain climber why he wished to reach the top of the greatest mountain, the adventurer replied, "Because it is there," a remark duplicated by Edmund Hillary, who, with Sherpa guide Tenzing Norkay, conquered the mountain in 1953. Mallory ominously added just before the expedition got under way, "for better or worse, we expect no mercy from Everest." He got none.

In late April 1924 the Everest expedition had set up its base camp near the Rongbuk Glacier. Six more camps, each one smaller than the last and manned by fewer and fewer climbers, were established as the party climbed through the spring. Two-man "waves" then attacked the mountain from Camp Six, which was only two thousand feet from the summit. (Mallory and the spunky Geoffrey Bruce

83

made the first attempt from 25,300 feet, but the Sherpa porters, superstitious of storms and mumbling about the mysterious *yetis*—the abominable snowmen—quit on them, and they were forced to turn back.) From Camp Six, which was at 26,800 feet, another unsuccessful attempt was made.

Mallory grew more and more determined to defeat the mountain, hurrying plans for a third attack, one which he, the most skillful mountain climber in the world, and a robust twenty-two-year-old Oxford graduate and brilliant athlete, Andrew C. Irvine, would mount on June 8. Mallory calculated that the snow monsoons would soon begin and cover the entire top of the mountain, making any assault impossible. On several occasions when he was making his preparations he was heard to say to himself that he would "stand on the top of *my* mountain" or die in the effort. Everyone knew Everest was *his* mountain, as if the flesh of George Leigh-Mallory and the rock and ice of the towering behemoth were two personalities in one man, in mortal combat to master each other.

Mallory, Irvine and eight Sherpa porters began to climb the last leg at 9 A.M. on June 6. Four of the porters returned late that afternoon. They told of the excruciating demands that the mountain made upon them—the devastating "high, thin air," the pressure against lungs and other organs as they trudged upward, the "mountain sickness," the dulled reflexes, errors in judgment, emotional strain. The oxygen bottles that Mallory and Irvine carried wouldn't last forever.

The remaining four porters returned to Camp Six on the morning of June 7, one handing N. E. Odell, the expedition's geologist, a note from Mallory, jubilantly exclaiming: "Perfect weather for the job!" Odell rose early the next morning, June 8, 1924, and began a vigil, staring through a powerful telescope at the summit. The top of Everest was shrouded by billowing white clouds.

At 12:50 P.M., the winds rose and the clouds were swept away, bathing the majestic peak of Everest in brilliant sunshine. Reported Odell three months later in *Current Opinion:*

> . . . there was a sudden clearing of the atmosphere, and the entire summit, ridge and final peak of Everest were unveiled. My eyes became fixed on one tiny black spot silhouetted on a small snowcrest beneath a rock-step in the ridge, and the black spot moved. Another

on the crest.

Obviously, Mallory and Irvine were cutting their way through the ice in their final dash to victory, "going strong" and only about 775 feet from the top. Mallory was pitting his enormous ability against *the* killer mountain and was winning, he and Irvine crunching upward on the sloping gable of the roof of the world, a place where no man had ever stood.

"The first black spot," said Odell, "then approached the great rock-step and shortly emerged at the top; the second did likewise. Then the whole fascinating vision vanished, enveloped in cloud once more." A snow monsoon quickly covered the mountain peak and with it Mallory and Irvine, who disappeared forever in the mists, theodolite observations fixing the altitude at which they were last seen at 28,227 feet.

Odell and others figured that the lashing blizzard certainly must have caused the two men to turn back. The geologist moved up the mountain from Camp Six as far as he dared go and kept shouting through the day and into the night to guide the men back. But by morning there was no trace of the two mountaineers.

In their disappearance Odell generously allowed the heroic pair their goal, telling reporters later that "I consider it very probable that they sheltered in some rock recess and fell asleep, and a painless death followed due to the excessive cold at those altitudes. . . . Considering all the circumstances and the position they had reached on the mountain, I am of the opinion that Mallory and Irvine must have reached the summit."

Forty years later Lowell Thomas wrote in *Book of the High Mountains* that "no subsequent expedition has ever come across a clue to the disappearance," speculating that "since they were roped together, the best guess is that one of them slipped, that they fell to their deaths together, that they lie entombed in the eternal ice and snow in the Himalayas."

The fate of Mallory and Irvine has proved to be *the* great disappearance in mountaineering, a mystery that in all probability will never be solved. The irony is that Everest can never be truly conquered, for scientists have learned that the mountain is *growing* by inches each year, a phenomenon that will always make the peak higher than the summit the last climber stood upon. But it was pure adventure Mallory sought, and he attained it, courting disaster all the way. This sense of lurking doom was best summed up in a little rhyme that Mallory and his companions prattled as they climbed in that fateful spring of 1924:

No game was ever worth a rap
   For a rational man to play
Into which no accident, no mishap,
   Could possibly find a way.

### The Lost Explorer of the Matto Grosso

The remarkable disappearance of George Leigh-Mallory was more than matched a year later when one of the world's last great explorers, Colonel Percy Harrison Fawcett, vanished into the fierce wilds of Brazil's Matto Grosso. This vast, jungle-webbed tract on a high plain in central Brazil, for the most part still uncharted today, haunted Fawcett for twenty years, drawing him with a siren song he could not resist, it was the sultry chant of riches and a lost city that may yet nestle in those dark regions.

Fawcett was no wild-eyed gold hunter motivated by greed, but a cautious, deliberate explorer whose aim was cultural discovery. Certainly, Fawcett's long career involved treasure. As a trained engineer in the British Army, Fawcett had been stationed in Ceylon at the turn of the century and spent much of his free time searching for the tombs and hidden treasure of the Kandyan kings. As a Founder's Medalist of the Royal Geographical Society he was "loaned out" to the Bolivian government to survey and determine the boundary between Bolivia and Brazil, an arduous and dangerous task that dragged on from 1906 to 1909.

The explorer became fascinated at this time with the almost mystical secrets of Brazil's forbidding interior, especially the seemingly endless and unknown jungle plateau known as the Matto Grosso. Somewhere inside that almost impenetrable wild, he believed, was a great, ancient city whose artifacts and spellbinding treasure would prove it to be the real cradle of civilization, its birth predating by more than five thousand years the first known cities of Egypt.

*Explorer Percy Harrison Fawcett vanished in Brazil in 1925 looking for what he thought to be the first civilization on earth.*

Fawcett was convinced that such a city existed—a city he called "Z"—because of a rare document that he unearthed about 1910 in Rio de Janeiro (Manuscript No. 512, Biblioteca Nacional). This incredible lost city, which purportedly rested on the side of an unreachable cliff, was discovered by a native of Minas Geraes who led a massive Portuguese expedition into the Matto Grosso in 1743, looking for the silver, gold and diamond mines located by the shadowy adventurer, Melchior Dias-Moreya, a half-Indian, half-Portuguese soldier of fortune who was known to natives simply as Moribeca and who had allegedly discovered in 1610 the staggering wealth of central Brazil. Moribeca was imprisoned when he would not pinpoint the location of the mines, and he died in 1622, his secret intact. The Portuguese expedition of 1743 in search of the fabulous mines went awry, the disoriented adventurers wandering north in error, through what is now the Matto Grosso. By accident, the Portuguese stumbled into a steep crevice and then climbed through an artificial breach in the cliff wall, following ancient paved steps.

Once through the cliff wall, the haggard adventurers beheld a giant city in ruins—wide streets, huge temples and enormous courts surrounded by majestic buildings. Mysterious inscriptions, copied by the amazed Portuguese and undeciphered to this day, decorated the buildings and temples. There was immense treasure, both archaeological finds and precious stones; a nearby river actually glittered with massive gold deposits. Lack of food and depleted supplies forced the Portuguese to abandon the city. Only three of them made their way, quite lost, to the coastal state of Bahia, where they emerged to tell the wild tale in 1754. The eleven-year odyssey was quickly forgotten except for a detailed report kept in the Rio library, the report that stirred Colonel Fawcett so many years later.

World War I interrupted Fawcett's careful plans to probe the Brazilian jungle for his lost city, but after serving on the Western Front, the English explorer returned to South America, launching his first expedition in 1920. The exploration failed when the colonel's companions broke down. He all but had to drag them back to civilization, complaining later that the explorer of the present day is soft in comparison with the hardy Portuguese pioneers and is dependent upon too many luxuries." It was Fawcett's habit to travel fast and with little equipment, living off the land and what friendly

Indians could be found, but there were few of these tribes in central Brazil. For the most part the natives in and about the Matto Grosso were illiterate and superstitious and would just as soon kill visitors as take their gifts and trinkets.

Fawcett would not give up his dream of finding the vanished city of Z and, in 1924, submitted to the Royal Geographical Society a new plan. He would be accompanied by his son Jack and another young Englishman, Raleigh Rimmel. The expedition would leave civilization at Cuyabá and travel north to the Paranatinga, moving down that river via canoe to about latitude 10 degrees south and then moving to the east on foot, crossing to the Xingu River, then to the Araguaya River, making for Port Imperial on the Tocantins and emerging from the Matto Grosso at Barra do Rio Grande on the São Francisco.

The three men would travel light, Fawcett insisted. (Most explorers thought him mad to enter the area without heavy supplies; an early-day expedition of 1,400 men with great quantities of food and equipment was simply swallowed by the Matto Grosso, all but three explorers starving to death.) The colonel explained to the Society, which would fund the trip, that "no expedition could carry food for more than three weeks, for animal transport is impossible owing to the lack of pasture and to blood-sucking bats." Fawcett could not be sure as to the exact location of Z; or, if he was positive, he was not about to tell anyone. Only three men in modern times knew of the city's whereabouts, he said,

> . . . so far as the general location and surrounding topography are concerned. . . . One was a Frenchman, whose last attempt to get there cost him an eye, and it is probable he will make no more; the second is an Englishman who, before he left the country, was suffering from an advanced stage of cancer, and is probably no longer alive; the third is the writer.

Porters were out of the question. "Most of the tribes fear and hate their neighbors," Fawcett told his sponsors, "and Indians will rarely accompany you beyond the limits of their own territory." Food was also a problem for a large group. "Game is nowhere plentiful in this country; there is usually enough to feed a small party, but never a large one."

Some questioned the reason for it all, the suffering in the waist-high jungle trail, the vicious attacks of swarms of virulent insects, the masses of snakes and other lethal animals, the jungle sicknesses, the fear of falling asleep in the wrong spot where swarms of blood-sucking bats might attack. Fawcett was, as usual, undaunted, and looked to the positive side of his near-impossible trek: "Science will, I hope, be greatly benefitted, geography can scarcely fail to gain a good deal, and I am confident that we shall find the key to much lost history."

The three explorers stepped into the wilderness at Cuyabá on April 20, 1925. By May 29 they reached the point where Fawcett had turned back—Dead Horse Camp—in 1920. It was from this point, at the dark edge of the Matto Grasso, that the world heard the last words of Percy Harrison Fawcett:

> Here we are at Dead Horse Camp [now named "Camp Fawcett"], the spot where my horse died in 1920. Only his white bones remain. My calculations anticipate contact with the Indians in about a week or 10 days, when we should be able to reach the waterfall so much talked about . . . our journey has been no bed of roses. We have cut our way through miles of *cerraba,* a forest of low dry scrub; we have crossed innumerable small streams by swimming and fording; we have climbed rocky hills of forbidding aspect; we have been eaten by bugs. . . . Our two guides go back from here. They are more and more nervous as we push further into the Indian country . . . We shall not get into interesting country for another two weeks. I shall continue to prepare dispatches from time to time, in hopes of being able to get them out eventually through some friendly tribe of Indians. But I doubt if this will be possible.

The possibilities existed for two years; it had been estimated that Fawcett's party would be gone that long in its quest for Z. By 1927, however, even the most stalwart believers (with the exception of Fawcett's wife, who never gave up hope of seeing her husband and son again) felt that Fawcett would never return.

Dr. Hogarth of the Royal Geographical Society publicly stated that

> we hold ourselves in readiness to help any competent and well-accredited volunteer party which may propose to proceed on a reasonable plan to the interior of Brazil in order to try for news of

Colonel P. H. Fawcett . . . I am forecasting a mission of inquiry alone, not one of relief. The latter is out of the question, as Colonel Fawcett himself stated emphatically, when he proposed to go where none but he could hope to penetrate and pass.

This announcement was immediately interpreted as an appeal for a search party. Thousands of adventurers volunteered, from the skilled to the crackpot, to cut their way through the jungle to retrieve the colonel and his companions. The Brazilian government believed that the Fawcett party, exhausted, and starving close to the Araguaya River, had "been killed by one of the various tribes which inhabit the banks of the River Xingu."

Yet reports poured in from all over Brazil that Fawcett lived. A Sergeant Roger Couturon (who for some reason also used the name Courteville), lately of the French Army, reported in the pages of the Rio newspaper *O Jornal* in November 1927, that he had been shooting alligators near Cuyabá

> when we saw a man on the right of the road, apparently exhausted with his hands on his knees. . . . He was a man of from 50 to 60-years-old with luxuriant greyish hair and a "pepper-and-salt" beard . . . He was wearing khaki shorts and trousers, such as those worn by scouts, with a wide-brimmed hat. . . . As I approached, the man continued to stare at his feet. To start conversation, I asked him if we were far from Cuyabá, but he did not seem to hear. His bare and hairy legs, on which a colony of mosquitos and insects had settled, were shod with enormous shoes that must have been very old. His heroic stoicism was so odd that I thought he must be a foreigner and addressed him at random in English—"I say, man, the mosquitos seem to take care of you[*sic*]." My remark produced its effect and he looked up at me. His face showed obvious signs of fatigue and general weakness consequent on fever, but his eyes were straight and forceful, and I had the impression that this man had been a soldier. . . . Finally, he replied: "Those poor animals are hungry, too." We went on our way, leaving the poor man calmly watching the mosquitos devouring his legs.

Couturon went on to tell different tales about the man he met, whom he believed to be Fawcett, that the colonel was living in luxury on a resplendent ranch in Brazil's interior, that he had given up on the civilized world and became a blissful jungle tramp, that he had gone mad in the jungle and that Indians who found him had made a white god of him. In Lima, some months later, the inventive Couturon insisted that he had met Jack Fawcett, who was living a life of ease and begged him not to inform the British government, since the Fawcett party were officially declared dead and Mrs. Fawcett was receiving a handsome pension. (Mrs. Fawcett never received a pension.) Such fanciful reports further confused the spectacular Fawcett disappearance.

A fellow of the Royal Geographical Society, Commander George Dyott, led an expedition of inquiry into the Matto Grosso in May 1928. Dyott's party was large and well-equipped, and doggedly followed Fawcett's three-year-old trail from Dead Horse Camp down the Rio Kuliseu. Here Dyott interviewed the chief of the Anauqua Indians, Aloique, who told him that Colonel Fawcett had reached the treacherous Kuluene River sometime in 1925. Both Jack Fawcett and Rimmel were by then physical wrecks and almost unable to talk. Fawcett, apparently obsessed with finding his lost city, practically carried both men across the river into the unknown regions lying east. For five days, the Anauqua and Kalapalo Indians who inhabit both sides of the river watched the camp fires of the white men. On the sixth day, Chief Aloique described through sign language, the Fawcett party's fires went out; they had been massacred, said the chief, by the fierce inland tribe of Suyás. The Kalapalos told Dyott that Aloique was lying and that he and his Anauquas had killed the three men. (Aloique's son was wearing about his neck a plate that bore the name of a supply firm that had furnished Fawcett with some airtight cases in 1924.)

Dyott never found Fawcett's remains; he became suspicious of Aloique and, under the cover of night, slipped away with his party in canoes down the Xingu, abandoning most of his equipment. He announced that Fawcett was, in all probability, dead. But few persons believed him until other explorers confirmed the story.

Stephen Rattin, a Swiss who had been trapping in the heart of the Matto Grosso in 1931, reported seeing a "tall man, advanced in years, with blue eyes and a long beard" living with an unknown tribe that dwelled north-northwest of Cuyabá, along the Iguassu Ximary, a tributary of the Rio São Manoel. In splintered English, Rattin squeezed out a brief conversation with the white man clad in animal skins while the Indians occupied themselves with getting drunk. The man, who oddly did not directly identify himself as Colonel Fawcett, explained that he was a captive and a "colonel in the English Army," and asked that Rattin contact Major T. B. Paget, a friend of his who lived in São Paulo, and inform him that he was alive but that his son was "asleep." (Paget had helped finance Fawcett's last expedition.) Rattin's English was less than poor, so the meaning of the brief conversation was difficult to determine.

Before being dragged off by the Indians, the white captive flashed a signet ring which Mrs. Fawcett later identified as her husband's. Rattin, whose piecemeal story sounded authentic to many, mounted his own expedition to rescue the white captive when he was told that the man he had met was in all probability Colonel Fawcett. The Rattin expedition was a failure.

Other expeditions ensued, one led by Vincenzo Petrullo, which confirmed the Dyott story of Fawcett's being murdered by Indians and another, in 1932, led by Robert Churchward. Peter Fleming, a mem-

*Bones brought back from the Matto Grosso in 1951 by searcher Orlando Vilas Boas, who claimed the remains were those of Colonel Fawcett; the teeth of the skull proved otherwise.*

ber of the Churchward expedition, a hunting trip only incidentally concerned with seeking Fawcett, penned a heady tale of his exploits in *Brazilian Adventure*, concluding that the Kalapalos, seeing the Fawcett party near death with fatigue and starvation, murdered the white explorers out of mercy. Fleming added, however, "there still remains an infinitesimal, a million to one, chance that Fawcett is still alive. If he is, we must assume that he is in some way mentally deranged. . . . Fawcett, whose powers of endurance and immunity to disease were extraordinary, might have lived," but "everything points to the whole expedition having perished in the summer of 1925, probably at the hands of Indians."

More expeditions, sometimes three in one year, reported different, odd fates for Fawcett and his companions. In April 1951, Orlando Vilas-Boas of the Central Brazil Foundation said that he had discovered the bleached bones of Colonel Fawcett after traveling into the heart of Kalapalo country. The bones were sent to England, where experts at the Royal Anthropological Institute determined that the remains were not those of the colonel, their findings based upon stature and teeth. Even as late as 1955, Edward Weyer, Jr., writing in *Jungle Quest*, reported meeting an aged white man in the Matto Grosso who might have been Fawcett.

Incredible stories still come from Brazil concerning this most famous of missing explorers, but Colonel Percy Harrison Fawcett's disappearance still remains a mystery. Fawcett or his remains (the colonel would be more than one hundred years old, his son, Jack, and Rimmel in their seventies) are as lost today in the wilds of the Matto Grosso as the fabulous lost city he sought.

### Halliburton and the Sea Dragon

Like Mallory and Fawcett, Richard Halliburton was a true adventurer. The Texas-born wanderer had no sooner been graduated from Princeton in 1921 than he embarked on extraordinary travels that took him to the most far-flung spots. Arm-chair travelers reveled in his tinged-with-peril exploits that seemed to be new renditions of old songs.

The trail of Ulysses from Ithaca to the Levant and back was duplicated by Halliburton. Like the romantic poet Lord Byron, Halliburton swam the Hellespont. He climbed Mount Olympus, scaled the walls of the Acropolis and jumped into the sacred Mayan well of Chichén Itzá. In recalling the great deeds of history, he strolled through the mists of Tibet and splashed in the forbidden pool in the gardens of the Taj Mahal (at night, so guards would not prevent him from daring the gods to destroy him for his transgressions). Halliburton even rode an elephant over the Alps, following what he thought was the original route taken by the Carthaginian general Hannibal. Each new adventure brought forth another book, seven in all, which sold in the millions, making Halliburton wealthy by his thirty-eighth birthday in 1938, the year in which he planned his last romantic adventure.

Halliburton wanted to sail an authentic Chinese junk from Hong Kong to San Francisco (which would host the World's Fair that summer), a distance of 9,000 miles. He thought the trip would serve well as the first chapter in a new book dealing with the "pre-Columbian discovery of America."

In Hong Kong, Halliburton was shocked by the types of junks available for the voyage. Most were broken-down vessels, unseaworthy and unreliable in any heavy storm. Captain John Wenlock Welch and engineer Henry von Fehren were hired to build a special junk for the voyage. More than $50,000 was pumped into the construction of the ship, its keel, hull and rudder especially reinforced for the trip.

Jittery friends told Halliburton that the voyage, attempted in midwinter, could easily prove disastrous. No junk designed had ever made the voyage. The Pacific was thoroughly erratic that time of year; storms came from nowhere and were suddenly gone, taking with them even sturdy ocean liners. Halliburton scoffed at the warnings and bravely told Horace Epes, manager of Consolidated News Features, which distributed his columns to fifty newspapers (and nine million readers), that a "storm could carry away our ship's main mast and wreck the junk's auxiliary engines and we could still make seventy miles a day on the open sea." He failed to explain how.

Though the junk, christened the *Sea Dragon*, was completed in record time, Halliburton spent weeks in preparing his vessel to face

*Everybody's favorite adventurer, Richard Halliburton, in Hong Kong in 1939. His specially built junk,* Sea Dragon, *is in the background.*

the unknown evils of the ocean. Superstition among the Chinese was honored through elaborate ceremonies at the Hong Kong dock where the ship waited. She had been painted a brilliant red with white and gold stripes along the rails. Her three mainmast sails were of gay orange, scarlet and white. The Chinese god of sailors, Tai Toa Fat, was placated by Halliburton, with the enthusiastic aid of several Chinese priests. Halliburton personally helped in nailing two enormous black eyes on either side of the prow in the tradition of the Chinese seafarer who gave his ships huge eyes by which to see through the storms and mists of the great Pacific. Gongs and drums were beaten by priests. Paper prayers were affixed to the masts. Firecrackers were religiously exploded on the deck. Priests washed the huge black eyes with rice wine. Then Halliburton and his crew of thirteen were ready.

On March 4, 1939, the 75-foot *Sea Dragon* sailed out of Hong Kong harbor with 2,000 gallons of water and two tons of food packed into her holds. Fuel drums for the auxiliary engines occupied all available storage space, enough for twelve days.

For a week there was silence. Then the crackle of the *Sea Drag-on's* radio sputtered on March 13: "1200 miles at sea. All's well." A six-day silence then shrouded the Halliburton journey. On the evening of March 19 came the message "Half-way Midway . . . arriving there April 5." This radio contact with the *Sea Dragon* was picked up in San Francisco.

High seas with forty-foot waves on March 23 turned part of the South Pacific into a cauldron that even the largest oceangoing liner of the day, the *President Coolidge*—let alone the *Sea Dragon*—found difficult to survive. The junk's master, Captain Welch, radioed his friend Dale Collins, executive officer of the *Coolidge*, which was struggling nearby: "Southerly gales, squalls, lee rail under water . . . wet bunks . . . hard tack . . . bully beef . . . having wonderful time . . . wish you were here instead of me."

It was the last anyone ever heard of Halliburton, the *Sea Dragon*, and the thirteen men who were with them. The U.S.S. *Astoria*, a cruiser, was dispatched to the area and searched more than 150,000 square miles of ocean, looking for the flamboyant adventurer and his crew. After some days the search was abandoned. *Coolidge* officer Collins reported in a hearing three months later: "If the *Sea Dragon* encountered such weather as we did on the night of March 23, and she undoubtedly did, there is small chance that the little craft survived."

Still, the many millions of readers who had thrilled to Halliburton's tales of wanderlust refused to believe that this hearty adventurer, the All-American boy, could disappear off the face of an earth he had so courageously traversed. It wasn't until October 1939, that a chancery court jury declared Richard Halliburton officially dead, the victim of a tropical typhoon on March 23 or 24, 1939. His exotic end was somehow fitting. The boy explorer of romance and the past sailed off into the yawning mouth of his own adventures.

### The Regions of Dim Hope

The disappearances of adventuresome titans such as Mallory, Fawcett and Halliburton have far from daunted their successors. These spectacular vanishing acts have served to stimulate, it seems, the wanderlust in other rough-and-readies, many of whom were snatched by the same fate that gobbled their mentors.

Like many before him, Jaroslav Renza was obsessed with finding the legendary gold deposits in the bush country of Australia and marched straight into the blistering heart of the desert in early 1954. Police and native trackers followed Renza's footprints for 150 miles before they found him completely exhausted but still trudging forward. He had to be subdued before he could be brought to a Perth hospital.

Alaska has myriad folk tales of lost treasure seekers, but for William C. Waters, a forty-two-year-old mail clerk from Erlanger, Kentucky, it was his lust for the vacation of his life that flopped into an Alaskan nightmare of meanderings and bare survival.

"I always wanted to see that Alcan Highway," Waters told friends, and by early June 1961 he had passed through Fairbanks and was traveling along the Steese Highway, heading for Circle, the northernmost point of the United States highway system. His abandoned car was found some weeks later 120 miles north of Fairbanks. On the front seat was found a booklet entitled "How to Camp Out." Authorities combed the subarctic woods for a month and found nothing. On July 21, a coroner's jury was convened for the purpose of determining Waters' fate, but in the tradition of the Yukon, where hope clings eternal, the jurors thought "there might just be a chance—however slim—that Waters was still alive." They refused to authorize a death certificate.

The chances *were* slim. Waters had wandered into the muskeg toward Big Lake, where he had heard the fishing was good. Leaving his car, he carried a machete, a hunting knife, rod and tackle box, and eleven matches. After Waters caught a pike he headed back toward his car but got lost by taking "a short cut" through a boggy marsh. "I didn't have a map—that was the stupidity of it," he said later.

The confused Waters began to follow Birch Creek, knowing that somewhere it joined the Yukon River. That somewhere was a hundred miles away. For ten weeks, eating only wild berries and rose hips (fruit of the wild rose), Waters staggered forward into hopeless terrain, his feet so swollen he could hardly walk. Then Waters collapsed and waited to die.

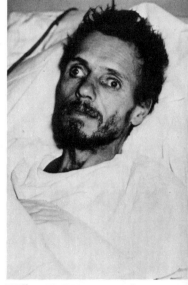

*William C. Waters yearned for an Alaskan adventure; he barely survived his excruciating disappearance in 1961.* (UPI)

97

The purring of a motorboat going down the creek revived him and Waters tried to signal its occupants. They did not hear his weak cries for help. Twenty-four hours later the boat returned. Waters was so emaciated and drained that he did not have the strength to crawl to the creek's edge. He shouted hoarsely only once, waved his hand, and then passed out. This time he was seen and saved.

As he slowly regained his health in a Fairbanks hospital, Waters was amazed by his rescue. "I didn't think anyone would look for me," he whispered. "I'm just a postal clerk."

A man of more illustrious background disappeared four months later. The object of a massive search along the shores of New Guinea was Michael Clark Rockefeller, the youngest son of Nelson Rockefeller, then Governor of New York. At twenty-three, Michael was a graduate of Phillips Andover and of Harvard. He had just served a stint with the Army as Private Rockefeller and was in peak physical condition, his six-foot-one-inch frame hard with muscle.

Following his father's unsuccessful bid for the Republican presidential nomination in 1960, Michael joined an anthropological expedition sponsored by the Peabody Museum of Harvard. He became entranced with the wood carvings of the Asmat tribesmen living along the shores of New Guinea. As an apprentice ethnologist, Michael returned to New Guinea in 1961 and, with a thirty-

*Michael Rockefeller in New Guinea in 1961. Was he the victim of Asmat cannibals?* (WIDE WORLD)

four-year-old Dutchman, Dr. René W. Wassink, and two loincloth-wearing Papuan guides, set out once more to locate the Asmat tribe.

The four men moved down the rugged, swampy coast in a 40-foot *proa* (two dugout canoes lashed together and powered by an 18-hp. outboard motor). Eleven miles from the coastal hamlet of Agats, a storm swamped the craft. The two terrified Papuan guides swam madly for shore. Wassink insisted on staying with the overturned boat, which had drifted three or four miles out to sea. Rockefeller told the Dutchman he thought he could swim to shore just as the guides were doing.

"I warned him about the crocodiles," Wassink later told Governor Rockefeller. "I told him I could take no responsibility for him."

Rockefeller stripped and then grabbed two five-gallon gas cans for buoyancy. He shoved off toward shore, shouting over his shoulder: "I think I can make it!" Wassink drifted more than twenty miles out to sea, where he was rescued. The Dutchman had watched Rockefeller confidently paddle landward. "I followed him until I could only see three dots—his head and the two red cans. Then he disappeared across my horizon."

The news soon reached Nelson Rockefeller, then going through the agonies of divorce after thirty-one years of marriage, he flew to New Guinea and organized search parties at Merauke. His daughter and Michael's twin sister, Mrs. Mary Strawbridge, accompanied Rockefeller. Natives were offered 250 sticks of tobacco—an incredible amount of wealth in those regions—if they would look for the missing Rockefeller. More than two thousand tribesmen shoved off in canoes and hacked their ways along the shoreline dense with jungle. Ships and planes scoured the cruel coast.

No trace of the young explorer was found. One of the red gas cans he used to float toward shore was eventually recovered far out to sea. It took little reasoning to conclude that Michael Rockefeller died in one of the lagoonlike areas along the coast, a victim of sharks, salt-water crocodiles, or drowning. (Film-maker Lorne Blair in 1977 absurdly claimed that Michael Rockefeller was killed by Asmat tribesmen just as he staggered to shore and that his body was hacked up and eaten by a subchief named Ari. Blair was making a film in New Guinea on Asmat art, when he allegedly stumbled upon the story. He put the question directly to Ari, who responded only by laughing, a noncommittal sign Blair interpreted as confirmation of Rockefeller's cannibalization.) "It would be a miracle if Michael is found alive," said Eibrink Jansen, the Dutch resident general, after weeks of search proved futile. That miracle never occurred.

The same kind of miracle would apply to the discovery of Thomas Gatch, balloonist extraordinary, who departed skyward on February 18, 1974. Gatch intended to be the first man to cross the Atlantic in a balloon, riding the swift stratospheric jet stream to Africa. It was a thousand miles west-northwest of the dark continent where a ship spotted Gatch's red balloon moving at terrific speeds high above. The balloon quickly sailed out of sight over the horizon. On March 6, the U.S. Defense Department inaugurated a sea-and-land search, which was abandoned when two freighters reported seeing part of the red balloon awash in the foaming sea.

Many people believe Gatch is alive. His sisters have offered $10,000 for information leading to his rescue. Marcia Kuhn, a friend of Gatch's in Laurel, Maryland, says she has seen him through ESP living a Robinson Crusoe-like existence on a nameless, deserted island. But hope is dim that Gatch will be found.

*Balloonist Tom Gatch preparing to sail the Atlantic in 1974; he vanished in the skies.* (WIDE WORLD)

# Carried Away

Kidnapping and abduction have been with the world since man crawled into his caves and drew his dubious past. Countless victims of such human terror were initially posted as missing; many who never returned or were found much later were so categorized out of convenience.

Kidnapping flourished in the early 1600s, when seamen were grabbed by press crews to man their ships. (The word *nap* was then a variation of *nab* and, coupled with *kid* meant to "nab the kid.") Abduction historically applied to the physical seizure of females, usually for immoral purposes. Irrespective of the definition, the missing person in such murky instances is one who disappears against his will and often into a hideous destiny.

## Little Ones Lost

During the 1880s and 1890s in West Ham, England, an ongoing epidemic of kidnappings and abductions plagued the terrified residents. The horror began at Eastertime, 1881, when a little girl named Seward vanished without a trace. The Director of Criminal Investigations in the district offered a huge reward for the discovery or return of the girl, but to no avail. In February 1882, 12-year-old Eliza Carter disappeared; some clues convinced constables that they were dealing with a fiend.

On February 4, at 10 A.M., Eliza left her sister's home to return to her parents' house on Church Street. She deposited some clothes at a laundry and was not seen again until 5 P.M., when, from the shadows of an alleyway she beckoned to one of her classmates returning from school. Eliza hurriedly and in hushed tones told her friend that she feared returning home because of some man. As she spoke she heard heavy footsteps and quickly fled down the alley.

*Eliza Carter, twelve years old, disappeared from West Ham, England in 1882, one of many children who vanished from that area.* (PENNY ILLUSTRATED PAPER)

By evening, the Carters were searching for their daughter in the dark streets of West Ham. They received one report that Eliza had been walking with a large, heavy-set woman who wore a long ulster and a black frock. It was the last identification made of the girl.

The next day the blue dress Eliza had been wearing was found on the West Ham football field. All the buttons had been ripped off. The Carters' highly publicized pleas for information about their little girl were never answered. Police insisted that some "inhuman creature" had abducted and ravished the girl before secretly disposing of her naked body. The mystery has gone unsolved.

Two months later the son of the local West Ham butcher, Charles Wagner, vanished. Police found the young boy's dead body some time later jammed between rocks at Ramsgate.

The final rash of West Ham disappearances occurred in the month of January 1890, when three girls disappeared at separate times. Only one, fifteen-year-old Amelia Jeffs, was found, her mutilated body discovered naked near West Ham Park. Police determined that the girl had been raped and then strangled. She had also fought desperately for her life, as evidenced by the flesh and caked blood found under her fingernails.

The first sensational kidnapping to arouse and anger the American public was the taking of little Charley Ross on July 1, 1874. Four-year-old Charley and his brother Walter, six, were playing in front of their home, an impressive Victorian mansion owned by a

*A contemporary rendition of kidnappers Joseph Douglass and William Mosher abducting 4-year-old Charley Ross and his brother Walter from in front of their Germantown, Pennsylvania mansion on July 1, 1874.*

Germantown, Pennsylvania, businessman, Christian K. Ross. Two men in a buggy stopped to greet them. They were not strangers, the men having stopped every day for a week to give them candy and exchange friendly remarks. This day the two tough-looking fellows suggested a quick trip to Philadelphia to buy fireworks—Independence Day would soon arrive, they pointed out. Charley and Walter jumped into the buggy too happy with the thought of having their own fireworks to notice the men drinking heavily from a flask of whiskey and making ominous remarks.

In Philadelphia, at the corner of Richmond and Palmer streets, Walter Ross was given twenty-five cents and told to go into a store across the street to buy firecrackers. The boy returned fifteen minutes later to find the carriage gone. He burst into tears. A kindly passerby took him home and the kidnapping of Charley was revealed. The police were called. The children's father agreed with officers that Charley could not have been kidnapped, that such a heinous crime was unthinkable, and that he would return soon after buying his own firecrackers.

Little Charley Ross did not return. Ross placed a little-boy-lost advertisement in the *Public Ledger*, offering a $300 reward for the return of "a small boy, having long curly flaxen hair, hazel eyes, clear, light skin and round face, dressed in a brown linen suit with short skirt, broad-brimmed straw hat and laced shoes."

A letter arrived on July 3, postmarked Philadelphia, and written in an illiterate scrawl: "Mr. Ros—be not uneasy you son charly bruster be al writ we is got him and no powers on earth can deliver out of our hand—You wil hav two pay us befor you git him from us —an pay us a big cent. to if you put the cops hunting for him you is only defeeting yu own end—we is got him fix so no living power can gits him from us a live—if any aproch is maid to his hidin place that is the signil for his instant anihilation—if yu reard his lif put no one to search for him you money can fech him out alive an no other existin powers dont deceiv yuself an think the detectives can git him from us for that is one imposebel—you here from us in few day."

Ross immediately informed the police. Within two days the frantic father received the kidnappers' demand—$20,000. The police, shocked by the first sensational kidnapping in American history, ransacked Philadelphia, conducting a house-to-house search and blocking all roads and railway stations while every child in the district was examined. Charley Ross remained lost.

Christian Ross was informed by the kidnappers that he was to board a train bound for Albany, New York, and stand on the rear platform. When he saw a signal from trackside he was to throw a bag containing the $20,000 overboard. Ross followed instructions and squinted at the darkness of the roadbed as his train shuttled northward. There was no signal, perhaps because the kidnappers had learned that the train was loaded with Philadelphia detectives.

Publicity on the case skyrocketed, and newspaper readers went into shock; across the land mothers and fathers locked up their children. Parents patrolled their homes at night carrying all manner of weapons, ready to repel any would-be kidnappers. Christian K. Ross waited and worried. He next heard from the kidnappers in a letter postmarked from New York City.

That city's police chief, George Walling, met with Ross and identified the ransom notes as those of a cheap crook named William Mosher. The crook's brother-in-law, William Westervelt, who had been discharged from the force for "improprieties," was called in and met several times with Walling and Ross, telling them he might be able to negotiate the return of Little Charley. Before dawn on December 15, however, Mosher and a fellow burglar, Joseph Douglass, were killed by police as they emerged from the cellar of a house that they had robbed in Brooklyn.

*Mastermind of the Ross abduction, William Westervelt.*

Before dying, Mosher admitted that he and Douglass had taken the boy: "We killed Charley Ross," he croaked with several bullets in him. "We did it for money." They were identified as the kidnappers by Walter Ross.

The more-than-helpful Westervelt, suspected of masterminding the kidnapping, was arrested and placed on trial. Several Germantown witnesses identified him as being at various sites in the company of a small boy who looked exactly like Little Charley. (Westervelt had no children of his own.) Though he shouted his innocence, Westervelt was given seven years in solitary confinement. He never muttered one word about Charley Ross's fate, though underworld sources insisted that the ex-cop had drowned the boy in the East River. When released, Westervelt vanished as thoroughly as his celebrated victim.

In 1900 a disappearance that equaled the public outcry over Charley Ross erupted in Omaha, Nebraska, when fifteen-year-old Edward A. Cudahy, Jr., the son of multimillionaire meat packer Edward A. Cudahy, Sr., vanished without a trace. On the night of December 18 Eddie was en route to a doctor's office to deliver secondhand magazines that his father had discarded. It was 7 P.M. by the time Eddie delivered the magazines and was returning home. Two men barred his path. They drew revolvers and announced, "We're detectives and you're a robber named McGee. We've been after you, McGee, and now we've got you! Come along with us!"

"You're crazy!" said Eddie Cudahy, trying to brush away the weapons.

The "detectives" ignored his pleas and bundled him into a buggy, telling him they were headed for "police headquarters." To prevent their dangerous prisoner from escaping, the men tied his arms, gagged and hooded him. Eddie Cudahy was taken to an old house, where he was handcuffed to a chair and given a plate of food. His captors, kidnappers after all, chuckled over their feat and broke open several bottles of liquor to celebrate the adventure.

The elder Cudahy waited until about 10 P.M. that night before phoning the doctor, who reported Eddie's arrival and departure. Next Cudahy called police to report his son missing. Almost the entire force turned out to conduct a meticulous search. They were joined by hundreds of Cudahy's employees, who had been ordered to hunt for the missing heir; Edward A. Cudahy was one of the most influential and richest men in Omaha.

No clue was found. Cudahy concluded that his son had been kidnapped, and he publicly offered a sizable reward if Eddie were returned. He then hired a score of Pinkerton detectives to search high and low for the boy.

The tycoon's offer evoked a dramatic response. A man wildly riding a horse past the Cudahy mansion hurled a ransom note demanding $25,000 in gold pieces for Eddie's return. "If you give us the money, the child will be returned as safe as when you last saw him," the kidnappers had written. "If you refuse, we will put acid in his eyes and blind him."

To further frighten the millionaire, the kidnappers reminded Cudahy of the terrible fate that befell Little Charley Ross:

Old man Ross was willing to give up the money, but Byrnes [Thomas Byrnes, of the New York Police Department], the great detective, with others, persuaded the old man not to give up the money, assuring him the thieves would be captured. Ross died of a broken heart, sorry that he allowed the detectives to dictate to him. . . . Mr. Cudahy, you are up against it, there is only one way out. Give up the coin. Money we want, and money we will get. If you don't give it up, the next man will, for he will see we mean business, and you can lead your boy around blind for the rest of your days and all you will have is the damn coppers' sympathy.

Cudahy delivered five sacks of gold to a remote spot at the outskirts of Omaha, and Eddie Cudahy was released that night. Swift and accurate police detection revealed the chief kidnapper to be a disgruntled ex-employee of Cudahy's named Pat Crowe, a cavalier fellow who had robbed trains before turning to abduction-for-profit. Crowe escaped with Cudahy's gold to Africa, where he lived through several harrowing adventures during the Boer War, fighting with the Boers against the British and becoming an underdog hero. Brazenly, Crowe returned to the United States and, after sending money to an Omaha attorney to repay the Cudahy ransom, announced to the press in 1906 that he was none other than Eddie Cudahy's kidnapper.

Crowe's dynamic display of new-found honesty, along with the growing public rancor against the trusts, of which Cudahy was a potent member, caused him to be acquitted. Ironically, Crowe became a celebrated lecturer and author, capitalizing on the antitrust theme popularized by Upton Sinclair's *The Jungle*. He never forgot his youthful victim either. Eddie Cudahy, on several successive birthdays, received a card and good wishes from Crowe, who was ever mindful to sign off as "your old kidnapper."

Nine years later another rich man's son disappeared in Sharon, Ohio—eight-year-old Willie Whitla, whose lawyer-father, James P. Whitla, was the nephew of steel magnate Frank Buhl. One day in March 1909 a swarthy little man arrived at Willie's school saying that he had been sent to pick up the child by Willie's father.

Willie was bundled up and sent along. By evening, the Whitlas knew that their son was in the hands of kidnappers, who had demanded by ransom note $10,000. Elaborate messages inserted in the personal columns of several newspapers, clandestine meetings in

*Kidnapper Pat Crowe, who threatened to put acid into kidnap victim Eddie Cudahy's eyes unless paid a ransom of $25,000.*

several cities, and wild treks by the father finally resulted in Willie's safe release in Cleveland. The kidnappers, who had obtained their loot, were apprehended in a Cleveland bar. Helen McDermott Bogle, a loud-mouthed slattern, and her tramp husband, James H. Bogle, wasted no time in getting drunk and were picked up by police. Mrs. Bogle was found to be carrying in the lining of her dress almost every penny of the ransom money. "I planned the whole thing!" she bragged.

Unlike Eddie Cudahy and Willie Whitla, many a kidnapped child did not share the joys of being reunited with their parents. Countless children were abducted without any contact being made. Typical was the disappearance of Arthur Philip Wentz, a seven-week-old baby boy whose mother Elsie left him in a baby carriage for a few minutes in front of a department store on New York's Third Avenue on July 29, 1919. Gone only five minutes, Mrs. Wentz returned to the street to find the baby carriage empty. Police interviewed several persons who had been standing outside the store at the time. The information gathered to this date appears on the police blotter: "The boy was stolen from his carriage by an unknown white woman, about nineteen years of age, blonde, dressed in white middy blouse, white skirt, no hat."

Halfway across the world, two years earlier, an even more baffling event occurred. British missionaries in Nepal received in the fall of 1917 an urgent message from a dying Hindu priest that he had a confession to make. The missionaries scurried to the priest's death-bed and found a fourteen-year-old white boy standing next to the Hindu. The priest moaned: "I took this child from a street in Wimbledon, England, in 1910." With that he died.

The boy, who could speak only a few words of English, said his name was Albert; that was all he knew of his background. Police in England and India conducted a three-year search for the child's parents but came up empty-handed. It was learned that "a number of boys had disappeared in Wimbledon around 1910," and none but Albert was ever found. Yet Albert's identity remained a mystery to his death some years ago in India.

Just as 1910 was a banner year in Wimbledon, England, for disappearing children, 1914 saw a remarkable number of youngsters vanish in the immigrant-glutted metropolis of New York. Much of this activity was attributed to the abduction of females to work in brothels, the then dreaded racket of "white slavery." Anna Standroup, age seventeen, was one of the many victims of this insidious criminal pursuit.

Anna was accosted while walking through Central Park one day in April 1914 by a man who promised to pay her handsome sums for posing as an artist's model. She was taken to a studio on 149th Street where apparently harmless photos were taken. She was then escorted to a flat at 124th Street, which was leased by a notorious madam named Ruth Waller. All of Anna's clothes were taken from her and she was a virtual prisoner, compelled to have sex with a host of men over a period of several months under the threat of death or, worse for that day, publicity, which would ruin the good name of her family. A chance raid on the brothel uncovered the missing girl. Ruth Waller, Andrew J. Arnold (the procurer), and Leo Kirschner, who had posed as the photographer, were arrested and drew long prison terms.

Some weeks after Anna Standroup's disappearance, little Yetta Levinthal, age thirteen, was abducted by a Negro after leaving school. "He grabbed me," Yetta told police some days later, "and told me he would kill me if I cried out." She was taken to a shanty near Jamaica Bay and for three days was sexually assaulted by Negroes who paid her abductor for the privilege. When she resisted, the kidnapper hit her bare legs with a club. The girl finally managed to escape and, though badly bruised and in a state of shock, managed to reach a point only a half mile from her home before collapsing. Some classmates discovered her and carried her home. The white slaver was never found.

Sixteen-year-old Mamie Nagle had been missing a month in 1914 before a small boy spotted her shivering on a window ledge of an apartment on Stanhope Street. The boy ran to a precinct station and told his story. Detectives raced to the apartment building, where they found William Knipschild, who denied any knowledge about the girl. The police heard screams from a rear bedroom, and there they discovered Mamie, begging to be rescued. An hour before she had stepped onto the ledge, intent upon suicide, a fate she preferred to that of forced prostitution. Knipschild and Adam Grosinger, an accomplice, were arrested and later sent to prison.

In the 1920s missing children later discovered to have been kidnapped met incredibly savage ends, their captors as psychotic and maniacal as the Jazz Age was confused, a time when the public at large abandoned all sense of propriety, an era that novelist F. Scott Fitzgerald aptly cited as having had "all wars fought, all gods dead, and all faith in mankind shaken."

These sentiments were proven accurate by two wealth-pampered Chicago youths, Nathan F. Leopold, Jr., and Richard A Loeb. Teenage scions of rich families, Loeb and Leopold abducted fourteen-year-old Bobbie Franks in May 1924, stabbing him to death and stuffing his mutilated body into a culvert at 118th Street in Chicago. Franks was taken haphazardly from a schoolyard. Any child from a wealthy family suited the kidnappers, and not for any ransom money. (A ransom was demanded after the Franks boy had been killed, only to make it appear that he had been taken by desperate characters in need of cash.) The abduction was conducted as an experiment in crime, conceived of as "the perfect crime" in the warped intellects of two idle rich brats—"moral imbeciles" they were later called. Both were caught through their own mistakes and fears and sentenced to life imprisonment. Had it not been for their stupendous lawyer, Clarence Darrow, Leopold and Loeb would, no doubt, have gone to the electric chair. (Richard Loeb was murdered by a fellow inmate at Stateville Penitentiary in 1936 after pressing homosexual attentions on him. Nathan Leopold was paroled in 1958 and died of a heart attack in Puerto Rico in 1971.)

Even more inhuman was Albert Fish, who confessed to having abducted 400 children and murdered them, also without demanding ransom. Billy Gaffney, a blue-eyed four-year-old boy disappeared on February 11, 1927. He was listed as among the missing until 1936, when Fish was trapped by police after mailing letters to the mother of another of his victims, Grace Budd. He had sexually molested Billy Gaffney, Fish bragged and, in 1928, kidnapped twelve-year-old Grace Budd from her Manhattan home, murdering her in a lonely cottage in White Plains, and carving up her body, which he ate piecemeal. This horrendous cannibal and extraordinary pervert was executed in Sing Sing's electric chair on January 16, 1936, an event

Fish looked forward to with great glee as "the supreme thrill. . . . The only one I haven't tried."

A year before cannibal Fish dragged Grace Budd to her dismal end, William Edward Hickman abducted twelve-year-old Marion Parker. Her father, Perry H. Parker, was a wealthy banker, and his twin daughters, Marion and Marjorie, were his greatest pride. Like the abductor of Willie Whitla two decades earlier, Hickman merely picked Marion up at her school, telling her that her father had sent for her. He demanded $7,500 for her return and this was eventually paid by Parker. Hickman, in what must be considered the most brutal delivery of a kidnap victim, met Parker on a lonely road and as their cars idled next to each other, held up the child who appeared to be sleeping. He took the money, drove a short distance, and placed the child alongside the road. Parker rushed up and threw back the blanket wrapped about his daughter. He let out a scream. She was dead. Hickman had strangled her with a towel and had barbarously cut off the child's legs.

Hickman was found and, following an egotistical confession, was convicted and sentenced to death by hanging at San Quentin. He rose from his prison cot at 3 A.M. on the day of his execution to listen to jazz records. Before he was led to the scaffold, Hickman grinned insanely at his guards and gloated: "I have committed the most atrocious crime in history." Few disagreed.

There would be more children, too many for normal shock and indignation to absorb: Charles Augustus Lindbergh, Jr., taken on March 1, 1932, and found dead on May 12, for which his abductor and murderer, Bruno Richard Hauptmann, was electrocuted on April 3, 1936; the abduction and murder of six-year-old Suzanne Degnan in Chicago on January 7, 1946, by William Heirens; the kidnapping of six-year-old Bobby Greenlease, Jr., in Kansas City, murdered by the calculating Bonnie B. Heady and Carl A. Hall on September 28, 1953, for which the killers were put to death by gas in the Missouri State Prison; the abduction from his home in Westbury, New York, on July 4, 1956, of thirty-three-day-old Peter Weinberger, who was later found dead along a roadside and whose killer, Angelo John LaMarca, was electrocuted in Sing Sing. The record is agonizingly unending.

Peculiar to the twentieth century are the disappearances of children who were victims of their friends, even relatives. One of the more spectacular cases involved Katherine C. Larkin, a thirteen-year-old Bronx girl who disappeared on August 7, 1914. Katherine, the daughter of mailman Martin C. Larkin, was last seen on or near Kingsbridge Avenue after attending mass at St. John's Roman Catholic Church. By nightfall squads of police and special detectives, along with fifty of Katherine's classmates, were busy searching the area. No trace of the missing girl was found, and authorities were further confused when Louis Krowick, a twelve-year-old neighbor, excitedly told them a fantastic tale in which Katherine was abducted by a suspicious gang. Louis saw "five men in an automobile near the church seize the Larkin girl, and drive away." The boy described the men as being dark; he thought they were Italians. The story made no sense whatever. Katherine's parents were poor, so a kidnapping for ransom was out of the question.

Yet detectives followed up the story and continued to search the neighborhood, especially the area around the church. Four days later, the police decided to comb nearby Public School 7. In the boy's washroom, four policemen clumped about checking commodes and closets. A Sergeant Meyer's attention was drawn to a heavy glass-plated lid covering a pit that gave access to the lavatory pipes. Meyer stared down and saw what he thought to be a human eye pressed against a hole where one of the lights of the trapdoor had been broken. He dropped to his knees and a weak voice cried out: "Mister, oh mister, take me out of here, won't you mister?"

School Superintendent John Davelle was summoned and rushed to the trapdoor with the key. Unlocking and lifting the lid the detectives found Katherine Larkin bound hand and foot. Police Commissioner Woods carried the badly bruised Katherine to her home. Mrs. Larkin was so excited to see her child that, as the Commissioner walked up the stairs of the Larkin home with the girl in his arms, she, "in her frantic eagerness, pushed both of her arms through the glass panel of the door.

Some hours later, Katherine told her story of terror. Following the

**111**

mass she was passing the school when the assistant janitor, a Negro named George W. Webb, approached her and, in a friendly way, asked if she would like to see his pet monkey. A curious child, Katherine was delighted and accompanied him to an empty school room on the second floor of the building, where he immediately raped her. He then bound and gagged her and dragged her to the boy's lavatory. There, he unlocked the trapdoor of the pit to the water mains—an area four feet square—and jammed the child inside. There were more than a hundred glass deadlights in this door. Webb punched out two of the deadlights to give the girl scanty air to breathe.

"He went away and left me," Katherine later told reporters, "and after a while I got my mouth and hands free by rubbing the bandages against the wall. I heard footsteps in the building, but I was afraid to call because the Negro had said he would shoot me if I did, and I thought maybe it was he walking. After a while he came back and when he found that I had rubbed the bandages off, he tied me up again. On Saturday he gave me a glass of water to drink and this is all I had. He never gave me any food at all. Later on I heard someone walking by and looking out [through the tiny broken deadlight] I saw the man had a white face and I called out to him."

Webb was charged with kidnapping, but refused to admit the abduction and attack. "She says I done it and I say I didn't. I guess my word is as good as hers in court." Police pointed out to Webb that the necktie, belt and handkerchief used to bind Katherine belonged to him. They had also found his coat in the pit.

In Webb's room police found a 38-caliber rifle that the janitor used to threaten Katherine. The final argument for guilt was clear, even to Webb: Other than the one held by Superintendent Davelle, Webb had the only key to the trapdoor of the pit in which Katherine had been held captive. The janitor broke down and admitted he had done the deed, that he had been drinking for hours before the kidnapping and intended to let the girl go, but that there were police swarming all about the school during her absence and there was no way to free her without implicating himself.

Webb was convicted of kidnapping and was sentenced to forty years in Sing Sing.

Katherine Larkin's horror story was repeated over the decades with alarming regularity. Elsie Dunlevy of Manchester, Iowa, was taken at age fifteen to live with her uncle, John Dunlevy, in Chicago in 1924. The uncle kept Elsie a virtual prisoner for almost two years inside his Broadway Street apartment. Not until the girl was seventeen did Elsie manage to smuggle a letter to her aunt, who informed the police. Dunlevy was arrested and sent to prison. Elsie had simply been listed as missing for two years.

Even more sinister was the disappearance in January 1976 of another Chicago girl, a fourteen-year-old high-school student, who was missing for two weeks. The girl, according to the story she later told police, was accosted by an unemployed dockworker, Charles Hansen, as she was going home from school. (The police of Chicago, as elsewhere, invariably withhold the names of under-age rape-abduction victims.) First Hansen asked where the nearest phone was located; then he drew a knife and forced her into his car. He then drove her to his apartment on South Hermitage Avenue and, according to the girl, locked her in a small closet, repeatedly raping and beating her for fourteen days. Taking advantage of his absence, the girl pushed the closet key out of the lock with a hanger, then pulled the key into the closet under the door and escaped.

The police managed to arrest the suspect after a half-hour, ten-mile chase through the streets of Chicago, twenty squad cars in pursuit of Hansen's speeding car. When police broke into Hansen's apartment they were greeted by a staggering arsenal that included twenty-five or more handguns, twenty shotguns and rifles, five thousand rounds of ammunition, several new gas masks, thirty pounds of gunpowder, twenty-five smoke grenades and fifty parachute flares. The suspect, according to the girl's testimony, apparently intended to make a fight of it if cornered in the apartment. Hansen, at this writing, is still awaiting trial.

Almost identical was the case of Abby Drover, who vanished on March 10, 1976, as she was going to school in Port Moody, Canada. The citizens of the area searched en masse for Abby. Reward leaflets flooded the district. Nothing was discovered.

One of the most aggressive searchers looking for the twelve-year-old was Donald Alexander Hay, a forty-three-year-old resident of Fort Moody and a neighbor of the Drover family. Hay knew all along where Abby Drover could be found: The girl was being held prisoner in a small dungeonlike room, 6 feet by 6 feet by 7½ feet high, beneath Hay's own garage, a foul-smelling, garbage-littered, sound-proof room into which Hay had dragged her. For 181 days Hay kept Abby prisoner, leaving her alone with packaged foods for weeks at a time. On other occasions the father of three savagely beat the child and sexually molested her.

Abby Drover's pure strength of will allowed her to survive the six-month ordeal. She busied herself with reading her school books over and over again beneath a single light; she exercised regularly; she spent hours determining whether it was day or night beyond her cell; she prayed herself into long sleeps.

On September 6, 1976, Port Moody police were called to the Hay residence to investigate a disturbance. They discovered a man climbing out of a shaft leading from the underground cell, working his way through an entrance concealed by a trapdoor behind two doors of an empty workbench cupboard in a garage. It was Hay. Behind the man the officers could hear the whimpering of a tiny human being. Constable Paul Adams stared into the pit in shock: "I looked down the shaft and here was this frail little thing coming up."

Hay was handcuffed and led to a lockup; Abby was rushed to a hospital, where she slowly recovered from the agony of her long imprisonment. In the pit, which Hay had outfitted with a dirty mattress, a portable toilet, and a sink with running water, police found a note that Abby had written to her kidnapper. It was penciled on pink letter paper. The girl had drawn a flower as a peace symbol at the top and headed it with "Happy days are always here." Abby had written:

> I know you think I'm stupid and like you say everybody is entitled to their own thoughts but I do believe in God and I do believe in friends. And I just wish you would be my friend. I also know that I will get out of here so I'm not worried. God has helped me so far and He will help me to finish. God works in mysterious ways but what He does is right. I know that you don't believe in God but I'll just say that God will be with you.

Donald Alexander Hay was convicted of kidnapping on February 3, 1977, and sentenced to life imprisonment. He was given another eight-year sentence for the statutory rape of a girl under the age of thirteen.

The most astounding recent rash of missing children began in

February 1976 in the Detroit area, when Mark Stebbins, age twelve, of Ferndale, Michigan, was abducted and later found murdered. Three more children in the Detroit suburban area were also taken and killed—Jill Robinson, twelve, of Troy, in December 1976; Kristine Mihelich, ten, of Berkley, in January 1977; and Timothy King, eleven of Birmingham, in March 1977. Police and a host of unofficial investigators swarming into the area have, at this writing, been unable to find a reason for the abductions and murders. Since there were no ransom notes, the idea of kidnapping was out of the question, and authorities concluded that the seven murders (including another three children abducted and killed in the Detroit suburbs) are the work of one man, a strange fanatic in that he washed his victims and dressed them neatly before depositing their bodies in lonely places.

### Missing for Millions

Tycoons and business magnates began to disappear with disturbing frequency in the early 1930s, most of them victims of kidnappers. Millionaire William A. Hamm, Jr., of the Minneapolis brewing family was kidnapped by the notorious Barker-Karpis mob on June 14, 1933, and ransomed for $100,000 three days later. The same gang snatched Minneapolis banker Edward G. Bremer on January 17, 1934, and received $200,000 a few weeks later when he was released. Oil man Charles F. Urschel was kidnapped in July 1933, by George "Machine Gun" Kelly and Albert Bates, and held for $200,000. The money was delivered some days later, and Urschel was turned loose. The Barkers and Kelly were eventually captured or killed, but the lucrative "snatch racket" accelerated to the point where gangsters were kidnapping each other for huge ransoms.

Around this time tough new antikidnapping laws, inspired by the Lindbergh abduction, made the death penalty almost mandatory. To be identified by the victim was too risky for most kidnappers who murdered, rather than released, their prisoners.

This was, no doubt, the reason why Thomas Harold Thurmond, who had never committed any crime in his life, murdered on November 9, 1933, his kidnap victim, Brooke Hart, a twenty-two-year-old department-store heir. Thurmond was arrested while arguing with Hart's father over the drop-off site for the ransom. Three weeks later more than 15,000 incensed residents of San Jose, California, lynched Thurmond and his partner John Maurice Holmes. Such violent retribution did not deter John Henry Seadlund from snatching Charles S. Ross, a wealthy greeting-card manufacturer in the fall of 1937, and receiving $50,000 ransom before murdering his victim and his own partner James Atwood Gray, and burying their remains in a pit in Spooner, Wisconsin. Seadlund was executed in Chicago in 1938.

The disappearance of Adolph "Ad" Coors III has never been fully explained, but it is thought that he was the victim of kidnappers who were reluctant to demand a ransom for fear of being apprehended. Coors, chairman of the board of the largest brewing firm in the Rockies, vanished on the morning of February 10, 1960, as he journeyed to Golden, Colorado. As hours passed, Mary Grant Coors, wife of the millionaire brewer and industrialist, and her four children, became alarmed and thought him abducted. The thought was not a new one in the Coors family; Adolph Coors, Jr., the missing man's father, had been the object of an unsuccessful $50,000 kidnap attempt in 1933.

It was dusk before state police had any evidence of foul play. Coors's station wagon with the motor still running was found abandoned on a dirt road near a bridge over Turkey Creek in desolate Jefferson County, just west of Denver. The millionaire's glasses and hat were found on the seat of his car, and, more perplexing, bloodstains were discovered on the railing of the small bridge. There were no signs of struggle.

More than one hundred state police, deputy sheriffs and volunteers fanned out across three counties, stalking through abandoned mines and edging over the frozen ridges. They found no trace of the missing millionaire. Sheriff Art Wermuth was convinced that the beer magnate had been kidnapped, and this speculation was strongly seconded by the missing man's father, who hurriedly returned to Colorado from a Honolulu vacation to tell newsmen, "It is just a matter of waiting for an offer. I am dealing with crooks who are in business. They have something I want to buy—my son. The price is secondary. It's like any other business transaction now. I cannot be emotional about this."

But the offer never came. Seven months later, F.B.I. agents announced that clothing belonging to the industrialist had been found in Douglas County, about fifteen miles south of Denver. There was a large amount of bleached bones in the area, thought to be mostly that of slain deer. Upon pathological examination, some of the bones proved to be that of "an adult human being." A pair of trousers containing money and a pocket knife with the initials "ACIII" was found in the area.

The grim recognition of Coors's inexplicable death came two days later, on September 16, when Castle Rock, Colorado, Coroner C. Douglas Andrews found a skull in the same district that had yielded the trousers and other skeletal remains. The Coors family's dentist, Dr. Arthur G. Kelly, stated that dental charts of Adolph Coors III matched exactly the dental structure of the skull that had been found.

In March 1961 Joseph Corbett, Jr., was found guilty of murdering Coors and was sentenced to life imprisonment.

*Millionaire brewer Adolph Coors III vanished in Colorado in 1960; his bones were found months later. (UPI)*

*Joseph Corbett, Jr. (center) listens in court as he is pronounced guilty of murdering beer magnate Coors. (UPI)*

Less sinister kidnapping befell countless sailors since man began to sail the oceans for profit and adventure. Typical of those unnaturally pressed into the service of unconscionable captains was George Miller, a twenty-year-old who left his home in Orange County, New Jersey, in July 1872 to purchase goods in New York for his father's business. Once in Manhattan, Miller visited some less-than-reputable dives to drink rotgut liquor and ogle the low courtesans. He was drunk when a press gang shanghaied him and put him aboard a merchant ship sailing for distant lands.

Miller's family heard nothing of him for thirty-five years and became resigned to the thought of his death; his father concluded that he had been murdered for the money he was carrying. In 1907, however, Miller appeared before his family a rich and powerful man. His prolonged disappearance, he sheepishly explained, was due to his own shame. He simply did not want to admit getting drunk and being shanghaied. Miller went on to tell how he jumped ship in Boston after visiting several exotic ports, and, rather than admit his indiscretions to his straitlaced family, joined a party of hunters going into the Maine woods. He became such an expert trapper and hunter that the Hudson's Bay Company hired him, and within a few years he headed his own fur business in which he made millions.

One bizarre kidnapping involved a man who had already made his fortune, one Jacques Villard, editor of the *New Age* and owner of a St. Louis correspondence school. The thirty-nine-year-old Villard visited Chicago with his wife on December 10, 1920. The couple checked into the LaSalle Hotel, and Villard immediately began advertising for a man of Polish extraction to serve as associate editor of his magazine and to aid him in his correspondence school.

Many applicants arrived at the LaSalle, most probably because Villard was offering a $10,000-a-year salary, a hefty income in those days. As the month went on, Villard continued his interviewing. He explained to his wife that job applicants in Chicago were not up to his expectations, and he might go to New York to continue his search. Mrs. Villard returned to St. Louis, reluctantly; she was apprehensive because her husband was a double amputee, having lost his legs early in life in an accident. He assured her that he would manage in his wheel chair and pointed out how bellboys were more than happy to carry him about. (Villard was a big tipper and made no secret of the fact that he was well-off financially, carrying several thousand dollars on him at all times.)

Not hearing from her husband in days, Mrs. Villard wired the La-Salle Hotel from St. Louis and was told by a desk clerk that Villard had been carted off, that "a tall blond man, apparently a Swede or a Pole, had carried him downstairs, paid his bill and taken him away with his luggage in a large black limousine." It seemed to be a clear case of kidnapping for Villard's wealth, about $2,000 in cash and $4,000 in jewelry. Unbelievably, it was thought that the legless editor had been shanghaied and held hostage until he agreed to give the lunatic who carried him from his hotel room the lucrative job with his magazine. A nationwide search revealed no clues as to the editor's whereabouts.

Villard solved most of the puzzlement when, on January 7, 1921, he was seen in the gutter of a lonely Chicago street, calling to passersby for help. Returning to St. Louis, the editor explained that he had been carried from his hotel room by a burly Polish fellow and held for ransom in a shanty on the outskirts of Chicago. He was tortured, he said, and was constantly threatened with death unless he convinced his wife to pay a heavy ransom. Oddly, none of the letters Villard wrote—ostensibly mailed by the kidnappers—ever were received by Villard's wife. The abductors did take away most of the cash and jewelry they found in the editor's hotel room. Apparently, the kidnappers grew disgusted with their plan and, alarmed at the publicity arising from Villard's disappearance, drove him into Chicago and hurled him into the street, where he was found minutes later.

Stranger than the Villard case, the disappearance (and apparent kidnapping) of Mrs. Dorothy Forstein from her suburban Philadelphia home in 1950 remains one of the most baffling. Married in 1941 to her childhood sweetheart, Jules Forstein, then a clerk in the Philadelphia City Council, Dorothy was an outgoing, ebullient person, as well as the devoted mother of two children, Marcy, an infant, and Merna, age ten, daughters by Forstein's previous marriage. (The first Mrs. Forstein died in childbirth.) The marriage was a happy one, and success came early when Forstein was made a magistrate in 1943. Another child, Edward, was born.

On the evening of January 25, 1945, after leaving her children with neighbors, Mrs. Forstein went shopping; she was seen joking with the local butcher and chatting with friends. Her neighbor Maria Townley saw her return home, and thought someone was with her, or walking behind her, as she made her way to the front door of her house. "It was getting dark and I didn't look too closely," Mrs. Townley recalled.

Seen or not, someone was with Dorothy Forstein that night. As she entered the dark three-story brick house, an intruder darted from the small alcove beneath the front stairs. Fists and a blunt instrument suddenly flailed at Mrs. Forstein, knocking her down, beating her into unconsciousness. As she fell, she knocked over the hall telephone, and an alarmed operator called the police.

Rushing through the open front door of the Forstein home minutes later, officers found Dorothy battered bloody on the floor. She had a broken jaw, a broken nose, a fractured shoulder, and a brain concussion. When coming to in the hospital, all the weak woman could mutter was "someone jumped out at me . . . I couldn't see who it was. . . . He just hit me and hit me."

Police Captain James A. Kelly of the Philadelphia Homicide Division went step by step over the attempted murder. It had to be intent to kill, he concluded, since no money or jewlery—nothing at all —was taken from the Forstein home. Magistrate Forstein was himself checked, but his alibi was unimpeachable. The children were too young to be considered suspects, and Mrs. Forstein had no known enemies; in fact, she was one of the best-liked residents in the area.

The attack was never solved and soon most everyone forgot the brutal incident—everyone except Mrs. Forstein, whose emotional makeup was permanently damaged by the beating. She became nervous and hypertensive, jumping at the slightest noise in the house, checking and rechecking the many extra locks put on the doors and windows following the attack.

Magistrate Forstein seldom left his wife and children alone, even though he was convinced that no one he came into contact with during his judicial capacities would harm him or his family. On the night of October 18, 1950, Forstein made plans to attend a political banquet. He called his wife and told her "I don't expect to be too late. Is everything all right?"

Dorothy assured Forstein that everything was fine at home and joked for a moment with him, seeming to be her old self. "Be sure to miss me!" she said before hanging up.

His wife's words were prophetic, as Magistrate Forstein learned when he returned to his home at 1835 North Franklin Street at 11:30 P.M. He was greeted by his two youngest children, Edward and Marcy, who were huddled together in a bedroom, crying in unison: "Mommy's gone!" The elder daughter, Merna, was away visiting.

At first Forstein thought his wife had visited a neighbor or a relative, but after several hours of telephoning he learned nothing. Captain Kelly was called once again into the lives of the Forstein family, and he quickly had his men check every hospital in Philadelphia, as well as rooming houses, hotels, rest homes and the morgue. Nothing was turned up. Kelly concluded that the woman was not in the neighborhood. She had left her purse, her money and her keys at home. The front door was locked. There was only the wild tale little Marcy Forstein told, one that the police earlier dismissed as being the product of a terrified imagination.

The girl, through convulsive sobs, told Kelly that "I woke up and it was late. I don't know whether I heard voices or whether I just woke up. I went to the head of the stairs and there was a man coming up. He went to Mommy's room in the front and through a crack in the door, I could see her lying on her face on the rug. She looked sick. The man turned her over on her back and picked her up. He put her over his shoulder so her head hung down his back. When I asked him what he was doing, he said: 'Go back to sleep, little one, your Mommy has been sick, but she will be all right now.'"

"And how was Mommy dressed?" Kelly asked the weeping Marcy.

"She had on her red slippers and her red silk pajamas—the ones she liked because they were so pretty. She didn't say anything." The girl, at the policeman's gentle prodding, went on to describe the stranger. "He had on a brown cap with a peak, not pulled down too much. And a brown jacket and something stuck in his shirt. I guess

**121**

*The much-bedeviled Mrs. Dorothy Forstein of Philadelphia whose 1950 disappearance remains one of the most puzzling on record.*
(UPI)

he was about as old as Daddy. I never saw him before. . . . He went downstairs and out the door. When I heard the lock snap, I went out and got Edward. We waited until Daddy got home."

It was incredible, but Marcy's explanation was the only one the Philadelphia police would ever have as to why Mrs. Forstein disappeared. Nothing was disturbed in the house. Not a single fingerprint was left anywhere, which seemed impossible to police, who figured that a man balancing a woman on his shoulder must have grabbed something to steady himself. And how would an abductor be able to make his way down a busy street carrying an unconscious woman in pajamas without arousing attention and suspicion? And how did the man even get into the Forstein home, since none of the locks was disturbed? Kelly remembered that in the case of the 1945 attack none of the locks had been disturbed either.

The child's story was repeatedly checked by psychiatrists and psychologists, and it was supported as being absolutely factual. The police made no progress. Dorothy Forstein's last known words were chillingly ironic: "Be sure to miss me!"

## 5

Alfred Tennyson's romantic notions about missing persons were heroically summed up in his 1864 narrative poem *Enoch Arden*, the story of a man who is lost at sea, survives on a desert isle, and returns after ten years, to discover his wife, who thinks of him as dead, happily remarried to Arden's boyhood chum. Arden, for the sake of his wife's continued bliss, observes brokenhearted from afar, and then departs without ever identifying himself. There have been many Enoch Ardens in real life, but they vanish for the darkest of reasons —out of fraud, corruption, and, as the purple-passioned writers of the previous century were wont to say, murder most foul.

### Trumped-up Tragedies

Swindling insurance companies through faked suicides or accidental deaths while the "victims" secretly survive has long been in practice, a criminal activity that keeps phalanxes of insurance detectives employed and scandal sheets in print. But it is no easy fraud. The perpetrator must establish an elaborate and believable set of circumstances to assure a broad acceptance of his or her own death. But finding no body, no real proof of death, the culprit knows, will prod the insurance sleuths to dissect every final detail before a policy payment is honored. It is always in the detail where the sham is found out and the "victim" is located.

Such was the case of Frank L. Birdsong, a well-to-do merchant, country squire, and Postmaster of Homeville, Virginia, who was declared legally dead a year after his apparent suicide by drowning in a river near his home in December 1920. Birdsong had taken out several insurance policies totaling many thousands of dollars and all but one of these, issued by the Penn Mutual Life Insurance Company, were paid off to Birdsong's estate.

When Penn Mutual's insurance investigator Jesse F. West, Jr., noticed that these insurance moneys were being siphoned from the estate, he began a four-year-long investigation that resulted in the discovery that the sixty-eight-year-old Birdsong was alive and well and living in Sarasota, Florida, under an assumed name. Birdsong no longer enjoyed the fruits of his own death after being sent to prison for swindling.

The case of Sam Abrams, a wealthy Manhattan businessman, was radically different. Abrams was trapped by fascination with his own death. In the late spring of 1928 Sam Abrams left his fashionable home on Manhattan's East Side for a Sunday swim. He did not return that evening, and the following Monday morning attendants cleaning out a bathhouse at the beach near Rockaway found Abrams' suit and personal effects. Police investigators originally thought the man had accidentally drowned or committed suicide but were perplexed when his body did not float to shore within a week. (Seldom and only under unusual weather circumstances are the bodies of drowned victims carried out to sea in that area.)

Then there was the odd way in which Mrs. Abrams reacted to police investigators Mrs. Abrams had actually informed police that her husband had been missing since Sunday night. When detectives arrived at her home to tell her that her husband's clothes had been discovered in the beachhouse she became instantly hysterical. According to the report: "She displayed all the outward signs of grief, wailing, wringing her hands, and shrieking. Later, when she became more calm, she told the detective that she had been under the impression that the husband had stayed overnight with his brother, who resided near the beach, and therefore she had not been worried by his absence."

Mrs. Abrams' telegraphed emotions that indicated knowledge of the death of her husband before it was confirmed, plus her immediate application for payment of $50,000 from his life-insurance policy, aroused more than casual suspicion. Even when it was publicly thought that Abrams had either committed suicide or had accidentally drowned, the bereaved wife was more concerned with collecting insurance money than worrying about the recovery of her husband's body.

Two months later, while New York police were still investigating the case and turning up no body or evidence, two cars collided in a downtown Montreal street and a man was removed unconscious from one of the autos and taken to a hospital. Officials searched the man's clothing to check his identity and found nothing except a fading newspaper clipping which told of Sam Abrams' disappearance and the finding of his clothes at the Rockaway Beach. As the authorities read the clipping, which described the missing man, they realized the description fit the accident victim perfectly.

Montreal police notified officers in New York. Revived, the accident victim was told that police in Manhattan were interested in him. Shaking with fear, Sam Abrams came back to life, admitting that he had faked his suicide with his wife's help to collect the life insurance. "I took that extra suit of clothes and dumped them in the Rockaway Beach undressing house. It seemed simple to disappear. Death by drowning and then $50,000! Huh, not so simple."

A similar happening on November 13, 1938, brought to the surface a man who had been declared legally dead for fourteen years, when John Edgar Davis was arrested in Pasadena, California, for a minor offense. Police routinely submitted Davis' fingerprints to the F.B.I. and were quickly informed that their prisoner was none other than Davis Rowland MacDonald, who was thought to have committed suicide on February 14, 1924, when his clothes were found on the Allegheny River bank close to Pittsburgh, where MacDonald had a large business. Beside his neat pile of clothes was found a note addressed to Clara MacDonald in which her husband lamented that he had "failed in business and as a man."

*Davis Rowland MacDonald vanished for fourteen years and emerged as John Edgar Davis in 1938. (UPI)*

Clara MacDonald had her suicidal spouse declared legally dead after divorcing him and remarrying. She subsequently collected three huge insurance policies on his life. MacDonald, who had been a much-bemedaled hero in World War I, a lieutenant in the Air Corps, had simply chosen to enrich his wife, who he knew would claim the insurance policies, by faking his own death.

George F. Knoop, of Las Vegas, Nevada, was also in trouble as a businessman and as a husband. He was financially drowning in debt, and to further his misery, he and his wife Janice could barely tolerate each other. The couple decided to end the marriage, along with George's official life, on March 27, 1964. On that day the thirty-one-year-old Knoop, a devout scuba diver, drove to Lake Mead near Las Vegas. He parked his car and walked slowly to the beach, careful to leave noticeable footprints in the sand, dropping his shoes and bathing apparel as he went. He entered the water and swam a long distance along the shoreline.

Knoop then left the water and strolled to a waiting car which was registered under the name of John L. Deviland, an auto which he, Knoop, had sold to Deviland, a fiction of his own mind and the imaginary person he instantly became. Knoop-Deviland then leisurely drove to Los Angeles, where he applied for and received a Social Security card in the name of John Deviland. With this new identity, Knoop-Deviland took up residence in El Segundo, California, where he worked as a machinist. He married an attractive brunette, a twenty-five-year-old divorcee with two children by a previous marriage. Knoop's brand-new life promised blissful freedom from the bitter cares of the past.

Also joyful over her new life was Janice Knoop, who returned to her home town of Cedar Falls, Iowa. When investigators determined that Knoop's death had been a case of accidental drowning, she collected $23,000 in insurance money, as well as sizable Social Security benefits. By then she was remarried to college teacher Chester McNelly.

An anonymous tip in January 1967 to California police revealed

*Insurance swindler George F. Knoop (left) steps from the "dead" and into prison in 1967.* (UPI)

that John Deviland was really George F. Knoop, a man who had staged his own death. Detectives investigated, and Knoop-Deviland was soon in custody, held on a Nevada fugitive warrant that charged him with failing to return the $150 worth of scuba equipment he used in his 1964 "death dive" into Lake Mead. The charge was, of course, an excuse to hold the man until his true identity could be determined.

This was established by Knoop's mother and sister, who visited him in jail. The women were not only shocked to discover that their loved one was alive, but angered over the fact that he had been living only five miles from their home for three years without ever contacting them. Both Knoop and his first wife admitted their joint plan to defraud the government and were given suspended sentences.

## White-Collar Wanglers

The quiet-mannered life of Atlanta, Georgia, exploded into mass frenzy on February 22, 1893, when the president of the city's most powerful financial institution, the Gate City National Bank, gave forth a startling proclamation. Said a tear-streaked President L. J. Hill:

> It gives us great pain to announce to the public that our assistant cashier, Mr. Lewis Redwine, has defaulted, but we are glad to say that his shortage will not impair our capital, and in view of the fact that there may be conflicting and exaggerated rumors circulated, we have invited the banks composing the Clearing House Association to thoroughly investigate the condition of our bank and ask our friends and the public to await their report, which will appear in the afternoon papers.

The news, however, published the following morning, was not heartening. The Gate City Bank was all but wrecked and had to close its doors. Redwine, a much respected thirty-two-year-old social lion, had worked for the bank all his adult life, inching through clerical jobs until awarded the post of assistant cashier. Late in February 1893 Redwine was summoned to President Hill's office. It seemed that there was an error in the books, an error that indicated more than $66,000 was missing from the bank vault.

Redwine stood outside Hill's office for a few moments then turned on his heels and, in the words of Georgia historian Franklin M. Garrett, "went instead to Buckalew's saloon on the ground floor of the bank. He downed a stiff drink in one gulp and disappeared into thin air."

Redwine's vanishing act was totally unlike his earlier conduct. He had been a quiet, conscientious young man whose long hours at work in the bank had earned him the trust and confidence of his employers. Yet it was soon discovered that the assistant cashier had been living far beyond his $1,500-a-year salary.

Two days after the posting of a $1,000 reward, the defaulting cashier was found in a boardinghouse on the outskirts of Atlanta. Redwine, who surrendered meekly, was living under the name of Lester. The cashier never explained what happened to the bank's money, and he was sentenced to a long penitentiary term for embezzlement. Upon the completion of his sentence, Atlanta's first great bank thief drifted through the South, dying on April 10, 1900. He is presently buried in an unmarked grave in Atlanta's Oakland Cemetery.

Disappearing cashiers from large banking concerns became more and more prevalent in the early years of the twentieth century. Dumont, New Jersey, was shocked to hear that one of its most respected citizens, one Thaddeus Stone, for twenty years cashier of the New York brokerage company of Moore & Terry, had vanished on June 29, 1914, with $10,500 of his firm's money. Stone hiding in his home, was discovered by detectives weeks later. He was convicted of grand larceny and sent to Sing Sing for five years. Stone gave as his excuse for the theft his sudden attraction to gambling and explained how Broadway sharpers fleeced him and his firm's money in a twenty-minute crap game.

Much more astounding was the case of the financier William Lustgarten, who in 1917 vanished from the Manhattan offices of the firm that he owned, leaving bookkeeping deficiencies that spiraled beyond $700,000. As president of the Tax Lien Investment Company of New York, Lustgarten had taken in more than one million dollars for various real-estate purchases since 1910. He had risen high in society, becoming an intimate of New York Mayor William Gaynor and a strong supporter of President Woodrow Wilson. He was also the head of several social groups and organizer of a curious fraternal group called the Loyal American League, which was chiefly a paper organization intent upon removing the "hyphen" from German-Americans. Lustgarten was also a man who enjoyed the lavish life and spent with abandon; he owned a stylish mansion, employed a dozen servants, drove about in the most modern autos.

The Delmonico life style ended on August 16, 1917. Lustgarten left a note stating that he could not account for "financial difficulties" and decided to end it all by "dropping into New York Bay." His hat, identified by his name embossed upon the inside band, along with other pieces of his clothing, was found floating in the waters. The financier was thought to be dead, a tragic suicide.

This fate was exploded as myth when two young women from Pearl River, New York, where Lustgarten had maintained a summer home, spotted the missing financier in Washington in July 1918. He was dressed as a private in the Army and was dining in a fashionable restaurant.

"Hello, Mr. Lustgarten," called out one of the women.

"Hello," acknowledged the hesitant missing man. He held a brief, nervous conversation with the women and then quickly excused himself. The report went out that Lustgarten was alive, and a dozen agencies busied themselves with tracking him down. The defaulter, however, alarmed by being identified, proved too slippery for pursuers. He obtained one transfer after another, moving from post to post until he succeeded in being sent overseas to serve on the Western Front, those tracking him always one step behind him.

Not until February 1919, when the war was over, did authorities run the elusive Mr. Lustgarten to earth, locating him in St. Nazaire, France, in the ranks of the 309th Engineers under the name of Corporal Allan H. Wilson. He was arrested and returned to the United States, where, because of heroic duty on the front lines, the Army ignored pleas to strip him of his rank. He was given an honorable discharge.

Lustgarten was then driven to the limits of Camp Upton, where he was let loose. As the wily embezzler stepped from Army property, a dozen sheriffs pounced on him and dragged him off to the Tombs in New York where he awaited trial. The wait was a short one; Lustgarten was quickly convicted of grand larceny.

Judge Crain scowled at the prisoner, who chose to wear his Army uniform while being sentenced. Crain took note of the gold service stripe, the wound stripe, and the honorable-discharge stripe on Lustgarten's sleeve, but he indicated that he was not impressed. It was not to the prisoner's credit, the judge roared, that he served in France when the whole purpose of entering the Army was to flee from the jurisdiction of the authorities and in order to conceal his identity. He gave the prisoner four to eight years in Sing Sing. Lustgarten gave the judge back a mocking salute and then marched with great ceremony between jailers from the court room. The vast holdings he had looted from his own company were never recovered.

Quite by accident another famous missing man who disappeared after filching funds, Edward Burke Scott, was discovered by his wife the one-time celebrated opera singer Kate Condon. She had been looking for him for twenty-four years, but by the time she located the lover of her youth he was dead by his own hand.

Scott had been the manager of one of impresario Charles Dillingham's traveling shows at the turn of the century. He was considered to be a brilliant and promising light in American theater, having graduated from Princeton at twenty and assumed at an early age the lofty position of drama critic for the *New York Press*. Dillingham thought him a genius and hired Scott to manage his top stars, May Irwin and Frank Daniels.

In 1903 Scott met and married in Toronto the lovely Kate Condon, herself the toast of operatic circles following bravura performances at the New York Metropolitan Opera House. The couple enjoyed only a few weeks' honeymoon before Kate moved west to complete a tour. In November, when she returned East and was frantically trying to locate her enterprising husband, Kate received a telegram from Scott's office informing her that he was missing. Also missing was about $10,000 from his accounts.

"I was convinced that he had been robbed or murdered," Kate breathlessly informed an anxious press, "as he usually carried large sums with him . . . I was never able to get any trace of him after that."

Two decades passed. Kate's career withered with her press notices and fading opera gowns. She went to live with her brother in Chicago, never again to marry. Then, in February 1927, the retired singer received an anonymous letter that informed her that a wealthy land speculator in New Orleans had just committed suicide, a man who was most likely her long-lost husband. Kate entrained to Louisiana and walked into the vault of St. Anthony's Cemetery in New Orleans. Edward Burke Scott was lying naked on a marble slab with a tag tied to one toe which said he was William B. Victor.

Kate learned that Scott, as Victor, had grown enormously wealthy as a land speculator and real-estate magnate in the South, but he had been careful never to reveal his background. He walked in rich apparel alone through the quaint streets of the French Quarter. He dined alone. He lived alone in a castlelike mansion, where his servants bustled in silence watching him move ghostlike from room to room, as if searching for something. One day in late 1927, Scott-Victor entered the exclusive Chess, Checkers and Whist Club, of which he was a prominent member, and just as enigmatically as he had disappeared twenty-four years earlier, calmly sat down at a table and then blew out his brains. Kate, however, did not return empty-handed to Chicago. Half of Scott-Victor's estate, about $100,-000, was awarded her. She returned to the Windy City in grand manner.

Chicago itself has had many a white-collar criminal vanish in an effort to elude capture and prison, but the most spectacular of these was Fred D. Hubbard, an articulate anti-Daley machine politician, who was elected to the City Council as a black reform independent in 1969. Hubbard's star rose and, in addition to serving as the alderman of the 2nd Ward, he was given the $25,000-a-year job of heading the Chicago Plan, a federal program to find construction jobs for minorities in Chicago.

In May 1971, Hubbard could no longer be found at home or in his office. He was gone, and vanishing with him was $110,000 from the coffers of the federal fund. For fifteen months the F.B.I tracked the missing man and finally apprehended him as he calmly threw in his cards in a Gardena, California, poker parlor. He was penniless when he entered prison to serve a two-year term for embezzlement; he said that he had gambled away every cent of the appropriated funds.

Upon his release, Hubbard carried from the federal prison in Terre Haute, Indiana, a bulky manuscript, a story he said concerned

*Chicago Alderman Fred Hubbard, who vanished in 1971 with $110,000 in Federal funds.* (UPI)

131

a politician who robbed from organized crime to help the poor. "I don't think anybody would buy it," he told reporters who walked him to the bus station, where he was given a $9.65 bus ticket for Chicago. One story the press did buy was Hubbard's consistent ability to disappear. When the Terre Haute bus arrived in Chicago, the onetime alderman was not on it, having disappeared once more. (At this writing, Hubbard is a Chicago cab driver.)

### An English Skull

Lydia Atley had a problem that seemed unsurmountable. The most attractive female in Ringstead, Northamptonshire, England, had fallen in love with a married man, a young landowning business-man named William Weekly Ball. The two had spilled their passions for each other in a dozen dark trysting places, and the torrid, highly illicit love affair was the gossip of the district. After a year of sagging romance, Lydia began to complain bitterly to a Mrs. Groom, a village neighbor, that Ball wished to get rid of her. Lydia vowed that he would pay handsomely for her shabby exit.

The scorned woman was determined to collect her love ransom and told Ball so. On the sultry evening of July 22, 1850, Joseph Groom overheard Lydia and Weekly Ball talking in angry tones as they walked through Ball's orchards. "I did not intend coming here to-night," Lydia was heard to say to Weekly Ball, "for I've got the feeling that you intend killing me. Isn't it so?" Groom strained from the other side of a hedge to hear Ball's response.

The swain's answer was in a tone so low that Groom could determine nothing. Then Lydia spoke again, her voice weak. "The Lord have mercy on me, if I am to die in my present state of sin." Another neighbor, John Hill, also walking abroad that beautiful night, heard the couple talking some time later as they continued their stroll through roses and honeysuckles.

Suddenly Lydia almost shouted: "I won't, Weekly Ball! I won't do or say nothing of the kind! It's yours, yours I tell you, and no one else's!" These were the last words ever heard from Lydia Atley's lips. That night she vanished.

Ball was arrested and questioned about Lydia's disappearance but he offered no solution, and since there was no trace of the girl or any sign of violence done to her, Ball was released. The years passed uneventfully, and the missing Lydia Atley was all but forgotten.

Almost fourteen years later a ditch-digger at his labors, one Richard Warren, of Ringstead, struck a hard object with his shovel while cleaning out a drainage canal. He uncovered a small white skull, and knowing the legendary disappearance of Lydia Atley from his village, raced off to his employer. Warren was immediately ordered to dig further and he soon uncovered an entire skeleton, that of a woman, medical examiners quickly concluded. The skull was examined carefully, and it was found to be missing one tooth, the same tooth Lydia Atley had had pulled only a short time before she vanished.

Suspicion was rekindled against Ball and the prosperous land-owner was arrested and tried in 1864 for the murder of the beautiful girl. Ball's defense counsels were shrewd. They pointed out that many a person in the village had lost a tooth on the left side of the mouth in the year Lydia disappeared and this single piece of evidence was no evidence at all. Moreover, the defense ordered the entire area where the skeleton was unearthed to be dug up. Many skeletons were discovered and it was claimed correctly by Ball and his attorneys that the site was often used by gypsies to bury their dead. The female skull and remains were, no doubt, those belonging to one of the myriad gypsies who traveled nomadic and unrecorded throughout rural England, the defense argued. The jury agreed, and Ball was set free.

The case of Lydia Atley was never resolved, but most experts of the case concur to this day that William Weekly Ball killed his beloved, who was pregnant, in order to hide his sexual escapade and then cleverly buried her in the unmarked graveyard where her remains would be thought to be that of just another poor gypsy. To the end of his days, Ball never spoke the name of Lydia Atley, but on occasion he was seen to walk about the gypsy burial site and pause, silent, as if in deep memory.

### The Vanishing Henpecker

Though the Lydia Atley mystery was one of the most memorable of the early cases of disappearance attributable to murder, such dark fate was no longer uncommon by the turn of the century. England was rocked by a similar occurrence in 1910, but this time the corpse, or what was left of it, was uncovered and identified in a spectacular fashion that was to mark the Crippen disappearance far above the average.

Hawley Harvey Crippen was a henpecked man if ever one existed. He was also a meek cuckold, the victim of a sex-craving megalomaniac wife. Born in Coldwater, Michigan, Crippen took his medical degree from the Hospital College of Cleveland. He was an ambiguous doctor, specializing willy-nilly in various parts of the anatomy.

This dry, withdrawn man met and married a flamboyant, florid, stage-struck woman named Kunigunde Mackamotzki in New York, where she was known in third-rate musical circles as Cora Turner. Cora longed to become an opera star, and Crippen more than humored her by paying for expensive music lessons. The couple moved to London at the turn of the century, where Crippen practiced dentistry and the "ear-cure" business, drawing most of his income as the manager of an American patent-medicine firm with offices on Shaftesbury Avenue.

All was quiet for seven years, and then Cora, who had taken the name of Belle Elmore, began to fanatically pursue a career as a classical singer. In the words of one chronicler, "Her voice matched that of her personality, and was loud, vulgar, unsubtle and lacking in feminine charm." She was an absolute failure, appearing only once during an actor's strike at the Bedford Music Hall in Camden Town. So inept and terrible was Mrs. Crippen's performance that she offended even a low-life audience conditioned to mediocrity and was quickly booed and hissed from the stage. Undaunted, Cora Crippen doggedly held onto the grandiose myth of her "talent" by busying herself, in the words of writer Filson Young, "with frequenting music-hall circles, reading the *Era*, retaining her 'stage' name of Belle Elmore, and adding to her already large stock of theatrical garments."

In addition, she lobbied for and won election to the post of treasurer of the Music Hall Ladies' Guild, a position that allowed her to meet every failure in London's stage world. From the desperate ranks of such fallen artists, Mrs. Crippen selected many male performers, all unemployed, and induced them to stay in her three-story house at 39 Hildrop Crescent, Camden Town, in North London —rent-free to those males who cared to share her bed.

To five-foot-four-inch Hawley Harvey Crippen such disloyalty was exceeded only by the humiliation his dominating wife heaped upon his thin shoulders. She compelled him to rise at 5 A.M., and before leaving for his office, clean the kitchen, make the breakfast and shine the boots of her "guests." (One of these guests, an American entertainer named Bruce Miller, was, at most times when Crippen was performing his domestic-servant chores, in bed with the unheralded diva.)

For three years, from 1907 on, Crippen endured the shame and the browbeating. The gentle man had small consolation, most of which came from his young secretary, Ethel Le Neve, who was as quiet and retiring as Crippen. Pliable, understanding, Ethel met with her lover-employer in dingy London hotel rooms where they consummated their birdlike passions.

Yet Crippen's unbearable home life did not alter. His posturing wife became an ogress of demand and domination. By December 1909 Cora threatened to leave and take with her their joint savings of 600 pounds. When Crippen learned that she had notified the bank of her purpose, he began to set in motion the plan for her permanent disappearance.

On January 31, 1910, Cora entertained two music-hall friends, Mr. and Mrs. Paul Martinetti. Following dinner, Cora chatted on endlessly about her nonexistent career. The couples then played whist until 1:30 A.M. Cora scolded the meek-mannered Crippen throughout the evening and then loudly demanded that he run into the street in search of a cab, since Paul Martinetti had a slight chill. The dutiful doctor did as he was bidden. Cora saw her guests to the door and watched them walk down the stairs of her house. "Don't come out, Belle," Mrs. Martinetti called up to Cora. "You'll catch a cold!"

What Mrs. Crippen caught was not determined until some months later. The Martinettis were the last to see her alive, for Cora Crippen disappeared completely. There were excuses, all provided by the dutiful Dr. Crippen. Two days after the Martinetti dinner, the Music Hall Ladies' Guild received a letter from Cora in which she

*The flamboyant opera apprentice Mrs. Hawley Harvey Crippen, better known as Belle Elmore when she disappeared in 1910.*

resigned her post and stated that she was in a great hurry to journey to America to visit a dying relative. The letter was written by Dr. Crippen, who said his wife was in such haste that she had no time to pen her missives. The music-hall artists were frantic with gossip. Something strange was afoot. Cora was not the kind to simply dash off to America without a full and lengthy explanation. To further mystify friends, Dr. Crippen pawned some of Cora's jewelry for 80 pounds. He then appeared at a benefit dinner with none other than Ethel Le Neve, who was wearing a brooch favored by Cora. On March 12, Ethel moved into the Crippen home, ostensibly as a housekeeper. Cora's furs and clothes were being worn by the new boarder when she went about Camden Town. To the horror of neighbors and friends, Dr. Crippen and housekeeper Ethel went abroad for two weeks, taking in the air and sun of Dieppe.

All of this aroused Cora's cronies so much that they petitioned Scotland Yard in June to investigate the strange disappearance of Mrs. Crippen. The intrepid Chief Inspector Walter Dew, accompanied by Sergeant Arthur Mitchell began to probe into the mystery. (Actor Stanley Ridges was to portray Dew opposite Charles Laughton's masterful performance as Crippen in the 1944 motion picture, *The Suspect*.)

Dew went to Crippen's office, where the dentist was affably cooperative. He recited his entire career for the persistent Dew, pausing only to pull an occasional tooth in an adjoining room. Crippen finally shrugged at the end of his day and told the Chief Inspector that he had, indeed, lied to Cora's friends. "It's extremely humiliating, sir, to inform you that my wife is not visiting any ailing relative in America. I've tried to protect her reputation and my own humiliation and failure. The truth is, sir, that Cora has left me for another man, a man better able to support her than myself." He inferred that the man was none other than actor Bruce Miller, who had recently returned to the United States.

Crippen further ingratiated himself with Inspector Dew by inviting him to lunch the following day. After the meal, the detective and the dentist, at Crippen's suggestion, adjourned to the doctor's house, where Dew was permitted a complete inspection. Dew stalked through the Hildrop Crescent floors, even looking over the garden and cellar. Nothing appeared suspicious, and Dew seemed to accept Crippen's explanation of his wife's absence. But the detective returned to Crippen's office three days later to clear up some remaining doubts. He was informed that the doctor and Miss Le Neve had departed.

Dew's doubts grew larger and, after repeatedly calling for Crippen and Miss Le Neve and finding them still out of town, the detective ordered a squad of his men to search Crippen's house. After three days of ferreting, the detectives were rewarded in the cellar on July 14. One of the bricks beneath a woodpile was loose and, raising this, Dew saw the earth had been freshly spaded. His men began to dig. A few feet down they found "something very unpleasant." Wrapped in a man's pajama jacket and covered with quicklime were grisly segments of a human body. The head and limbs had been severed and never were recovered. There were no bones at all, the body having been filleted, and, it was later established, burned in the kitchen grate. Were these the only remains of the vanished Cora Crippen? Inspector Dew had no way of knowing, for so little was left that it was impossible to determine which sex the deceased had been. However, traces of hyoscine, a poisonous drug used normally as a nerve depressant and hypnotic for delirium tremens and as treatment for meningitis, were found in the stomach of the body. Dew learned that on January 17, 1910, Dr. Crippen had visited the chemical firm of Lewis and Burrows and had purchased five grains of the deadly drug, signing for it with his own name. (The overuse of such a drug by Crippen on his shrewish wife was in keeping with his gentle character, for hyoscine merely induced a peaceful sleep that ended in death.)

Inspector Dew definitely identified the dead woman as Cora Crippen. Her doctor husband had neglected to destroy a piece of his wife's stomach which clearly showed an old abdominal scar which she was known to have had. (This gruesome evidence was later exhibited at Crippen's trial, passed shudderingly from juror to juror on a soup plate.)

Finding Crippen and Miss Le Neve, however, turned out to be as difficult as locating the missing Cora. Thousands of circulars describing the couple blanketed England and the continent. Hundreds of wild sightings were reported to Scotland Yard. All were false leads. Then Dew received a curious wire from the captain of the liner *Montrose*, still at sea and en route to Quebec from Antwerp. Captain Kendall had noticed a peculiar couple among the *Montrose's* passengers. (Kendall was later the unfortunate skipper of the *Empress of Ireland*, which was rammed in dense fog in the St. Lawrence River by the collier *Storstad*, suffering a staggering loss of 1,024 passengers on May 29, 1914.)

John Philip Robinson who was traveling with his teen-age son aroused Kendall's suspicions by doting too affectionately on the boy whose delicate features and shy mannerisms were certainly feminine. Also curious were the clothes the boy wore—they were much too large, compelling the graceful lad to hold up his trousers with a safety pin. Kendall was sure that Robinson and son were the runaway Crippen and Ethel Le Neve.

Dew lost no time after receiving Kendall's wire. As the only policeman who had met and could recognize Crippen, he sailed immediately for Canada on the *Laurentic*, a much faster ship than the *Montrose*. Arriving in Canada first, Dew met the *Montrose* when it docked, and was led to Robinson's cabin by a beaming Captain Kendall, proud of his own detective abilities.

"Good morning, Dr. Crippen," the Inspector stated calmly as he faced the bogus Mr. Robinson. "I am Chief Inspector Dew of Scotland Yard. I believe you know me."

Nervelessly, Crippen responded in a monotone. "Good morning, Mr. Dew."

"I am arresting you for the murder and mutilation of your wife, Cora Crippen, in London on or about February 1, last."

Crippen and Miss Le Neve were taken in tow back to London, where they were both charged with murder. Throughout the five-day trial, which began on October 18, 1910, the quiet doctor maintained his innocence. His main concern was the freeing of his mistress; he repeatedly insisted that she knew nothing of the murder. Following his conviction and death sentence, Crippen begged the authorities to spare her. In one yearning letter he wrote: "In this farewell letter to the world, as I face eternity, I say that Ethel Le Neve has loved me as few women love men, and that her innocence of any crime, save that of yielding to the dictates of her heart, is absolute. My last prayer will be that God will protect her and keep her safe from harm and allow her to join me in eternity."

Miss Le Neve was found not guilty some days later, and Crippen went to the scaffold to be hanged on November 23, 1910, consoled with the news of his lover's freedom. His last request was that her photograph be placed in his coffin; it was. Ethel Le Neve did not appear at Crippen's funeral. She vanished after her release and was never heard from again.

The Crippen disappearance and murder were a preamble for the glut of missing women who disappeared from their Paris homes from 1914 to 1919, their lover and killer a small snake-eyed sensualist named Henri Désiré Landru, known later to a world horrified at his crimes as Bluebeard. Ten of the missing women were murdered, dissected and burned by him, it was proved in court. (Two hundred eighty-three were listed in Landru's meticulously kept notebooks as being swindled by him.) The mass killer was cavalier onto the guillotine about the whole thing. "The women never reproached me," he said, referring to his sexual exploits.

A decade later, another missing lady in America not only caused sensational headlines, but her disappearance indirectly led to the downfall of the powerful Tammany political machine and the end of the happy, gin-stained reign of gentleman James J. Walker, the bon vivant mayor of the City of New York.

*Henri Desire Landru, better known as Bluebeard, was responsible for the death of at least ten missing ladies.*

### An Escaped Butterfly

Onetime show girl, part-time blackmailer, and full-time grade-A call girl Vivien Gordon vanished on the eve of her date with prosecutors probing the affairs of Tammany Hall and its dapper front man Mayor Walker. Her case against political grafters and vice cops on the take was condensed in a little black book, which boasted names, dates, payments, and sexual misconduct that dated back a decade. Vivien had provided the sex.

Strong-willed as a child, Vivien ran away from her upstanding Detroit family and her convent school at age fifteen. The bright lights of the theater beckoned, and she was soon working in show business, chiefly as a chorus girl in burlesque. She met John Bischoff, then a salesman, and wed him. The marriage produced one child, Benita, but Vivien had no time for her daughter and husband. She left for New York to seek the fortune that had eluded her on the stage. She found it in bed.

As one of New York's leading madams of the 1920s, Vivien Gordon met most of the political sachems running Manhattan, men who talked so much in the boudoir that Vivien felt compelled to write down their words in her little black book for future use. Unlike Polly Adler, whose chief interest was prostitution, Madam Gordon used the information she had collected to bring in more revenue. She became an expert blackmailer, drawing thousands of dollars each month from more than five hundred "sugar daddies" who paid her to keep quiet. (Vivien's blackmailing operations actually shocked prostitution queen Polly Adler, who later stated in *A House Is Not a Home:* "I knew her only as an attractive brunette in the same business as I, out to feather her nest quickly.")

With money readily available, Vivien resumed her role of part-time mother and took her child Benita to live with her. When the child was six Vivien was arrested for prostitution and sent to the Bedford Reformatory for Women. John Bischoff took custody of little Benita, but as soon as Vivien was released she began a violent hair-pulling crusade to retrieve her daughter. She was declared by the courts to be an unfit mother. Vivien shrieked that she had been framed on the vice charge that sent her to prison so that her child could be taken from her.

Out of either rage or self-vindication, Vivien in February 1931 visited with Irving Ben Cooper, an assistant to the crusading Judge Samuel Seabury, and promised to expose the widespread extortion practiced by the police vice squads. In the words of Herbert Mitgang in *The Man Who Rode the Tiger*, "she told him that she had been framed in the past on a prostitution conviction. She arranged to come to his office again with evidence." Seabury and his aides were then gearing up operations to destroy the corrupt Tammany machine and its happy-go-lucky advance man, Mayor Walker.

Vivien did not return to see Cooper in two days as she promised. She promptly vanished. Detectives looked everywhere and found no trace of what the newspapers later termed the "misled woman who followed the tinseled path." Then, on the wintry night of February 28, 1931, the body of a well-dressed, attractive woman was found in Van Cortlandt Park in the Bronx. She had been strangled to death, a clothesline cord drawn so tight about her neck that it was embedded in the flesh.

Received at the City Morgue, officials could not, at first, determine the victim's identity. The woman was five-feet-two-inches, blue-eyed, and weighed 135 pounds. She had brown hair with a reddish tint to it. This was no ordinary grifter killed for a few dollars, authorities knew. She was handsomely gowned in a black velvet dress trimmed with yellow lace at neck and cuffs. She wore white kid gloves and black silk stockings. Her fingerprints were taken and sent to police headquarters. They matched those of a woman arrested and jailed on vice charges, Vivien Gordon.

New York's press exploded. A chief witness against the machine and police corruption had been silenced with murder. Until the killing was solved, boomed Police Commissioner Edward P. Mulrooney, there would be "a stain on the shield of every policeman in New York."

Found in Vivien's apartment was her fatal black book showing the names of hundreds of men, many of whom were highranking public officials. James D. Horan in *The Desperate Years* recalled how "as investigators dug deeper, a network of crime and corruption was revealed. Vice cops were found on her payroll; others were listed with an indication that they could be bought for a price."

All of the sordid details of Vivien Gordon's twisted life were jammed into print. Her daughter, Benita, living with her father in Audubon, New Jersey, became hysterical with shame as she read the newspaper accounts. The teen-age girl, like her mother, began keeping a diary, but its tragic entries were brief and ended suddenly. On February 28, Benita scrawled: "Mother found dead. Terrible things are being said." On March 1, the distraught girl wrote: "I guess I will have to change my name." Then, finally, Benita entered her last line: "March 3, 2:15 P.M. . . . I'm tired . . . I've decided to give it all up . . . I'm turning on the gas." The suicide of Vivien Gordon's daughter caused almost as many sensational headlines as had the madam's own death.

Though Vivien's murderer was never apprehended, her intention to "bust up" the corruption in the city was more than completed by Judge Seabury. One of Mrs. Gordon's associates, a Chilean procurer named Chile Mapocha Acuna, called the "Human Spittoona" by

*When bordello madam Vivien Gordon disappeared in New York in 1931 most thought her murdered; they were right.*

the press, took on Vivien's job. Acuna, who cost the Police Department $40,984 to keep him in fancy hotels and theater tickets while testifying, picked out in a courtroom twenty-seven policemen whom he had served as a stool pigeon or had paid off to "look the other way." Dozens of policemen were either sent to prison or kicked off the force. John C. Weston, prosecutor in the Woman's Court, was only one of the powerhouse officials to fall in the Gordon disappearance and murder case. He subsequently confessed that he had accepted more than $20,000 for scuttling cases. The vice squad was abolished.

Acuna, who was first suspected in the Gordon killing and later acquitted, was to author the biography of a pimp; it was appropriately called *Women for Sale*. Before dying of natural causes, the procurer bragged to newsmen: "You know, down in Santiago [Chile] the people think I'm a big hero. I'm a crusader."

If the sleazy Acuna was a hero to whoredom, then Dr. Harry C. Zimmerly, four years later, could consider himself a glowing martyr to the then illegal operation of abortion. The fact that Zimmerly killed at least one of his many butchered patients in his savage surgery was, no doubt, incidental. Zimmerly thought so, and he found others to echo his opinion.

In March 1935, Dr. Zimmerly brought to his rural, squalid home in Mechanics Grove, Pennsylvania, one Mrs. Gladys Lawson of Calvert, Maryland. The mother of two was to undergo an abortion. Mrs. Lawson was never seen alive again. Following a massive search for the prominent Maryland woman, missing for almost a month, investigators arrived at Dr. Zimmerly's ramshackle house. His housekeeper, Miss Blanche Stone, panicked immediately and informed authorities that her employer had used "instruments on Mrs. Lawson" and that, on March 15, 1935, she heard "moans and cries" from Mrs. Lawson's room on the second floor of the doctor's house. To housekeeper Stone the doctor merely commented: "She's gone. If anyone asks about Mrs. Lawson you are to say I took her back to Lancaster, where I picked her up at the train station."

The doctor's handyman, Richard Parker, went even further and shocked inspectors by telling them that he had sharpened a butcher knife with which the doctor cut up Mrs. Lawson, who had died as

*Dr. Harry C. Zimmerly, found guilty of operating illegally on Mrs. Gladys Lawson, who had been missing for weeks in 1935. (UPI)*

142

a result of his attempts at performing an abortion. "I saw him hacking away at the body," said Parker, shuddering.

Zimmerly at first protested his innocence. Yes, Mrs. Lawson had been to see him about treatment for an undisclosed ailment, but she had vanished after he had looked after her for a few days. He had no idea where the missing woman might be. Parker and the police did; a hole was dug up under a nearby barn on the Zimmer property and many human bones, all identified as those of several women, were unearthed.

The bones, plus hair and teeth were examined by experts and were determined to be that of Mrs. Lawson and others. Damned by Parker's testimony, Zimmerly was convicted but not of murder. He was given seven-and-a-half years in prison for "performing an illegal operation."

In more recent times people have vanished and later have been found murdered for much more than the protection of a medical practice run amuck. On March 4, 1977, a young university student in Chicago, Taweeyos Sirikul, disappeared completely after showing his 1976 car in hopes of selling it. Sirikul was approached at home by a short man guessed to be twenty-two years old who wanted to purchase his car. The two rode off in the auto for a test drive. Three weeks later the body of Sirikul was found in a storage locker on the far-south side of Chicago. He had been stabbed to death. His car remains missing, and so does his killer at this writing.

Only three days after Sirikul's badly decomposed body was discovered in Chicago, a party of rock hunters searching the barren area near Mountain Springs, Nevada, turned up a corpse buried under a small pile of rocks. The body was that of Al Bramlet, who had been the secretary-treasurer of Local 226 of the state's Culinary and Bartender's Union and had been missing for three weeks. As the leading union powerhouse in and about Las Vegas, the sixty-year-old Bramlet had reportedly tried to extort money from the crime syndicate for allowing them to partake in union spoils, especially in Las Vegas.

Getting off a plane in Las Vegas on February 24, 1977, at McCarran International Airport following a one-day visit to Reno, Bramlet

*Union leader Al Bramlet was a powerhouse in Las Vegas before he vanished in 1977. (UPI)*

was met by three men. Bramlet called his daughter and told her he would be home in thirty minutes. He never arrived.

Whether or not he was murdered by syndicate killers is not known at this time, but whoever performed the murder was thorough. The missing man was discovered to have been shot in the head several times with a silencer-equipped handgun (according to an informant). His head was then crushed and he was stripped and buried in the isolated district. At this writing Andrew Hanley and his father, Thomas, are charged with the Bramlet murder and are awaiting trial.

Bramlet's end was as noble as his beginnings. The most powerful union leader in Nevada, a man who ruled his union with an iron fist for twenty-four years, had begun his career in Peoria, Illinois, in the depths of the Depression during the middle 1930s as a pot washer.

### Vanishing Villains

The murderers escaping their crimes and convictions are myriad in the past fifty years but such events were fairly uncommon in the nineteenth century, so much so that disappearing killers caused sensations in mass memory that lasted for decades. One of the most notable in the volatile history of Atlanta, Georgia, involved a flamboyant character named William J. Myers, as bold and nerveless a killer as any on record in that city.

Myers met Forrest Lee Crowley in September 1894, when both young men were fishing on the Chattahoochee River. The enterprising Myers was not fishing by accident but had planned to encounter Crowley at the time, striking up a conversation in which he posed as an agent for an Atlanta livestock dealer. Crowley, whose father was a prosperous merchant trading in livestock, was interested in selling some of his animals. Myers offered a handsome price. On the morning of September 18, 1894, Crowley, accompanied by his father, Seaborn Crowley, and a driver, herded their mules to Atlanta to sell them to Myers.

Myers informed Forrest Crowley, whom he knew to be carrying more than $500 in cash, that they and the mules must go to a rural spot outside of town, where they would meet the man who would purchase the animals. The elder Crowley remained in Atlanta to conduct some business as his son and Myers drove out of town in a rented buggy, the mules being driven behind them.

It was noon when Seaborn Crowley accidentally bumped into Myers on a downtown street. "Mr. Myers," said the old man, "where is my son Forrest."

Myers smiled. "I saw him an hour ago on East Alabama Street."

The father scurried to Alabama Street but could not locate his son. He chanced to meet Myers about an hour later in front of Folsom's Hotel on Marietta Street. The father could not help notice that Myers' apparel had changed drastically; he no longer wore the drab, threadbare clothes of that morning but sported a brand-new suit (it was later learned that Myers had rented a room in Folsom's for an hour to change and then raced out without paying the fifty cents for the room). Again the elder Crowley asked about his son.

"Oh, last I heard was that he hired a buggy to go into the country." Myers tipped his hat respectfully and walked away in a jaunty manner. Alarmed, Seaborn Crowley followed the youth to the train depot. He watched nervously as Myers boarded the East Tennessee train. The elder Crowley raced to the police station and told Chief Connolly of his suspicions, that his son had "met foul play at the hands of Will Myers."

A massive hunt was immediately conducted for the young Crowley. Chief Connolly learned that Myers and Crowley had driven in a buggy beyond West End near the West View Cemetery. The following morning police trailed the buggy tracks down several dirt roads, the marks from the carriage quite visible in the mud created by a rainstorm the previous night. In a deserted field wild with goldenrod and sedge grass, the elder Crowley and Detective E. M. Cason found, beneath a bush, the body of Forrest Crowley. He had been beaten, shot and robbed. The hunt was on for Will Myers.

The murderer, however, had so completely vanished that the police of a half dozen cities where he was thought to be living could find no trace of him. Some days later in Cincinnati the local police received word from a barber that a man answering Myers' description had forced a great deal of money on him to have his hair dyed. Detectives traced the man to a dingy hotel, where he was registered under the name of J. C. Cunningham. He was really Will Myers, he admitted, and was hiding from a killer.

"Oh, I know all about that murder in Atlanta," Myers said calmly. "Of course I had nothing to do with it." Though he refused to talk further, Myers consented to return to Atlanta to face charges without waiting for requisition papers. His conduct on board the train heading for Georgia was peculiar for a man arrested on murder charges. According to one report Myers "propped his feet on the back of the seat in front of him and puffed away at a big cigar, seeming to feel safe and happy as though he were going on a pleasure jaunt."

To police in Cincinnati and Atlanta, Myers told the same story. He had met a gambler, he said, named Brown Allen. He was introduced to Allen's attractive sister whom he trysted with, his lovemaking interrupted by Allen, who broke through a door. Caught in flagrante delicto, Allen, employing the old badger game, demanded at the point of a pistol that Myers pay him $250 for despoiling his sister's virtue. Myers claimed he gave the gambler $25. Allen insisted that Myers go to his friend Crowley and get the balance. The youth went to Crowley, he said, and asked for the money and was refused. Allen, incensed upon hearing this, set a trap for Crowley near Westwood.

"Allen was in waiting," Myers insisted, "and when he saw Crowley he killed him. Allen then returned to where I was waiting, and, hitting me in the face with a pocketbook, said, 'I've killed him and there is your part,' at the same time handing me $31."

Preposterous said the police; so did a jury. No such person as Brown Allen ever existed. Yet even after Myers was convicted on heavy circumstantial evidence he clung to his tale of the mythical gambler Allen.

Awaiting execution, Myers received several new trials, but his death sentence was upheld. On October 21, 1895, Myers was visited by a friend of his mother's. The Fulton County jail rules, however, prohibited women from entering the jail proper, and Myers was taken to the front office facing Fraser Street. Only one heavy iron door barred his path to freedom. As the wife of another prisoner was led out, the iron door opened wide for her. Myers leaped from his chair and dashed fifteen feet to the door, knocking down the elderly jailer and sprinting into the street.

The unarmed jailer got to his feet and ran after the escaped prisoner. Myers tore up and down several streets, the heaving, puffing jailer in pursuit and screaming at the top of his lungs. Atlantans strolling leisurely by thought both men to be drunk and ignored them. Myers finally outdistanced his aged pursuer and vanished in an alley. It was the last anyone ever saw of William J. Myers, convicted killer, or victim of a gambler's murderous passion for money. The Atlanta police looked diligently for Myers for a decade but the case is still open today.

If the Atlanta police were perplexed for eight decades over the disappearance of Will Myers, the New York police were positively dumbfounded by the mysterious vanishing act of wealthy, middleaged Dr. Charles Brancati, along with his erstwhile but near mythical friend, one Luigi Romano. The case, according to investigators, was downright eerie.

Brancati had immigrated from Naples, Italy, with his three brothers, Oreste, Edward and Ernesto, at the turn of the century. They settled in the thickly populated Italian community on the East Side of Manhattan. He worked his way through the Columbia College of Physicians and Surgeons as a dishwasher. Upon graduation he served his fellow Italians and slowly grew rich, acquiring many apartment buildings and great amounts of stocks and bonds. His personal estate by 1928 was estimated to be more than one million dollars.

The doctor never married and lived alone with a taste for the grand manner. He purchased the old Gouverneur Morris mansion that overlooked Long Island Sound from a knoll in the Throgs Neck section of the Bronx. Outside a busy practice, Brancati had few friends, chiefly the brokers who handled his investments.

On Sunday morning, November 19, 1928, George Rheinish, Brancati's handyman, was summoned by the doctor from the small cottage he occupied with his wife, Daisy, on the estate. It was urgent, Brancati insisted, that Rheinish drive him to the Pelham Parkway subway station. He had to get to his office at 411 East 116th Street without delay. As Rheinish drove his employer to the station he

*The mysterious and wealthy Dr. Charles Brancati walked into a New York subway in 1928 and was never seen again.* (UPI)

**147**

noticed the doctor was sweating and twitching nervously. Oddly, Dr. Brancati alighted from the car and shouted to Rheinish: "Paint the place, the whole house!" He slipped from sight and was never seen again, dead or alive.

Rheinish dutifully painted the mansion in colors he thought Brancati would like—horrid rococo hues and designs—but the doctor never returned to disapprove. But he was heard from; letters were received by his brothers postmarked Passaic (New Jersey), Canada, and finally London, four months of letters. Then nothing.

The Brancati brothers finally went to the police, and detectives were soon stomping through the old Morris mansion. The place was a wreck, dust and dirt everywhere, furniture topsy-turvy, and papers littering the floors, as if someone had been searching the mansion for something. No clues to Brancati's whereabouts could be found, but a curious sight greeted the detectives when they entered the doctor's upstairs bedroom.

There were bullet holes in a wall and a spent slug on the mantlepiece. There was a threatening letter, undated and unsigned, on a chair which began with the address: "You Big Villain." The letter was full of obscenities and profanities. There were references to a woman who had jilted the letterwriter and caused his violent hatred. "If you don't put her out," the writer concluded with a threat, "I'll cut your throat like a sheep's."

Detectives looked about the room and were further puzzled by what greeted them. According to one report, "In a chair, near the middle of the room, littered with torn scraps of papers, were eight pairs of trousers freshly pressed and neatly folded. On the floor were three dozen bottles of ginger ale, a pair of woman's slippers, a manicure set, several volumes of medical books and some surgical instruments."

Nothing could be made of such curious debris, but police soon concluded that Brancati had been kidnapped, especially when they learned that more than $225,000 had been withdrawn from the doctor's account from the brokerage firm of Hardy & Company, and transferred to one Luigi Romano. The order for the transfer came by letter from Brancati himself a few days following his disappearance. Executives at Hardy & Company did not doubt the order, since some weeks before he vanished Brancati had brought a small, dark man to the brokerage firm, introduced him as Luigi Romano, and stated that he might in the future be transferring funds from his account to this man.

Police traced the money to a bank where Romano kept an account. Some weeks after he had deposited the $225,000, he withdrew all but about $200. The kidnapping theory evaporated when federal authorities who had been called into the case informed New York police that Brancati had a record dating back to 1923, when he had been arrested as leader of a counterfeiting ring. He was also associated, it was learned, with none other than gambler Arnold Rothstein and helped Rothstein to establish a nationwide dope ring.

An international search for the ubiquitous Romano was as fruitless as the one conducted for Brancati. Neither man was found, and in the end the police felt that Brancati had been involved in the murder of Rothstein on November 4, 1928, at the Park Central Hotel, only a few weeks before his disappearance. This was the reason for his disappearance. No matter, Dr. Charles Brancati was legally declared dead in January 1932, after a three-year search that failed to find a single shred of evidence that he existed. Luigi Romano remains a mystery to this day, if he, in fact, ever existed at all.

One killer who certainly did exist was Robert Coleman Johnson, of Madeira Beach, Florida, a commercial fisherman and worker for a chemical firm, who went meekly into custody when police arrested him for the bludgeoning death of his wife, Phyllis, on August 21, 1966. That very day authorities were shocked to discover from the prisoner's own mouth that he was not only Johnson but a distinguished lawyer from Huntington, West Virginia, named William Henry Waldron, Jr.

Johnson-Waldron had vanished from his home and practice leaving his wife and two children after embezzling $7,000 from a bank in West Virginia. He was last seen on December 26, 1950, as he emerged from a cab that had taken him to his private club. Some days later Mrs. Waldron received a letter from her husband in San Diego; he deeded his home to her. Waldron's family struggled to repay the bank and, after having done so, charges against the missing lawyer were dropped.

The fact that he was no longer sought as an embezzler was not known by Johnson-Waldron, but the memory of his crime undoubtedly plagued him, branding him an escaped criminal for sixteen years. In the minds of many such malefactors, one major crime established against them may illogically be accepted as leading to another, even murder. Perhaps it was easier for Johnson-Waldron to beat his wife to death while thinking he was still a much-wanted fugitive. The killer did pay for his second offense. After being found guilty of second-degree murder, Johnson-Waldron was sentenced in Clearwater, Florida, on February 2, 1967, to twenty years in the state prison at Raiford.

William Bradford Bishop, Jr., a distinguished foreign-service officer in Washington, D.C. had a mental problem wholly different from that of lawyer Waldron, one that caused high tides of depression and made of him an exhausted insomniac. It had to do with personal ambition and the always nagging thought that time and youth were fleeing, and, no matter how doggedly Bishop pursued these goading intangibles, he was falling more and more behind. Despite his fears, Bishop's career was, up to the time of his disappearance in 1976, anything but a failure. A Yale graduate, Bishop served with Army Intelligence during the early 1960s and entered the State Department in 1965.

By that time he had married his high-school sweetheart, Annette Kathryn Weis, and had three sons. He rose through the ranks of the Department, taking posts as a foreign-service officer in Addis Ababa, Ethiopia; Milan, Italy; and Gaborone, Botswana, Africa. He was working in Washington by 1976. Everything in Bishop's life seemed ideal. He had a happy marriage and his career had advanced with incredible speed for a man his age.

Yet at age thirty-nine, Bishop was drowning in self-doubts, and an acute sense of being passed over in the Department, not having had a promotion in five years. He thought it a "terrible blow," stated one friend. Inwardly, the man appeared to be tearing at the seams. He had a long history of using sleeping pills to overcome chronic insomnia. He had seen a psychiatrist to deal with long periods of depression and had even consulted a hypnotist, learning self-hypnosis in an effort to induce sleep. "It's real jolly," Bishop, an only child, wrote once to his mother, Lobelia, as he explained his method of self-hypnosis. "Honest to Christ, you think of all those years of not sleeping and sleeping pills and all you have to do to sleep is put your second finger of your right hand between the second and third of the left hand. Life is weird and ridiculous and lovely."

As the years rolled by, Bishop began keeping a diary in which he plunged into introspection and self-consciousness. He regulated his life by the hours, allowing himself so much time to work, to watch the TV news, so much time to exercise by playing tennis and walking, so much time to get drunk, so much time to "collect quotes, words, epigrams." All of this he entered into his diary, all of it had a glowing purpose, one of "enormous new capacity for love of self . . . a whole new confidence and style, an intellectual and moral integrity, a much more efficient and directed working new—the real self."

This strange fanaticism of self, an idolatry of self to dispel fears and doubts, as it were, ended on March 1, 1976, when Bishop left the State Department Building in Washington, telling fellow workers that he had the flu and was going directly to his Bethesda, Maryland, home. What he had might have been something entirely different, a malady of the brain that compelled him to go to a Sears store and purchase a five-gallon gas can which he later had filled at a Texaco Service Station. Hours later Bishop's entire family died— his wife, three sons, and mother—all bludgeoned to death in their Maryland home. Their bodies were found burning the following day in a ditch outside Columbia, North Carolina, and Bishop's station wagon was discovered abandoned two weeks later in the Great Smoky Mountains near Gatlinburg, Tennessee. Bishop himself was not seen again.

The F.B.I. has named him the berserk killer of his family, and agents are, at this writing, looking for him. Bishop, federal investigators reason, was certainly alive after his entire family had been killed. His BankAmericard was used on March 2, 1976, in Jacksonville, North Carolina, where sporting goods were purchased. The signature on the card's receipt has definitely been identified as that of Bishop. Agents have interviewed thousands of persons but have come up with no trace of the State Department official. According to *Washington Star* reporter Mary Ann Kuhn, "the prevailing theory among investigators is that Bishop, an experienced camper, left the car and began walking in the half-million acres of forest and wilderness [of the Great Smoky Mountains]. They believe he is somewhere in that great mountainous region—probably dead, perhaps by suicide."

One clue to Bishop's confused thinking in relation to his apparently happy home, his wonderful family, and his sterling government career was something he once wrote to his mother after reading an interview with writer Truman Capote. "He [Capote] said, in effect, that anyone who is totally happy would have to be incredibly stupid. True?"

And William Bradford Bishop, Jr., one of the strangest missing persons of our day, prided himself on his intelligence.

## 6

Disappearances of a permanent nature that are attributed to murder present the most exasperating mysteries in the annals of the missing. Reasons for the extermination of those never found, or suspected of being found in the form of rotting bones decades, sometimes centuries, later can provide full-time occupations for the curious. But in the end, the mystery remains, and the unanswered question of "why?" hounds the sleuth probing into cryptic endings, into authentic tales that, in the words of one hunter of missing persons, "are best left dangling." Still the riddles left by such dark disappearances chant for solutions.

### The Cellar Skeletons

Such was the mystery of the nun of Gibraltar in the 1630s. One Alitea de Lucerno, who, after incurring her noble Spanish family's wrath for falling in love with a swain, one Silvano, a member of a clan feuding with her own family, was removed to a convent on "the rock," where she was expected to spend the rest of her days in meditation for her sins. Silvano followed her to Gibraltar, after becoming a friar. They were reunited in a confessional and attempted to flee dressed as civilians by boat to England. Members of the bloody Inquisition, however, disguised themselves as boatmen and slew the lovers after the appropriate amount of torture had been administered to the "heretical pair." The bodies then disappeared, never to be found. In 1838, workmen repairing the stone slabs of the governor's mansion, which stood on the site where the convent had been, uncovered the bones of a woman, an old iron cross still clutched in the bones of the right hand. The remains have always been thought to be that of Alitea de Lucerno, murdered and secretly buried by Inquisition thugs in the very convent she sought to escape. Yet absolute proof is still lacking.

Much-haunted, say occultists, is the rectory at Borley, in Essex, England, which also gave up the remains of another murdered nun when a female skull and jawbone were discovered in the cellar on May 29, 1945. It would be hard, almost impossible, to convince many local inhabitants that the grim find was anything other than the mortal fragments of Marie Lairre, who had been spirited away

153

from her convent in Le Havre, France, by a demented fellow named Waldergraves, who owned Borley Manor, which later became the rectory. Waldergraves, for no given reason, married and then reportedly strangled Marie Lairre to death on the night of May 17, 1667. He buried her bones in the cellar. Although the lovely French lady was simply declared missing by her tight-lipped spouse, the gruesome artifacts found in 1945 seem to support the murder story.

Human bones most often are the only testimony of unsubstantiated murder of the missing, but they do form a link to the crime and a trail to the suspected killer or killers. This was the theory advanced when a skeleton was found in 1937 in Vicksburg, Mississippi. It was quickly concluded that the remains were those of one Lex Brame, Jr., a lawyer in his middle thirties from Jackson, Mississippi, who was last seen in 1907, sitting on the bank of the Mississippi in back of a Vicksburg hotel. He was reading a copy of Eugène Sue's *The Wandering Jew*. His murder, unlike the religious overtones of those of the missing Alitea de Lucerno and Marie Lairre, was thought to be inspired by reasons of race hate by a gang of Jew-baiters. The bones thought to be Brame's were found in the cellar of one of the members of the suspected gang.

Religion and race, however, are rarely causes for the murder of those who disappear. Usually, the motive is that eternal corruptor, money, which has moved many a culprit to elaborate murder, thoroughly cloaking the deed by forever hiding the telltale corpse. This type of killer, it seems, has a penchant for disposing of the missing victim by burial in cellars. An early and spectacular case of this sort involved a French priest, Father Étienne Lafont, whose good intentions to set the crooked straight apparently made of him a troubled ghost no cellar floor could contain.

A wastrel named de Bougainville, addicted to gambling, spent his last francs at the gaming tables of a Paris casino in 1789 and then promptly killed himself, leaving his seventeen-year-old daughter Julie to fend for herself. The destitute girl was aided by a family friend, Father Étienne Lafont, who persuaded the sisters of an Ursuline convent to take her in as a novitiate. Julie would, undoubtedly have faded into the obscurity of the religious order had not her uncle Alexis de Bougainville died in Brazil, leaving her a fortune of 24,000 pounds.

The lawyer in charge of the uncle's estate, M. Dupré, however, conspired with the stepson of the dead uncle, Alphonse Bertin, to deprive Julie of her fortune. Quite simply Dupré insisted that Bertin, who received only a pittance of his stepfather's estate, marry the novice nun (she had not yet taken the veil) and thus acquire her inheritance. Bertin balked. He was in love with a trollop named Josephine Ramon. Discard her, demanded the well-meaning lawyer. Bertin gave in and agreed to marry Julie de Bougainville.

One night in August 1789 the lawyer Dupré was awakened by his client Bertin, who stood in his doorway. According to one account Bertin's "face was scratched and covered with blood, his clothes were torn and muddy, and he was out of breath and trembling all over." The young man explained to the shocked lawyer that his condition was the result of his lover's wrath over being jilted. Josephine Ramon had become so incensed when she heard that he was to marry Julie de Bougainville that she tried to kill him. But now his mind was made up; Bertin was determined to marry Julie and asked Dupré to arrange the wedding. The lawyer scurried off to the convent.

The Mother Superior of the convent suprised the lawyer by telling him that Julie had disappeared the night before. While wondering what to do, the lawyer turned to see a policeman enter and inform all present that Julie de Bougainville had been found—in a ditch a mile from the convent. She had been brutally slain. It was explained that the girl, dressed in her habit, probably fell victim to a rampaging mob, for the French Revolution was in full swing and the religious were as hated as the aristocracy, and priests and nuns were being killed by revolutionaries out of hand just as were the nobles.

Found in the murdered girl's hand was a letter written by an anonymous friend, telling Julie that her uncle Alexis had left her an enormous fortune, and that Mother Superior and lawyer Dupré had plotted to rob her of her inheritance. The letter instructed her to go at once to the Château D'Aix nearby and look for a young man wearing "a green blouse and soft glazed hat." He would conduct her to the author of the letter, a dear friend of her father's. The girl was apparently en route to the letterwriter when she was waylaid and murdered.

Another piece of startling evidence, however, pointed the finger of guilt at none other than Alphonse Bertin. Found clutched in Julie's dead hand was a piece of cloth that inquisitive police experts matched with Alphonse's bloody, torn cloak when searching his premises. This was the same cloak, Alphonse had said, that had been shredded by his jilted mistress, Josephine Ramon. The handwriting in the letter that drew Julie de Bougainville to her death and that of Alphonse Bertin, experts agreed, were the same.

Bertin was placed on trial, but he insisted that he was innocent, that Josephine Ramon had plotted the entire affair to steal his stepfather's fortune. As he stood in the dock, Bertin pointed out Josephine in court, stating: "she was the only person to whom I ever mentioned the will of Alexis de Bougainville."

"Liar!" screamed the injured Josephine. "You never said a word of it to me!"

Bertin went on to state that his cloak had been intentionally torn by Josephine so that she and her accomplices could plant the piece of garment in the hand of the murder victim, thereby implicating him.

The court was disinclined to believe Bertin and sentenced him to the then heavily used guillotine. Confessor of the Ursuline Convent, the elderly Father Lafont, who had first rescued Julie de Bougainville from destitution, interceded for Bertin. He felt the youth was not guilty of the murder. He insisted that Josephine had imitated Bertin's handwriting and had sent the letter to Julie. Further, he stated, an accomplice named Jules Bart and, perhaps another, had murdered the girl. So convincing was Father Lafont's arguments that Bertin's death sentence was commuted to life as a galley slave.

Alexis de Bougainville's fortune then passed to Eugène Le Gros, Alphonse Bertin's cousin and one who had taken a great interest in the murder of Julie de Bougainville and Bertin's subsequent trial. To the amazement of Father Lafont, not long after receiving the vast inheritance, Le Gros married none other than Josephine Ramon. The plot not only thickened but boiled over when Josephine's onetime handyman Jules Bart took sick and from his deathbed begged Father Lafont to hear his confession. The priest did hear Bart's confession, which included his part and that of others in the murder of Julie de Bougainville. The details of the confession were never made public, for Father Lafont, only hours after he stepped from Bart's bedroom, vanished as if into thin air.

In contrast, the fate of Eugène Le Gros was quite well known. He was dragged from his cab one day by revolutionaries who recognized him as a onetime Royalist officer and was hanged from a lamppost. Josephine escaped in the same cab, half-crazed by the sight of her husband dangling with eyes bulging and blue-black tongue jutting.

Not long after that Josephine Le Gros took ill in her villa, one purchased with the de Bougainville fortune. She raved in her delirium about assassins, a missing priest, and a ghostlike figure whose unearthly steps she could hear coming up from the cellar. Her physician thought best to call in a priest, but most of the clerics in and about Paris had been guillotined by the mob. He finally located the Abbé Delmar, who hurried to the side of the dying woman.

Josephine, when she first spotted the Abbe as she came out of a dozing sleep, screamed in wild fright. The priest calmed her. She squinted and said, "I recognize you now. You are the priest who once came to my house. I thought at first—" Her voice trailed off and she cocked her head, as if listening for something. "There . . . There . . . do you hear that?" she said in a horror-stricken voice. "It's him! He's come out of the cellar and he's coming up the stairs. Those stealthy steps follow me everywhere. I can even hear them in my sleep! Oh, save me from him, Father, save me!" She became hysterical and it took the Abbé several minutes to quiet her.

Then Josephine Le Gros pushed herself upward on her elbows. "Listen, he is going back to the cellar. The steps grow fainter and fainter. But he will return when you are gone." She flung her arms about the Abbé. "Oh, say you won't leave me! You won't, will you, Father?" She pulled away and looked wide-eyed at the Abbé. "Father, do you believe the dead can come out of their graves and pass through locked and bolted doors?"

The Abbé spoke hesitantly: "If they could in scriptural days, my daughter, they assuredly can now."

"I know they can, Father! I know they can, for *he* does! He comes right up here, although the door of the cellar is both bolted and locked! I saw to that myself. Promise me, Father, that you will go down into the cellar and sprinkle his grave with holy water. Perhaps that will keep him quiet!"

The Abbé was in a quandary. "Who is *he* you talk about?"

Josephine sank deep into a pillow. "I can't say . . . I can't say . . .

No one . . . Nothing." She collapsed into deep sobs. The Abbé finally withdrew. Josephine's wild ravings were not in keeping with her illness, according to her physician, a Dr. Petit. Both priest and doctor went to the police and told an inspector their suspicions. The police returned to the house to find Josephine Le Gros dead. No one was with her at the end. She was stretched across her bed with a look of absolute terror on her face.

Police in the cellar of her house broke through a locked and bolted door and, once inside a foul-smelling dungeonlike room, began to dig. In hours one of the turning spades struck a human head. The body of an elderly man was then unearthed, but his features were unrecognizable. The person who had coated the body with quicklime had seen to that.

Was this the body of the missing Father Étienne Lafont? The French authorities never knew, but they were convinced that Father Lafont had been correct in this theory. Josephine Ramon and Eugène Le Gros had plotted the death of Julie de Bougainville. Jules Bart, with Le Gros's help, murdered Julie and placed the letter and piece of cloth in her hand—items obtained from and forged by Josephine —and pinned the guilt on the hapless Alphonse Bertin.

It no longer mattered. The de Bougainville fortune was divided by the revolutionaries. Alphonse Bertin never spoke of the bloody inheritance. He was too busy escaping from prison with the help of friends and fleeing to America, where he became an upstanding merchant.

### Homicide for Profit

Another Frenchman, one Louis Aimé Augustin Le Prince, who might have been the father of the motion picture, vanished like Father Lafont on the brink of a discovery. For years Le Prince, who had studied under Louis Daguerre, the famous pioneer of photography, had been perfecting a camera and projector with sixteen lenses. He, not Edison, who was later to receive the full credit, first developed the idea of perforating film strips with four holes per frame. This film pioneer was one of the first to employ celluloid film rather than the traditional glass plates. Le Prince was also the first inventor in the field of motion pictures to achieve the projection of pictures.

On March 30, 1890, Le Prince displayed his amazing process by projecting pictures onto a large screen before many officials at the Paris Opera House. (The new invention was patented under his name in France on January 11, 1888, Patent No. 188,089.) The effect was electrifying, and the inner circle to which Le Prince had confided realized that he was the father of cinematography. Yet the public at large was never to know his name.

Louis Le Prince was about to announce his discovery to the world as he boarded the Dijon train in September 1890. He was a distinguished-looking man, almost six feet, four inches tall, and he stood out in the crowd as he carried his luggage onto the train. He never arrived in Paris. No one ever saw Louis Le Prince again, and his marvelous invention was subsequently credited to the Lumière brothers, whose cinematographic inventions were first shown in March 1895, almost five years after Le Prince's disappearance. Speculation exists to this day that Le Prince was murdered for his invention and that his body was actually thrown from the Dijon train as it passed over a river. French and English detectives searched doggedly for the missing inventor, but no clue was uncovered as to his whereabouts, not even his luggage. No one was ever charged with Le Prince's possible murder.

In the words of film historian C. W. Ceram (Kurt W. Marek), Le Prince's

> disappearance remains to this day one of the riddles of criminology, and is really worth a film itself. There is no doubt that destiny cut a thread in this case—for it may be assumed that Le Prince would have perfected his apparatus before five years were out, and thus become the uncontested winner of the race [to own the motion picture process].

The unknown father of cinematography was presumed to be dead seven years after his disappearance.

As much as European detectives were deservedly upset over the disappearance of Le Prince, New York detectives were completely baffled when Manhattan money-man Aaron A. Graff vanished on August 8, 1924. Graff, who ran a one-man loan business at admittedly

**159**

usurious rates, had been missing for more than a week, according to his wife, before police were called in to investigate.

Detectives quickly learned that Graff was in the habit of loaning large sums of money to finance brothels and other unsavory enterprises, and, because of the class of persons he associated with, they concluded that he had been murdered. Prostitutes and gamblers were interrogated by the score, but no clues turned up. One plainclothesman going through Graff's personal papers found a note due August 1, 1924, the very day Graff disappeared. The note had been signed by one John Lugosy, who operated a radio-cabinet shop on Sixth Avenue. When checking at Lugosy's home on Twelfth Street, just around the corner from his shop, detectives were told by the cabinetmaker's wife that she had not seen her husband for days; John Lugosy had also disappeared.

Searching the cabinet shop, detectives found nothing to arouse their suspicions. The shop's basement was another matter. In an L-shaped catacomb that was filled with rubbish and led to the shopkeeper's home, detectives found a covered box.

"Oh, I don't think that will interest you," Mrs. Lugosy told them. "My husband uses that box for melting varnish. He uses the varnish on his cabinets."

*Police carrying away the butchered remains of New York businessman Aaron A. Graff in 1924.*

They ignored her and pried off the lid. Peering inside the zinc-lined box, one officer squinted in the flickering light. "My God," he groaned as the perfectly preserved face of the dead Aaron Graff stared back at him from beneath a layer of hardened varnish. From this grisly box the officers removed portions of Graff's body, which had been dismembered and cut in half with a dull saw. Poking about in the nearby rubbish the detectives also found the implement. States one report: "Portions of Graff's flesh still adhered to the teeth of the blade of the saw." Homicide officers were soon searching for cabinetmaker Lugosy, but he was never found. It was assumed that, failing to pay Graff the amount due him, he merely murdered and slaughtered his creditor and then vanished.

Jewels, not money, figured in the disappearance of Henry Levy in 1931. Levy was the kind of jeweler who carried his stock in a case, occupying only a desk in an office with other jewelers. At first it was speculated by Manhattan police that Levy had absconded with his own unpaid-for merchandise, but his upstanding character denied this. He was later found floating in waters about Glen Cove, New York. The fact that Levy apparently had been murdered for his jewelry case and then quietly dumped into the ocean was not startling or new. Innumerable killings for the same motives and employing the same methods have been performed over the decades. The twist to this case was that Mrs. Levy, following her husband's much-publicized disappearance, was contacted by what most authorities consider to be the strangest extortionist on record.

In his first call, the man with a deep, booming voice stated that Levy had been kidnapped and was being held for $10,000 ransom. "After I get the money, Levy will be released," added the extortionist. "Now keep your trap shut about this! Let out a peep to the cops, and your man will be bumped off. Don't forget!"

The caller rang up Mrs. Levy some days later; the nerve-wrenched woman was near collapse while awaiting instructions on how to deliver the ransom. The delivery plan, outlined in the extortionist's next call, was a classic. Mrs. Levy was to go to a certain cigar store in Queens and there pick up five pigeons in a box. She was to wrap a $1,000 bill around each leg of each pigeon, making a grand total of $10,000. The pigeons were to be let free to fly home at once. Mrs. Levy was actually in the process of delivering the money according to this bizarre plan when police convinced her that the caller knew nothing of her husband's whereabouts. They were proved right five months later when Levy's body bobbed to the surface, long dead before the extortionist ever called Mrs. Levy, according to pathologists.

Eugenia Cedarholm, who left a handsome estate of $40,000 when she disappeared, took twenty-six years to surface, if indeed, the bones found in the back yard of a Long Island home were ever hers.

Following the death of her mother, Miss Cedarholm operated a boardinghouse briefly at 37 Prince Street, Long Island City. The attractive twenty-six-year-old woman vanished one day in November 1927. One of the boarders in the Cedarholm house, sixty-year-old Edward Lawrence Hall, suddenly began collecting the rents each month, as well as cashing checks purported to be written by the missing landlady. When police investigated they discovered that Hall had forged the checks, and he was quickly tried and convicted. Hall was given a stiff twenty years' imprisonment in Sing Sing for forgery, being a second offender, as well as for showing contempt for the court in his refusal to state where Eugenia Cedarholm could be located.

Hall did admit before stepping into Sing Sing that he had married the pretty landlady and "taken her away," but he gave no more information. Almost two years later Hall was ready to talk, stating: "I refused to speak in public to protect her." He went on to say that he left her in Pueblo Beach, Florida, after marrying her. That was all. A check of that Florida area turned up no Miss Cedarholm. Hall went back to jail.

This disappearance would have faded on the back pages and eventually been lost to memory but for a Long Island man digging up his back yard to plant some shrubs in 1953. He struck bones and called in authorities. The bones found in John Cummings' back yard on Prince Street, only a few doors from Miss Cedarholm's old address, were human all right. But whether or not they belonged to the long-lost Eugenia was never determined. Edward Lawrence Hall could not say either; he died in prison, still protecting the woman he claimed he loved.

Agnes Tufverson too was much loved by her flamboyant husband, so much so that she apparently lost herself permanently in the welter of his affection. She was a successful corporation lawyer in New

York, and her disappearance on December 20, 1933, has haunted Manhattan's Missing Persons Bureau almost as much as that of Judge Joseph Force Crater. Her quixotic husband, Captain Ivan Poderjay, a Yugoslavian officer, added to the confusion of the police with resounding gusto.

The couple fell in love in late 1933 and were married in the Little Church Around the Corner on December 4. Agnes called her two sisters, Sally and Olive Tufverson in Detroit to inform them that she was going to London, where she would live on her husband's fabulous estates.

Oddly enough, Poderjay thought it would be a good idea if Agnes withdrew her life savings from the bank; the love-struck woman emptied her account of $25,000. This money the new bride happily gave to her dashing Yugoslavian captain, not as a gift, Poderjay later pointed out to police, but as the price of some invaluable Yugoslavian stocks and bonds he had turned over to her.

By December 20, the bride was among the missing. She apparently did not sail with her husband to England. On that day a taxi driver drove Poderjay and Agnes to a New York pier, from which they were to sail on the liner *Hamburg*. As the police later discovered, alerted by the worried sisters who had not heard from Agnes, Poderjay sailed alone and not on the *Hamburg*, but on the *Olympic* two days later.

Detectives began the unpleasant task of checking every female body fished from the rivers. None matched Agnes' description, a forty-three-year-old, 135-pound, 5-foot-6-inch woman with dark-blue eyes and brown, bobbed hair.

It was then learned that Poderjay was a devout bigamist, having married Marguerite Susanne Ferrand in London in March, 1933, nine months before wedding Agnes Tufverson. He was located in Vienna, Austria, and held on bigamy charges. Before he was returned to the United States, Austrian authorities heard that he had married women in Yugoslavia and Denmark and were preparing to send him to those countries for trial first. Poderjay sneered at such claims, insisting that "I had only mistresses in Belgrade and Copenhagen. You don't hang a man for that." Found in Poderjay's Vienna apartment were most of Agnes' luggage and much of her clothing and jewelry. One room of his apartment was described by the press as a "sadistic room" with special equipment for inducing pain—whips, pliers, prongs, studded boots. Obscene photos adorned the walls.

Returned to the United States to face bigamy charges, Poderjay met the press on board the *President Polk*. He played an unusual air of nonchalance. One newsman noted how he "pranced and smiled, waved his hat, flashed his white, wide-set teeth, shook his heavy growth of dry, black hair, streaked with gray." Poderjay yelled to reporters: "Make it snappy! I must look nice for the girls."

"Say, listen, Poderjay," one veteran newsman interrupted. "Is this dame Tufverson dead?"

The Yugoslavian captain scowled, his white-blue eyes went cold. He shook his fist. "Bah! Rubbish!"

Questioned by New York's Assistant Chief Inspector John J. Sullivan, who later termed Poderjay a "cheerful liar," the captain denied any wrongdoing. Yes, he had married Agnes Tufverson, even though he had earlier wed Marguerite Ferrand. Miss Tufverson, he

*Flamboyant as ever, Ivan Poderjay, one-time Yugoslavian officer and chief suspect in the mysterious disappearance of Agnes Tufverson, bids hello to police and press upon arriving in New York aboard the* President Polk *in 1933. (UPI)*

explained, told him as a lawyer he could marry her, that his previous marriage was not legal. He insisted that Miss Tufverson was alive, even though they had separated in England. (In Vienna, Poderjay had told Austrian police that he had taken pity on Miss Tufverson and married her after she told him of a previous break with a lover and that she intended to travel "around the world" after reaching Europe. He also said he married the woman to prevent her from committing suicide; she was depressed at being a spinster. He also said that she begged him to marry her only for the time it took to get to Europe; she would then have the marriage annulled. Agnes' two sisters received a telegram on January 2, 1934, ostensibly from their sister, which stated: "Sailing for India by way of France." Poderjay thought that's where she went, India. The Tufverson sisters thought he, Poderjay, had sent the telegram.)

In a speedy trial, Poderjay was convicted of bigamy and sentenced to Sing Sing for seven years. Judge George L. Donnellan peered down from the bench at Poderjay and stated: "It is my judgment that this defendant should be before the court on another charge"; prosecutor Irving W. Halpern had been broadly hinting of murder. Halpern pointed out that Poderjay's stateroom on board the *Olympic* had a seventeen-inch porthole just above the water line through which a body could have been easily shoved.

"Her disappearance," stated Halpern, "was not voluntary, but directly caused by the defendant, who had no affection for her, and could profit financially by her death." Halpern further enlightened the court with the fact that though the thirty-five-year-old Poderjay was judged sane in a ten-day study by Bellevue Hospital psychiatrists, he "had a penchant for wearing women's clothing . . . he is thoroughly egocentric."

Moreover, Marguerite Ferrand knew all about Poderjay's second marriage, having met Miss Tufverson on a boat train between London and Southampton six months before the marriage.

Poderjay was sent to prison on the bigamy charge only. He refused to discuss the whereabouts of his poor Agnes. A year later he became enraged in his cell and had to be subdued by guards when he learned that the Yugoslav War Minister had ordered him demoted to private. He was released on February 1, 1940, and immediately held a press conference in which he claimed Agnes was

**165**

still alive and, if he was not deported, he would produce her "in sixty days."

"Some say you killed Agnes," a reporter stated.

"The whole case is now a complication. It is pure nonsense to say I killed her. I heard from her seven months ago. I will bring her to life, if it pays." A strange look came into the Yugoslavian's face. "I'm a bachelor now," he said dreamily. "But I am going back to Paris to Miss Ferrand. I will marry her now properly. I have a brother who is a Jesuit priest in India. He is going to marry us. But if he does, I will be considered a bigamist there, for I married Miss Tufverson in a church." He appeared to newsmen as if his mind had snapped. "We were never in love," Poderjay said of Agnes Tufverson. "She was my lawyer and we were very big friends."

Poderjay insisted that he was innocent of bigamy, that his marriage to Marguerite Ferrand was illegal. He was asked why then had he pleaded guilty to bigamy. The ex-captain shook his fist: "The newspapers and the women's clubs were down on me, I tell you! I had to take the rap for something! That Agnes! I have proof that she is still alive but she's too smart for me. The police are not interested in finding her and never were."

Deported some days later to Yugoslavia on the liner *Washington*, Ivan Poderjay had lost his vivacity, grumbling "I am glad to get away from this country." Agnes Tufverson was too smart for everyone, it seemed, for not a trace of her exists to this day.


### Tales of Three Judges


John Lansing was an institution unto himself when it came to the founding of the United States, a direct descendant of Gerrit Lansing, who raced from religious persecution in the Netherlands to the wild haven of America as early as 1640. John Lansing was admitted to the practice of law in 1775, just at the time of the American Revolution; he served as military secretary to General Philip Schuyler. He was elected to six terms in the New York Assembly and was mayor of Albany, New York. As his blinding political star rose, Lansing could not help but incur enemies, lots of them. And one or more of these seething adversaries came to be responsible not only for his disappearance but also for his murder.

No doubt most of Lansing's opponents stemmed from the time he held his lofty post on the New York Supreme Court, where he served as a judge from 1790 to 1801; he was chosen chief justice in 1798. Following his judgeship, Lansing became chancellor of the state, and he held that position until 1814, when he reached the constitutional age limit of sixty.

A fair, cultured gentleman, Lansing was nevertheless severe and unyielding in his judgments. One of his most devastating acts was sending John V. N. Yates, a distinguished member of the Albany bar, to jail for contempt, a decision that was later overturned by the New York Supreme Court in a bitterly fought battle.

Other enemies rose out of Lansing's unwillingness to take orders from his political backers, chiefly the powerful George Clinton family. Several times Lansing refused to follow Clinton's dictates, even refusing the governorship of New York in 1804 and, by doing so, alienating Clinton, Thomas Jefferson and Alexander Hamilton. Clinton, who was seeking the vice-presidential nomination to run with Jefferson, thought to elevate Lansing to the governorship so that Lansing would, in turn, appoint his nephew De Witt Clinton to his vacated post of chancellor, as well as throw his gubernatorial support to Clinton's vice-presidential nomination. By stepping away from the New York governorship, Lansing dashed Clinton's hopes and drew upon himself the Clintons' permanent wrath; he also indirectly aided Aaron Burr's nomination to the post of governor.

Upon his retirement, Lansing became a regent of the University of the State of New York and acted as a consultant in the business affairs of Columbia College. In his declining years, this most respected of American jurists, one could believe, was safe to live out a peaceful, rewarding retirement. Those about him liked and admired him. Biographer Dumas Malone described him in those last days as "a large, handsome man, dignified and kindly in manner, a good conversationalist and a favorite in society." Yet on December 12, 1829, this paragon of American politics and jurisprudence vanished and was never seen again.

Lansing had been looking after certain affairs at Columbia College, staying in New York at one of the better hotels. He left the hotel at nine in the evening and as he stepped into the foyer the hall-boy brushed his coat. He was carrying some letters that he intended to post on the Albany boat at the foot of Cortlandt Street. The hall-boy was the last person to see Lansing alive. Though an intensive hunt for the jurist was conducted, nothing was ever found of him. Commented author T. W. Barnes: "There was nothing in his character, temperament, or antecedents to warrant the belief that he had committed suicide."

Then what happened to Judge Lansing? Journalist and thoroughly corrupt political leader Thurlow Weed had the answer, one handed to him by "a gentleman of high position." Lansing had been murdered, Weed later stated, by a group of powerful persons. The overwhelming proof of the murder was supplied to Weed by his august informant, but on the promise that Weed would never make their identities known while they lived. Weed promised not to reveal the names of the highly respected killers until 1870. In that year, Weed backed away from naming Lansing's killers. In a gush of gobbledygook that passed for acceptable rhetoric in that era, Weed stated: "While it is true that the parties named are beyond the reach of human tribunals and of public opinion, yet others, immediately associated with them and sharing in the strong inducement which prompted the crime, survive, occupying high positions and enjoying public confidence. To these persons, should my proofs be submitted, public attention would be irresistibly drawn." In short, out of fear of either reprisal or a loss of the political spoils in which he shared, Weed refused to name the killers, protecting as usual his own interests. No one in 1870 thought to brand Weed a criminal accomplice to Lansing's murder by virtue of his withholding evidence, but then again such brazenly unscrupulous attitudes soon became the hallmark of American politics, which grew a century later into Richard Nixon's tower of ugly babble.

Where the missing Judge Lansing was done to death by members of his own social caste, the upstanding Circuit Court Judge C. E. Chillingworth of Florida disappeared in 1955 due to the tireless efforts of a fellow justice.

Judge Chillingworth had spent thirty-four years on the bench. He had been stern but fair, placing emphasis on the law, always the law. Most of Chillingworth's judgeship had been centered in Palm Beach and Broward counties, and he was particularly known for his promptness, an unbending trait even his wife and three grown daughters had learned to respect.

Seldom if ever could the judge's court attendants ever remember Chillingworth being late; so, when he failed to appear for a hearing in his West Palm Beach chambers on June 16, 1955, the alarm was immediately sent out. Police and family members converged on the judge's fashionable seaside home at Manalpan, an exclusive area twelve miles south of Palm Beach. What detectives found in the Chillingworth home—or what they did not find—stunned and amazed them. Both the judge and his wife were gone with only a few physical traces that they had returned the previous night at ten-thirty after dining with friends. Sheriff's inspectors determined that the couple had undressed and had neatly hung up their clothing, retiring in pajamas. Their money and jewelry remained untouched on bedroom bureaus. Nothing was missing except the two humans who had inhabited the home.

*Circuit court Judge and Mrs. Charles E. Chillingworth vanished from their West Palm Beach, Florida, home in 1955.* (WIDE WORLD)

Outside were a few slim clues. A beach lamp that lighted the back area to the water was broken, and on the wooden stairs and walkway leading to the sea, investigators found splotches of blood and two rolls of adhesive tape. One footprint, distorted as if a person had been struggling, was found in the sand next to what appeared to be the marks of a boat that had been beached at the water's edge.

At first authorities deduced that the couple had drowned, even though Chillingworth and his wife rarely went out into deep water, since they were poor swimmers. Planes and helicopters soon roared and buzzed over the waters behind the Judge's home, pilots and observers scanning the clear sea for bodies. Scores of surface vessels were sent over the waters and went as far as the Bahamas looking for the missing couple. Skin divers and deep-sea divers explored the depths. In the end nothing was found.

For weeks, police expected a ransom note to arrive and even went so far as to name a Methodist minister, the Reverend Harry Waller, to act as intermediary. But officials were doubtful about the kidnapping from the beginning; Chillingworth did not have the kind of money that would profit abductors. Even when a staggering total of $113,000 in reward was offered by friends, family, county and state, no new leads developed. Florida authorities sat back and shook their heads. The Chillingworth disappearance was a complete mystery. It probably would have remained in the unvisited limbo that claimed Judge Lansing had it not been for a startling conversation between Brevard County Sheriff's aide James Yenzer and an old friend, Joseph Alexander Peel, Jr., in late 1960. Yenzer was told that he would receive a handsome sum of money if he would kindly murder an habitual criminal named Floyd Albert Holzapfel (pronounced *holds-apple*), known to both Yenzer and Peel as "Lucky."

Yenzer stalled and later contacted the wanted felon Holzapfel, luring him into a drinking fest inside a motel room that was wired for sound. Yenzer and another undercover man, P. O. Wilber, got Lucky drunk; once in his cups, Holzapfel spewed forth a tale that caused his listeners' flesh to crawl.

Holzapfel and a few of his friends had murdered Judge Chillingworth and his wife all right. They did it, like Hemingway's thugs in "The Killers," for a friend, a very powerful pillar of the Florida community, who was annoyed with the Judge's rigid ways.

The killing had not been easy. Holzapfel and his accomplices arrived late on the night of June 15, 1955, at the beach behind the Chillingworth home. They crept into the house intent upon slaying only the Judge, but the crotchety old man struggled so fiercely and loudly in his bed that he woke up his wife, who started to scream. The killers had to bash her into unconsciousness; it was Marjorie Chillingworth's blood the sheriff's men found the next day on the walkway, blood gushing from her wound as she and her husband were dragged, mouths taped, out to the beach and into the waiting boat.

Once in deep water, clouds shrouding the moon and the movement of the murderers, Marjorie Chillingworth was wrapped in chains, and weights were attached to them. She was rolled into the ocean and sank immediately. The Judge was another matter. So fiercely did he struggle with his assailants that he almost succeeded in knocking Holzapfel and friends into the sea. They barely managed to get the chains and weights about him before tossing him into the water.

Judge Chillingworth would not die easily. To the astonishment of his killers, he did not sink but, wrapped in chains and weights as he was, began to swim to shore. The killers paddled furiously after him and, just as he was about to reach shallow water, one of them reached out in desperation with a paddle and split his skull. Only then did the Judge go down.

Finishing his murder tale in a drunken stupor, Lucky Holzapfel passed out. He was arrested for murder on October 4, 1960. Within hours he tried to commit suicide by cutting his wrists but his efforts were as awkward as the murder of Judge Chillingworth. He lived to stand trial.

Holzapfel's employer in this and other murders was, of course, Joseph Peel, the man who had politely asked Yenzer to kill him. Investigation into Peel's background was painful. He came from one of the most respected families in Florida. He had been West Palm Beach's only municipal judge and from that sacrosanct position, police learned, took bribes and kickbacks from every illegal operation in the area, from moonshining to lottery-ticket sales.

Judge Peel stood for no nonsense from those who interfered in his lucrative rackets. When a twenty-two-year-old informer named Lew

*Dapper former judge Joseph Peel, Jr. (right) arranged the Chillingworth deaths; he is shown at the time of his 1960 trial. (WIDE WORLD)*

Harvey caused dozens of raids on stills producing moonshine in which the judge had an interest, Peel ordered Holzapfel to murder him. Harvey's bullet-ridden corpse showed up in a canal outside Palm Beach in November 1958. Holzapfel was sent to South America until the manhunt for Harvey's killer dissipated. Peel sent his killer regular checks to South America, but when he stopped mailing the money, Holzapfel returned and began to blackmail his employer. This was the reason why Peel went to Yenzer and asked him to kill his troublesome henchman.

Judge Chillingworth had always been troublesome to Peel, investigators learned. During a 1952 divorce case, Peel instructed his client to lie. The case was tried before none other than Judge C. E. Chillingworth, who helped to establish perjury and send Peel's client to prison. The Judge's oral rebuke of Peel was so devastating that its repercussions destroyed his law practice and forced him to resign from the bar. Peel later became a municipal judge, but Chillingworth knew of his link to organized gambling and several times threatened to expose him. But by then Peel had professional killers like Lucky Holzapfel on his payroll and he simply eliminated a nuisance by ordering Chillingworth murdered.

Joseph Peel stood trial for his crimes and was convicted twice and sentenced to two life imprisonments for the killing of Chillingworth and his wife. His not-so-dutiful stooge, Lucky Holzapel, did not live up to his name. He went to the electric chair.

Judge Joseph Force Crater, considered to be the "missingest man in New York," had striking similarities to Judge Lansing and Judge Chillingworth. Like Lansing a century before him, Crater sat as a justice on the New York Supreme Court; like the unbending Judge Chillingworth, Crater was a fiend for punctuality. All three Judges were Methodists; but there the similarities end. Contrary to the up-standing dedication to honesty mirrored in the lives of Lansing and Chillingworth, Joseph Crater was undoubtedly corrupt, a jurist whose nocturnal habits, underworld connections, participation in kickbacks, bribes and payoffs belied his moral office and his re-spected image, all reasons most given for his dramatic disappearance on the night of August 6, 1930.

Crater's beginnings suggested nothing of the bizarre oblivion into which he would step at age forty-one. Born of German extraction in 1889 in Easton, Pennsylvania, Joseph Force Crater did not endure the usual struggle against poverty or even middle-class financial difficulties. His mother Lelia Montague Crater, however, refused to lavish gifts and money on her son, although his produce-merchant grandfather, J. F. "Pa" Crater, was reputedly worth $500,000.

Frank Crater, one of Pa's four sons, raised a large family himself, having three sons and a daughter. The daughter, Margaret, was shy and retiring, but Joseph, the eldest, Douglass and Montague were always unpredictable, each with a propensity for odd adventures. Douglass ran away during World War I and joined the Royal Naval Air Force and, as a British pilot, rose to the rank of lieutenant. He was the wildest of the three sons and the first to die when his speed-ing Paige sports roadster went out of control and crashed into several trees outside Trenton, New Jersey, in 1922. Montague, the youngest boy, broke away from two prep schools before he ran away and joined the Marines. At the age of fifty, Montague was to take a de-gree in sociology from the University of Washington.

Joe, his father's doting pride, was something of a genius whose childhood ambition had always been to be a judge. Joe Crater not only was graduated first in his high-school class but won a full scholarship to Lafayette College, where he earned a Bachelor-of-Arts

*Joseph Force Crater, the "missingest man in New York." (UPI)*

degree in 1910. By that time, the Crater fortune had dwindled and Joseph Crater was reduced to tutoring and applying for student loans to work his way through Columbia University's Law School, where he took his degree in 1913.

As a young lawyer working in Manhattan, Crater attacked his work with the vengeance of a man whose eyes were riveted on that bench, and not just any judgeship but—and many of his admiring fellow lawyers thought he was a likely candidate for it—a seat on the United States Supreme Court. One of the most learned young men skilled at interpreting the intricacies of the law, Crater willingly took on the sweaty tasks of writing impressive, concise briefs for less facile lawyers without recognition or thanks. Though pride, arrogance and vanity were imbued in him, Crater's shrewd appraisal of powerhouse politicians running New York—men for whom he had a secret, deep contempt—led him to act as a suave, agreeable minion who happily took on involved legal chores to advance his career.

And the man was impressive despite his somewhat "different" appearance. Crater stood slightly over six feet and at the time of his disappearance weighed about 185 pounds. He had brown eyes and had false teeth in both jaws. His head was unusually small, which compelled him to wear a size-6⅞ hat. Also strange was his scrawny, elongated neck, which demanded a size-14 collar. From his days as a young lawyer practicing exclusively in the appellate courts to the time of his judgeship, Crater sought to hide his giraffelike neck by wearing old-fashioned high white collars, detachable chokers of white linen later made popular by President Herbert Hoover. The rising barrister was addicted to spats, and his courtroom appearances were something out of a men's-fashion show; Crater was always impeccably attired in a cutaway coat and striped trousers. His thinning brown hair, flecked with gray at an early age, seemed to be plastered down with pomade and was parted in the middle as was then the vogue. Crater's courtroom demeanor was always proper and succinct. He endeared himself to every judge he argued before by speaking "quietly and logically and as briefly as possible," according to writer Jack Alexander.

In 1917 Crater met a slim, attractive blonde, Stella Mance Wheeler. She was unhappily wedded at the time, and Crater, acting as her lawyer, obtained a quick divorce for the woman. Exactly seven days later, on March 16, 1917, the lawyer married his client. The marriage produced no children, but it was, according to all reports, a happy one. Crater's habits were hardly those that would annoy a normal wife. He seldom drank and then only sociably. He never smoked cigars or cigarettes, occasionally trying out a pipe (which was more for studied image than personal pleasure). He was outwardly the ideal mate, kind, generous and considerate at all times toward Stella.

Two passions, other than his wife, seemed to stir the punctilious Crater. He was an avowed clothes horse, spending most of his extra money on the latest fashions in suits, ties, shirts, although these were of a conservative nature. Women, especially long-stemmed, ample-bosomed models and chorus girls along the Broadway circuit, took up most of Crater's spare time. Early in his blossoming career, Crater took pains to keep such extramarital relationships secret.

As far as Robert Ferdinand Wagner, a justice of the New York Supreme Court, was concerned, Crater's womanizing was not known. Crater was the most promising lawyer Wagner had seen working in Manhattan in years. When Wagner hired Crater in 1920 to act as his personal secretary, the young counsel's star began to light up political heavens. Crater became president of the prestigious Cayuga Democratic Club in the Nineteenth Assembly District, a post he was to hold for ten years and one which gave him tremendous allies in the all-powerful Tammany machine.

When Wagner, whose son was to become mayor of New York, went to the U.S. Senate in 1927, he reopened his law firm of Wagner, Quillinan and Rifkind. Crater returned to private practice, renting space in Wagner's offices and becoming the workhorse of the organization, although he was not a partner. Crater specialized in receiverships and, as such, grew rich, making as much as $75,000 to $100,000 each year. Crater was named as Assistant Professor at Fordham and New York Universities. He became an exceptional law-school lecturer in this sideline and was known as one of the most lively, amusing and thoroughly entertaining speakers in the schools.

Crater began to live high. He and his wife moved into a luxurious apartment at 40 Fifth Avenue. The Craters purchased a small woodland estate at Belgrade Lakes, Maine, where they spent their summers in quiet sun-basking, except when Crater had to journey to the city to see one of the many showgirls he dated. He also befriended the ill-fated madam, Vivien Gordon, but most of Crater's trysting was confined to one woman, an ex-model named Constance Marcus, whom he had met at the Cayuga Club. The sexy brunette became his favorite mistress, although she was married. Crater settled that problem just as he had with his wife years before; he contacted a fellow lawyer and arranged a divorce for Constance, who was more than grateful. "Joe and I just continued seeing each other from then on," she told reporters later. "I can't ever remember his having done anything like what you'd call wooing me. It just seemed natural and inevitable to us. I honestly felt like a wife." Crater paid a portion of Mrs. Marcus' rent for seven years up to the time of his disappearance, and helped finance her small dress shop. He visited her regularly at her apartment, or sometimes the amorous couple met in hotel suites. But the enterprising lawyer was always cautious and secretive in his movements; his wife Stella reportedly never knew of the Marcus affair or the string of other girls Crater saw. The family chauffeur, Fred Kahler, later testified that Crater always gave him vague instructions from the deep-cushioned back seat of his 1927 limousine. He never told Kahler to go to a specific address, but generally alighted from the car at intersections, giving directions to be picked up at such-and-such a corner.

To pay for his extravagant passions, Crater involved himself in more and more shady deals, according to most reports, transactions that would be vaulted to scandals in later years by the Seabury Investigation. One such unsavory deal involved the twelve-story brick Libby's Hotel, on the Lower East Side of New York, which went into receivership, costing its stockholders great losses. Crater, on February 2, 1929, was named receiver of that property and managed it for five months until, on June 27, 1929, it was sold for a bid of $75,000 to the American Mortgage Loan Company, a subsidiary of the American Bond & Mortgage Company. No cash was paid for the hotel, although the deed was turned over; accumulated taxes, water rates, and other assessments on the building exceeded the purchase price. On August 9, 1929, only two months later, the hotel was sold by the American Mortgage Loan Company to the City of New York for $2,850,000. (The City did not pay this amount until January 12, 1931.) Certain city officials deemed the destruction of the hotel necessary to a street-widening project. Crater's subsequent payment for handling the receivership was $10,286.02, an amount paid to Crater's wife long after his disappearance.

The street-widening project was never begun. The Libby's Hotel deal was an obvious and typical Tammany swindle according to Fiorello La Guardia, who became mayor of New York largely due to Seabury's destruction of the corrupt Walker regime. La Guardia had broadly hinted that this trumped-up transaction was only one of the many swindles Tammany politicians had devised to line their pockets. Asked when the street-widening project might begin, Mayor La Guardia snorted: "Page, Mr. Crater!" (Crater was later portrayed in the smash musical *Fiorello!* as "Judge Carter," a profile that might have amused the theater-loving Crater.) Though Crater had received all the legal fees he was entitled to over the hotel transaction, it appeared from a strange note found after his disappearance, that he expected much more.

Crater's skirt-chasing did not stop over the years, and neither did his ruthless drive toward a stellar judgeship, a position "by which I will be remembered," as he termed it. In early 1930 Crater learned that New York Supreme Court Justice Joseph M. Proskauer was to resign his high post and that he, Crater, was being considered for the job. Although the position paid an annual salary of only $22,500 a year, one fourth of Crater's average income, the lawyer went after the post with a personal campaign that approached fanaticism. He lobbied his Tammany friends to urge Governor Franklin D. Roosevelt to appoint him to the vacant post, especially seeking aid from Martin J. Healy, who controlled the district in which Crater presided over the Cayuga Club. He asked his friend Magistrate George F. Ewald to do what he could for him. He even enlisted the help of his mistress, Constance Marcus, who made speeches on his behalf at women's clubs. Crater induced the New York Bar Association to recommend him to the Governor, but his strongest support came from his old mentor, Senator Robert F. Wagner, who exercised strong influence on Roosevelt and convinced the Governor to appoint Crater to the vacated judgeship on April 8, 1930. Crater had every expectation that he would run in the November election and, with Tammany's influence, be elected to the fourteen-year-post.

Everything seemed right in Joseph Force Crater's world; he was about to realize his lifelong ambition. And who knew? There was every reason to think that he might one day sit on the United States Supreme Court.

Reformers disgusted with the sinkhole politics practiced by Tammany and the Jimmy Walker regime, however, had other plans. There was talk of the Libby's Hotel deal being a giant political swindle. Then Magistrate Ewald, Crater's old crony, was indicted with his wife on a charge of office-buying; it was alleged that he had paid $10,000 to politician Healy for his judgeship, the equivalent of a year's salary in that post. (The case against the Ewalds was later dropped when the jury failed to agree. Ewald resigned, apparently under fire, leaving the post of magistrate in disgrace, much the same way as his predecessor Albert H. Vitale. Vitale was removed because of his association with gambler Arnold Rothstein. The political reputation of Martin J. Healy was permanently stained, as was his position of Deputy Commissioner of Plants and Structures.)

It would later be pointed out as an indictment of Judge Crater's corruption that he had, on May 27, 1930, drawn $7,500 from his bank account and sold securities worth $15,779.86 through his broker Arthur E. McCabe. At the bank and at the brokerage house Crater insisted upon being paid in thousand-dollar bills. The total amount, investigators later concluded, approximated the Judge's yearly salary of $22,500. Since it was commonly known that office buyers had to pay one year's salary of the post they were purchasing, Crater's abrupt withdrawals of money indicated that he was buying his judgeship, many insisted, and from none other than his political sidekick Healy.

Crater seemed to sense the mounting storm and, immediately upon the closing court session at the end of June 1930, he and his wife departed for their woodland retreat in Maine. It was going to be a long, hot summer in New York. Judge Crater, against his expressed desire to spend a season in the sun, left his Belgrade Lakes resort in July and traveled to Atlantic City, New Jersey, where he spent a rather raucous but undocumented weekend at a hotel in the company of two men and four women. It was while on this pleasure trip that two significant events occurred. Crater saw the preview of a new musical, *Dancing Partner,* which was scheduled to open on Broadway the following month. It was rumored that he met and became enamored of one of the girls in the show, a stunning, leggy brunette. The second occurrence was more painful. Crater emerged from a cab one night in Atlantic City and, as the door was being abruptly closed, had the tip of the right index finger permanently mutilated when it was crushed.

Something else was crushed when Crater left his retreat on August 1 and traveled back to New York to say *bon voyage* to Senator Wagner, who was leaving for a month's vacation in Europe. Emerging from Wagner's offices on lower Broadway, Crater seemed to be extremely nervous. He had been counting on Wagner's support in the fall election for the state Supreme Court plum. Gordon Manning, writing later in *Collier's*, stated that "according to friends of the judge, Crater came away from that meeting somewhat depressed. Was it possible, they wondered, that the Senator was forced to tell Crater then that, because of impropriety in public or private life, he was unacceptable to the party for nomination as Supreme Court judge?"

This speculation, in light of Crater's astonishing exit into nowhere, was upheld by many, though Wagner later denied any such personal appraisal of the judge's conduct. "We did not talk politics the day Crater came to my office," stated Wagner. "Our chat was quite good-humored and informal. Politics was not mentioned." (It must be remembered that Wagner also denied ever urging F.D.R. to nominate Crater for the vacated judgeship when it was known that he did exactly that.)

Joseph Crater returned to Maine and sat about quietly at the beach, keeping his thoughts to himself. On Sunday, August 3, he received a mysterious phone call from New York and appeared visibly upset. When his wife, Stella, inquired about the call, Crater, who was already dressing to rush back to New York, replied: "I've got to straighten those fellows out," one of the many enigmatic statements he was to make in the last three days of his known existence. The judge, who could not drive a car, left his limousine in Maine and took the train to Manhattan. Before departing, Crater told his wife that he would be back at the Lakes by Saturday, August 9, to celebrate her birthday. She would never see him again.

The following day, Crater, staying at his Fifth Avenue apartment,

**179**

informed his Puerto Rican maid that she should return on August 7 to clean up. For a man on vacation, Crater suddenly became absorbed in his office duties, attending to routine business in his chamber on August 4. He took time out to write a short letter to a niece at a girls' camp in Maine. That afternoon he was seen lunching at a restaurant near the county courthouse. Later he visited his physician in Greenwich Village to see about the finger he had damaged during his Atlantic City partying in July.

August 5 saw Crater again busy in his private chambers. He lunched with another jurist and dined at the home of his doctor, where he played cards until 12:30 A.M. On this same day a stunning well-dressed woman, calling herself Lorraine Fay, consulted with lawyer Samuel Buchler, stating that she wanted to file a $100,000 breach-of-promise suit against Judge Crater. Buchler heard the woman out and then advised her that she had no cause for action. Lorraine Fay was never identified and was not seen again.

### "Calling Mr. Crater"

Wednesday, August 6, 1930, was to be one of the busiest days in the life of Judge Joseph Force Crater, and the last day, as far as the world was concerned, he would exist. He rose about 9 A.M. and went to his large closet. From more than thirty neatly pressed almost-new suits, all tailored by Vroom, Crater selected a dark-brown double-breasted suit with thin green stripes. He put on his traditional high stiff collar and slipped into pearl-gray spats. He grabbed a Panama hat before leaving his apartment. By 11 A.M. Judge Crater was in his office, the door locked. He was in a near frenzy as he began packing stacks of papers from his important files.

Crater summoned his attendant Joseph L. Mara and sent him to cash two of his personal checks at two different banks, one of $3,000 drawn on the jurist's account at the Chase National Bank, another for $2,150 drawn from his account at the Empire Trust Company. Mara returned shortly with the money, $5,150 in large bills and handed the cash in two envelopes to the Judge. In an untypical gesture, Crater didn't even bother to count the money, but merely thrust the envelopes into his coat pocket. (Later conjecture had it that this money was used to pay off the so-called Lorraine Fay to drop her breach-of-promise suit.) He appeared to be in a great hurry as he packed his volumes of documents.

After filling six gusseted cardboard folders and his own briefcase, Crater realized that he needed room for more documents. He called his secretary, Frederick A. Johnson, and borrowed Johnson's briefcase to carry more papers. His only visitor that day was a friend, Wagner's legal associate Simon F. Rifkind. The office encounter was a brief one; Rifkind, who was later to become a federal judge, was merely paying a social call. When he left, Crater resumed his packing. A little after noon, Crater called Mara again to his office and told him to help carry the six portfolios and briefcases outside to a taxi. As he left, the Judge made a point of reminding his secretary Johnson to lock his office.

Mara and Crater lugged the packed documents to the Judge's apartment. (Mara never saw what files were taken by the Judge, since Crater had been most secretive and had made sure the flaps were securely sealed.) After Mara placed the portfolios and briefcases on a chair in the sitting area of the swanky five-room suite, Crater turned to him and said: "You may go now, Joe." His words were pronounced as distinctly and slowly as if he were delivering a lecture at Fordham. "I'm going up Westchester way for a swim. I'll see you tomorrow." The remark was later thought odd since Crater was in no way athletic and disliked swimming.

Mara departed, and Crater was left to ponder the cryptic contents of his hurriedly packed files. Nothing was known about how Crater spent that last afternoon. Given the events of the last few weeks, it is not difficult in hindsight to speculate that he was worried, perhaps terrified, of investigations that might lead into his private affairs and possible malfeasance of his judgeship. No other conclusion seems possible in light of his gutting his office files of documents that might later appear to incriminate him.

Early that evening Crater, taking his typical mincing steps, walked into the Arrow Theater Ticket Agency on Broadway and approached Joseph Grainsky, an agent and the Judge's friend. Crater asked for a ticket to *Dancing Partner*, which was being performed at the Belasco Theater on West 44th Street. Grainsky told him that none was available, but he would try to locate a ticket and leave it for him under Crater's name at the box office that night. Perhaps Crater wished to renew his acquaintance with the girl in the show whom he had met in Atlantic City.

It was a few minutes before 8 P.M. when Crater walked into Billy Haas's restaurant at 332 West 45th Street, just beyond Eighth Avenue. After checking his Panama hat, Crater was making for a table when he was hailed by a friend, William Klein, a lawyer for the Shubert brothers. With Klein was a Shubert showgirl, Sally Lou Ritz, onetime member of the *Artists and Models* company. Crater appeared in excellent spirits, Klein later reported, and dined with the couple, enjoying his usual drink of orange juice, along with a frothy conversation about show business, one of his favorite topics. Crater told Klein and Miss Ritz that he was returning to Belgrade Lakes for a three-week vacation before August 25, when his court reconvened.

Crater looked at his yellow-gold square-shaped wristwatch and suddenly remembered his arrangement to see *Dancing Partner;* he thought he could catch the last act if he hurried. It was 9:15 P.M. Klein and Miss Ritz, on their way to the Shubert office down the street, walked from the chophouse with Crater and waited at the curb with him until he hailed a cab. Getting inside, the Judge waved a friendly goodbye, and the cab sped off westward down 45th Street. His friends waved back, not knowing that they were the last persons in the world known to have seen Joseph Force Crater alive.

Someone—it might have been Crater—picked up the ticket at the Belasco Theater box office that agent Grainsky had put aside for the Judge. It was never known for sure who exactly occupied that theater seat; the box-office attendant could not remember.

Days rocked on, and there was no sign whatever of Crater. Mrs. Crater, not hearing from her husband by August 9, the day he promised to return to their Maine cabin, began to call friends in New York. She expressed her worries to Simon Rifkind, who said he would check around. No one, other than Stella Crater, appeared to be alarmed about the Judge being gone; Crater once before had absented himself for three weeks.

When Mrs. Crater received no word about her husband, she sent chauffeur Kahler to New York to investigate. On August 20 Kahler wrote stating that he had checked the Fifth Avenue apartment but Crater was not there and appeared not to have been there for quite some time. Mrs. Crater became frantic and hired private detectives to look for her missing husband. They found exactly what the chauffeur uncovered—nothing. Mrs. Crater was advised to keep quiet for a while until Crater returned; news of his disappearance, she was strongly advised, would jeopardize his upcoming election.

Rifkind and other business associates and friends grew more and more alarmed as August 25 approached, the deadline for the Judge to return to his duties on the bench. The court sessions opened on that date without Judge Crater presiding. Two days later, on August 27, Supreme Court Justice Louis A. Valentine, disturbed at Crater's failure to attend a full-scale meeting of the judges, rang up Mrs. Crater in Maine. She poured out her frantic story.

It was the old *New York World* that first broke the fabulous tale of Crater's disappearance on September 3, 1930, almost a full month

*Perhaps the most famous missing-persons poster in history advertised for the return of Judge Crater who, most authorities speculate, was secretly murdered over illegal money matters.*

# $5,000.00 REWARD

The CITY of NEW YORK offers $5,000 reward to any person or persons furnishing this Department with information resulting in locating Joseph Force Crater

Any information should be forwarded to the Detective Division of the Police Department of the City of New York, 240 Centre Street, Phone Spring 3100.

**JOSEPH FORCE CRATER**
JUSTICE OF THE SUPREME COURT, STATE OF NEW YORK

DESCRIPTION—Born in the United States—Age, 41 years; height, 6 feet; weight, 185 pounds; mixed grey hair, originally dark brown, thin at top, parted in middle "slicked" down; complexion, medium dark, considerably tanned; brown eyes; false teeth, upper and lower jaw, good physical and mental condition at time of disappearance. Tip of right index finger somewhat mutilated, due to having been recently crushed.

Wore brown sack coat and trousers, narrow green stripe, no vest; either a Panama or soft brown hat worn at rakish angle, size 6⅞, unusual size for his height and weight. Clothes made by Vroom. Affected colored shirts, size 14 collar, probably bow tie. Wore tortoise-shell glasses for reading. Yellow gold Masonic ring, somewhat worn; may be wearing a yellow gold, square-shaped wrist watch with leather strap.

EDWARD P. MULROONEY,

Phone Spring 3100.

Police Commissioner

after he had vanished. The following day the N.Y.P.D.'s Bureau of Missing Persons was asked by Simon Rifkind to search for the missing Crater. At that time their now massive and celebrated File No. 13595 was opened.

More than 10,000 circulars that gave a detailed description of Crater were sent to police chiefs and sheriffs across the country, as well as foreign consulates. (The poster, later claimed to be a classic in definition and detail, neglected to state that Crater had a distinctive identifying mark, the Greek initials of his college fraternity, Sigma Chi, tattooed on his left arm.) Squads of detectives roamed the city and state looking for the missing judge. Detective Leo Lowenthal was the first man to inspect the Crater apartment. Lowenthal, who had unofficially checked on the Judge's whereabouts at the request of Crater's friends before he was officially declared missing, found little in the Fifth Avenue apartment to make him suspicious. Everything was in order. The Judge's clothes, except for the suit he was wearing, were still in his closet. He had left his monogrammed pocket watch, pen, and card case on his dresser. Lowenthal concluded that Crater had left these prized possessions behind, since the day of his disappearance was a sultry one and he wore no vest in which to carry them.

The taxicab drivers in the city were canvassed and mounds of trip tickets were checked. No one recalled having Crater for a fare. This was odd in itself, since New York cab drivers have made it a tradition to remember personalities who have traveled with them. Crater, in addition to his unusual appearance, was a well-known night-clubber whom any driver along the Broadway route would remember.

Rewards totaling $7,500 were posted, and still no one came forward. As the months of 1930 dwindled, it became evident to almost everyone that Judge Crater might never be found. More than three hundred persons were interviewed, and thousands of telegrams, letters, depositions were taken. The grand jury looking into the case strained to read the two thousand typewritten pages of testimony taken during its forty-five sessions.

Detectives never found the documents Crater took from his offices on the day he vanished. A systematic search of Crater's files failed to determine exactly what papers the judge so feverishly packed and secreted away with him. Mrs. Crater had never seen them and neither had her chauffeur. Stella Crater was in no condition to talk further. She suffered a nervous collapse and stayed in Belgrade Lakes until coming to the city on January 31, 1931.

Stella Crater was no more than five minutes inside her Fifth Avenue apartment when she miraculously uncovered something scores of police were unable to find, a manila envelope addressed from her husband to her, plucked, Mrs. Crater stated, from a secret drawer in her bedroom dresser. The contents of the envelope caused more than a stir at police headquarters and in the press. Inside the envelope there were $6,619 in cash and three checks for $500, $19 and $12. There were stock certificates, bonds and several insurance policies on Crater's life, with a face value of about $30,000. The Judge's sixteen-line will, written five years earlier, left everything to Stella. Most startling was a three-page note to Stella marked "Confidential" from Crater, maddeningly undated. Written on three sheets of legal foolscap in pencil, the note was certainly in the Judge's handwriting, although it seemed to be written in haste and under great pressure. Commented District Attorney Thomas C. C. Crain when examining the note, "Crater must have been in a very nervous state . . . the writing is really scribbling, the margins are ragged, the

*Stella Crater, who miraculously found the judge's last note long after he disappeared.* (UPI)

proper names are difficult to decipher, there are many abbreviations."

Essentially the note listed twenty-one of Crater's supposed debtors. His personal loans to these persons ranged from $6,000 to smaller amounts. One entry read: "I loaned————$5,000. His note is enclosed. It is to be paid September 10. Be sure and get in touch with him. He will pay it at once." Crater also mentioned that, in addition to the regular fees due him for the Libby's Hotel receivership transaction, he expected a great deal more in payment. "There will be a large sum due me for services when the city pays the 2¾ millions in condemnation. Martin Lippman will attend to it—keep in touch with him." (Lippman, an attorney for the American Mortgage Loan Company, denied, as did all the debtors Crater listed, any obligation to the Judge, other than his legal fee, which was paid; the American Mortgage Company went into bankruptcy in September 1931.)

At the bottom of Crater's note, the Judge had once more written and underscored the words *This Is All Confidential*. He added: "I am very whary. Love, Joe." No doubt he meant "weary," but those who ardently believed later that he had been murdered could interpret the misspelled word to mean "wary."

The delivery to police of this packet was a bombshell, especially when detectives came forward stating that they had searched the entire Fifth Avenue apartment from top to bottom and had not uncovered the envelope. Detective Edward Fitzgerald reported that, months before Stella Crater's find, he had personally examined the secret dresser drawer and found nothing but a few items of little consequence. "I remember it particularly well," Fitzgerald recalled in retirement, "because the drawer in front was covered with a bureau scarf and contained some women's clothing and a palm fan. It was a hot day when we were there, so for a joke I took out the fan and tossed it over to my partner so he could cool off. There was no envelope in there then."

That the envelope was delivered before September 10, 1930, was evidenced by Crater's mentioning in his letter the $5,000 note due on that upcoming date. That the envelope was delivered—either by Crater himself or a trusted friend, who had somehow gotten into the locked apartment—after Crater's disappearance on August 6, was clear, since Fitzgerald and other detectives who searched the secret drawer examined it on September 4, 1930. Further compounding this provocative message from the unknown was the fact that the three checks found in the envelope with the cash, according to Kermit Jaediker writing in the *New York Daily News* in 1971, were all dated August 30, 1930, three weeks after the judge's disappearance.

All of the material in the astounding envelope would normally have been in Judge Crater's safety deposit box, one which only he was authorized to open. When the box was finally examined, it was found to be empty.

There the great vanishing act ended and the many legends began. It was said that Crater voluntarily absented himself to avoid impending scandal and because he was worn out with the vicious in-fighting of politics. To his mistress, Constance Marcus, who last saw Carter on July 24, but had expected to dine with him on August 6, the night of his disappearance, Crater had many times sighed: "My idea of being at peace with the world, complete, everlasting peace, is to go into a monastery and never come out again." During his last visit, the Judge told her: "I feel that I've already quit the world, Connie. Don't try to drag me back." Police Commissioner Edward P. Mulrooney agreed with the voluntary-disappearance theory, emphatically announcing without explanation that "Crater's disappearance was premeditated."

Most others down through the years, however, have opted for murder, especially Mrs. Stella Crater, who eloped to Elkton, Maryland, on April 23, 1937, with an electrical engineer named Carl Kunz. Two years later, on July 6, 1939, Surrogate Judge James A. Foley declared Crater legally dead. (This was two years beyond the normal waiting time for such rulings.) That same month a New York lawyer representing Mrs. Kunz, Emil K. Ellis, maintained that Crater had met death "by external, violent, or accidental means" and was eager to prove murder in court so that his client, the ex-Mrs. Crater, could collect double-indemnity payments from the Judge's two insurance firms, Mutual Life Insurance Company of New York and the Fidelity Mutual Life Insurance Company.

Ellis stated that he had learned that Crater had been a blackmail victim and that the $5,150 he drew from his accounts on the day he disappeared was to pay off a former show girl who threatened to expose his wild sexual exploits. The girl turned down the money, demanding more, according to Ellis, and then introduced two thugs to convince Crater to produce a greater amount of cash. Crater struggled with the gangsters, Ellis insisted, and was accidentally hit too hard and killed. His body was hurriedly taken to New Jersey where a phony death certificate was issued and the corpse was cremated.

The insurance firms turned down the claim and finally settled with Mrs. Kunz for a total of $20,561, $5,000 from Fidelity and $15,561 from Mutual. Nothing more was heard from the long-suffering Mrs. Kunz.

In 1955 writer Murray Teigh Bloom followed an unusual path down the murder-theory lane and consulted Dutch medium Gerary Croiset, who had successfully solved many crimes for the police in the Netherlands. Bloom placed a photo of Crater face down in front of the medium who touched the back without even looking at the judge's face. Said Croiset from his trance: "This man is not alive . . . I see him sitting in a chair raised above the floor . . . two men sitting below him, one on each side. He has to do with criminals but not as a lawyer . . . he was murdered long ago . . . maybe twenty-four, twenty-five years ago. . . ."

Croiset drew a crude map and Bloom matched this to the areas about the city of New York. The medium had drawn an X where Crater, whom he had never heard of, was allegedly buried. It roughly matched the area of Westchester, the place where Crater had told his attendant Mara he was going for a swim the day he vanished. Further investigation led Bloom and N.Y.P.D. officials to look over a house in Westchester which many political sachems of the 1920s and early 1930s had visited to attend wild parties. It was reported that Magistrate Ewald and Crater had gone there often. Holes were dug up about the house but no telltale bones were unearthed.

Before and since that time, Crater has been reported being seen all over the earth. He was seen to be panning gold in California and Alaska, to be driving a taxi in a dozen cities. He was a Hollywood race-track tout, an amnesia victim in Missouri, a constant traveler on ocean liners and trains. He became the subject of standing nightclub jokes such as "Judge Crater, call your office." To "pull a Crater" was permanently established in the vocabulary as meaning to disappear.

The Bureau of Missing Persons in New York has handled, since its inception in 1917, more than 30,000 cases a year. Almost all of these disappearances are solved one way or the other. There are only a few hundred files that remain open and File No. 13595, dealing with Judge Joseph Force Crater, is still today the Bureau's most famous unsolved case. Crater, whose corpse may be no more, thanks to murderers (the most likely story), or who may reside today at age eighty-eight as an elderly monk in a monastery, would have liked his special kind of immortality, for in his absence he has attained the goal of his ambition. He is remembered.

# 7

## The Search for Wealth

Deep within most of us lurks the lust for riches. We seek the fabulous treasure troves, or sly business fortunes, or inheritances rendered in the dark. Countless hordes have stalked El Dorado and thousands of other fantasy pits of wealth that subtly encourage the patience and persistence of the seeker on the promise of yielding that inevitable pot of gold. The anticipation of discovery is the magic lure, the fine madness in which many have become lost inside their golden pursuits. It is not always a matter of hidden treasure; often the one who disappears in the name of wealth secretly seeks to become a captain of industry. The motives of these missing are often vague, sometimes totally inexplicable.

With pirate Edward Davis, there was no mystery in his thrust for riches. He and his barbaric crew plundered scores of ships and towns along the coast of Central America carrying his loot to a terrible, tiny dot in the Pacific.

### Quest at Cocos

The freebooter thought Cocos Island was known only to him and his followers. Davis had good reason to think so. The stark island, barely twenty miles square, that squats two hundred miles off the steamy coast of Costa Rica, is to this day wholly uninhabitable. Most of the place is of volcanic rock coated with dense, flesh-ripping underbrush. The air above the jutting rock is thick with insects and flying sand. The sun is blocked by green and brown creepers interlocking with gnarled branches entwining in a hideous distortion of nature. Cocos Island is one of the ugliest and deadliest spots in the world, a place which prompted one visitor to exclaim: "The first thing it reminded me of was an open grave."

There is nothing to recommend Cocos to the human race, except what is hidden somewhere in its damp, dark earth, perhaps the greatest fortune in the world—three enormous fortunes really, secreted by those who disappeared, and over the centuries searched for by those who also disappeared.

The vanishing acts connected with Cocos began with its first known visitor, the bloodthirsty Captain Davis, who sailed quite by accident out of course and found the island in 1709. Beyond the normal sea lanes, Davis made Cocos his headquarters, and he buried deep within it the great booty he had taken over a decade. Davis made out a meticulous record of his hoarded treasure before it was entombed: 700 bars of gold, 20 water kegs filled with golden doubloons, and more than 100 tons of Spanish silver coins.

Davis, like every visitor after him, found the island unbearable. He and his crew sailed away in search of more prizes, intending to return more loot to Cocos. Neither pirate Davis nor his crew, down to the last man, was ever seen again.

Another pirate, an insane, incredibly cruel mariner who went into fits of laughter while torturing his prisoners, one Benito Bonito, called Cocos home for a short time in 1819. Bonito had captured 150 tons of pure gold from a Spanish ship off Acapulco, Mexico. He sailed immediately for a spot he had heard rumors about since childhood, Cocos Island.

Anchoring in Wafer Bay, Bonito buried his treasure somewhere on the island. He then slaughtered most of his men (their bones were found later by explorers) and sailed off with a skeleton crew, who were, one by one, systematically murdered, obviously to prevent any of them from returning to Cocos for the treasure. The fate of pirate Bonito is in doubt to this day. Although he was reported killed in a sea battle with a British frigate, several accounts state that he, alone, made his way back to Costa Rica and mysteriously vanished there while attempting to raise an expedition that would take him back to the island and his blood-soaked booty.

The third great treasure, brought to Cocos by a man destined to vanish along with his entire crew and ship, consisted of the collected wealth of Lima, Peru. While the great South American liberator Simón Bolívar marched toward Lima, city officials panicked and hurriedly gathered up their immense wealth, including tons of jewels and solid gold from Lima's magnificent cathedral. All of the church's treasures, including a life-sized statue of the Virgin Mary made of solid gold and encrusted with thousands of diamonds, were loaded aboard the British brigantine *Mary Dier*. The treasure has been estimated as being worth from $30 to $100 million. (The hoard was overwhelming: a shoulder-high, 14-ton wall of gold, formed of ingots; seven giant solid-gold candlesticks studded with jewels, chests brimming with Spanish doubloons, uncut stones, ornaments.)

191

The *Mary Dier's* master, Captain Charles Thompson, was soon overcome by greed, and, instead of making for Panama where he was to deliver the treasure, he headed for Cocos. He made a pinpoint map of the area where he buried the treasure, then departed with his crew. The *Mary Dier* and her entire crew promptly vanished. Some reports had it that the ship was sunk by Spanish pirates, other accounts stated that the ship foundered in a hurricane.

Twenty years later, Captain Thompson, apparently the only survivor of the missing *Mary Dier*, mysteriously turned up in Newfoundland, and he had his Cocos map with him. He appeared to the residents to be mad with his tale of untold riches waiting to be recovered in the Pacific. No one was interested in joining his expedition to recoup the vast wealth. In 1840, Thompson, like his crew and ship two decades before him, vanished and this time permanently. Rumors had it that he died of alcoholism, or a fever. More likely, he was waylaid by cutthroats who murdered him for his precious map.

Since that time, hundreds of treasure seekers have crawled over hardscrabble Cocos Island, many of them vanishing after reaching the place, their bones mingling with pirate skeletons. And the fantastic treasure on Cocos—perhaps as much as a half billion—remains as missing today as the three greedy freebooters who put it there.

### An Embarrassed Preacher

In complete contrast to the kill-for-riches characters who were swallowed by the mystery of Cocos Island, the Reverend Benjamin Speke sought no earthly wealth whatever—which was, incredibly enough, the reason for his strange disappearance. Speke was the brother of John Hanning Speke, African explorer, whose discovery with Sir Richard Burton of Tanganyika and the Victoria Nile had brought fame to the family name. The preacher brother, Benjamin, was in no way adventuresome; he was a quiet, introspective creature who dwelled in sleepy Somersetshire, England, with his parents and gently administered to the spiritual needs of his devoted parishioners for eleven years. Yet this same man absented himself over riches and created England's first great manhunt for a missing person.

At breakfast, on the morning of January 8, 1868, Benjamin Speke informed his parents that he would journey to London that day to attend the marriage of a friend. He would return the next day, he promised. His groom took him to Chard Station, where he caught the eleven o'clock express. Speke was careful to tell his servant to return the following night with the dogcart to pick him up at the station.

Upon his arrival in London, Speke went immediately to the home of his brother-in-law in Eccleston Square. His luggage was taken to his room, but the Reverend did not enter the house. He spoke briefly to a footman, telling him that he was going to walk to Warwick Street, a fashionable thoroughfare of clothiers, to purchase a new hat for tomorrow's wedding. He mentioned he "had some business in Westminster" after that.

It was 6:45 P.M. when Speke left the hat shop, instructing the proprietor to send on the hat he had bought to the Eccleston Square address. With that the Reverend Benjamin Speke strolled down the street, turned a corner, and vanished.

*The British clergyman Benjamin Speke's disappearance in 1868 sparked England's first great missing-persons manhunt.* (ILLUSTRATED POLICE NEWS)

Scores of policemen began to comb the narrow streets of London when it became clear that the Reverend might not return. No trace of the man was found. Some days later a workman went to the police and turned in a worn top hat which he said he had picked up in Birdcage Walk on the night of January 8. He had discovered the shabby hat at about 7:30 that night, a few hours after the preacher had disappeared. When he read about the missing parson in the press, which made the disappearance into front-page news, the workman immediately brought the hat to authorities. He had noticed the name Speke printed on the hat's lining.

Speculation on the case abruptly shifted from disappearance to murder. Stories were recalled about other well-to-do strangers who had been ambushed by garroters in the Birdcage Walk area, a sinister, dark district where the underworld scum of London collected and preyed upon helpless passers-by. The tale of a well-to-do London clergyman named White was remembered with chilling horror.

White had been accosted by a man in a hansom cab while he was walking in Trafalgar Square one day. On some pretext, the stranger asked the parson to journey with him to a Bow Street address. White had to attend to some important business, he told the man as he begged off. The next day, however, the clergyman went to the Bow Street address only to discover that no man answering the description of the man in the cab lived there. The whole thing had obviously been a ruse to lure the parson to his doom for robbery's sake. White's narrow escape was repeated some weeks later when a woman begged him to rush to her home in Fetter Lane, one of the most dangerous slums of the city; she wanted her dying child baptized.

The clergyman began walking to the address alone, but fortunately he was met by a constable who warned him that even policemen did not enter the Fetter Lane area unless in squads. Accompanied by the constable, White went to the address. There was no mother worried about the spiritual state of her sick daughter and there was no daughter. Standing about nearby White and the constable did see, according to one historic account, "slatternly women and evil-looking men, many of whom had closely cropped heads, as if but just out of prison." Had not the policeman accompanied White, said the press, he surely would have been killed for his money. That, no doubt, was what happened to Reverend Speke, most concluded. Dead, poor fellow, murdered for his purse.

The manhunt for Speke did not lessen; hundreds of constables and detectives searched for the missing minister all over England. On January 21, Police Sergeant Soady of Cornwall was making his rounds in the village of Padstow. He took special interest in a fair-haired man who appeared to be a cattle driver. Soady thought the man bore an amazing resemblance to a thief named Ayre, who was wanted for stealing in the town of Hull. Summoning Inspector Opie to make an identification the two officers watched the man, who appeared dazed and whose movements seemed erratic and confused. Then, based upon wanted posters, Soady arrested the strange cattle-driver who was found to be carrying a large sum of money.

The man would say nothing, not even stating his name. He was taken to the town of Bodmin. There officials compared the stranger with pictures of the thief Ayre. He was not the man, they resolved, but he bore a strong likeness to a missing clergyman named Speke.

"Are you the parson Speke?" the man was asked.

The stranger's hands shook, his lips quivered. "Yes, I am Reverend Speke. I'm sorry for all the bother I've made."

Flabbergasted, police asked why he had absented himself. Speke slowly replied that he had come into great wealth when some property was left to him by an obscure relative. His family, his friends, he said, no longer cared for him as a human being; the riches newly lavished upon him had destroyed his happy life, and he had vanished to begin a new life all over again by going incognito to America. He explained that he had decided to travel about England, the land dearest to his heart, for one last look before departing. That is why he was discovered in the guise of a cattle drover.

England was agog with wonder over Speke's adventure, for here was a man who vanished not to seek his fortune but because he was ashamed of having one. Little is known of what became of the embarrassed clergyman except that he underwent a medical examination that determined that he had what a contemporary quaintly termed "a slight kink in the brain," diagnosed as hypochondriasis.


### A Bevy of Bonanzas

There was no shame at all in fourteen-year-old Mary Clay, who vanished from her home in 1907. Mary, unusually bright and almost a full-blown woman, immediately set herself up as a visiting member of German royalty with her small savings and made her fortune for several years as Marguerite von Graff, alleging that she was the nineteen-year-old daughter of Countess von Graff who lived in "Donna Castle" in the Blitzen Mountains of Germany.

Mary, before she was recognized by an old classmate, successfully gleaned a young fortune from admiring and naïve young men of wealth whose romantic disposition toward royalty, a mania of the era, caused them to shower the attractive girl with jewelry and money. When exposed, Mary returned to her New England home to live a life of ease.

Paul Gesner's disappearance from Stapleton, Staten Island, on December 2, 1919, was also aimed at fortune, but was clouded by an unexplained corpse. A motorboat at Bay Ridge was found not long after Gesner vanished and inside the boat police found a corpse, which was identified as that of the missing man. The body was buried as that of Gesner, and his family became resigned to his death.

Two years later, on March 23, 1921, the fifty-one-year-old Paul Gesner, healthy, and smiling, walked through the front door of his home. His wife fainted, his in-laws went screaming into the night, and his children sank to their knees and prayed fervently.

"What's all the fuss about?" Gesner complained. "You'd think you'd at least say hello."

When sanity was restored to his household, Gesner, an accomplished inventor, patiently explained that he had gone to Dayton, Ohio, determined not to return until he had compelled an automobile company to settle handsomely for stealing the right to produce an engine that he had designed. He had won a long legal battle and was awarded an enormous amount of money. Ending his story, Gesner yanked from his pockets wads and wads of money, which he threw ecstatically into the air until his front room floor was coated with greenbacks. Again his wife fainted. (Gesner never could explain how that corpse got into his motorboat.)

The scene was duplicated seven years later when, on November 15, 1930, a man came to the door of 23 Brownville Avenue, in Lynn, Massachusetts. A young woman answered the bell.

"Does Nora Rush live here?" he inquired.

"Yes," the young woman replied hesitantly.

"And are you Mary Ellen?"

"Yes." Mary Ellen Rush looked closely at the man as he casually stepped inside. Nora Rush, Mary Ellen's mother, came into the parlor, where the man sat smiling in an easy chair. For several minutes there was silence as the woman studied the man. He turned his head briefly and Mrs. Rush gasped, recognizing the profile. It was her husband Edward Rush, who had been missing since 1895.

"Where have you been ?" Mrs. Rush stammered.

"Around the world many times. It's a tale out of the Arabian Nights." Rush went on to explain that he had tired of his life in Lynn and merely walked off one day, following an argument with his wife, to seek his fortune, finding it as far away as India, China and the South Seas. Gone for thirty-five years, leaving when his daughter Mary Ellen was two and his daughter Josephine was four, Rush seemed not at all repentant about his absence. "I left on impulse and returned on impulse. It's that simple."

Mrs. Rush stated that she had waited all those years, thinking he might return. She suddenly looked at the clock and said that she was due at Whyte's Laundry, where she had scrubbed clothes for twenty-seven years in her battle against poverty.

"No need of that," Rush said as he brought forth fistfuls of jewels and stacks of bills in large denominations. "I am rich. You are rich."

### Lost to the Great Reef

No hearth or family existed for Harry Bell Lasseter, prospector extraordinary, to return to; only a solid-gold reef in the middle of the uncharted bush country of Australia drew him forward and into the ranks of the missing. This amazing mountain of wealth caused Lasseter to disappear twice, the first time in 1929.

Down on his luck, Lasseter worked up a small grubstake and, with a few mules, pushed into the blazing interior of Australia in search of gold. Most who knew him thought he would never return, that he would certainly perish in his crazy quest for wealth and, as the weeks and then months passed and there was no sign of Lasseter, the prospector was listed by authorities as missing.

Harry Bell Lasseter, however, was far from missing. He was certainly lost and almost without water as he staggered across the blistered bush country. One day he came to a small mountain and went to sleep in its shade. In the morning the prospector noticed that the bright sunlight literally "bounced" off the mountain. He began to claw away at the lower rocks. Speechless, Lasseter learned that the rocks and the whole mountain—or reef as mountains are called in Australia—were solid gold, a mountain of gold poking its way out of the desert sand, the biggest single gold deposit in all the world, he thought, worth billions.

At that moment, though the world thought him at best missing, worse dead, Harry Bell Lasseter considered himself the richest man on the globe, a true-to-life Count of Monte Cristo, but there was no way on earth he could move the gold with him. Loading his pack mules with as many solid gold rocks as they could carry, Lasseter headed back for the coastal town of Alice. He again got lost on his way and his mules broke loose.

Lasseter somehow managed to hang on to one mule and miraculously made it back to civilization. He staked his claim on the mountain of gold, guessing its location. Assayers blinked in wonder at the few chunks of gold rocks he had manage to retrieve.

Geologists listened to the man who had been posted missing for months. Lasseter's mountain of gold, they told him, was probably the center of the gold belt that ran down to the panned-out Kalgoorlie goldfields of the early 1920s. Experts figured the reef to be about 800 miles straight west of Alice in uncharted territory. A conservative estimate valued Lasseter's strike to be worth a half billion dollars.

The prospector quickly organized another expedition. This time he purchased several trucks and hired a dozen helpers. He would not come back, he swore, with just a handful of gold rocks, but tons of it. With the money from such a haul, Lasseter said, he would build a railroad straight to his mountain of gold and ship the entire reef in pieces back to the coast.

Lasseter's expedition set off in high spirits. Then silence. For more than a year no one heard from the prospector or the men who had so hopefully gone with him in search of the fabulous mother lode. Again the goldhunter was officially listed as missing. Another truck expedition set off to find him early in 1930. Three hundred miles from Alice in the stark, heat-killing bush country, searchers found Lasseter's abandoned trucks. All supplies were gone. Skeletons were found nearby; none of these was Lasseter's remains.

The search party pushed on. In another 200 miles the expedition came to the Rawlinson Ranges and there, in a cave, they found all that remained of Harry Bell Lasseter. He had left a note saying that he was only 300 miles from his gold mountain. (His brief diary stated that he was only "five days" from "the reef." By truck this would be a distance of 300 miles, thus making the distance from Alice to the reef roughly 800 miles, as the geologists originally estimated.) Lasseter's end was a grim one; he had been captured by aborigines and held captive in the cave for several months until he slowly starved to death.

The prospector's diary revealed how his men had gone mad with gold fever and had begun to argue and then fight openly before they were halfway to the reef. It ended with a mass shootout, with only Lasseter escaping from the blood bath. He was then picked up by aborigines, who took all his food and supplies.

Lasseter's reef is still there, out in the bush country geologists argue today, waiting for more goldhunters to step into the "land of the lost."

### End to Two Hunts

Fred Jaques, a coal miner in Seaton Sluice, England, had never thought of stepping into the void of those seeking great fortunes, but the birth of his only child, John Charles, changed all that. Fred's wife, Marion, died in childbirth and he became so overwrought at her death in 1902 that he left England to wander aimlessly through the world, seeking great treasures. "On the day of my wife's funeral," Jaques was to say much later, "I handed the baby to my sister Louise to look after. Then I sold the house, packed up and went to sea. I was very young, very sad, and very lonely."

The treasures that Jaques searched for seemed always to elude him; hidden gold, secreted jewels were always in the next port, under the sands of the next island. He himself became as lost as the treasures he sought. His sister Louise divorced and, not hearing from her brother Fred, whom she reported missing, put the seaman's child up for adoption.

Fifty-one years later, in November 1953, Jaques, then seventy-seven, had lost all dreams of wealth. He was making his living in South Shields, England, as a glazier, living alone with only a nervous and aging cat named Dimpy for companionship. Called to fix a broken window pane, Jaques was invited to share a pot of tea. He slowly told the neighbor the story of his wanderlust for wealth and the son he had lost.

"Why, that's funny," responded the neighbor. "I heard almost the same story from a bus conductor right here in town. His name is Jaques, too."

Fred stared in disbelief. He suddenly got up and went hurriedly out of the house, searching for the bus driver. He met the fifty-one-year-old-man, examined his birth certificate and then saw a photo of the driver's mother. It was his own wife's photo. John Charles Jaques was indeed alive. The old man not only was reunited with his son but was happily introduced to a daughter-in-law, five grandchildren and a great-grandson of one year.

Fred Jaques, fortune hunter, found his second quest—that for his son—incredible in its conclusion. Both Fred and his son John Charles had lived in the same small town for the past twenty-five years and only a few blocks away from each other. "It's odd," Fred said to his son, "to think that you must have given me a bus ticket hundreds of times, and neither of us ever wondered who the other was."

## 8

Knowledge—especially the kind that involves the clandestine operation of government or the machination of wheeler-dealer operators; no matter whether the knowing serves patriotic aims or narrowly selfish designs—has caused many a person's disappearance. Very few of the principals in such cases ever have reappeared to explain their absence; and the pertinent information that they possessed has in most cases irretrievably vanished.

One of the earliest of these cases has been told in many languages and has myriad variations. It began and ended in the gay festival that was Paris in 1889, the year the Eiffel Tower was completed to celebrate the Great Exposition.

### The Vanishing Lady

An Englishwoman and her daughter arrived in Paris and registered in a fashionable hotel. Crowded as Paris was at that time, the woman managed to obtain two separate small suites, on the third and fourth floors of the hotel. The mother, who had apparently been suffering from a strange ailment, immediately took to bed when shown into room 333. She asked her daughter to call for the house physician.

The doctor arrived and examined the woman privately, the mother insisting that her daughter not be present. Emerging from the bedroom of the suite, the doctor informed the young woman that her mother was desperately ill and that he required a special medicine that was kept in his office on the other side of town. The physician asked the daughter to take a carriage to his office, obtain the medicine and bring it to him. As the excited daughter rushed outside to a waiting carriage it never occurred to her that the doctor could just as well have sent a hotel steward, or his own driver, for the medicine.

The carriage ride was painfully slow, and it took all of four hours to arrive at the physician's office, obtain the medicine from the doctor's wife after presenting her with a note for it, and return to the hotel. (The daughter later insisted that the carriage driver, who was in the employ of the doctor, deliberately took his time returning, purposely taking out-of-the-way routes that brought the carriage into hooting throngs of Exposition celebrants.)

Rushing to room 333, the daughter threw open the door, looked about in amazement, and nearly collapsed. The entire room, from plush wall paper to ornate furniture, was different. Not only was her mother no longer in the bedroom, but another family, eyeing her with indignant glares, occupied the suite. The young woman went to the lobby and asked to see the manager.

"Where is my mother?" she demanded of him.

"I have no idea whom you are talking about."

"We arrived here today," the daughter pointed out, getting more anxious by the minute. "My mother became ill, and the doctor sent me for medicine. The room my mother was in has all been changed and now there are other people in suite 333."

"But you arrived alone," said the manager. He turned the register about and showed the young woman her own signature. Her mother's signature was not there.

"We both signed this book," said the daughter. "My mother signed her name just above mine." Above her name was that of a stranger's. "There is something terribly wrong here. Get the house physician."

The same doctor who had sent the daughter on her tedious errand arrived and blinked at her without recognition as they stood in the lobby. The daughter retold her story.

Shaking his head, the physician stared directly at the fear-gripped young woman and said: "I never attended to your mother and, further, I have never met you before in my life."

With a scream that brought gaping silence to the crowded lobby, the daughter raced from the hotel and went to the British Embassy. Officials there patiently listened to her story but did nothing; neither did the police or the newspaper editors whom the girl contacted. All were convinced she was suffering a nightmare, an hallucination.

The young woman went mad, was declared insane, and was removed to an English asylum, where she died raving about a plot that never existed for anyone except herself. Yet there was a plot—many of them according to several versions.

Yes, the mother had been a guest at the hotel. She was ill and she knew what horrible malady had befallen her—the plague. She had contracted the deadly disease aboard the ship that had brought her and her daughter to Paris from India. The mother, to prevent her daughter from witnessing her death, as well as becoming suspected of being a plague-carrier herself, acted in collusion with the doctor in sending the daughter on her bogus errand. When the mother died an hour after the young woman departed to retrieve the medicine, the doctor took matters into his own hands. He feared panic among the tens of thousands of visitors to the Exposition, the very ruination of the Exposition itself, should word get out that a plague victim had died.

He and the management of the hotel, along with the police and most authorities, ordered suite 333 completely redecorated and refurbished during the daughter's absence. The Englishwoman was placed inside a sealed coffin and buried in an unmarked grave. The register at the desk was completely rewritten to show only the daughter's signature.

Verification of this fabulous story has been impossible, albeit reporter Karl Harriman of the *Detroit Free Press* wrote the story for his American paper the year in which it supposedly happened. Years later he could not remember whether he had heard about the disappearing Englishwoman or merely invented the tale. The *London Daily Mail* investigated the story in 1911 and reported that the facts concerning the vanishing lady were accurate but cryptically added that it could not identify the missing person.

Novelists and film makers have rehashed the tale a dozen times since that terrifying afternoon in Paris. Mrs. Belloc-Lowndes used the story as the basis for her 1914 novel *The End of Her Honeymoon*. In this melodrama, English newlyweds arrive at a Paris hotel, their suite next to that of the visiting Tsar of Russia. While the wife is out shopping, an anarchist explodes a bomb he is making in an adjoining room, which kills him and the newlywed husband. Authorities hurriedly redecorate the room and put a lid on the event to prevent the Tsar from knowing that he was to be assassinated.

The wife, who thinks her husband has jilted her, learns much later of the real events. The terrific explosion was conveniently covered up by the ear-splitting thunderclaps of a storm ensuing at the precise moment the anarchist's bomb went off.

A less heady version found its way into the pages of *She Who Was Helena Cass*, by Laurence Rising. Novelist Ethel Lina White employed the same tale with a much broader spectrum that incorporated international intrigue and espionage in *The Lady Vanishes*, which Alfred Hitchcock made into one of his most remarkable films in 1938. Still, no one knows to this day who the lady was and if, indeed, she disappeared in a world of angry virus, mad bombers or artful spies. Of Juliet Stuart Poyntz, sleuths understood too well her disappearance. Her strange society was replete with spies; she was one herself.

### The Reluctant Traitor

Juliet Stuart Poyntz was fifty-one years old when she vanished. At the time, she was considered to be one of the ten top Communists in America. She had prepared long and hard for her position in the hierarchy of the American Communist Party. She left Omaha, Nebraska, at about the turn of the century and settled in New York. Juliet attended Barnard College and subsequently taught there. Under a fellowship from the General Federation of Women's Clubs, she studied for two years in England, at Oxford University and the London School of Economics.

Politics obsessed Juliet Poyntz, and she became an active member of the Socialist party by 1909. It was ironic, some thought, that the far-left-leaning Juliet married Dr. Frederick Franz Ludwig Glaser, a German consulate attaché in 1913. Not so, experts on espionage argued decades later. She intended to use Glaser to spy on German operations in the United States.

At the time of the Russian Revolution in 1917, Juliet dropped out of the Socialist party and became one of the founders of the more radical Workers party. By then she was a full-blown Bolshevik. In 1922 Juliet leaped headlong into the Communist movement in America. She became one of the most trusted party members in the United States and was asked in the late 1920s and early 1930s to carry out delicate secret missions for the Russians, traveling several times to Moscow and once traveling to China as a spy for the Comintern. Juliet even found time to run for the post of New York State Attorney General on the Communist ticket.

Juliet's big moment came in 1934, when she underwent intensified training in Moscow. She was to become a full-fledged espionage agent in America. Her job, according to Ronald Seth, author and master spy, was to return to New York "with the assignment of finding new agents for the American networks."

Something then went wrong. Juliet Poyntz was not fully committed to her task. While in Russia, she had witnessed the ruthless tyranny practiced by Stalinists and was repelled by the ferocious purges carried out by Stalin against the old-line Bolsheviks in the middle 1930s.

Suddenly, Juliet openly quit the Communist party. She was disgusted with its brutality, she told acquaintances. She was thinking of writing her memoirs. That choice document, if it was ever put to paper, was never seen, and neither was Juliet Stuart Poyntz. One day in late May or early June 1937, Juliet walked out of her Manhattan apartment in the American Women's Association clubhouse with only the clothes on her back. Her disappearance was not reported for six months, until her lawyer, Elias Lieberman, announced that she was gone. He had searched her rooms, he said, and found all her clothing, luggage and valuables intact. He checked her bank account, and her money was untouched. (The amount of $10,500 remained untouched until Miss Poyntz was officially declared to be deceased in 1944, when it was awarded to her sister Eulalie Poyntz.)

New York police spread investigating squads throughout the city, invading Communist newspapers and barging into cell meetings. Nothing was uncovered. Then one Carlo Tresca, fiery editor of *Il Martello* (*The Hammer*), a veteran New York radical, and leader of the anti-Fascists in America, stepped forward to tell the world that Juliet Poyntz had been "lured or kidnapped" to Soviet Russia because "she knew too much."

*Carlo Tresca insisted that Juliet Poyntz had been kidnapped by Soviet agents in 1937; Tresca himself was later assassinated.* (WIDE WORLD)

> I knew Miss Poyntz very well [Tresca said in a wild news conference]. Shortly before she resigned from the Communist party she confided in me that she could no longer approve of the things under the Stalin regime in Russia, that she was withdrawing from party activity. Her critical attitude was well known to the Communists here, and this made her a marked person, similar to other disillusioned Bolsheviks who have turned upon the party. I need only recall the case of Ignatz Reiss, prominent Russian Communist official, who was assassinated near Lausanne last summer after he

205

had threatened to make public documentary material exposing the Zinoviev-Kamenev and Radek-Piatakov trials as frame-ups.

The man who I am convinced lured or kidnapped Miss Poyntz to Soviet Russia because she knew too much of the inner life of the Communist movement in this country also had a hand in helping to engineer the Reiss assassination. It is also interesting, in connection with the Poyntz case, to recall the kidnapping last year in Barcelona by members of the Soviet G.P.U. [later N.K.V.D.] of Mark Rein, son of the Russian Socialist leader Raphael Abramowitch, and the assassination in Spain of Andreas Nin, Trotskyist leader, last year.

Tresca later went on to insist that Juliet had been taken, undoubtedly by force, aboard a Soviet freighter bound for Russia and was most likely murdered before the ship left port. (Tresca himself was later, in 1943, shot and killed as he strolled down a New York street. His killer was named by many as Carmine Galante, the man who is considered to be the head of the Mafia syndicate in the United States today.) The abductor's name was never publicly revealed by Tresca or the grand jury he talked to about the case. The assassin was considered by many to be one of the Soviet's top foreign agents, a ruthless exterminator of dissatisfied Communists here and abroad. His identity mattered little in the ensuing years; Juliet Poyntz was permanently listed in the gallery of the missing in the dark times before World War II. Her fate was shared by many another would-be spy.

### Mr. and Mrs. Robinson

In November 1937, when Juliet Poyntz was declared missing, another set of spies vanished. During that month a Mr. and Mrs. Donald L. Robinson arrived in Moscow from New York. Mr. Robinson, his passport stated, was a writer doing historical research. The couple registered at the National Hotel, close to the American Embassy. Donald Robinson suddenly vanished from his hotel room on December 2. Mrs. Robinson returned to her room to find her husband gone. The hotel officials, responding to her alarm, quietly informed her that Mr. Robinson had somehow developed pneumonia on the spot and had been removed to an unknown hospital, where he had "been placed in an iron lung" for his health.

Next Mrs. Robinson disappeared. U.S. Embassy officials could not locate either of the Robinsons for days. They were then informed that the couple were being held on charges of using fraudulent passports. Closer investigation disclosed that the Robinsons were not Robinsons after all; their real names were Mr. and Mrs. Adolph Arnold Rubens, and their passports had, indeed, been falsified, made by three men in New York close to the Communist Party. The Rubens had used the names of two children who had died several years earlier.

Rubens was never officially seen alive, but his wife, Ruth Marie Rubens, was discovered, in February 1938, to be an inmate of the Butirki Prison. Loy W. Henderson, Chargé d'Affaires of the U.S. Embassy in Moscow, visited her in her cell.

*The forged passport photos of Donald and Ruth Robinson, last seen in Moscow in 1937.*

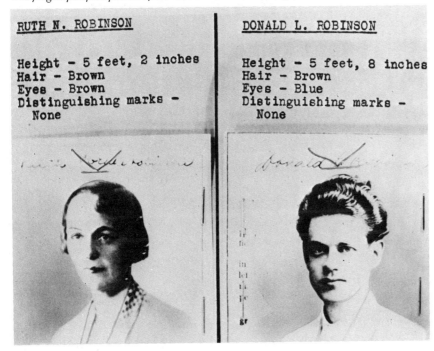

RUTH N. ROBINSON

Height - 5 feet, 2 inches
Hair - Brown
Eyes - Brown
Distinguishing marks - None

DONALD L. ROBINSON

Height - 5 feet, 8 inches
Hair - Brown
Eyes - Blue
Distinguishing marks - None

At first the woman would relate no information about why the couple had traveled to Russia. She did admit that the passports her husband had procured for them were false. Russian guards prohibited her from saying more. Mrs. Rubens, United States officials were next informed, was being held in Lubianka Prison for espionage; she and her husband, insisted the Soviets, had come to Russia for the sole purpose of spying. Upon her release in 1939, Mrs. Rubens met briefly with United States newsmen.

The woman was seemingly annoyed at having to answer questions about her husband. He was a spy, unquestionably, in her mind, she stated. Rubens, a Latvian by birth, had been very reserved throughout his married life, his wife remembered. She went on to describe him as a "profascist and anti-Communist." When asked why she thought her husband had such political beliefs, Mrs. Rubens stated: "Why, he often played a phonograph record at home, 'Giovinezza,'" the Italian Fascist hymn. Neither of them, she insisted, had anything to do with Communists in America.

Mrs. Rubens, who was later to take out Russian citizenship and never return to America, the land of her birth, went on to state that her interrogators were very kind to her. "They told me my husband was a spy. I said then he must be an American spy. The examiners just laughed at that and said, 'No.'"

"They told me my husband did not love me when he married me but married me only because I was so antifascist that I would serve as a blind for his profascism. I don't know. But I know he loved me afterward, and they told me that, too."

She had asked to see her husband, who she said was also in the same prison. According to the soft-spoken Mrs. Rubens—she appeared incredibly naïve to newsmen, who thought she was acting—Rubens was brought to the examiner's office to meet with her, an unusual procedure granted only because Mrs. Rubens was an American citizen. "When I saw my husband he was crying, and that is unlike my husband. I never saw him cry before. I asked him whether he was a spy. He answered with tears on his face, 'I am a criminal in the Soviet Union.'"

From that moment to this, Rubens was never seen again. Some days after Mrs. Rubens gave her remarkable interview, she too disappeared forever. The New York trial of three men who had provided the Rubenses, as well as countless others, with phony passports came to an end; lawyer Edward Blatt, photographer Ossip Garber, and Aaron Sharfin were sentenced to the maximum penalty of two years in prison. None of the convicted men said a word throughout their trial or at their sentencing.

That Rubens was dead seemed to be confirmed in a letter Ruth Marie Rubens sent to her daughter by a former marriage, Ruth Braman. It was dated June 16, 1939, and took two weeks to arrive in the United States. Quite simply, Mrs. Rubens stated: "Nooky [her nickname for Rubens] won't be with us anymore, and I need a helper very much." It was the last communication received from the woman.

Editor Carlo Tresca had about as much to say about the Rubens affair as he had about Juliet Poyntz. The whole thing was a Stalinist plot, he told the press. "The purpose of the Robinson frame-up was to create a spy scare in the United States," said Tresca in 1937, "with two objectives in mind: to speed the movement for war by the United States against Japan as a measure advantageous to Stalin's foreign policy and to involve or smear opponents of the Stalin regime and Stalinism in the United States."

Not until 1948, with the House Un-American Activities Commit-

*In 1948 self-admitted spy Whittaker Chambers (right), shown with Richard Nixon, then a Congressman from California, and investigator Robert Stripling of the House Un-American Activities Committee, cleared up the baffling Robinson disappearances.* (WIDE WORLD)

209

tee hearings booming, was more light shed on the Rubens disappearance. Whittaker Chambers, in his almost nonstop testimony, remembered Mr. Rubens quite well. He was certainly not profascist, but one of the most accomplished Russian agents in the espionage ring operating in America during the middle 1930s. He traveled under many passports and was never a United States citizen (or a Latvian, for that matter). He was known as Robinson, Rubens, "Ewald" and "Richard."

As "Richard," the man had established a bogus front, The Fawn Press, for which he acted as publisher, a cover from which he operated, among many spying duties, the making and distribution of fake passports for Russian agents traveling abroad.

The fantastic story that Mrs. Rubens had told American newsmen was then certainly a contrived one, a tale that was designed to protect Russian or American-born Communist spies still operating in the United States. Rubens had not left the United States in 1937 to spy on Russia; ostensibly he had been called for in-depth briefing—or, at least, that's what the Moscow directive appeared to suggest. In reality, Rubens had been suspected, along with Poyntz and others, of being anti-Stalin and, once lured to Moscow, was simply arrested on a trumped-up passport charge and later liquidated as an enemy of the regime. The fact that the Manhattan men who manufactured the fake passports allowed themselves to be sent to jail to complete the Soviet ruse, speaks dramatically for their dedication to the Party.

Such demoniac plotting was not, however, for the down-home public of 1937, where spies and counterspies were easily identified in any Warner Brothers film, the evil they embodied obvious to any schoolboy. It was with the same naïve faith that the public sorrowfully accepted the loss of one of America's great heroines, the pure vanishing by misadventure of an unsullied creature of the blue sky.

### *"Look, dear, it flies"*

At the age of ten I saw my first airplane. It was sitting in a slightly enclosed area at the Iowa State Fair in Des Moines. It was a thing of rusty wire and wood and looked not at all interesting. One of the grown-ups who happened to be around pointed it out to me and said "Look dear, it flies," I looked as directed but confess I was much more interested in an absurd hat made of an inverted peach-basket which I had just purchased for fifteen cents.

Thus wrote Amelia Mary Earhart in 1937; her initial contact in 1908 of what was to become the love of her life deserved nothing more than a cursory glance. But that love of flying was a slowly-developed passion, one that first beckoned with adventure, then obsessed her with ambition, and finally swallowed her with childhood's headstrong dreams of glory, which she as an adult refused to abandon.

Born in Atchinson, Kansas, on July 24, 1898, Amelia's early life was dominated by her grandfather, a wealthy Kansas judge. Her father, Edwin Stanton Earhart, who married Amy Otis, Amelia's mother, in 1895, was a ruined man early in life. As a youthful lawyer, Earhart had dreams of some day becoming a member of the United States Supreme Court, but his attempt to provide a life for Amelia's mother in the grand manner displayed by Judge Otis created enormous financial pressures.

Earhart found lucrative employment in settling claims for the railroads, but the slow death of his own ambition led him to drink. By the time his second daughter, Muriel Grace, was born, the lawyer was a hopeless drunk. The family drifted from city to city—Des Moines, St. Paul, Chicago—as Earhart's fortunes disintegrated.

For the most part, Amelia's childhood was rooted in the stately home of her Grandfather Otis—something out of another era, one of gentle, uncaring grace. His huge white antebellum mansion stood on a bluff that towered over the Missouri River. In its library, little Amelia lost herself, particularly dispelling her worries about her troubled father by stepping inside the romantic works of Scott, by blinking down sleep over the harrowing images of Dickens. "I was a horrid little girl," she later recalled. "Perhaps the fact that I was exceedingly fond of reading made me endurable."

After attending six schools, Amelia was graduated from Chicago's Hyde Park High School in 1916. Then, as was the tradition of the day, and at her mother's command, Amelia entered the Ogontz finishing school in Philadelphia, where she was to be trained in the peculiar etiquette of pleasing some future husband. She was espe-

211

cially inept at such parlor-room niceties and left the school at every opportunity. On one such brief escape, Amelia visited her sister Muriel, who was attending another finishing school, St. Margaret's, in Toronto.

In Canada, Amelia saw for the first time the tragedy of World War I, young wounded men from the Western Front stumbling and limping down the streets on canes and crutches. Canadians, by that year of 1917, had been bleeding and dying in Europe for three years. The angelic ardor of Nurse Edith Cavell suddenly burst inside Amelia, and she gave up everything to work as a nurse's aide for the Canadian Red Cross.

It was in Toronto that Amelia became enraptured of the flying machine, during a fair that featured stunt pilots, all of them war aces. Amelia described her own romanticism and attached it permanently with those pilots when she wrote in *Last Flight:* "These men were the heroes of the hour. They were in demand at social teas, and to entertain crowds by giving stunting exhibitions. The airplanes they rode so gallantly to fame were as singular as they."

With an astonished heart, Amelia found she could not take her eyes from the double-winged planes cavorting in the skies over Toronto. She and another nurse

> watched a small plane turn and twist in the air, black against the sky excepting when the afternoon sun caught the scarlet of its wings. After fifteen or twenty minutes of stunting, the pilot began to dive at the crowd. Looking back as a pilot I think I understand why. He was bored. He had looped and rolled and spun and finished his little bag of tricks and there was nothing left to do but watch the people on the ground running as he swooped close to them.

The pilot saw everyone, including Amelia's friend, scamper across the field as he zoomed downward, all but one. Amelia held her ground, defiant it seemed, waiting. He and his machine could not make her run. His engine screaming, the pilot dove directly for her.

> I remember the mingled fear and pleasure which surged over me as I watched that small plane at the top of its earthward swoop. Common sense told me if something went wrong with the mechanism, or if the pilot lost control, he, the airplane and I would be rolled up in a ball together. I did not understand it at the time but I believe that little red airplane said something to me as it swished by.

Although she enrolled in medical courses at Columbia University in New York in 1919, Amelia was by then a captive of the skies. She traveled to California the following year to visit her father, who was then combating his drinking problem by steady work and participating in an early Alcoholics Anonymous program, an effort that prompted Mrs. Earhart to join her husband in a last attempt to salvage the marriage. Her father took her to an air meet, where she watched barnstormers pace their flimsy Jennies and ancient wartime Spads.

A dashing flier named Frank Hawks, who was to write his name in the skies of a hundred stunt shows, was the first to take Amelia into the air. When only a few hundred feet from the earth, she realized that flying was the only thing in life she wanted to do and resolved to raise the $500 fee for a twelve-hour flying course. With her father's help, Amelia enrolled as a student with female pioneer pilot Neta Snook, the first woman to graduate from the Curtiss School of Aviation.

From John Montijo, a former instructor in the Army, Amelia took her advanced training, and under his patient guidance she soloed in 1921. The woman flier took youthful pride in her ability to manage an airplane and even greater vanity in her swaggering appearance, dressing just as had the wartime pilots who first snared her

*Amelia Earhart (right) with her flying instructor Neta Snook in 1920 after her first flight. (* NAPA, CALIFORNIA, *Register)*

213

imagination. She joyously stepped into the flier's regalia, one she was seldom to discard for the rest of her days—boots, khaki pants, leather helmet and goggles, and a knee-length patent-leather coat that she saved $20 to purchase. The coat looked too new, so she applied grease to it and slept in it for several days until it took on that "veteran appearance."

Nothing was fake, on the other hand, about Amelia's gift as a pilot. She was cool under pressure, nerveless said many experienced male pilots who came to marvel at her. She worked long and hard at mastering one plane after another. Her life became flying.

But there were few jobs for male pilots, let alone female fliers in those early days before commercial aviation. (Even men like Lindbergh had a hard time finding employment in the air, grabbing anything that might happen along, from stunt flying in an air circus to flying the mail in battered crates that went to pieces in the smallest storms.) To support her dream, Amelia took several secretarial jobs and even worked in a dark room, while she learned photography.

With her savings, plus money provided by her doting father, Amelia purchased her first airplane, a sport biplane built by William Kinner and called the Kinner Canary. Amelia performed every conceivable test on herself and the plane, purposely going into spins, stalls and forced landings. It was during that year that Amelia Earhart crashed for the first time. (There would be three more in her career.) The motor failed in a borrowed plane and she merely cut the engines and slopped into a cabbage patch. And there were triumphs. Amelia set the first of her records, ascending to 14,000 feet, the highest altitude ever reached by a female flier.

All of the sky dreams were interrupted when Amelia's parents were again separated. Amy Earhart had tried to reestablish a union with her husband in California, but Edwin resumed his drinking, and the couple divorced in 1924. Amelia sold her plane and, heartbroken, bought a yellow Kissel sport car in which she and her mother motored to Medford, Massachusetts, to live with sister Muriel.

Trying to resume medical studies proved a failure. "I didn't have the qualities to be an M.D.," wrote Amelia years later. "I lacked the patience. I wanted to be doing something, not preparing for it." She dropped out of Columbia University on April 25, 1925. Under the

Massachusetts University extension program, Amelia Mary Earhart,
would-be flying genius, settled down to teaching English to for-
eigners in factories in and about Boston. She seemed destined to be
grounded for life.


## Into the Air


In the spring of 1928, a British socialite, Mrs. Frederick Guest,
whose husband had been in the Air Ministry under Lloyd George,
bought a trimotored Fokker airplane named *Friendship* from Commander Richard E. Byrd. Mrs. Guest intended to be the first woman
to fly the Atlantic Ocean, as a passenger, not a pilot. The dangers of
early-day flying, however, were pointed out to the intrepid Mrs.
Guest, and she was persuaded to allow another woman to take her
place. Since Lindbergh, an American, had been first to cross the Atlantic a year earlier, it was only fitting, thought the good-natured
Mrs. Guest, that an American female make the trip.

A sort of talent hunt then commenced, with George Palmer Putnam II, of the G. P. Putnam's Sons publishing company, leading the
hunt. Snooping about Boston, Putnam was told of a startling lady
pilot named Amelia Earhart, who had already logged five hundred
hours in the air and was the first woman to be granted an F.A.I.
pilot's license. Amelia was found and asked if she wanted to be the
first lady to fly the Atlantic. She accepted with alacrity, jubilant at
being able to leave her dreary language work.

Putnam looked Amelia over and, beyond what he knew of her
flying skills, saw in her a promotable item. She bore a strong resemblance to the clear-eyed, clean-cut rangy Lindbergh. He envisioned
her as a "Lady Lindy" and not only set Amelia up for the flight but
signed her to a book contract. (Putnam had already scored a tremendous publishing hit by signing up Lindbergh for $10,000, which pro-
duced the best-selling *We*, the story of the Lone Eagle's solo flight
to Paris.)

The flight's pilot was Wilmer L. Stultz, the flight mechanic Louis
"Slim" Gordon. Amelia was the lone passenger. Stultz, known as
"Bull" to his friends, was a long-time air veteran, who was addicted

to candy and alcohol. He was to receive $20,000 for his labors; Gordon was to get $5,000. Amelia would have the fame.

On June 3, 1928, the heavy tri-motored plane lumbered into the air above Boston and slowly made its way to Trespassy, Newfoundland. Bad weather kept the flying trio earthbound for three weeks. Stultz got drunk and almost drowned himself by falling off a pier at dockside. (He drank more than a fifth of brandy a day.)

Amelia's miserable experience with an alcoholic father helped her to aid the drunken pilot. A sober Stultz finally lifted the *Friendship* from the Newfoundland fog on June 17. Amelia busied herself with taking down copious notes of the trip; they were to appear in her book *20 Hours, 40 Minutes.*

Ebullience bubbled from Amelia during that trip in which Stultz fought one storm after another. From her cramped cabin position, Amelia wrote: "I am getting housemaid's knee kneeling here gulping beauty. . . . Marvelous shapes in white stand out, some trailing shimmering veils, the clouds look like icebergs in the distance. . . . How marvelous is a machine and the mind that made it. I am thoroughly occidental in this worship."

His flying mastery at its peak, Stultz gently landed the *Friendship* at Burry Port, Wales. Cheers were heard from England to the United States, and Amelia Mary Earhart was world-famous. She discarded her usual male attire to slip into a dress loaned to her by a Welsh native before newsmen snapped her photo. She returned to the United States, staying at the Putnam estate in Rye, New York, where she finished her book, which was published in 1929 and was ironically dedicated to Mrs. Dorothy Putnam. Within two years, the Putnams were divorced and George Palmer Putnam was spending almost every waking moment with Amelia.

Six times Amelia Earhart refused to marry him, but his money, flattery, his hosts of famous friends, his high-society perch, and his power position finally wore down the woman aviator. They were married on February 8, 1931. The "aviatrix," as female fliers were then called, handed Putnam a note just before their wedding in which she, more or less, stipulated the ground rules of their strange relationship. Among her directives, Amelia stated:

*Amelia being helped from the cockpit by her publisher-promoter husband, George Palmer Putnam, in 1931 after she had successfully completed two transcontinental flights.* (WIDE WORLD)

In our life together I shall not hold you to any medieval code of faithfulness to me, nor shall I consider myself bound to you similarly. If we can be honest, I think, the difficulties which arise may be best avoided. Please let us not interfere with each other's work or play, nor let the world see our private joys or disagreements. In this connection I may have to keep some place where I can go to be by myself now and then, for I cannot guarantee to endure at all times the confinements of even an attractive cage.

(There were many affairs, rumors had it, that occupied Amelia's six remaining years of life, associations with her navigator, Fred Noonan; with Eugene Vidal, father of novelist Gore Vidal; and with Hollywood stunt pilot Paul Mantz, who was later to be killed while flying the weird contraption used in the motion picture, *Flight of the Phoenix.*)

Putnam, twelve years older than Amelia, abided by her terms. He spent the next six years promoting Amelia in one high-handed scheme after another. Selling his interest in his publishing house to a relative, Putnam went on to promote the sale of all manner of items in Amelia's name, from lightweight *Friendship* luggage to mannish clothes, with buttons on women's jackets shaped like airplane rivets.

217

Amelia busied herself with flying, her first love. With Putnam backing her financially, Amelia purchased the best planes available and in one, a red, Lockheed Vega monoplane, she took off from Harbor Grace, Newfoundland, on May 20, 1932, and landed in a meadow in Londonderry, Ireland, 14 hours and 56 minutes later, the first woman to solo the Atlantic. Only months later Amelia established a record in transcontinental flight for women. She flew nonstop from Los Angeles to Newark, New Jersey, in 19 hours and 5 minutes, a distance of 2,448 miles. She beat her own record by two hours in 1933.

More than 10,000 hurrahing admirers met Amelia in January 1935, after she flew from Hawaii to Oakland's Bay Farm Airport in 18 hours and 15 minutes. She became the first to solo from Los Angeles to Mexico City some months later. Hardly had her engine cooled when "Lady Lindy" was again in the air, flying solo from Mexico City to Newark, New Jersey.

Amelia Earhart had more fame than one human could tolerate. World-famous politicians, scientists, educators, movie personalities, social wizards begged her presence. She dined with President Roose-

*Triumph and glory belonged to Amelia as she rode through a New York ticker tape parade in 1932 held to celebrate her being the first woman to fly solo across the Atlantic.* (WIDE WORLD)

velt and even took Eleanor Roosevelt up for a moonlight ride among the clouds.

All was hers, much more than Amelia ever expected when she first climbed into that cockpit behind Frank Hawks those long years back in California. Only one challenge remained, a dream that Amelia had possessed since youth—to fly around the world. To that end, on March 20, 1936, she purchased from Lockheed for $50,000 the most powerful nonmilitary plane of the day, a twin-engined, 10-passenger 10-E Electra airliner. She had the plane stripped and larger gas tanks installed, to give the plane a 4,500-mile range. A complete navigation room with the latest instruments on board was installed aft in the main cabin. She called the plane "my flying laboratory," but what she intended to study on her around-the-world jaunt has caused ceaseless debate to this day.

Amelia's world flight began on May 29, 1937. Her Electra made its way across the United States. It departed Miami and flew on to Puerto Rico, Venezuela, Dutch Guiana, Brazil, then across the Atlantic to Africa, landing at Senegal, then across Africa to Karachi, India, then Burma, the Dutch East Indies, the island of Timor, then Port Darwin, Australia. From there, Amelia and her navigator, Fred Noonan, flew to Lae, New Guinea. More than 7,000 miles remained by July 1, 1937, the most difficult in the next nonstop flight to tiny Howland Island, 2,556 miles across open water.


### Farewell to Amelia

As she stood on the shores of the New Guinea coast, that night of July 1, 1937, Amelia Earhart was thirty-nine years old. Her boyish face was amazingly unwrinkled. Her gray eyes still sparkled, and that bright, toothy smile made her, to all the world, everybody's kid sister—a little wild, perhaps, but pure, steadfast and true.

Into her log she wrote by bright starlight:

> Not much more than a month ago I was on the other shore of the Pacific, looking westward. This evening, I looked eastward over the Pacific. In those fast-moving days which have intervened, the whole width of the world has passed behind us—except this broad ocean. I shall be glad when we have the hazards of its navigation behind us.

Glad, indeed. The last sweep of Amelia and Noonan's arduous journey would be over a stretch of water that no one had ever before flown. Outside the normal shipping lanes, the route to Howland Island was seldom traversed by ships. It was one of the loneliest and most desolate areas on earth.

The destination was an almost impossible pinhead to find in a rippling cushion of water. Howland Island was a mere half-mile wide and only two miles long. At high tide, the United States possession stood a scant fifteen feet at its greatest elevation. Noonan had no qualms, even though the flight would be AE's (Amelia's newly acquired and favorite nickname for herself) longest in her flying career. The navigator had long experience in the Pacific, guiding Pan American's *China Clipper* in her maiden flight from San Francisco to Manila in years previous. He would have his chronometers to aid him, as well as the direction finder. There would also be radio

*The last known photograph of Amelia Earhart, taken at Lae, New Guinea on July 2, 1937 shortly before the aviatrix and her navigator, Fred Noonan (extreme right), flew off into oblivion.* (WIDE WORLD)

bearings sent out to the Electra from ships and shore stations. The Coast Guard cutter *Itasca* had been stationed at Howland Island for that purpose. The U.S.S. *Swan* was standing by, too, stationed between Howland and Honolulu. The U.S.S. *Ontario* was between Lae and Howland.

The weather cleared somewhat by dawn of July 2, enough AE felt, for the last leg of the journey to begin; she wanted to land in California on the Fourth of July, an apt day of celebration for her country's birth and her around-the-world accomplishment. Loaded to the brim with 800 gallons of gasoline and 70 gallons of oil, the Electra sat poised at the end of an airway strip carved from the New Guinea jungle, a 3,000-foot runway that ended abruptly at a cliff that shot straight down into the sea.

Wearing her traditional slacks and a plaid shirt, Amelia, slim, agile, running her hand through her tousled, tawny hair, climbed aboard, followed by Noonan. They cheerfully waved goodbye to the Dutch officials and natives gathered to see them off.

Behind the controls, Amelia revved her engines. The Electra rolled forward, gathering momentum and speed. The heavily laden craft barely lifted itself from the runway, becoming airborne just 150 feet from the lethal end of the strip. Those on the ground watched the plane buzz eastward into what appeared to be an increasingly overcast sky. Perhaps it had not occurred to AE, but her times and dates were slightly out of order. It was 10:30 A.M., July 2, on Lae when she took off. Because of the international dateline, however, Amelia's takeoff, according to the waiting *Itasca* at Howland was registered at 12:30 P.M., July 1. There would be plenty of time to make America by Independence Day; Amelia and Noonan were actually flying into yesterday.

Commander W. K. Thompson, skipper of the *Itasca*, was informed a few hours later through a radio dispatch from the Coast Guard Commandant in San Francisco that Amelia Earhart was in flight toward Howland. Thompson had stationed four men on constant alert for Amelia's signal. The Electra's radio schedule called for Earhart's call letters, KHAQQ, to be broadcast with messages on 3105 kilocycles every fifteen and forty-five minutes past the hour. Homing signals and weather reports were to be broadcast by *Itasca* to Amelia every hour and half hour on 3105 and 7500 kilocycles.

For some unexplained reason, Commander Thompson seemed nervous. He made a point of contacting the direction-finder unit ashore at Howland several times to inquire if it had picked up anything from KHAQQ. Nothing had been heard. It was 1:12 A.M. when Thompson wired San Francisco: "Have not heard Earhart signals but see no cause for concern as plane is still about 1,000 miles away."

At 2:45 A.M. a voice, distant and hardly discernible, broke through the crackling static on wavelength 3105. The anxious seamen in the *Itasca's* radio room leaped for the controls, hunching forward and holding their sets, as if to squeeze out a clearer signal. "Cloudy and overcast" came the thin piping of Amelia's voice, "... headwinds."

Thompson immediately flashed to San Francisco: "*Itasca* heard Earhart plane at 0248."

The next expected signal at 3:15 A.M. did not come. At 3:30 A.M. *Itasca* radioed the faraway Electra its weather report. Thompson discarded the scheduled routine as his worries mounted. He added to the weather report: "What is your position, KHAQQ? *Itasca* has heard your phone. Please go ahead on key. Acknowledge this broadcast next schedule."

At 3:45 P.M. another signal came through. Amelia was still using voice transmission and had apparently not received the *Itasca's* last message, since she made no acknowledgment. Her voice seemed even more distant: "*Itasca* from Earhart ... *Itasca* from Earhart ... overcast ... will listen in on hour and half hour at 3105."

Again *Itasca* asked for key transmissions, but Amelia remained on oral transmission, her words very faint, muffled, garbled. What startled Thompson was that the experienced flier gave no position or bearing. Later someone remembered that Noonan was having trouble with his chronometers before the Lae takeoff, something to do with radio interference that prevented exact settings and threw off position-fixes from the stars. If Amelia was flying in storms and could receive no ship- or shore-to-plane communication, that left only dead reckoning. Thompson knew what that meant. One degree deviation from flight plan would send a plane a mile off course for every sixty miles of headway. Tiny Howland, in that instance, could be easily overshot by Amelia and Noonan, and they would then fly into a landless vast area of ocean and, most likely, oblivion.

Earhart's signals stopped. Commander Thompson ordered a ground

crew to clear the runway at Howland of clustering dodo birds. The
skies over the *Itasca* were bright and clear when the dawn broke.
Still no Electra came into view.

At 7:42 A.M., Amelia's voice broke the silence in the radio room.
Jittery and high-pitched, she nearly shouted: "KHAQQ calling
*Itasca*. We must be on you but cannot see you. Gas is running low.
Only about thirty minutes left. Been unable to reach you by radio.
We are flying at altitude of one thousand feet."

Then, about fifteen minutes later, AE's signal came in at its strong-
est level. "KHAQQ calling *Itasca*. We are circling but cannot see
you. Go ahead on seventy-five hundred either now or on schedule."

Thompson ordered a steady stream of "A" signals sent out immediately. For the first time, Amelia acknowledged the *Itasca* transmission. "We are receiving your signals but unable to get a minimum
[bearing]. Please take a bearing on us and answer with voice on
3105." She sent out her steady signals, but the sound drifted and
faded before a bearing could be determined.

According to dead reckoning, Amelia and Noonan would have calculated the 2,556-mile distance from Lae since their takeoff eighteen
hours earlier. From AE's reference to having only thirty minutes' gas
remaining, Thompson figured the Electra must be within a hundred
miles of Howland. To the south by thirty-eight miles lay Baker
Island. If Amelia overshot Howland in that direction she was bound
to sight Baker. To the north there was nothing, and it was here
that Thompson charted a block of ocean for a possible search and
rescue.

For the last time, at 8:45 A.M., the earth heard Amelia's voice. She
was obviously confused, frightened, desperate. Her words approached babble. "We are in line of position 157-337 . . . will repeat
this message. We will repeat this message at 6210 kilocycles . . .
Wait: Listening on 6210 kilocycles. We are running north and
south." The signal abruptly ended.

Thompson now realized that Amelia had overshot the island and
was headed—her plane running quickly out of gas—into a no-return
area of sea. He ordered his ship out of Howland harbor and dashed
northward. He shot out messages to Washington, D.C., and San
Francisco: "Earhart unreported at 0900 . . . Believe down. Am searching probable area and will continue."

223

Waiting at Fort Funston in Oakland was Amelia's husband, George Putnam. He tore Thompson's message from the radio operator's hands and grimaced. To reporters he emphasized: "Even if they are down, they can stay afloat indefinitely. Their empty gas tanks will give them buoyancy. Besides, they have all the emergency equipment they need—everything." True, the Electra carried food and water rations, a two-man rubber boat, life belts, a Very pistol, flares, and a signal kit. But it was thought that if the huge plane was down it would sink rapidly in the high seas, empty gas tanks or not.

Before *Itasca's* signal was received for a seaplane to be sent from Honolulu to help in the search, the Navy commander in Hawaii had already been instructed by Admiral William D. Leahy, Chief of Naval Operations in Washington, to "please render whatever help you deem practical in search for Earhart and Noonan."

The seaplane was sent out and so was the enormous battleship *Colorado,* accompanied by several smaller craft. From San Diego steamed the fast carrier *Lexington* with its scores of planes waiting on deck to join the search.

As the word flashed across the country, "one of the ten most reported news stories of the twentieth century" took place. Newspaper headlines screamed the disappearance: "Lady Lindy Lost!", "Earhart Down in Pacific," "Amelia's Plane Vanishes," "Earhart Disappears."

The seaplane from Hawaii was forced to turn back after hitting a freak ice storm. The *Itasca*, the *Colorado* and her sister ships, plowed the ocean north of Howland. Nothing was seen. For more than a week the U.S. Navy scoured by plane and ship 262,281 square miles of Pacific Ocean. Millions waited and wondered. Silence was followed by more silence until, on July 12, when seventy-six planes returned to the deck of the *Lexington* without a sighting of the lost Amelia and Noonan, the Navy called off the search.

Amelia Earhart's disappearance officially ended in a terse Navy statement: "Lost at sea." More provocative were the series of undying legends of the lost flier. They persist to this day, a few astoundingly logical.

The most believable of the stories indirectly insisting that Amelia did not perish as reported in 1937 was first made public by, of all sources, RKO Studios in 1943, which produced a film entitled *Flight for Freedom*, starring Rosalind Russell. Miss Russell gave the Earhart myth more than encouragement by portraying the flier to near duplication. It was the film's contention, and that of several writers decades later, that Amelia purposely flew off course, heading not for Howland but for the Japanese Mandates, islands that, through agreement, the United States could not inspect. The United States knew that the Japanese were building up huge armed forces in the islands they occupied, but it did not know if airstrips for bombers had been prepared. The RKO story had the aviatrix begin the last hop of her around-the-world flight with the intention of crash-landing on "Gulf" Island, which would prompt the U.S. Navy to ignore past agreements, steam into the forbidden area and rescue the pilot, all the while accomplishing the real mission of photographing the massive buildup of the Japanese war machine. Miss Russell, learning that the Japanese have discovered the ruse, and intend to pick her up before the full-scale rescue mission gets under way, heroically dives into the ocean near the island. She is killed and the search of the area by the United States military takes place anyway.

Astonishing as this fiction might seem, there is much to support belief that Amelia Earhart was indeed on a secret mission to photograph the Japanese-occupied islands, especially Saipan and/or the island fortress of Truk. As late as 1949, Amelia's mother stated: "Amelia told me many things, but there were some things she couldn't tell me. I am convinced she was on some sort of government mission, probably on verbal orders."

Those orders, it was claimed, came directly from the President of the United States, Amelia's close friend, Franklin D. Roosevelt, who wanted to use AE's around-the-world flight and subsequent crash in the seething Japanese island area as an excuse to more closely examine the hidden war machine. Investigative reporter Fred Goerner believes this story quite possible. There was, for instance, a young woman who was captured on Saipan in 1937 and was taken to Japan to be executed as a spy. Similar compelling stories emanated over the years from other Japanese-occupied islands. Natives and Japanese officers who survived the war recalled seeing Amelia as a prisoner and witnessing either her imprisonment or her execution in Japan. Writers Joseph Klass and Joseph Gervais even advanced the theory of total survival in their *Amelia Earhart*

*Lives,* in which they contend AE is alive and well and living, for arcane reasons, incognito in New Jersey.

Given the logic of the sacrifice-flight story, one could easily conclude that Amelia would not be kept alive by Japanese captors in 1937. Her knowledge of their secret war preparations would be enough to assure her death. There is much to suggest this was Amelia's true end—testimony of fellow prisoners in the Japanese military prison on Saipan, certain equipment that may have come from the Electra wrecked on a small Japanese-controlled atoll in the Gilbert Islands, and bones that may be all that remain of "Lady Lindy."

Added to this was the fact that Howland Island was almost an impossible spot to reach from Lae, and, after Amelia's carefully prepared, meticulously flown journey nearly around the world, the island was selected only because it could not easily be reached, and because it was in the path that led to the Japanese-held islands. The flight to Howland, one might easily conclude, was a ruse. Amelia Earhart was too good a pilot to depend on landing there, and too good a pilot to have allowed her equipment to malfunction and her flight to become confused if she *had* to land at Howland. To say that AE simply lost her way is to say that she was not one of the greatest airplane pilots ever to take to the air, which she certainly was.

In the last forty years, hosts of reporters have attempted to gather the real truth from officials in all branches of the services in Washington. They have obtained flat denials from official sources of any knowledge of the Earhart flight being an intelligence probe. But that, as was the case with British frogman Lionel Crabb, who appears later in this chapter, is the standard fare served up by governments for their failures and embarrassments. As far as the author is concerned the Earhart disappearance is still open and awaiting a definite answer.

For George Putnam, who waited seven days in the radio room at Fort Funston before giving up hope, Amelia, his wife and sky hero, was dead in 1937. Wistfully he looked from a window that faced westward toward the Pacific. He opened up a letter Amelia had given him with instructions to read it only if she failed to appear. With bloodshot eyes, Putnam read aloud: "Please know I am quite

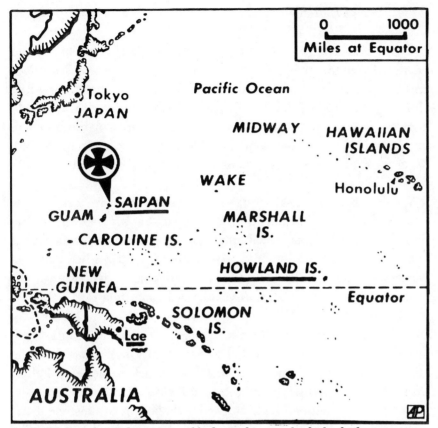

*Amelia Earhart's last flight was ostensibly destined for Howland Island. The cross on this map pinpoints the island of Saipan, a Japanese stronghold at the time and the aviatrix's most likely destination.* (WIDE WORLD)

aware of the hazards. I want to do it—because I want to do it. Women must try to do things as men have tried. When they fail, their failure must be but a challenge to others."

All the heady promotion had gone out of Putnam. He stood before reporters an exhausted man. "If she's gone," he said slowly, crying, "this is the way she would have wanted it." He remembered how she often told him: "When I go, I'd like to go in my plane. Quickly." Putnam shook his head, still for the moment disbelieving Amelia Earhart was no more. "Only, it was to have been her last flight . . . she said absolutely, the last one."

"Now this has come. . . . I must go," said Father Henry Borynski as he put down the receiver. The Roman Catholic priest had been chaplain for nine months of the small Polish community in Little Horton, a suburb of Bradford, England. Father Borynski was a well-known anti-Communist who had encouraged with volatile speeches and sermons his one thousand parishioners, all exiles from Poland, never to return home to live under the dictatorship of a Stalin-backed regime.

When Father Borynski answered the phone in his rectory on July 13, 1953, he listened briefly, then hung up and addressed his cryptic remark to housekeeper Elizabeth Beck. He immediately put on his hat and overcoat and left his house. Minutes later Father Borynski was seen standing on a Little Horton street corner, as if waiting for someone. It was 4 P.M., and it was the last time the priest is known to have been seen.

Father Borynski's disappearance puzzled many an Englishman and caused an uproar in the Polish community he served. That he absented himself or committed suicide was quickly ruled out. Father Borynski was a devout priest who took his responsibilities seriously. That he was kidnapped and returned to Poland for punishment because of outspoken attacks on the Communist regime in his native land, of which he knew many secrets, was a distinct possibility. Lending itself to this theory was the fact that Father Borynski had departed so quickly that he left his most precious priestly possessions behind in the rectory—his prayer book, crucifix, certificate of ordination and his priestly garments—not to mention the 300 pounds in his bank account.

What stumped Bradford City police, as well as Scotland Yard, was that the priest was so easily identified; he was a huge man stood six feet tall and weighed no less than 200 pounds. Attired in his priest's clothes, such a man, concluded inspectors, would certainly be seen if he were being abducted.

Days later reports of sighting Father Borynski began to trickle into the Yard. One account had it that Father Borynski was seen on the moors in Scotland, wandering through the mists. Another reported that he appeared "gray with fear" on the streets of Glasgow as several sinister-looking men hustled him along. He was reported in Lancashire and in Oldham. In Little Horton there was even a strong rumor that another priest had murdered Borynski out of envy.

The elderly priest held a press conference on August 11, 1953, at the high tide of this gossip, his face red with anger as he thundered to reporters, "The police think I murdered Father Borynski. I did nothing of the sort!"

The most believable report of the priest's sudden disappearance is that he was seen getting into a black car in Brandford. Several "foreign-looking" men were inside. The auto sped away toward London just in time to meet the Soviet ship *Gribojedov*, which then sailed for Leningrad. On board the ship, documentation proved, were two strange travelers not on the passenger list. One of these men, it was claimed, was a professional assassin for the Polish Communists, who reportedly murdered with cyanide pellets fired from a gas pistol two important Russian refugees who were attempting to escape to Germany. The other passenger, the story goes, was none other than Father Borynski, who was murdered by the assassin on board the *Gribojedov*, his body carved into tiny pieces and fed through the dollar-size holes that opened on the ship's boilers. None of this was ever fully substantiated.

The priest was certified as dead in 1959. The British government to this day has, however, a closed-door policy on the Borynski case. When Parliament Member Henry Kerby, an expert on Polish and Lithuanian affairs, rose in the House of Commons to ask embarrassing questions about the missing priest, he was answered in a typical and perfunctory manner by the Government. Any disclosure of facts from the investigation into the disappearance "would not be in the public interest."

Certainly in the private interest of Dominican Republic dictator Generalissimo Rafael Leonidas Trujillo was the disappearance of Dr. Jesus de Galindez who is known to the world of the missing as the "vanishing Ph.D."

Dr. Galindez, born in Madrid, had been an ardent antifascist all his life. He had fought with the Loyalists against Franco during the Spanish Civil War, deeply involving himself with the Basque Republic which was overrun by Falangist, Fascist and Nazi legions. As a refugee in 1939, Galindez emigrated to the Dominican Republic,

*Dr. Jesus de Galindez, volatile opponent of the dictatorship of Generalissimo Rafael Leonidas Trujillo in the Dominican Republic, vanished in March, 1956 after teaching a class at New York's Columbia University.*

which was then seeking professionals to staff its education departments.

The hard-working Galindez, then a teacher, had risen by 1946 to the position of legal adviser to the National Department of Labor, serving as Secretary of the Dominican Minimum Wage Committee. He made his sympathies with the common worker obvious when he sided with striking sugar workers. Galindez was promptly fired from his position by the Trujillo dictatorship, a one-man rule that yielded to the Generalissimo more than forty million dollars each year for his private coffers.

Departing for New York, Galindez became a publicly avowed enemy of Trujillo and one of the most active leaders against the oppressive Dominican Republic regime. The forty-two-year-old Galindez taught political science in the graduate-student division at Columbia University, but mostly busied himself with a polemical book that was to expose the corrupt dictatorship in the Dominican Republic, and which he entitled, *The Era of Trujillo*. Into the work, Galindez poured his special insider's knowledge of how the Generalissimo ruled by strong-arm methods, torture, terror and murder. The professor knew he was in danger. Trujillo's agents in America had not hesitated to kill the dictator's enemies on United States soil. On October 2, 1952, while Galindez was working on his long manuscript, he heard that his friend Andres Resquena, who published an anti-Trujillo newspaper, had been shot to death in the lobby of his Manhattan apartment. The killer escaped, but there was no doubt in Galindez's mind that the murderer had been one of the Generalissimo's hired assassins.

Two days after Resquena was killed, Galindez wrote a letter to nobody in particular to be opened if anything "happened" to him. In it Galindez stressed that if he should be murdered or vanish, the persons responsible were in the employ of Trujillo. He buried the letter in his personal files, hoping that the time would never come for it to be read. That time was less than three years distant. On the wintry night of March 12, 1956, Dr. Galindez concluded his classes at Hamilton Hall at 9:20 P.M. He accepted a ride from Evelyne Lang, one of his students, to Columbus Circle, where he usually caught the subway.

Alighting from the car, briefcase in hand, Galindez walked slowly toward the subway entrance at Seventh Avenue and 57th Street. The heavy snows obliterated him from view in seconds. That was the last seen of Galindez. His disappearance was reported to police five days later by friends.

The professor's clothes, personal belongings, money and papers were found undisturbed in his rooms. A thirteen-state alarm went out for him. Galindez was nowhere to be found. Shortly, the story broke that Galindez might have been killed for a vast amount of money he had been hoarding. As a representative of the Basque Government-in-Exile, Galindez had raised more than $1 million to aid the refugees of his native country. The money, reporters soon learned, had been faithfully sent to the Basque organization in Paris. "Every cent has been accounted for," stipulated José de Aguirre, president of the Basque group. (Galindez had spent $32,103 for personal expenses in his fund-raising activities, expenditures he duly reported to the Basques.)

Why then did Galindez disappear? There were still no answers on June 6, 1956, when Columbia University conferred *in absentia* one of its 203 Ph.D. degrees upon Jesus Maria de Galindez. But there were rumors by the bushel. Thugs had ambushed the professor for the money in his pocket the night he disappeared. He had gone to Spain to lead the underground battle against Franco. There was a report that he had smuggled himself into Budapest to spy for or against the Communists. The Galindez disappearance quieted for a while. Then, on December 4, 1956, a twenty-three-year-old American pilot named Gerald Lester Murphy vanished in Ciudad Trujillo.

Ambassador to the Dominican Republic William Pfeiffer personally investigated Murphy's disappearance. The pilot's car had been found abandoned at the edge of a cliff overlooking the ocean. Pfeiffer located one of Murphy's fellow fliers, who complained that Murphy was a loudmouth, that he had bragged about completing secret flights at the direct orders of dictator Trujillo. Pfeiffer informed officials of the Dominican Republic and Murphy's colleague was quickly jailed. Within days, an unconfirmed report had it that he had hanged himself in his cell out of remorse. His suicide note told how he had accidentally killed Murphy.

The matter would have ended there, except that F.B.I. agents and other investigators routinely checked Murphy's immediate past and uncovered a startling bit of information. The young pilot had made an important flight from Long Island to the Dominican Republic on the night of March 12, 1956, only hours after Professor Galindez vanished. The probe went further.

Murphy was relatively well-off before he disappeared in the Dominican Republic, a questionable state of affairs for a myopic youth whose poor eyesight had prevented him from flying in the Air Force or for commercial airways. Raised in South Dakota and Eugene, Oregon, Murphy barely eked out a living as a draftsman and later, after he had painfully earned his commercial-aviator license, as a pilot for an air-taxi firm located in Miami, Florida. In early 1956, Murphy was broke; yet, only days after he made the flight to Ciudad Trujillo, he had come into a good deal of money, purchasing a new Dodge convertible for $3,412, landing a posh job as a copilot with Compañia Dominicana de Aviación, the Dominican Airline, and making furious plans to marry a beautiful airline stewardess he had just recently met, one Celia "Sally" Caire.

All of Murphy's good fortune (and Galindez's bad) stemmed from that March 12 flight. Investigators learned that Murphy had chartered a twin-engine Beechcraft D-18 for $800 on March 5, stating that he was going to pilot some New York businessmen to Miami. Murphy had the plane dispatcher make out the receipt for the charter to "John Kane." Later that day Harold French, an old friend of Murphy's, accidentally bumped into the pilot, who was with two swarthy-complexioned men. One of the men with Murphy was Arturo Espaillat, the Dominican consul in New York City.

French saw Murphy on and off during the next few days and was told by the gregarious pilot that he was about to conduct a strange flight from Miami to the Dominican Republic. He did not give French details. On March 10, Murphy had additional gas tanks installed on his D-18, stating that he would need the 1,500-mile range the tanks allowed for a possible "trip to the Azores."

On the morning of March 12, Murphy flew the D-18 from Newark, New Jersey, to Zahn's Airport at Amityville, Long Island, arriving there at 10:30 A.M. He waited all day in his plane. Just after midnight, an ambulance appeared on the strip and an unconscious man strapped to a stretcher was put on the plane. Night watchman at the airport, Anthony Frevelle, who helped put the passenger aboard remembered that "he could not move a muscle." Murphy took off immediately.

It was almost dawn when Murphy landed at Lantana Airport in West Palm Beach, Florida. Mechanic Donald Jackson had received a call from New York days earlier telling him to be on hand to refuel the D-18. As he filled the gas tanks, Jackson noticed the passenger inside the plane tied down in a stretcher. The mechanic later stated that he smelled something like potent drugs inside the cabin, calling it a "peculiar stench."

After paying $95 for the gas, Murphy was again airborne, landing that evening at Monte Cristi Airport at the Dominican Republic. The passenger was removed, and Murphy's fortunes instantly fattened with money and position.

Gerald Murphy's bright prospects would, no doubt, have continued to blossom had it not been for his wagging tongue. He had bragged to la Maza about his top-level flight, and he even went so far as to tell his sweetheart Sally that the man he had flown to the Dominican Republic from the United States was the archenemy of Rafael Trujillo, one Professor Galindez.

But federal investigators could get no further. All trails stopped in Ciudad Trujillo. The Dominican Republic officials denied any knowledge of either the Galindez or the Murphy disappearance. In the United States an official investigation into the double disappearance produced no new evidence. Still, the public clamor was loud in insisting that Trujillo was linked to the missing men.

The dictator answered by hiring publicity agent Sidney S. Baron, who employed the prestigious lawyer Morris Ernst to investigate the affair. Ernst went to work on the case and, in unison with William H. Munson, former New York State Supreme Court Justice, produced a massive "Report and Opinion in the Matter of Galindez," which cost $562,855. Trujillo happily paid the bill, especially delighted with the conclusion reached by Ernst and Munson that there "was not a scintilla of evidence" that tied the Murphy and Galindez disappearances together. "Whitewash," screamed Trujillo's critics, but they would have to wait more than six years to be proven right.

In March of 1964, Charles O. Porter, looking into the Galindez-

233

Murphy cases, interviewed the former warden of the Dominican prison outside Ciudad Trujillo. In the presence of several United States embassy officials, the onetime warden told how Galindez was abducted by Trujillo's thugs, drugged, and put aboard Murphy's plane. A nurse named Ana Gloria Vieira, who had administered the knockout drug, accompanied the captive and Murphy on the secret flight, hiding in the back of the plane. Miss Vieira, the official said, was also with Galindez when he was revived and driven to *La Fundación*, the country estate of Dictator Trujillo.

Groggy, the professor was led into Trujillo's marbled office, an enormous room of pillars and towering gold candlesticks. The Generalissimo glowered from behind a massive desk. He stood up, pounded his heavy fists onto the desk and screamed, "Your life now is as worthless as an empty page in that book you were writing!" The dictator motioned several guards forward and pointed at the hapless Galindez. The guards opened fire with automatic weapons, pouring hundreds of bullets into the professor. His bloody corpse was then dragged in a sheet across the marble office floor and taken to an unmarked grave. Trujillo, according to nurse Vieira, was beside himself with rage at the bloodstains left on the floor.

The nurse herself met with a violent, albeit predictable end in August 1956. Trujillo, wanting to rid himself of any witnesses, had Miss Vieira beaten to death. Her body was then put into an auto and sent over a high cliff. The burning car, with the charred corpse of Miss Vieira inside, was found days later. Friends of the slain nurse raised embarrassing questions. Trujillo's agents had again bungled their assignment. Miss Vieira did not drive.

Murphy's mouth assured him of a similar fate. He was arrested when he attempted to leave the country on December 1, 1956. Taken to the Dominican prison, the pilot was dragged from his cell hours later for "interrogation." One of four guards immediately hit Murphy in the mouth. In the words of the ex-jailer, "The pilot crumpled to the floor. The two policemen placed a rope around his neck and each pulled it until Mr. Murphy was choked to death."

So ended the Galindez disappearance. Trujillo squirmed for years in the evil comfort of having silenced the words of a cultured, fragile critic. The dictator went to his death, assassinated in 1961, thinking the story forever suppressed. Jesus de Galindez's book, *The Era of*

*Trujillo* was subsequently published in Chile and became a best-seller throughout South and Latin America.


## To Russia With Malice


Lionel Kenneth Philip Crabb was anything but the low-profile-stiff-upper-lip-type officer of the British Royal Navy. He was more in tune with the wandering, listless Ernie Mott, anti-hero of Richard Llewellyn's *None But the Lonely Heart.* Early in youth, Crabb forsook queen and country, traveling throughout the world, picking up odd jobs here and there; he wrote advertising copy, he pumped gas in the United States and worked for an art gallery back in London. But always, Crabb liked to be near salt water. He was "Navy-struck" since age eight. When World War II erupted, Crabb was first denied military service because of his poor eyesight. But in 1942 he cajoled and wheedled his way into the bomb-disposal service at Gibraltar.

Crabb's wartime service was nothing less than spectacular as he almost single-handedly cleared the bottoms near Gibraltar of mines and fought Italian frogmen in the deeps while removing the secret fascist weapon from the hulls of British warships—delayed-action limpet mines. What made Crabb's feats seem all the more impossible was the fact that he was small for his job, less than five-feet six-inches, with a torso that slimmed away from a massive head and shoulders to legs of almost finlike proportions; Crabb was also one of the most inept swimmers in the Royal Navy.

Following the capitulation of Italy, Crabb's reputation was such that the entire section of Italian frogmen he had been battling for over two years refused to surrender to any one but Lieutenant Commander Crabb. From them, Crabb learned everything about the German mines beneath the Italian harbors, which he promptly helped to clear.

A grateful country not only awarded "Crabbie"—or "Buster," as the frogman was known to his friends—the distinguished George Medal and the Order of the Empire, but also kept him in the service long after the war ended, using him on rescue missions such as the times when the British submarines *Truculent* and *Affray* sank. (It was Crabb who suggested using for the first time an underwater TV device to locate the *Affray*.) He was also used, according to most reliable reports, as one of the frogmen who secretly inspected the modernistic hull of the Russian cruiser *Sverdlov* when that ship visited Portsmouth Harbor in honor of Queen Elizabeth's coronation. (The British were most anxious to learn how the new Russian cruisers could maneuver so well with only two screws, as well as discover the type and placement of their new sonar devices.)

By 1956, however, Lionel Crabb was washed up as a frogman. At forty-six, gone flabby and winded most of the time from heavy smoking and drinking, Crabb was a beached hero without pension or trade. He picked up odd jobs and even served as a consultant to the makers of the movie *Cockleshell Heroes*, which, according to writer Herbert Brean, "he hated because it was about the Royal Marines and not the Navy."

Selling furniture to the many *espresso* coffee shops then popular in London became Crabb's full-time employment, a job he loathed. In early April 1956, the despondent frogman came to life. He was seen in various London pubs, telling friends that he had a "little job" opening soon in Portsmouth, one that would pay him only 60 guineas but would be professionally rewarding all the same. To some he went further and said he was "going down to take a dekko [look] at the Russian bottoms." The Russians, in this instance, happened to be the three Soviet ships arriving on a goodwill tour with Soviet Premier Bulganin and Communist Party Chief Khrushchev on board.

Before Crabb's departure for Portsmouth, his employer Maitland Pendock brought the salesman's attention to a check written by a "Bernard S. Smith," a customer to whom Crabb had sold furniture. It carried the wrong date. Crabb told Pendock that he would see Smith in Portsmouth and obtain a correctly dated check.

The frogman did see Smith, if that was ever his name, in Portsmouth. Both Crabb and Smith, who was described as "a tall, fair-haired man of about forty," registered at the Sallyport Hotel near the harbor on April 17, 1956. Crabb, among his luggage, carried his sword-cane, which was monogrammed with a crab, an item he never traveled with unless on official frogman business.

Crabb apparently went through a trial dive somewhere in the

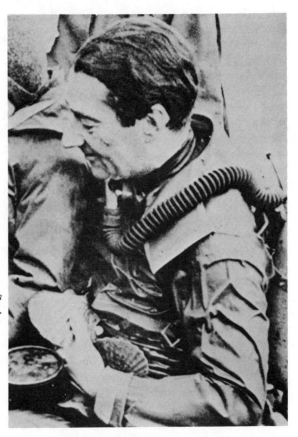

*Britain's great underwater frogman, Lionel Crabb, was lost beneath two Russian warships in 1956.*

harbor. That night he remarked over the phone to Pendock: "Well, I'm not as old as I thought." But there were cryptic last-minute letters he dashed off that seemed full of foreboding. To the publishers of his upcoming biography, he noted: "Lots of trouble. Chaos complete." To his mother, the frogman had mysteriously written: "I am going on a job . . . but it is a simple mission . . . I'll be back in about two days . . . Please tear this letter up."

Frogman Lionel Crabb was not back in two days or ever. He was seen again, if Soviet officials were to be believed, on the morning of April 19, 1956, at about 7:30 A.M. By that time the sleek Russian cruiser *Ordzhonikidze* and her escort destroyers *Smotryashchy* and *Sovershenny* had anchored in Portsmouth Harbor. Soviet seamen on watch on board both destroyers were startled to see the calm waters part and an object shoot upward between the ships.

One writer described the scene thus: "He popped like a cork to the surface of Portsmouth harbor . . . a shiny, snouted figure in the rubber suit of a navy frogman . . . Then, with a kick of his long, black flippers, he dove down into the dark, dirty waters of the historic English port."

Although Lionel Crabb was reported seen the following day at one of his favorite haunts, the Nut Bar of Portsmouth's Keppel's Head Hotel, for all practical reasons, the man had completely vanished. The Russians, it was later claimed, had killed Crabb, sending down their own divers as he inspected the cruiser's new hull as he had the *Sverdlov*'s three years before. Yet that would not explain the strong note of protest put forward by Russian Admiral V. F. Kotov, who reported the sighting his men had made of the frogman, nor the diplomatic notes the Soviets deluged the British government with in the ensuing weeks; had they killed Crabb, they certainly wouldn't have announced his presence near their ships.

The mysterious Mr. Smith, who had accompanied Crabb to Portsmouth, was seen to return to the Sallyport Hotel later during April 18. He checked himself and Crabb out of the hotel, paying the bill, and taking Crabb's and his own luggage with him. Mr. Smith was never again located.

When the British press learned of Crabb's disappearance, reporters ran wild over Portsmouth. By then most doors were closed to them. A Navy official had arrived at the Sallyport Hotel before them and ripped four pages out of the hotel's register, pages that contained the names of Crabb and Smith. All official avenues of information from the Navy were barred.

Though the British press was prevented by the Government Secrets Act from unearthing evidence of the frogman's espionage, the Russians kept demanding an explanation. Prime Minister Anthony Eden was finally compelled to act, replying to Soviet notes with a terse reply, one of usual British diplomatic argot which meagerly apologized in its conclusion: "Her Majesty's government express their regrets for this incident."

Two weeks after Crabb's disappearance, on May 4, Anthony Eden rose in a hooting House of Commons and angrily stated: "It would not be in the public interest to disclose the circumstances in which Commander Crabb is presumed to have met his death. While it is the practice for the Ministers to accept responsibility, I think it is necessary in the special circumstance of the case, to make it clear that what was done was done without the authority or the knowledge of her Majesty's Ministers. Appropriate disciplinary steps are being taken." He refused in the following weeks to speak another word about Crabb's disappearance.

What happened can only be surmised. The spy mission carried out by Crabb apparently was not sponsored by the government, a deduction that is supported by the fact that Crabb was paid a mere 60 guineas for the job and that Eden had promised to take "appropriate disciplinary steps." Crabb's friends decided that he had been in the employ of a special right-wing group conducting their own investigation of the Russians or an overzealous British government official who thought to accomplish an intelligence coup on his own.

Marshall Pugh, Crabb's official biographer, believed that the frogman died while under the Russian cruiser as a result of not using a "dicky," a second diver to help him, and was employing improper equipment. Death came undoubtedly from oxygen poisoning. Crabb's body either floated out to sea some days later or sank into the muddy recesses of Portsmouth harbor.

Writer J. Bernard Hutton insisted in *Frogman Spy* that Crabb was captured by the Russians, drugged, and flown to the Soviet Union, where he was brainwashed and began a career as a Soviet underwater spy, living out his life as Lieutenant Lev Korablov, a story that the British Admiralty branded a total fiction.

Something was found a year later that officially passed for Lionel Crabb. A headless corpse without hands and wearing a diver's suit was discovered floating off Chichester Harbor in Sussex on June 9, 1957. A coroner's investigation of the grotesque corpse officially declared it that of Lionel Crabb. The body was buried under Crabb's name on July 6, much to the edification of an unnamed British officer who had finally ordered: "Get that man underground."

## The Prof Who Went Poof

In the United States another dark intriguer, named Thomas Riha, caused as much consternation in spy circles as had the aquatic Mr.

Crabb, especially when his disappearance on March 15, 1969, was covered up by the C.I.A. for reasons that remain unclear to this day. The Riha case would take the combined imaginations of Eric Ambler, Dashiell Hammett and Raymond Chandler to fictionalize, except that it is real with cyanide murders, suicide, purported espionage, forgery, and the involvement of the F.B.I., the C.I.A. and a United States senator, not to mention the most oddball disappearance in the annals of those who knew too much.

Exactly what Thomas Riha knew is still under debate. Whatever it was, it had to do with Russia or, at least, the secrets held behind the Iron Curtain. Riha, born in Prague, Czechoslovakia, in 1930, immigrated to the United States in 1947. He became a United States citizen and took his Bachelor's and Master's degrees at the University of California at Berkeley. Riha took his doctorate from Harvard University in 1962, and as a professor of Russian history, he taught at the University of Chicago and at Marburg University, in West Germany before joining the faculty at the University of Colorado in 1967.

While living in Boulder, Colorado, where the university is situated, Riha's life exploded with the bizarre and the inexplicable. Strange people traveled to Colorado just to be near the flamboyant professor. Although he was married to one Hana Hruskova, also born in Czechoslovakia and fifteen years younger than Riha, the professor's old girl friend, Gloria Forest McPherson Scimo Tannenbaum, arrived from Illinois to keep him company during his lonely hours. The string of names clinging to Mrs. Tannenbaum like wet seaweed was the result of several marriages. She was known in Boulder as Galva Tannenbaum. Riha called her "the colonel" because of her bossy ways. Galva called Riha "Tom Cat" because of his apparent sexual promiscuity. The fact that the thirty-nine-year-old Galva had served more than two years in the penitentiary at Dwight, Illinois, for forgery and embezzlement in 1959 did not bother the forty-year-old professor. He was a happy-go-lucky sort, one who felt there was room for all kinds of people and behavior in this tired old world.

There was room, too, for Riha's nephew, Zednek Cerveny, who moved to nearby Lyons, Colorado, after escaping from Czechoslovakia in 1968 when the Russians invaded. According to one report, Galva insisted that she had something to do with effecting Cerveny's escape, convincing "the professor she was an officer in the United States military intelligence who could help him get his nephew Cerveny into the United States."

Things became extremely active for Professor Riha in early 1969, beginning one night when his twenty-five-year-old wife, Hana, ran screaming from her home. Neighbors rushed up to the frantic woman. Her words tumbled together as she hysterically explained that friends of Riha's were trying to kill her. There was an overpowering smell of ether on her clothes. Mrs. Riha immediately left Colorado to stay with friends in Brooklyn. Shortly before this traumatic event, Riha and Hana, married only five months, were suing each other for divorce. A week after Hana's departure, Riha, on March 15, 1969, vanished from the face of the earth. Though the professor failed to show up for classes on March 18, almost everyone he knew insisted that he was alive. "He's somewhere between Montreal and Toronto in a summer-resort sort of place," Galva Tannenbaum informed writer Champ Clark, who was looking into the disappearance some months later.

The then president of the University of Colorado, Dr. Joseph Smiley (later head of the University of Texas at El Paso) reported to inquiries that he thought Riha was "alive and well," stating that his information was based upon what "I consider reliable sources," in Washington who had sworn him to secrecy. "I repeat my real regret that I can't go beyond what I have said. A confidence is still a confidence."

When one of the professor's college colleagues talked to the Denver office of the Immigration and Naturalization Service, he was told that Riha was definitely alive. The same person contacted that office some months later and was cautiously informed that it was "better not to be interested in the Riha matter."

Galva Tannenbaum was definitely interested in Riha's estate. Only a few weeks after the professor vanished, Galva called nephew Cerveny and told him that his uncle would never return. The two met, and Galva dramatically handed Cerveny two pistols, stating matter-of-factly that she was a brigadier general in military intelligence. She then insisted that Riha's holdings be liquidated. The professor had asked her to dispose of his personal effects, she told Cerveny.

*Galva Tannenbaum, the unsteady link to the disappearance of Professor Thomas Riha from the University of Colorado in 1969.*

241

The professor's car was sold to a Denver public-school official. The signature on the auto's title assignment appeared to be Riha's. His house was then sold. Galva had all the furniture in Riha's home and his personal papers moved to her own house. Appearing to be the soul of generosity, Galva then turned over Riha's art collection, statuary valued at about $19,000, to the Denver Art Museum. She also gave away the professor's 1,000-book library to Loretto Heights College in Denver. Mrs. Tannenbaum suddenly began to receive at her Denver home all the royalties accruing from Riha's three-volume work, *Readings in Russian Civilization*, published in 1964.

Riha's lawyer became suspicious when letters arrived, allegedly written by the professor, but in a different handwriting and use of grammar. That Galva was not entitled to Riha's personal effects and furniture was made quite clear. (Mrs. Riha won her divorce settlement suit on September 30, 1969, for $5,000, but this was never paid.)

Oddly, some of Galva's closest friends began to die in ugly ways. Gustav F. Ingwerson, a Denver painter, inventor and plastics designer, died of potassium-cyanide poisoning on June 16, 1969. The seventy-eight-year-old Ingwerson left small amounts of money to his family, but his will also provided for Galva; she and her two children received through the will stock and personal possessions that included a color TV, a cuckoo clock, and a dinosaur bone. Adding more mystery to the Riha disappearance was the unexplained discovery of the professor's engraved wedding ring, which was found in Ingwerson's home.

Ingwerson's will appeared to be witnessed by none other than Zednek Cerveny; Riha's nephew later denied witnessing the document in a Denver Probate Court. (Cerveny was delinquent in reporting his uncle's disappearance, not informing the Missing Person's bureau until October 1969, almost seven months after Riha vanished.) Cerveny was later to tell a reporter from the *Rocky Mountain News* that "my uncle's body is probably somewhere in the mountains." He did not explain why he thought so.

Another close friend of Galva Tannenbaum's, Mrs. Barbara Elbert, age fifty-one, and a native of Denver, died almost three months to the day of Ingwerson's passing. Mrs. Elbert was found dead in her apartment on September 13, 1969. Cause of death was sodium-cyanide poisoning.

Although the Denver police suspected Galva of being directly involved with the Ingwerson and Elbert deaths, as well as the disappearance of Riha, there was little evidence to link her to murder. The hasty disposal of Riha's belongings however, was another matter, plus Ingwerson's questionable will. Authorities brought charges against the unpredictable Galva, charging her with forging Riha's signature and faking Ingwerson's will.

Galva went on trial and instantly pleaded not guilty by reason of insanity. A Boulder District Court took little time to find Mrs. Tannenbaum legally insane and ordered her confined at the Colorado State Hospital in Pueblo. Early in March 1971, Galva began to give away her possessions to other inmates. She then sat down and wrote a farewell letter to her lawyer, John Kokish, of Denver. In it, she told her lawyer that "it doesn't matter really, but I will tell you this. I didn't do Tom or Gus or Barb in. I went nuts with hurt over losing them. . . . Everything that has made me feel good about myself has been taken away. Life is very cheap." With that Galva Tannenbaum stretched out on her bed and swallowed a small pill, cyanide. (Where she obtained the poison was never determined.) Her suicide further confused efforts to solve the Riha disappearance.

For months after the professor vanished, hundreds of police and reporters conducted an exhausting search for his body. They trekked up mountain roads and crawled into abandoned mine shafts. One reporter from the *Denver Post*, on the supposition that Galva had murdered the professor, completely dug up Mrs. Tannenbaum's earth basement in her East Denver home. Not one hair of the professor's was found.

Even more confounding was the way in which certain federal agencies appeared to cover up the disappearance. University officials, along with Denver and Boulder police, it was reported, were dissuaded from looking for Riha after a while, having been assured by "reliable sources" in the Federal government that the professor was alive and well. Although the F.B.I., C.I.A. and the State Department all denied any involvement in the disappearance, later court documents show that an F.B.I. agent stationed in Denver instructed a C.I.A. agent to "calm this thing down. . . . Get out to the press that Riha is alive and well."

When the late J. Edgar Hoover heard of this, he demanded that the Central Intelligence Agency inform him of the identity of the F.B.I. agent. The C.I.A. refused. The *Denver Post* doggedly stayed with the case and, in 1975, at the newspaper's request, U.S. Senator Gary Hart, of Colorado, brought up the Riha case. Hart raised the question of the professor's disappearance while the Senate Select Committee on Intelligence Activities was grilling James J. Angleton, the C.I.A.'s former chief of counterintelligence and Charles Brennan, the former director of the F.B.I.'s intelligence division.

The results were astounding. The C.I.A. admitted that it had told university president Joseph Smiley that Riha was alive and well after his disappearance. Angleton then submitted a C.I.A memo that told of a "possible sighting of Riha in Czechoslovakia in 1973." C.I.A. representatives then admitted that the agency, in 1958, when Riha was an exchange student in Moscow, thought of using the professor as a spy but abandoned the idea. Both the F.B.I. and the C.I.A. flatly denied ever having anything to do with Galva Tannenbaum. The C.I.A., strangely enough, went out of its way to state that it had "no information to suggest that Riha was a Soviet agent, or for that matter, a double agent."

Senator Hart reached his own conclusions: "Riha is, most probably, living somewhere today in Eastern Europe, possibly Czechoslovakia. . . . Why he left the U.S. remains unclear."

It all seemed quite clear to Galva Tannenbaum as she lay dying on her asylum bed four years earlier. The last words from her mouth, heard by hospital authorities were of Riha. "I didn't kill him. . . . That son-of-a-bitch! He's in Russia! He just made it!"

The most frustrating of disappearances are those wherein the absentee, if returning alive, gives no explanation for vanishing and takes his reasons with him to the grave. In such off-beat cases, family, police and private investigators are left to offer their own vexing apologies or excuses. Sometimes, in such oddball disappearances, the missing person is compelled to pay a stiff price—the loss of love, or family fortune, and even legal prosecution. For the most part, it matters little to those who disappear. Their going into a void chiefly of their own making and their inexplicable visit inside the unknown are somehow either precious or hellish enough to insure a permanent silence that leaves wild speculation to provide the answers. It is this type of disappearance that is most populated, literally millions of persons drifting each year in and out of this perplexing category of the missing.

### For Singles Only

Single adults seem to be the most likely to stumble, for no apparent reason, into the limbo of the lost; their very lone existence, separated from family ties, works all too well in covering their trails and obliterating their motivations.

A sensational case of this type in 1880 left newspaper readers wondering for weeks. One day in August the Florida interisland steamer *City of Dallas* anchored in Jacksonville to pick up passengers traveling to Brunswick Bay. One of the travelers getting on board in Jacksonville was a shabbily dressed young man of about twenty-eight years of age who gave his name as Henry L. Edward.

Edward was on deck that night wearing a long linen duster and carrying a cane, which he struck upon the deck in cadence with his own steps. He spoke to one member of the crew at 10 P.M. By dawn, Henry L. Edward was gone. It was thought that he might have leaped overboard, but a half dozen officers and crew members watching every section of the ship certainly would have seen him, let alone heard the splash since the "night was clear and beautiful and the sea as smooth as glass," according to *The New York Times*. The placid ocean would also have prevented him from falling overboard. One life preserver on the wall of an outer deck was later found missing and this further confused the Edward disappearance.

Crew members inspected the young man's berth and found only a coat and a vest. Inside the vest was found a three-cent piece. The report ended on a laconic note: "The missing man appeared to be in low spirits, but as many passengers come on board the steamers in Florida in the same mood, no particular attention was paid to him."

John K. Van Arsdale, Jr., son of a prominent Texas rancher and oil man, was also a missing traveler, leaving home at the age of twenty-six, and wandering through the backwaters of Oklahoma, until he settled briefly in Fort Smith, Arkansas, in 1908. From that point, Van Arsdale permanently vanished; he was still being sought in the late 1940s as an heir to a $30,000 inheritance.

Another traveler, Albert Daniel Rounds, while in his early twenties, left Sioux Falls, South Dakota, in 1914. Rounds was the son of Charles Albert Rounds, a distinguished Washington, D.C., newspaperman. The son was heard from only once, shortly after his disappearance. His family received a postcard from Decatur, Iowa, which tersely stated: "Going farther West, will send address when I have one." That address never arrived.

Neither did that of Miss Carrie T. Selvage, a forty-three-year-old Indianapolis teacher, who vanished on March 11, 1900. At the time Miss Selvage was hospitalized for nervous tension. Twenty years later, workmen converting the hospital in which Carrie was a patient into a garage discovered in a second attic the skeleton of a woman sitting in a rocking chair. Still about the bony remains was a ragged, dark-blue flannelette wrapper and black felt house slippers. Carrie's brother identified the skeleton as that of his sister, by the clothing, but what perplexed the coroner was how and why the woman got into the rarely frequented attic. He speculated that she was either carried there for sinister reasons or "went to the place of her own accord and starved herself to death."

A year after Miss Selvage's remains were uncovered, Juanita McHargue, a preacher's daughter, vanished from her family's home in Dunkirk, New York. The twenty-one-year-old stenographer left the McHargue residence in June 1921 and was the subject of a massive police search for four years. She suddenly popped up in

April 1925 in the New York City home of her brother, William R. McHargue. Juanita would give no reason for her disappearance except to tell reporters that she was "experimenting with independence."

For James Kelly, son of a wealthy plantation owner, a visit to his father proved to be a path into oblivion. Kelly's fortunes were the reverse of his father's; he lost one investment after another, steadily going broke. By the time he was forty, James Kelly had even lost the girl he wanted to marry. On July 19, 1927, Kelly left his home in Dallas, Texas, intent on visiting his father, who lived in Terrell, a distance of fifty-five miles. He never arrived and remained missing, leaving an unclaimed estate of $19,000.

Money also seemed to matter little to Philip T. Van Biber, a thirty-eight-year-old bachelor, described by his banker father as "an electrical genius." Van Biber, whose average income was more than $30,000 when he disappeared on September 18, 1930, walked away from every known relative and friend in the streets of Newark, New Jersey. Van Biber was scheduled to call on several Newark jewelers to arrange for installations of security systems; the man left his home without his wallet or a dime in his pockets.

As the dark years of the Depression deepened, hundreds, then thousands vanished, single men and women homeless on the roads, deserting farms that had turned to dead land during the great dust storms, losing jobs as factories and businesses by the score failed each day.

Those who had been in the ranks of the missing for years before the Depression caused little stir when they were identified. Julia Napier of the Bronx was typical. The forty-year-old divorced woman had been lost to relatives and friends for a decade until she was found dead in a furnished room, the cause of her demise listed as "poisoned alcohol." When police finally did unearth a Napier relative, a well-to-do contractor in New Jersey, the uncle merely stated, perhaps giving some insight as to why Julia disappeared: "Bury her in Potter's Field. Even that is too good for her."

One man, John Kachnycz, of Pittsburgh, was buried before his time, a strange situation that the courts refused to alter, a typical indifference of the conscienceless era of the 1930s. Kachnycz, who left home in 1929 for no apparent reason, was officially recorded as "dead" after a friend identified the picture of a man killed in a brawl as Kachnycz. One of those in the donnybrook was tried for murdering Kachnycz and was acquitted. The missing man turned up in 1936, embarrassing neighbors, who had collected benefits under insurance policies on Kachnycz's life. He attempted to find the man tried for "murdering" him but that man had vanished, too. Kachnycz then went to the courts to prove that he was still alive. Legal technicalities were so involved that Kachnycz gave up and once more left Pittsburgh, never to be seen again. So far as court records were concerned, the man remained "dead."

James Sarsfield liked vacations and traveled for two weeks with pay from his plumbing job in Normal, Illinois, every year since 1915. The Depression ruined most of Sarsfield's holidays. He had lost not only his own life savings in an investment house that collapsed during the crash, but also that of his friends, who had deposited their money with the bankrupt firm at his suggestion. Sarsfield thought of himself as jinxed; two of his fiancées had died only weeks before the date set for their marriage. His brother and sister-in-law both died in 1933. "My next vacation" the life-weary plumber said to friend John Grifford, "will be the longest on record." Sarsfield took the train to New York, where, on August 18, 1939, he vanished. Sarsfield's last gesture was to send his friend John Grifford a souvenir cigar from the World's Fair mailing office.

Fred Strow of New York City had no one, positively no one in the world, to whom he could send cigars. He died in a squalid room on Bedford Street in 1940, and police prepared to bury Strow in a pauper's grave. As officers searched his room for any trace of known relatives they uncovered, hidden in tin cans and cigar boxes, five bankbooks showing large deposits in New York banks, as well as mortgage certificates on large buildings around Washington Square. Said Strow's indignant landlady: "We never knew he had money. He had no friends and no one ever came to see him. . . . Why, people in the house used to give him food." Strow had apparently been missing from his native town in Germany for more than forty years.

No one cared if the lonely old bachelor Strow was alive or dead. Since the miser had few acquaintances, there was little discussion over his passing. There was no concern whatever when the lone-living Dr. Bernard M. Bueche, one of the leaders of the town of Spotswood, New Jersey, vanished into thin air on July 14, 1964, even though the doctor had established the most thought-provoking building ever seen in Spotswood, a bizarre structure that gave the town a national, albeit absurd, identity.

Dr. Bueche appeared from nowhere in 1955. It was known that he was a graduate of the University of Michigan Medical School and had taken his residency in New York City. He quickly built up the most successful practice in the town, mainly because of his willingness to make house calls. Single, brooding, Dr. Bueche was seen often wandering the fields about Spotswood, his flaming red hair escaping from the edges of an atrocious coonskin cap. He seldom spoke; he talked to his many patients only when necessary.

With the blossoming funds from his practice, Dr. Bueche decided that he wanted to build a hospital. He went to architect Robert O'Neill and asked him to draw up plans for a twenty-room clinic. O'Neill, thinking the doctor was joking, thought to humor him by putting together a whimsical structure on paper, a rambling building on stilts. To the architect's surprise, Dr. Bueche fell in love with the plans, turning over a bag of money and ordering O'Neill to go ahead with the building.

The blue-paneled monstrosity, decorated in plastic, was completed in 1959, and Dr. Bueche moved into it, having his office and living quarters in the same building. Two more doctors and a dentist joined him. Five years later, in July 1964, Dr. Bueche went to the dentist and said he would be away for some hours. He took nothing with him. Dr. Bueche never returned. He left behind all his medical equipment, his car, his personal belongings, and money, plus the most exotic building in Spotswood, or most any other town for that matter.

The town offices and police department finally occupied the $250,-000 "white elephant," but Dr. Bueche never saw the Spotswood officials move in, despite the fact that the F.B.I. conducted a nationwide search for him. He is missing to this day. Spotswood residents reacted to Dr. Bueche's disappearance as they had to his dream building, Mayor Donald Brundage summing up the town's attitude with: "Why should anyone care about Dr. Bueche?"

*Wandering Wives*

Disappearing wives, as compared to husbands, have historically been in the minority. For no reason, both low-income housewives and society matrons drift off, their stays in limbo either usually brief or for great periods of time. Mrs. Ella Berentsen was a good example of the short-take disappearance. Wife of a wealthy executive in Mount Vernon, New York, Mrs. Berentsen suddenly got out of bed on the night of January 15, 1921, at 9:30 P.M. Her maid watched her quickly leave her mansion wearing a brown velvet evening gown trimmed with white lace, a white wool sweater, a sealskin coat trimmed with beaver, and a large hat. Mrs. Berentsen was absent for only three days.

She was reported being on a Manhattan subway train. One person answering the statewide alert that had been sent out, insisted that Mrs. Berentsen was aboard the ferry to Weehawken. Richard R. Berentsen found his wife through an employee working at Manhattan's Hotel Lucerne, where she was staying. She had paid for her room with a diamond bracelet and refused to tell either her husband or police the reason for her disappearance.

Mrs. John Torrance, of Pasadena, accompanied her husband on a vacation to La Jolla, California, in 1925. After the couple checked into their hotel, John Torrance went to the reading room. When he returned to his suite his wife was absent. For two weeks California police combed the state. On February 11, Mrs. Torrance's body was found floating in the kelp beds off La Jolla. There was no sign of foul play. Her husband was both stunned and perplexed; his wife never went bathing, because she could not swim.

Mrs. Anna Fellows' repeated disappearances were equally mystifying. In 1926 reporters in Cambridge, Massachusetts, came across seventy-year-old William B. Fellows, who had been searching for his wife for twenty-three years. He had married Anna Moran in 1876. Anna left home after three years of apparent wedded bliss. More than twenty years later, Fellows recalled, he returned home one day to find her in the kitchen making dinner. She offered no explanation for her disappearance and Fellows, a very understanding type, asked for none. Anna lived contentedly with Fellows for another three years and then, in 1903, she vanished again. He was never to find her.

William D. Foley also thought his life with his spouse Mamie McCann Foley was a happy one and could never puzzle out why she vanished with their infant son, David, in 1915. After waiting twelve years, Foley asked a Jersey City court to declare her dead. Just at the hour the court was about to make such a decision, on November 6, 1927, while Foley was away on business in Canada, Mamie Mc-Cann Foley and her thirteen-year-old son David arrived in court to prove they were still very much alive. Mrs. Foley informed the court that she and her son were living in Hoboken, but she refused to give her address or the reason why she had vanished a decade earlier. The woman, her son in tow, then marched out of the courtroom and back into her inexplicable vacuum.

A case that still baffles the literary set today involved Barbara Newhall Follett, a poet and novelist, who left her husband and Brookline, Massachusetts, home without a word on December 7, 1939. She never returned, and no trace of her was ever discovered even though her father, Wilson Follett, a famous critic, appealed to her and the readers of the *Atlantic* for her safe return in a moving open letter. "A scheme of things in which I do not know where you are," wrote Follett, "do not know probably *that* you are—it changes, I assure you, the shape of my sky."

But even such eloquent appeals went totally unanswered. Her mother and a psychologist speculated in a later work, that Barbara had returned to the Maine woods she loved so much and which filled the pages of her books, and that there she perished in the snow and was permanently shrouded from human view by a kind wilderness.

What stirred and prompted Barbara Follett may have been the catalyst for the disappearance of Mrs. Gertrude Jones more than two decades later. On a bright Sunday morning, May 10, 1964, Mrs. Jones stepped around her husband Bruce, who was repairing the front stairs of their home in Tamalpais Valley, California. She mumbled an almost incoherent "goodbye" and set off walking down the road, carrying a handbag that contained about $30, her husband's will, and her birth certificate. A neighbor returning from church stopped his car and asked Mrs. Jones if she wanted a lift. She refused to look in his direction, uttered not a word, and kept walking, a stroll into emptiness that has not been explained to this day.

### Husbands Who Hurried Away

One of the more famous of early-day missing husbands was a wealthy London baker elegantly named Urban Napoleon Stanger, whose strange disappearance still remains a mystery. Stanger, a native of Kreuznach, Germany, moved to London with his young wife, Elizabeth, in 1871, establishing a bakery in Lever Street in Whitechapel, the same area that was to be terrorized by Jack the Ripper some years later. The hard-working Stanger prospered and appeared happy, even though his thirty-five-year-old wife, according to rumormongers, was carrying on an affair with the baker's young assistant, Franz Felix Stumm.

On the night of November 12, 1881, Christian Zentler, a neighbor, was passing the Stanger bakeshop shortly before midnight. He saw the baker talking with Stumm and two other men. Stanger then abruptly entered his shop and turned off the gaslights while the three men walked off. It was the last ever seen of Urban Napoleon Stanger.

Some days later Stumm moved permanently into the Stanger household, living openly with Mrs. Stanger and wearing the baker's clothing. As the months passed Stumm took complete control of Stanger's affairs and finally took over the shop, changing the proprietor's name to his own. Although such unexplained activities aroused suspicion of neighbors and police alike, no investigation was made.

In April 1882, Mrs. Stanger's lawyer, Wendel Scherer, placed an advertisement in all the newspapers and had thousands of handbills posted announcing a reward of fifty pounds for information leading to Napoleon Stanger's discovery.

There was no response. Stanger's close-mouthed wife briefly told inquiring constables that her husband had gone to bed with her on the night of November 12–13, 1881, jumped from the covers at 1:30

A.M. and left his home and shop without a word. His replacement, Stumm, grumbled that the master baker had "gone back to Germany," and that he was "heavily in debt." Stumm made no bones about the fact that Stanger had been in debt to him, that Stumm had been financing the money-foolish Stanger for years.

It was then discovered that there was more than 300 pounds still in Stanger's bank account, that the baker had no creditors, and that the baker had left behind all his personal belongings and valuables when he vanished. Further refuting Stumm's claims in the summer of 1882 was a legal action in which John George Geisel and William Evans, Stanger's attorney, charged Stumm had forged checks with Elizabeth Stanger in an attempt to defraud the baker's estate.

Stumm went on trial and was convicted of the forgery; he was stoic about the ten-year prison sentence handed down to him by Judge Hawkins, smiling at the justice from the dock and remarking sarcastically: "Thank you. I am much obliged to you."

Mrs. Stanger argued for Stumm's release but was unsuccessful. Never placed on trial herself, Elizabeth Stanger returned to the bakery to live out her life. Many concluded that she and Stumm had killed the baker and destroyed his body in one of his own ovens. This, however, remained gossip. And Napoleon Stanger remained missing.

Stories of sudden disappearances of husbands apparently happy in their married lives fill endless columns of newspapers around the world. Magazines, books, handbills, reports by the thousands detail the abrupt departures of these men and in their wake wives and children are left in shock, bewilderment and eventual despair of ever seeing the men again.

Charles E. Austin, a businessman in Yonkers, came home to take a bath on March 28, 1905. An hour later Austin said to his wife: "I'm going out for a moment. Be back shortly. Keep supper for me." He never returned. James J. Judge, a Bronx policeman in full uniform, left his large family on December 2, 1910, and vanished as he turned a corner. John McHugh, a Manhattan streetcleaner, went to work on August 13, 1913, kissing his blind wife goodbye, never to return, even leaving his week's pay uncollected.

Wives who are victimized by their husbands' unexplained disappearances are engulfed by strange reactions, from incomprehensible despondency to utter wrath. When Fred R. Howard, a master plumber in East Orange, New Jersey, left his home with a pair of overalls under his arm on his way to a job, his wife Minnie went shopping for their dinner. After waiting two years for Howard to return, Minnie sat down and wrote: "Being tired of the lonely, anxious waiting and unable to endure it any longer. I am going away, God knows where." Minnie, duplicating her husband's actions, then promptly disappeared forever.

Jacob and Sarah Bowers were in their sixties, living out comfortable lives in Brooklyn on a pension when, in 1910, Jacob went out for a cigar. Sarah waited eighteen years for him. At age seventy-eight she was pushed into a courtroom in a wheelchair to demand that her marriage be annulled—which it was. William and Charlotte Whitehall, also of Brooklyn, had been married since 1899. Whitehall left home in 1908, but continued to see his wife, supporting her and his children until 1913, when he completely vanished. Mrs. Whitehall waited until 1922 before going to court to have her marriage dissolved. Just as the matter was to be decided, William Whitehall marched into court and politely asked: "Is this case on?"

Sarah Whitehall and her married daughter almost collapsed from the sight of Whitehall, thinking him dead. The reunited family suddenly stood up and walked out of the courtroom together, leaving the judge to stammer: "This is the end of this proceeding."

Queens resident Sydney Denning said little about his wife's avid animal collection over the many years of their marriage. Denning once computed his wife's pet menagerie as being 28 dogs, 16 cats, 43 pigeons and numerous chickens and geese waddling underfoot. One day in 1923, Denning made room for more animals by disappearing. He returned three years later to the front door of his home late at night. Failing to get inside, Denning sat down on the front steps and waited. A passing neighbor recognized him and told Denning his wife was in jail. She was charged with fraud, the neighbor explained, having identified a corpse found in an outhouse as that of her husband and collecting $10,000 in life-insurance money from Prudential and Mutual life insurance companies. Denning began to laugh so uproariously that he went into convulsions and a doctor had to be called to quiet him. The missing husband's roaring guffaws aroused the army of pets inside his house who began a din of barking, meowing, squawks and squeeks that could be heard for blocks. Denning then promptly disappeared one more, and final time.

Some women will not give up on missing husbands. When Chicagoan Harry N. Lanning, a supervisor for the Container Corporation of America, vanished on February 14, 1947, his wife immediately offered a large reward for information leading to his discovery. She placed advertisements describing Lanning in newspapers across the country and had hundreds of thousands of wanted posters distributed in every major city in the United States. A bartender in Queens, New York, who had received one of Mrs. Lanning's posters only days before, recognized the missing husband on the night of February 16, 1949, and tipped off police. Lanning,

*Absentee Harry Lanning of Chicago in 1949 with his wife Elsie, who spent a fortune to track him down in New York where he was working as a dishwasher under an alias.* (UPI)

255

who gave his name as Harry Manders, was arrested on a trumped-up charge of forgery until Mrs. Lanning could be contacted. Some days later Mrs. Lanning arrived in New York and identified her husband, who admitted his true identity. "I never had amnesia," he said, but was "at a loss" to explain his disappearance. He returned with his wife to Chicago.

The same kind of determination to find her missing husband was evidenced by Marianne Hanno, of East Hills, Long Island, after her husband, Lewis H. Hanno, who owned a string of lucrative repair shops, utterly vanished on January 16, 1956. Mrs. Hanno placed an ad in the personal columns of the New York newspapers which read: "Lewis H. Come home or contact us. Everything will be all right. Children crying. Your loving wife."

Hanno, who had abandoned his expensive car on board the Staten Island Ferry, read the notice and called his wife. He was in Fort Worth, Texas. The couple and their children relocated in Dallas, Texas, where Hanno worked in real estate. His wife, expecting their third child, received a call from Hanno on February 5, 1959. He was in Phoenix on business. After their short chat, the onetime New York shopkeeper and Dallas real-estate broker, again vanished.


### Going Together

Wives and husbands disappearing together for no apparent reason are rare occurrences. One of the most sensational of such cases involved Mr. and Mrs. Andrew Toth, of Manhattan, who completely vanished on August 16, 1943, in a mysterious walk to the grocer's, a disappearance that still has N.Y.P.D.'s Bureau of Missing Persons wondering. Toth, a Hungarian house painter by trade, was distrustful of banks. Both he and his wife Elizabeth worked and were known to be frugal savers; gossiping neighbors believed that the Toths carried as much as $5,000 on their persons at all times. This may have been a reason for the double disappearance. Toth was also a violent anti-Nazi who would boldly storm into the drinking spas in Yorkville to publicly denounce Adolf Hitler, a tactic that did not endear him to the populous German community there. He

*Elizabeth and Andrew Toth, whose mysterious 1943 disappearance in Manhattan was never solved. (UPI)*

and his wife, who shared Toth's political views, may have been killed by pro-Nazis, police theorized.

That the Toths vanished willingly was easily refuted. All their personal belongings remained in their apartment at 318 East Seventy-eighth Street, along with a refrigerator full of food (something that would certainly upset the left-over-saving Mrs. Toth), along with a small bank account of $372. Also left behind was Toth's eight-year-old daughter Margaret by a former marriage, who was kept in a Catholic home for children. Toth was a doting father; he had been to see his daughter only a day before he and his twenty-nine-year-old wife disappeared. If the Toths were murder victims, there was not a shred of evidence to prove such a crime. Such victims, remarked N.Y.P.D. Captain John G. Stein, "have been killed for a lot less [than the alleged $5,000], but their bodies rarely stay hidden very long . . . somebody went to a lot of trouble to do a perfect job on this pair." But murder was never proven, and the bodies of the Toths were never unearthed.

257

The 1970 disappearance of Mr. and Mrs. Edward P. Andrews, of Arlington Heights, Illinois, has equally baffled Chicago area police. Andrews and his wife, Stephania, both sixty-three years of age, had been married for six years. Andrews, a semiretired bookkeeper, had been married four times previously, and his wife, a credit investigator, had been married once before, twenty years prior to her marriage to Andrews. The couple's employers described them as hard-working and trustworthy. They dressed in high fashion, and were not heavy drinkers.

In the evening of May 15, 1970, the Andrewses attended a cocktail party given by the Chicago chapter of the Women's Association of the Allied Beverage Industries, receiving tickets from a friend. The affair, held in the Chicago Sheraton Hotel, ended at 9:30 P.M. The Andrewses were seen to leave the hotel's garage at that time. Persons attending the party later stated that Andrews seemed to be ill, complaining that he was hungry, after having only canapes to chew on during the party. Mrs. Andrews appeared to be crying by the time the couple reached their black-and-yellow 1969 Oldsmobile, which was parked in the underground garage of the hotel.

The garage attendant saw the couple drive away on lower Michigan Avenue, going south on the underpass toward the Michigan Avenue bridge that spans the Chicago River. It was a drive into a very dead end. The childless pair were never seen again. Their Arlington Heights house, their extensive bank accounts, their stocks and bonds (and fourteen credit cards), had not been touched and remain intact to this day.

What happened to the Andrewses? The police in their original probe into the mystery speculated that Andrews, sick at the wheel of his car, may have lost control and somehow plunged the auto into the Chicago River. The river was dragged and sounded by experts using a special boat with electronic equipment. The search was fruitless, and the couple remain missing.

### The Very Young

Countless children run away each year seeking adventure, riches, and the wide, wide world they suspect awaits them with thrills and laughter. Most have their reasons for departing à la Huck Finn. Most return home in a few days, or invariably contact parents and friends to inform them of their safety and location. Sometimes the authorities perform that task for the runaways with expected adult annoyance. Few children completely vanish without motive.

John Patterson, a fourteen-year-old boy in Albany, New York, was one of these, disappearing on September 1, 1873, while running an errand for his mother. The youth was anything but capricious, without a bone of wanderlust in his body. Devoted to his mother, young Patterson was a homebody who found his delights and entertainment in books, yet he vanished without a trace. His mother offered a $500 reward for information leading to his discovery, but never heard a word about him. She spent several years haunting morgues and viewing bodies of youths drowned in a tragic and senseless search for her boy.

When seven-year-old Warren McCarrick, of Philadelphia, vanished on March 12, 1914, police first feared that he had been kidnapped. The son of a city employee, Warren simply walked away from his home. His parents offered $6,000 for his return, but no information was received. Not until June 16 was the McCarrick boy again seen, this time floating dead in the Delaware River. How the lad wound up in a river three months after he disappeared was a question that stumped police officials. One fantastic theory had it that the boy had fallen into a sewer and was carried down the Schuylkill River, which transported him to League Island, and from there his body was washed into the Delaware, but many experts stated that it would not take three months for a body to float that distance. Another theory insisted that a "German farmer," who had written to Warren's father that he had slain the boy, had buried Warren in a shallow grave and dug up the body in early June and tossed it into the Delaware. In the end, the reasons for the boy's disappearance and death were still unclear.

The explanation that Charles Romer, a Brooklyn resident, gave for the repeated disappearances of his daughter Mary was even more impossible. Mary, age fifteen, was picked up by police as a vagrant in Jamaica, New York, on August 21, 1921. She gave her name as Ellen Collins and insisted that she was seventeen years old. She was placed in a jail cell. After she had been identified from

**259**

newspaper photos, Charles Romer was asked to pick her up. Romer arrived and not until he confronted his daughter did she admit her true identity. Mary Romer refused to explain why she vanished on this and other occasions. "It's all right," her father told newsmen. "Mary always runs away in August . . . when the moon is full."

Another fifteen-year-old, Isabel Bennett, who was President Warren Harding's second cousin, ran away from her posh Manhattan home on the ominous Friday the thirteenth in November 1925. Her mother, Mrs. Frank Bent (she had remarried, after divorcing Harding's first cousin, John B. Bennett), told police that she thought her child had been kidnapped. A nine-state alert went out, and Isabel was quickly picked up in Norfolk, Virginia. She had run away with her friend Sara Cohn, but when asked why she had disappeared, the girl only blurted out, "I don't know; it was for no reason at all."

It was the same story with sixteen-year-old Irving Schiff, who vanished from his home in North Bergen, New Jersey, in 1924. He was discovered a year later in New Orleans as a member of a traveling band. The youth did not give any reason for his sudden departure. The New Orleans Chief of Police ventured his own opinion: "The lad was lured from his home by jazz, plain and simple."

The fate of even smaller, younger children who disappear is ever perplexing searchers. They seem to toddle into another world as did LaVern Enget and Steven Damman. The four-year-old Enget boy went out to the pasture to help his farmer father bring in the cows one evening in October 1954 and did not return. First neighbors helped the Engets, whose farm was near Powers Lake, North Dakota, to search the fields. The search intensified daily until three thousand persons, forming a human chain, moved across every inch of the Enget place. Two helicopters and forty-two light planes circled above the area. Specially trained dogs, some sent by the Canadian Mounties, picked up the little boy's scent several times, but it either faded out or trailed back to the house. In the end he was gone.

On October 31, 1955, Mrs. Marilyn Damman stepped into a supermarket near Mitchel Field, Long Island, leaving her three-year-old son Steven on the street. Ten minutes later she emerged with her groceries to find the boy nowhere in sight. Again a massive search ensued with more than one thousand persons, most of them airmen, combing the area, but the blond-haired, blue-eyed Steven was not sighted. And soon, he too was gone.

## Scholars Slipping Away

Disappearing students form another, albeit smaller, contingent of the lost whose reasons for vanishing are vague or nonexistent. The first of the famous cases in this dark arena occurred on March 15, 1907. Albion Davis Pike, twenty-one years old, of Lubec, Maine, quietly walked off the Harvard campus into nothingness. To quote a report of that day: "The disappearance of a handsome, young man, dressed in the height of fashion, is one of the least probable things in police annals, but that is just what he did. He did not smoke, drink or associate with dissolute characters." He also did not return, ever.

*Steven Damman, whose mother lost him forever at a Long Island shopping center in 1955.*

A brilliant high-school student, Harold Frank, was on his way to an Eastern college in 1919 from Denver, Colorado. He was not seen again. Ben W. Kimble, a student at Rice Institute at Houston, Texas, left abruptly in the middle of his sophomore year in 1922. His brother Abe received a wire from Ben, who was in Los Angeles, telling Abe to meet him in El Paso and that he was sending his clothes along. The clothes arrived, but Kimble never did. On November 13, 1925, Alice M. Corbett, of Utica, New York, a Smith College junior, left her Northampton, Massachusetts, dormitory and completely vanished.

The most celebrated case of missing students in this century was that of Richard Colvin Cox, a sophomore cadet at West Point, who vanished inside the Academy grounds on the evening of January 14, 1950.

The Point was not and is not an easy school from which to escape, its schedules for each student tightly adhered to and guarded. Almost every waking moment of a cadet's life, Cox's included, is controlled by a system of checkpoints, of signing in and out for specific

*Richard Colvin Cox, a West Point cadet, disappeared on the Academy's ground in January, 1950. (UPI)*

day-to-day, hour-to-hour destinations. Authorities at the Point always know where their cadets are—or almost always.

Cox was certainly not a student expected to take liberties with the ultraconservative and militaristic system at the Point. Born and raised in Mansfield, Ohio, Cox was an excellent high-school student, graduating with honors and dreaming mightily of someday entering West Point. He enlisted in the Army in 1946 and was eventually assigned to duty with the 27th Constabulary Squadron stationed in Germany. Through hard work and top-rated performance, Cox rose to the rank of sergeant. His superiors granted his deepest wish when they recommended him for the competitive Army examinations for West Point. His grade was superior. Ironically, Cox's mother had, almost at the same moment, secured an appointment for him through the recommendation of an Ohio Congressman.

The hope of a lifetime came true in June 1948, when Cox entered the Point. For two years he stood in the top third of his class, displaying exceptional perception in military science. He also proved to be an excellent athlete, joining the track team and becoming one of the Point's best long-distance runners. Cox had no known bad habits, and the only company he kept outside of his fellow classmates was that of family members and his pretty girl friend, Betty Timmons, whom he planned to marry at the Point upon graduation. There was nothing but harmony and success in the life of the twenty-two-year-old Cox until early in 1950.

On January 7, Cadet Peter Hains, Charge of Quarters, B Company, took a phone call from a man who asked: "Do you have a Dick Cox in your company?" When Hains replied in the affirmative, the man requested that Hains inform Cox that "George, who served with him in Germany, is here." Hains *thought* the man said his name was George. Cox never referred to this visitor by any name, calling him simply "that man" or "my friend."

When Hains first informed Cox of his visitor, the cadet seemed puzzled, commenting, "I have no idea who that could be." Cox did recognize the visitor at 5:30 P.M. when he met him in Grant Hall, a cavernous beam-ceilinged place that was used for guests. Officer of the Guard in the hall, Cadet Mauro Maresca, was the only person other than Cox to get a good look at "George." He was just short of six feet, weighed about 185 pounds, had fair hair and a light complexion. He was hatless and wore a trenchcoat. "Cox and the visitor shook hands," Maresca later told curious investigators from C.I.D. "They seemed glad to see each other. After a few minutes they walked to the coat rack and while Cox was putting on his coat the visitor kidded Cox about how he looked in his uniform."

The cadet and his guest left the hall to go to dinner, ostensibly the Hotel Thayer, which was just inside the south gate of the Academy, the only available dining spot outside the cadets' mess hall. Cox returned by 7 P.M. He apparently had been drinking, because he fell asleep over his study books. (Cox was not a drinker; three drinks were his limit and would cause him to fall asleep.) As a practical joke, Cox's roommates, Joseph J. Urschel and Deane E. Welch, decided to take the sleeping cadet's picture when tattoo sounded at 9 P.M. At the shrill noise, Cox suddenly woke up. Welch took his picture, which was to be a precious discovery for investigators, taken as it was almost on the eve of one of the most mysterious disappearances in modern times.

Cox was so startled by the sound of tattoo that he leaped up and ran into the hallway, shouting something that sounded like "Alice!" He may have shouted *Alles kaput* ("All is ended"). His roommates were not sure.

"Who the hell is Alice?" asked Welch.

Cox did not answer but went to his neatly rolled up mattress and bedding, turning it down and falling on it without bothering to undress or crawl between the sheets. In the morning, before breakfast, Richard Cox talked about his strange visitor with Welch and Urschel, telling them: "This guy I saw last night was in my outfit in Germany. He'd been a Ranger before that. We weren't close friends. Kind of a morbid guy, too. He'd had a few drinks last night —he wouldn't let me out of the car until I had some, too—and he was boasting how during the fighting as a Ranger he had slashed and emasculated some of the Germans he killed. He'd also lived with a girl in Germany, got her pregnant and then hanged her."

The routine life Cox led at the Academy did not alter in the ensuing weeks. He maintained good grades and seemed to have no fears or apprehensions, although he did remark that he hoped "he wouldn't have to see that fellow again." But Cox did see the fellow again, about 5 P.M. on January 14, a Saturday, meeting "George" at the east sally port of his barracks. About an hour later, Cox was in his room, telling Welch that he was having dinner again with "George" even though he didn't like the visitor who was ruining his study hours and was "eccentric," to say the least.

"He didn't act apprehensive," Welch remembered, "just sort of disgusted. I guess he just figured it was an excuse to get out to eat at the hotel." Welch looked back at his roommate Cox to see him pensively buttoning up his long, gray overcoat as he stood in the alcove next to his bed. It was 6:18 P.M., according to Welch, who looked at his watch before leaving the room. Cox, Welch remembered, "looked kind of lackadaisical." It was the last anyone ever saw of Cadet Richard Colvin Cox. Although he had signed out for a "DP" (dinner privilege) an hour before Welch saw him last, no one remembered seeing the cadet leave the barracks, let alone walk toward the Hotel Thayer. That he met "George" for dinner was never determined; there was no record of Cox dining at the Hotel Thayer. He was not seen by the sentries guarding the gate, nor was there any record of anyone like "George" driving out of the Academy's limits.

Although Cox did not return by the regular hour of 11 P.M., some leniency was exercised on a Saturday night, and the duty officer overlooked the matter. When Urschel and Welch awoke the following morning and noticed that Cox still had not returned to his bed, they informed the tactical officer. The New York State Police were called in and a thirteen-state alarm was sent out. The C.I.D. immediately entered the case. Public appeals for information on Cox were widely spread three days later.

Every cellar and attic, every building on the post, as well as the entire grounds of the Point, were searched by dozens of regular soldiers. Helicopters whirred over the area day and night. Delafield Pond was completely drained in a two-week operation. Still no trace of the missing cadet was found. The biggest dragnet in West Point history went on for two months, but Cox remained the only cadet at the Academy ever to disappear permanently.

For years, reports of seeing Cox in hotel lobbies from Maine to New Mexico, in a Brooklyn swimming pool, in an Atlanta bus terminal, flowed into the C.I.D. A record 1,500 leads were checked and found bogus. A widely printed photo of a Sergeant Cox, appearing

*Soldiers searching the grounds of West Point for Richard Cox.* (UPI)

in December 1950, serving in Korea and holding up frozen under-wear, caused officials to investigate the battle zones. The soldier's fingerprints were checked, but he was the wrong Cox.

An equally industrious search for the mysterious "George" was conducted, C.I.D. checking back through the years in the muster rolls of Ranger battalions. He, like the famous missing cadet, was never found. The C.I.D. has never closed the Cox case, and the cadet is still listed as AWOL.

Cox was a strong young man, "hard and lean," according to West Pointers, and it is doubtful whether "George" easily overpowered the cadet. But for what purpose? Kidnapping for money? Cox had little cash, and his family was not wealthy. One theory had it that "George" did kidnap Cox and has kept him a prisoner ever since out of some sort of warped envy of Cox's role as a cadet, an idea too fantastic for belief. Whatever, many believe still that "George did it," whoever "George" was.

*The Impish Impresario*

Of all the confused, mystifying cases of persons who vanished for no reason at all, from countesses to clerks, from tycoons to tots, the cream of this missing crop boils down to an extravagant creature named Ambrose J. Small, entertainment impresario extraordinary, whose vanishing act on December 2, 1919, created one of the greatest sensations in Canadian history. The raffish, roguish Small, without a doubt, would have had it no other way.

Small, born in 1863, was introduced to hard work at age thirteen, working as a dishwasher in Toronto's Warden Hotel, a modest enterprise managed by his father, Daniel. In early manhood Small's uncanny ability to manage the hotel's bar and handle the bookings of minor acts determined his life's work. On the side he took a job as an usher at the Grand Theater and quickly moved up to the posts of assistant manager and booking manager. His taste ran to the florid and spicy melodramas of the day; he never hesitated to sign up pedestrian successes such as *Bertha the Sewing-Machine Girl* and *School for Scandal.*

As Ambrose Small prospered he began to buy interests in small theaters in and about Toronto. His real ambition was to own the Grand Opera House, but his offers were several times refused—which made Small, a towering egotist, all the more dedicated to possessing the building.

Racing became a passion for Small when he was in his thirties. He bet large sums and was considered a plunger who took great risks in making his wagers. He scooped up $10,000 in one race that was said to have been fixed, and further, he was said to have been the jocular fellow who fixed it. His reputation in gambling circles was less than sterling. Said his biographer Fred McClement: "Ambrose was building around himself an envelope of hate and distrust."

Small's reputation with women, especially the leggy chorus girls working in the local theaters, was that of an expansive, fun-loving wencher. He was not unattractive, standing five feet, six inches, and having bright-blue eyes and a luxuriant walrus mustache, which he wore at the time of his fabulous disappearance. To everyone's surprise, the womanizing Small, just before his fortieth birthday, suddenly married Teresa Small, wealthy heiress to a brewery fortune. Perhaps it was no surprise when Small began to purchase theaters by the droves, using Teresa's money and booking the biggest-named talent available into his theaters.

A great fortune began to accumulate for Ambrose Small, and he finally realized his dream by purchasing the Grand Opera House. Inside a few years, the building theatrical magnate grew weary of his marriage and began to resume his reckless gambling, but winning just as heavily as he wagered. He returned to his wenching, ordering a special secret room to be constructed adjoining his offices in the Grand Opera House. Inside this small room were heavy drapes to muffle sounds, a deep Oriental carpet, a well-stocked bar, and one of the most exquisite beds in the city of Toronto, a bed fitted with satin sheets and pillows. To this room Small took many a beautiful courtesan, but not his long-standing mistress, Clara Smith, who was horrified years later to discover the existence of the secret room; she and Small, she insisted, trysted only in her apartment.

Though he soon became a millionaire, Small was a much-hated man. He made his own prejudices well known to even total strangers, pointing out that he disliked children (he was impotent), wanted nothing to do with Catholics, and to give anything away, even to legitimate charities, he thought foolish.

As a gambler, the theater mogul grew more and more daring, but his winnings incredibly mounted. Small kept informed of the doings of every racetrack in the United States by avidly reading *The New York Times*. He was more interested in his wagers than in his business, consistently tardy for any appointment dealing with his theatrical empire, which now included almost every theater in Eastern Canada. The impresario secretly enjoyed keeping people waiting. He would purposely stroll through the most expensive shopping areas while business associates twiddled thumbs in expectation of his arrival. On one occasion he dallied before an important appointment to buy a $9,000 car and a $10,000 pearl necklace for his wife; he literally spent his way to work each day. Small always paid by check and never carried money, a policy carried through from his youth, when many a mugger waited on dark streets to waylay and rob nocturnal businessmen such as himself.

The high life Small wallowed in began to take its toll. His hair began to gray and recede, his complexion became reddish with tiny veins exploding in his cheeks and nose, apparently a result of prodigious drinking. It was about this time that Small employed a private secretary named John Doughty, a slippery, conniving fellow who knew most of his employer's dark habits and had some startling secrets of his own. His actions were more than suspect in the last month of 1919.

For several months during that year Ambrose and Teresa Small had been negotiating the sale of the Small chain with a British-owned firm, Trans-Canada Theaters Limited. The business deal was finally concluded on December 2, 1919. The Smalls received a check for $1 million, with an additional $700,000 to be paid to them in annual installments over the next five years. Ambrose concluded the meeting by lighting a cigar and endorsing the check. His wife, Teresa, also endorsed the check and deposited it in the Dominion Bank at 11:45 A.M., a deposit that raised the eyebrows of every teller present. That afternoon, Small told his lawyer, E. W. M. Flock, that he was going to inform his loyal secretary Doughty that he had not only been retained as secretary and booking manager by the new firm but that his salary would be increased.

Flock saw the millionaire later that evening, at 5:30 P.M. Small was in a jubilant mood, slapping his lawyer on the back and offering him a cigar to celebrate the sale of his chain. The lawyer declined (he did not smoke) and then bolted through the glass door of the Grand Opera building's foyer to catch a train. He turned for a moment and saw through the swirling snow the happy Small waving to him. Minutes later Small, bundled against the rising storm, braved his way through the biting snow to the corner of Adelaide and Yonge, going to the newsstand operated by Ralph Savein. He wanted his copy of *The New York Times* to check the racing results. Small was habitually the first person to buy the paper, which was delivered each day by train. On this day, Tuesday, it was due to arrive sharp at 5:30 P.M. But the train did not arrive; it was delayed by a monster snow storm in New York.

Ambrose Small swore. "I never heard him curse like that before," Savein later told an investigator. "He stormed away in an ugly mood, I can tell you."

As the magnate pushed his 140-pound frame against the blasting wind and snows, the newsdealer looked after him, the last human to glimpse the living form of Ambrose Small.

It was days before Small's disappearance was discovered. His wife and friends merely wished to ignore his dallying, it was thought later. Small had undoubtedly strayed off with another doxy and had overstayed himself. When the disappearance became official the largest manhunt in Canadian history went into high gear. Teresa Small offered a $50,000 reward for information that would lead to the finding of her husband; it was a staggering amount and it inspired almost every private investigator and crackpot sleuth to join the many hundreds of legitimate detectives seeking the lost tycoon.

Detectives were also seeking the redoubtable secretary John Doughty, who had, ironically, disappeared on the very day that his fortune-loving employer vanished. Investigators discovered that Doughty had left his office on the afternoon of December 2 and promptly absented himself, but not before going to the Dominion Bank and, using Small's key to his private safety-deposit box, withdrawing $100,000 in negotiable Victory bonds belonging to Small. (Doughty was found a year later working in Portland, Oregon, where he labored in a paper mill under the name of Charles B. Cooper. He was tried for the bond theft and given a five-year prison sentence but was cleared of having anything to do with Small's disappearance.)

*Theater magnate Ambrose Small, lost in a Toronto snowstorm in 1919.*

Reports about Small became fantastic tales that suggested haunting abduction and terrifying murder. George Soucy, a publishing employee in Toronto, was positive that he saw Small being forced into a car by several men late on December 2. Also on that same night, insisted caretaker Albert Elson, four men were burying something in the frozen ground in a ravine only a few blocks from Small's Glen Road mansion. A Mrs. Mary Quigley, a cleaning woman, swore to police that she saw a notice posted in the Convent of the Precious Blood, located on St. Anthony Street, which requested "prayers for the repose of the soul of Ambrose J. Small" several days *before* the press or public knew of the disappearance.

Police were devastatingly thorough in their search for the missing man. Every place of business in Toronto was checked. Every city in which Small had a theater, six in all, were combed. Toronto Bay was dredged several times. The basement of the Small mansion on

Glen Road was dug up. (As late as 1944 investigators were still on the case, digging up the basement of the old Grand Opera House in search of the mogul's bones.)

Mrs. Small was officially interrogated. She thought her husband had come to a dark end brought about "by a designing woman." Teresa had known all about Ambrose's infidelities. She ignored them when her husband promised to quit seeing Clara Smith after Teresa had found obscene letters the mistress had written to her lover. Teresa had found a black box containing the letters and purposely left them exposed on a dining room table so her husband would know of her discovery. Small came upon the box and letters and destroyed them, leaving a note for his wife which read: "Teresa, Dear Teresa . . . Don't bother your dear little head about this rotten stuff anymore. It's all over." That was in 1918. Teresa did not know at the time of her husband's disappearance that Ambrose Small had gone right on seeing Clara Smith, dining with her on December 1, the night before he vanished. (Clara Smith knew nothing of her lover's disappearance, police concluded.)

By 1920 detectives were desperate to solve the riddle, but all leads turned out to be false or the work of hoaxers. On his visit to the United States in 1920, the masterful creator of Sherlock Holmes, Arthur Conan Doyle, was asked by a reporter of the *New York World-Telegram* what he thought of the Small disappearance.

"A very interesting case," responded Doyle.

"Would you lend your talents to the case?"

"By Jove, I might if I was asked, but no one has approached me on the matter."

This was enough for Eastern papers to banner the headline: "Sherlock Holmes May Enter Small Mystery." The *Chicago Tribune* picked up the fanciful thought and ran the head: "World's Greatest Detective to Solve Small Case." A West Coast paper, staggering in the chain reaction, yelled from its front page: "Sherlock Holmes to Reveal Toronto Mystery."

But no one, indeed, ever asked the great Doyle to solve the Small puzzle. Six years later, however, police, still anxious to find an answer, employed a Vienna criminologist, Dr. Maximilian Langsner, to use his "thought process" to find the missing Ambrose. The eccentric Viennese doctor was put up in the best Toronto hotel while conducting endless seances and "astral trips" to the place where poor Ambrose could be found. Directed by his wacky divinations, police furiously dug up half the countryside but found nothing. Langsner, pausing between mouthfuls of steak and onion, explained that the detectives were clouding his vision. After running up staggering bills, the clairvoyant criminologist departed Toronto while the public roared with derision.

Since that time, Ambrose Small was "seen" in hundreds of places. He was living it up on the Riviera, a girl under each arm and champagne bottles protruding from his dinner jacket. A mind reader saw him buried in Toronto's city dump. Harry Blackstone, the magician, swore he spotted Small gambling in a Juarez gin joint. In 1923, a Toronto court pronounced Ambrose Small dead, but his spirit through imposters went strutting on for decades.

# 10

*Stepping
Right
Up*

"I am Ambrose Small!"

It was in April 1926, and the man on the phone talking to a reporter on the *Toronto Star* was calling from Albion, Indiana.

"Where have you been?" inquired the incredulous reporter.

"They grabbed me and put me in a loony bin in Wisconsin... that was December 1919. I just got out... I escaped." The caller went on to explain that he was then known as Charles E. Morse. He had been held in the asylum for the criminally insane at Waupon, Wisconsin. He pleaded to be saved. A series of calls to Albion by detectives, reporters and even Mrs. Small convinced everyone in Toronto that the caller was indeed the missing theater mogul. He was most convincing, this Charles E. Morse. He knew, or seemed to know, everything about Ambrose Small, his wife Teresa, his business dealings, his associates. He even knew that Ambrose Small banked at the Dominion Bank of Toronto, from which he had days earlier demanded, by telegram, that $5,000 be sent to him without delay, stating that he was the flamboyant tycoon in person.

Reporters and investigators from Canada and several Midwestern cities descended on Albion to view the amazing survivor. Nearly everybody gleefully agreed that the man was the missing Ambrose Small. As a routine precaution, Morse's fingerprints were taken. They were much different from Small's. Someone pointed out that Morse looked awfully well preserved. Authorities at Waupon, who came to pick up their charge, nodded yes, he was in good condition; he should be, since he was twenty years younger than Small.

Morse was first held on charges of attempting to obtain money under false pretenses. He was then returned to the asylum. (The unhinged Small impersonator was steeped in the tycoon's disappearance; his padded prison cell at Waupon was found to be littered with clippings and stories about the missing man.) The Morse-Small kind of impersonation was not a new game. For centuries grand imposters have stepped forward to present themselves as the missing legitimate heirs to great estates and vast fortunes. Theirs is the most reckless of adventures, requiring astounding mental capabilities, as well as acting talents that no stage in the world can deny.

The earliest of these tantalizing tales engulfs a French youth named Martin Guerre during the 1550s. Guerre lived on his father's great estate outside the town of Artigues in the district of Rieux. At six- teen he married a beautiful girl named Bertrande Rols, who was only thirteen years old. (Early marriages were the custom then.) For almost ten years no child was produced between the youthful couple, a situation that caused great concern and dread among the couple's families and the townsfolk. They were enchanted some said, or under a devil's spell. They were fed holy cakes, and special masses were said for them. The so-called enchantment remained un- broken.

Then, when Guerre was about thirty, Bertrande bore a child, whom they named Sanxi. Shortly after the birth, Guerre, for un- explained reasons, stole some grain from his father, who would readily have given it if the son had asked. Fearing his father's wrath, Guerre left home and was listed as missing for eight years.

One day, a stranger arrived in Artigues. His face was weather- beaten and bearded, but he spoke of his boyhood in the area and startled the residents with his knowledge of Martin Guerre, so much so that he was instantly thought to be Guerre.

During Martin's absence, his father had died and, far from being angry over the missing grain, had left his vast holdings to his son. Peter Guerre, the dead man's brother, who had been managing the estate, rushed to view the stranger and joyfully pronounced him to be his true nephew. Guerre's four sisters also insisted that the stranger was Guerre. Bertrande, who had remained a recluse during her husband's eight-year absence, upon seeing the stranger, took little time in admitting that, yes, here was her long-missing spouse. The stranger moved into Guerre's great house and lived for three years with Bertrande, who had two children by him.

All was not well, however. Peter Guerre had publicly acknowl- edged the stranger as Martin, but he repeatedly refused to give his nephew an accounting of taxes and incomes from his lands, retaining his proprietorship of the Guerre estate. This so angered Martin that the two fell into violent arguments and, on one occasion, Peter knocked Martin down with an iron bar and would have killed him had it not been for the intercession of Bertrande. From that moment on, Martin Guerre's life was in high jeopardy.

Shortly after the birth of Bertrande's second child by the new Martin Guerre, a soldier arrived in Artigues stating that the Martin Guerre living in the family mansion was nothing but an imposter, a clever look-alike who had fooled the entire Guerre family. The real Martin, the soldier stated, was known to him as an intimate friend; he was alive elsewhere, having lost a leg in a war in Flanders.

This bit of news threw the community into an uproar. Bertrande, who sent for the soldier and talked with him, later remarked that the man who was living with her as her husband was authentic. "If it isn't Martin Guerre, then it is the devil in his skin!"

There were many devils in the land in that superstitious era, some of them, it was whispered, living inside the shells of dead humans. From the subsequent actions of Peter Guerre, he might have qualified for the role of one of those caculating demons.

Using the statements of the visiting soldier, Peter Guerre retracted his identification of the stranger as his nephew Martin Guerre. He lobbied mightily for a full investigation by authorities and a public trial. A trial did commence in Rieux. On the indictment sheet the man calling himself Martin Guerre was listed as one Arnold Tilh, a native of Sagias, who was commonly known in that town simply as Pansette. Dozens of witnesses stepped forward to talk about the known scars, moles, discolorations and other physical defects the real Martin Guerre was known to possess. In equal number, those who identified the accused as being Guerre were contradicted by those who stated he was an imposter. Martin's child Sanxi was brought into court and it was pointed out that he bore no resemblance whatsoever to the accused. When Bertrande took the stand and was asked whether or not the accused, a man she had lived with and loved for three years, was her husband she startled the court by making no reply; she merely lowered her head and remained silent. This act was interpreted by many in the court as a reaction to the many threats made by Peter Guerre.

At this juncture, the accused stood up and addressed the court in a clear voice: "If Bertrande, after thus receiving me back and living with me perfectly happily for three years, is now one of my accusers, it can only be because she has been intimidated and forced to turn against me by my enemies, of whom my uncle is the most bitter. I once had the misfortune to quarrel with him and ever since then he has sought every opportunity to do me harm."

The high point of the trial occurred when the man with the wooden leg, who claimed to be Martin Guerre, arrived in Rieux and confronted the accused in court. They were almost exact twins. The new Martin Guerre stood in the middle of the court, insisting that he was the true claimant to the Guerre millions. Although his demeanor in court was excitable and somewhat confused when answering certain questions, Guerre's sisters turned the tide for the newcomer. Shown into court, the four women first hesitated. Then the oldest sister flung her arms about the peg-legged man and pro-

*The look-alikes who claimed to be the missing Martin Guerre.*

claimed him the real Martin Guerre. Her sisters followed suit. The prosecution pointed out that the imposter who had taken Guerre's position and lands was a poor swordsman and had no knowledge of the Basque tongue; Guerre, as a youth, had been excellent with a sword and spoke Basque fluently.

Bertrande settled the matter in a dramatic, climaxing appearance. In the words of Charles Dickens, writing about the case in *All Year Round:* "She stopped at the threshold as soon as she saw the unexpected man, and evinced sudden and powerful emotion. She burst into tears, threw herself at his feet, stretched out her arms, and, sobbing loudly, she begged his forgiveness. He was her lost husband, the real Martin Guerre."

The imposter Tilh rose and stood next to Bertrande, imploring her to make a proper decision; she ignored him. The game was up. Tilh, knowing he would be tortured by authorities to exact a confession, admitted that he and Martin Guerre had served together in the army, sharing the same tent. Guerre had related every detail of his life to Tilh, including his most secret relations with Bertrande. When Tilh returned to Sagias, many stated that he was Martin Guerre, who was known in that town. First Tilh treated the remarks as a joke, but when they persisted he "made a study" of Guerre and then purposely journeyed to Artigues to impersonate Guerre and take over his fortune and estate.

The High Court of Toulouse, on September 16, 1560, ordered the imposter executed. There was much ceremony in Tilh's death, as was the tradition of humiliating the guilty in that punitive time. Tilh, wearing only his shirt, was forced to crawl on his knees to the church door in Artigues, bareheaded, barefoot, a rope around his neck, a burning taper in his hand. He was then led through the town while citizens heaped rubbish and verbal abuse on him. Kicked up the stairs of a gallows erected in front of Martin Guerre's house, the condemned man looked up to a balcony where, by order of the court, Bertrande and the new Martin Guerre stood. Said Tilh, "Forgive me for my crimes, I beg of you." He was then hanged in such a way that he slowly strangled to death. His body was later taken down and burned.

That ended the great adventure of the Guerre imposter. Or did it? It was long said after Tilh's death that the man with the wooden leg was also an imposter, that Martin had been murdered by a gang of ruffians seeking his purse when he first left home after stealing his father's grain, and that the vindictive uncle, Peter Guerre, had sent the soldier to Artigues to spread the lie that the peg-leg man was the true Guerre, and that this man had been paid by Peter Guerre to usurp the false claimant Tilh. Bertrande and Martin Guerre's sisters, many concluded, had been forced, under the threat of death, to acknowledge the new imposter with the wooden leg as the true Martin Guerre. This was all said, but nothing was done about the suspected conspiracy. The state had already triumphed in setting the Guerre matter right, and the course of this personal history had been officially determined. If evil persisted in yet another bogus Martin Guerre, played out by the man with the wooden leg, it was of no concern to the courts. The man with the wooden leg lived out his life as Martin Guerre and happy to do so, being loved, rich and acknowledged.

### The Probable Marshal Ney

Many of those who present themselves as long-missing persons suddenly returned are motivated by the desire to possess the wealth of the vanished. Rarer are the claimants who seek something less definable, more heroic, something desperately tragic—a place of distinction in history, the seeming immortality of another. Such imposters attempt to usurp an identity in order to inherit position and status even though it be only awarded them on their tombstones. Most, like J. Frank Dalton, who in 1948 tried to convince the world that he was the legendary outlaw Jesse Woodson James at age one hundred and one, are proven frauds. A few remain enigmatic to historians and detectives alike, looming ghosts that will not fade.

The most distinguished of these in American history died twice: once in the windswept Luxembourg Gardens outside Paris on December 7, 1815; then in a small town in North Carolina on November 15, 1846.

As the carriage jiggled its way toward the spot of his execution, Michel Ney had ample time to review one of the greatest glory-filled lives in the history of his native France. Born in 1769, Ney had enlisted in the French army at seventeen and had risen through its motley ranks through the Revolution and the early days of his beloved Emperor Napoleon I. Bonaparte came to respect and love Michel Ney, a man he called "the bravest of the brave," making him a marshal of France. Ney returned that love by fighting from Madrid to Moscow for Bonaparte and France; it was Ney's dogged legion that covered the awful, bloody retreat from Russia, a defensive action that saved the Grand Army from complete annihilation.

When Napoleon was exiled to Elba, Ney swore allegiance to Louis XVIII. The Bourbon king in return elevated Ney to the peerage. Yet Ney's love for his old commander was too strong, and when Bonaparte returned to the soil of France after one hundred days, Ney, instead of arresting the Emperor, placed himself and his troops at Napoleon's disposal. It was Marshal Ney who led the last great gallant charge of the Old Guard at Waterloo.

Though urged to escape to America following Bonaparte's arrest and final exile to the barren island of St. Helena, Ney chose to stay in the country of his birth. After a quick trial, he was condemned to death by the Chamber of Peers. Though the Marshal's old enemies, the Duke of Wellington included, beseeched the king to exile Ney instead of killing him, Louis XVIII was implacable in his vengeance. The night before the execution, deputies roused the King from his sleep, again petitioning the monarch for the soldier's life, stating that they feared a general uprising of the citizens if such a national hero were imperiously slain. Louis's answer was typical of the unfeeling Bourbons. He rolled his fat carcass over his silk-sheeted bed and roared: "Let me hear when I awake that the traitor has paid the penalty for his crime."

At a little after 9 A.M. the following morning, "the bravest of the brave" stood against a wall in the Luxembourg Gardens, a firing squad before him in a thin line. The Marshal had asked that his executioners be from the ranks of his old veterans—which they were, a reluctant, sorrowful squad indeed. The captain of the guard approached Ney and asked if he wished to have a blindfold. Enraged, the Marshal half-shouted: "Are you ignorant that for twenty years I have been accustomed to face both balls and bullets?"

Ney took one step forward. He loudly announced: "I protest before God and my country the sentence which has condemned me. I appeal from it to man, to posterity, to God." With magnificent military bearing, the Marshal squared his shoulders and turned briefly to the Commandant of Paris, ordering: "Do your duty!" He faced the firing squad and said to the troopers about to raise their rifles, many of whom were weeping: "My brave comrades, when I place my hand upon my breast, fire. See you take sure aim at the heart." He removed his hat. "Soldiers! Straight to the heart! Fire!"

With a thundering volley Marshall Ney fell, another martyr for France. Yet the death of the great hero was privately contested almost immediately. Though the official report stated that Ney had been killed by "twelve balls, nine in the breast, three in the head," the report from the hospital, where the body was taken for examination, stated that the body had been unmarked by bullets.

Some weeks later, one of Napoleon's soldiers, who had deserted in 1815 and had become a seaman, one Philip Petrie, was attracted by a passenger boarding a ship sailing from Bordeaux to Charleston, South Carolina. Petrie, who had served under Marshal Ney, approached the passenger. "Are you not Marshal Ney of the Grand Army?" inquired Petrie.

The passenger turned to the soldier-turned-sailor and said tersely, "Marshal Ney was executed two weeks ago in Paris." Petrie went off shaking his head; the passenger was an exact look-alike of his old commander. (It is important to note that this story was not told by Petrie until 1874, shortly before his death.)

The ship docked at Charleston on January 29, 1816, and Peter Stuart Ney disembarked. (Ney had been nicknamed "Red Peter" by the devoted soldiers under his command.) This same man was identified by refugee members of Napoleon's court in Georgetown, South Carolina, in 1819 as the one and only Marshal Ney, but he vanished before officials could question him. Late in 1819, Peter Ney appeared in Mocksville, North Carolina, where he became a teacher, holding that position for three years. In this isolated community, the highly cultivated Peter Ney appeared extremely sensitive to any mention of Bonaparte. Napoleon's death in 1821 almost spelled the end for schoolteacher Ney, as one of his former students, Colonel John A. Rogers, later testified in 1888.

I was in the schoolroom in 1821 [Rogers remembered] when a newspaper was brought to him by one of the boys containing the announcement of Napoleon's death at St. Helena. He read it, turned deathly pale, fainted, and fell to the floor, exactly as if he had been shot. Some of the older scholars threw water on his face, which soon revived him. He dismissed his school, went to his room, and shut himself up for the rest of the day. He burnt a large quantity of papers—perhaps everything that he thought might lead to his identity. Among other things burnt was a very exact likeness of the Emperor Napoleon. The next morning, Mr. Ney did not make his appearance as usual, and my father went to look after him. He found him with his throat cut. The blade of the knife that did the work was broken in the wound. This probably saved his life.

Recuperating from his suicide attempt, Ney told Rogers' father some weeks later: "Oh, Colonel, with the death of Napoleon my last hope is gone." This remark was considered mysterious, for the schoolteacher did not explain what hopes he had. More than ten years later the teacher added a bit more information. By then he had moved to Virginia and then back to North Carolina. When hearing that Napoleon's son had died he burst out with, "young Napoleon is dead, and with him dies all hope of ever going back to France, of again seeing my wife and children and home and friends." That evening his students discovered him burning a lengthy manuscript. When asked what it was, the teacher replied through sobs, "The story of my life."

The story of that life, or a part of it, if it is to be believed, was related by Peter Stuart Ney on his deathbed in 1846 in North Carolina. There were many who came to believe the man who had come to their community to teach their children. They remembered how he appeared in 1821, a man with blue-gray eyes, auburn hair (from which the nickname "Red Peter" emanated), who stood almost six feet tall, a man who was as marvelous a swordsman as was Marshal Ney, a man who knew every detail of Napoleon's campaigns, as well as the most intimate information about the Emperor, a man who fluently spoke, in addition to his native French, the same tongues as Marshal Ney—Greek, Latin and Hebrew. Peter Ney also bore the same battle scars as were known to be on the body of the Marshal.

Was the man dying on that frontier bed really the grand Marshal

or merely a deluded nobody reaching for the history of another to
make his passing significant and his memory eternal? (Ney had often spoken of the importance of "posterity," even, it will be recalled, at the time of his execution.) This is how the claimant put it, after explaining that the Duke of Wellington had saved him from the firing squad and arranged his escape:

> Louis XVIII was full of revenge. He ordered that some of my old soldiers, whom I had often led into battle, should be my executioners. The thing was so revolting to Frenchmen that a plan was formed for my escape. The officer appointed to superintend my execution told my friends to apply for my body for interment. They did so and the necessary permission was granted. I was to give the command "fire," and fall as I gave it. I did so. The soldiers who had previously been instructed, fired almost instantly, the balls passing over my head and striking the planks or walls behind. I was pronounced dead, hastily taken up, put into a carriage, and driven off to a neighboring hospital. That night I was disguised and left for America.

Peter Ney then went on to relate that he thought he might be apprehended when a sailor recognized him on board his escape ship from Bordeaux to South Carolina. (This remains a startling statement since it was made twenty-eight years before Petrie made his story public.)

Historians looking into this tale found that Mrs. Ney acted strangely following her husband's death. When Louis Napoleon took the French throne in 1848 he ordered the graves of all of Napoleon's trusted followers to be enshrined with magnificent monuments. Madame Ney refused to be part of the ceremonies honoring the alleged grave of her husband. She also neglected the grave, never visiting it. And upon her death, even though family plans had determined she was to lie beside her husband, Madame Ney was buried elsewhere. Mrs. Ney was devoted to her husband and his memory, and never remarried following the 1815 execution, so her actions were not those of one having deep-seated animosity toward Ney.

The most startling evidence pointing to the North Carolina schoolteacher's claim as being genuine was presented by David Carvalho, one of the world's great experts in handwriting, the same expert who detected the errors in the infamous *Bordereau* of the Dreyfus case. Carvalho was given lengthy samples of writing by

Marshal Michel Ney and Peter Stuart Ney to examine. The handwriting genius conducted an exhaustive study. His results have plagued missing-persons authorities ever since.

> I applied the same tests that I have applied times without number when some man's life depended upon my findings [Carvalho was quoted as saying]. I am of the opinion that the writer of the specimens of the four pages purporting to be those of Marshal Ney and the writer of the specimens on the four pages purporting to be those of P. S. Ney are one and the same person; the variations of hand being largely due to style of pen used, the quill, gold and steel all being represented, which produces the different quality of line without hiding away the idiosyncrasies of the writer.

If schoolteacher Peter Ney was truly who he claimed to be, one would certainly inquire of the French government, Who, then, is in the earth beneath that gray slab marked simply "Ney"?

### The Two Tichbornes

No more fabulous imposter laying claim to a missing person's identity existed than the incredibly presumptuous Arthur Orton, who, with sheer will and audacity, attempted to take over one of the great British estates, stealing for himself enormous lands and an income from a massive fortune that paid more than one million dollars a year.

The real heir to this golden spoon was Sir Roger Doughty Tichborne, an aesthetic, slightly pompous youth, who was born in Paris on January 5, 1829. His mother, Henrietta Félicité, was French, although the daughter of an Englishman, one Henry Seymour, a wealthy businessman, who left his fortune to her. Roger's father, James Tichborne, was the third son of the renowned Tichborne family, which possessed a baronetcy that dated back to 1135. Roger, as was expected of a high-born son slated to be the eleventh baronet of Tichborne, was dutifully enrolled in a distinguished British school, the Jesuit College at Stonyhurst, much to his English-hating mother's disgust.

Following three years of military training, young Roger in 1849 was commissioned an officer in the Sixth Dragoons, also known as the Carbineers. The Tichborne scion scorned the rough-hewn ways of soldiers, having his uniforms tailor-made and preferring, to the coarse companionships of troopers, the company of gentlemen and socially acceptable females, not the least of whom was his first cousin Katherine Doughty, the woman he loved. Her Roman Catholic family, especially Roger's uncle, the redoubtable Edward Doughty, objected to the marriage; the Church of Rome looked with stern disfavor on the marriage of first cousins.

Roger persisted in his love affair, being discreet to mention his affections for Katherine to only a select few. The Doughtys pointed out to their daughter that the Tichborne heir was dissolute. He smoked and drank to excess and "wasted most of his time reading French novels." Roger would have to mend his ways before they would approve of the marriage. It was proposed that a wait of three years would be suitable. If, by that time, Roger and Katherine still loved each other, the wedding would be approved.

Roger agreed, stating that he would enjoy a world tour. With three years of time to spend, along with a hefty monthly allowance, Roger made plans to sail to South America. The twenty-four-year-old Tichborne arrived in Rio de Janeiro in the spring of 1854. From Rio, Roger sailed with the *Bella*, a new cargo schooner, for New York by way of Kingston, Jamaica. The *Bella*, her captain and crew of forty, as well as all passengers, Roger Tichborne included, were lost at sea when the ship apparently capsized due to improperly stowed tons of coffee. Wreckage of the *Bella* and an empty lifeboat were later found floating at sea. Thus ended the wedding plans of Katherine Doughty (who later became Lady Radcliffe) and the bright rich future of Henrietta's "darling Roger."

*Wealthy Sir Roger Doughty Tichborne, last seen on the ill-fated* Bella *sailing for New York in 1854.*

Roger's father, James, had fallen heir to the estate, but died. Alfred Joseph Tichborne, in light of Roger's being lost at sea, became the new Tichborne heir in 1862. Yet Lady Tichborne refused to believe that Roger, most precious of her children, had died in the sea. Her maternal faith and intuition told her that Roger somehow had survived. She heard rumors that the missing ship *Bella* had given up survivors, who had been taken by ship to Australia. One of these, she knew, must be her long-lost son.

So desperate was Lady Tichborne to have her son returned to her that she advertised widely in newspapers around the world for information regarding Roger, offering a large reward for such information and indiscreetly mentioning in the notices that her son was heir to the fabulous Tichborne estate.

One of Henrietta's advertisements was seen by a butcher named Castro, who was living in Wagga Wagga, New South Wales, Australia. He wrote Lady Tichborne that he had been shipwrecked in the Pacific many years earlier, that he had suffered some memory loss but that he felt sure he was her missing son. Coupled to this claim was the ironic fact that an ancient Negro named Boyle, who had once been a servant on the Tichborne estate, and was living in New South Wales, insisted that Castro was the authentic Roger Tichborne; though many years had elapsed, he could not fail to recognize the young master. Castro, still in Australia and carrying on lengthy correspondence with Lady Tichborne, who was living in her beloved Paris, employed Boyle as his body servant and proceeded to pump him of every minute detail about the Tichborne estate and family history. The naïve Boyle responded by draining his memory. It was almost a year, from the time Castro began his correspondence with Lady Tichborne and his claiming to be Roger, before *"the Claimant,"* as he would later be called, decided to play his cards. Castro sailed for England, arriving on Christmas Day 1866.

The reborn Roger immediately went to the Tichborne estate and, helped by one Rous, a clerk for the old Tichborne attorney, totally familiarized himself with the vast holdings he hoped to inherit. When he finished walking the grounds, interviewing servants, and absorbing the history of the family, the man next sailed for Paris, where he sent Boyle to contact Lady Tichborne, explaining that he, Roger, was too ill to leave his hotel suite. In a mad rush, the emotion-soaked Henrietta, met with the Claimant.

Only one as clever as the butcher Castro could have set the scene so expertly, one in which Lady Tichborne, blinded by her emotional desire to see Roger alive, would accept almost anyone as the heir to the Tichborne estate. Bram Stoker, the author of *Dracula*, wrote of the meeting in his *Famous Impostors*:

> The deluded woman professed to recognize him at once. As she sat beside his bed, "Roger" keeping his face turned to the wall, the

conversation took a wide range, the sick man showing himself strangely astray. He talked to her of his grandfather, whom the real Roger had never seen; he said he had served in the ranks; referred to Stonyhurst as Winchester; spoke of his suffering as a lad from St. Vitus' Dance... but did not speak of the rheumatism from which Roger had suffered. But it was all one to the infatuated woman.

Lady Tichborne overlooked Castro's errors, so joyous was she to have her son back from the dead. She explained away his inaccuracies as the mistakes that one makes after mental stress, writing to a friend that "he confuses everything as if in a dream." But she recognized him as her son and the legal heir to one of the greatest fortunes in England, endowing him immediately with a one-thousand-pound-a-month allowance.

Thus enriched, Castro, thinking Lady Tichborne's identification to be the worst of it, sailed for London to do legal battle with the other Tichborne heirs in what was to become the longest trial in legal history to that time. Hundreds of witnesses went on the stand

*Arthur Orton (nee Castro), who insisted he was Roger Tichborne, greeting the curious masses on his way to the longest court battle in English history.*

to either affirm or deny that the Claimant was the missing Tichborne. The testimony took up ten thousand printed pages as the Claimant battled through two marathon trials (1871 and 1874) at a cost of ninety thousand pounds, an expense finally borne by the family.

The Claimant centered his argument of Roger Tichborne's survival on an obscure rescue at sea, insisting that he had been saved, along with the crew and passengers of the sunken *Bella* by a vessel named the *Osprey*, which took them to Australia. Exhaustive checking did not uncover any ship named the *Osprey*. The discrepancies increased as the Claimant rattled on day after day, week after agonizing week.

It was the sensation of London. Thousands, from working-class citizens clawing for seats with grimy hands to members of the peerage beating aside crowds with walking sticks, fought for places in the court gallery. Much of the Claimant's testimony was impressive, but he relied all too heavily on Lady Tichborne's shaky identification of him as her son.

Sir John Coleridge, who later became Lord Chief Justice, mercilessly prosecuted the Claimant on the stand, his own cross-examination taking up twenty-two days. Coleridge's bulldog indictments were ruinous for the Claimant's chances. In one courtroom assault, Coleridge flared:

> The first sixteen years of his life he has absolutely forgotten; the few facts he had told the jury were already proved, or would hereafter be shown, to be absolutely false and fabricated. Of his college life he could recollect nothing. About his amusements, his books, his music, his games, he could tell nothing. Not a word of his family, of the people with whom he lived, their habits, their persons, their very names. He had forgotten his mother's maiden name; he was ignorant of all particulars of the family estate; he remembered nothing of Stonyhurst; and in military matters he was equally deficient. Roger, born and educated in France, spoke and wrote French like a native and his favorite reading was French literature, but the Claimant knew nothing of French.

One condemnation was heaped upon another but the Claimant held his head high and insisted that he was Roger Tichborne. His mere physical appearance was enough to doom him. Although the

Claimant stood about Roger's height, five foot, nine inches, his girth was enormous. Where Roger Tichborne weighed 160 pounds and was known to have a woman's waist of twenty-three inches at age twenty-five (which made it necessary for his tailors to make special suspenders for him), the Claimant was as broad as the House of Commons, weighing a ponderous 364 pounds. He possessed none of Roger's scars or marks, including a telltale tattoo on the right forearm reading "RCT" below a cross, anchor and heart for "faith, hope and charity." Another physical peculiarity about Roger was not evident on the Claimant. Roger's earlobes were attached; the Claimant's earlobes were free. Where the Claimant gushed love for Lady Tichborne, Roger had never displayed anything but acid contempt for his mother.

Toward the end of the second trial, the prosecution identified the imposter as one Arthur Orton, pointing out that the intials "AO" had been tattooed upon the Claimant's left arm. The arm was examined, but the initials were not present. There was, however, "a mark which was sworn to be the obliteration of those letters."

The Claimant tried to counter by besmirching Katherine Doughty, who was sitting in the gallery turning various colors of red. He stated that he, as Roger Tichborne, had seduced her and made her pregnant. Katherine had then tried to force him to marry her and this was the real reason he departed on his around-the-world trip. The prosecution made short work of this fantastic claim and went on to expose the Claimant as one Arthur Orton, a lowly butcher's son from Wapping, who was born in a shop's back room in 1834. Orton, it was pointed out, traveled to Valparaiso in 1848, staying with a family named Castro, the name he used when he lived in Wagga Wagga. He returned to England in 1851 to apprentice as a butcher under his father. He left the following year for Australia. In 1854, Orton stopped writing to his family. (It was in this year that Roger Tichborne was lost with the missing *Bella*. Though the court insinuated that Orton had possibly taken up a life of crime at this time, prosecutors did not, other than hint at the fact, relate that the butcher may indeed have met the real Roger Tichborne, who just might have survived the sinking of the *Bella* and been stranded in Australia. Later testimony pointed out that Tichborne had been identified in Australia and had sold a ring he was known to have worn; he was also seen in the company of Arthur Orton in one of the bush country stations. The implication of all this was that Orton had murdered the young man after prying from him his family background, preparatory by a decade to impersonating the wealthy absentee.)

Orton's case collapsed on February 28, 1874, when the jury stepped out for only a half hour's deliberation. They returned a verdict stating that the defendant was not Roger Tichborne, but Arthur Orton, and that he was guilty of gross fraud. Orton was sentenced to fourteen years' penal servitude. He spent ten years in prison, and when he emerged he still insisted he was *the* Roger Tichborne. By then the public was no longer interested. Orton sank into miserable poverty. In 1895, Orton finally gave up his colossal impersonation, swearing out a lengthy confession of his fraud which appeared in *People Magazine* of that year. England's greatest imposter died on April 1, 1898, in his ramshackle lodgings in Shouldham Street, Marylebone.

The final enigma presented itself at Arthur Orton's burial, one that gave rise to the theory that though he was not Roger Tichborne, Orton may have been an illegitimate child of the Tichborne household. Though he had fully and publicly confessed his swindle three years before his death, the Tichborne family baffled the world by allowing the following inscription to be placed on a metal plate hammered into the top of Orton's coffin. It read: "Sir Roger Charles Doughty Tichborne; born 5th January, 1829; died 1st April, 1898."

### The Changing Mr. Speer

On rare occasions, an imposter will not claim an inheritance but will seek to assume the identity of another for pure day-to-day profit. One recent ongoing case involves a missing scientist whose inventiveness may have spelled his untimely doom.

That Michael Carr Speer, of Evanston, Illinois, was a genius there could be no doubt. Speer, with an IQ of 162, had entered college on a scholarship at age fifteen and went on to receive a doctorate in chemical engineering from Stanford University. The positions this engineering wizard held over the next years were all high-level and sensitive, much of the work in quasi-secret areas. By the time he was forty-two, Speer was still a bachelor, and had changed his name to Farlan Speer.

Nothing was amiss in Speer's life until he excitedly visited his parents on October 25, 1975, in their Lincoln Park home to inform them of a new position he had obtained through a Bethesda, Maryland, firm, a job that called for the handling of a mineral-development project in Haiti. Speer, as the top engineer, would oversee fifty or sixty workers and earn an annual salary of between $50,000 and $60,000. Speer's Maryland contact was a man simply called "Jim" by Speer.

On November 17, Speer called his parents, Paul D. and Helen Speer (Paul Speer is one of this country's leading financial consultants), to tell them that he was going to meet "Jim" in Oklahoma before going on to the Haitian job. He promised to write or call home with information about his address. It was the last the Speers ever heard of their son.

Worried, the family contacted their son's friends in Washington, who said they had received a phone call from someone who said the engineer's plans had been altered, that he was not going on to Haiti after all but would be relocating in Europe on a hush-hush job. When the friends pressed for contact with Speer, the caller, a man with a husky voice, grew curt, telling them they could only contact him in the future through a post-office box in a small town near Oklahoma City, Oklahoma.

Helen Speer began sending letters to the post-office box, but she received no response, and the letters were never returned. On June 17, 1976, with his son absent for more than seven months, Paul Speer contacted investigators in the Oklahoma City area to look into his son's disappearance. The financial consultant explained his delay in seeking help, thinking that his son might be in a very secretive job which is not unknown to persons with his special training. "He could have gotten a job with the C.I.A. or a Howard-Hughes–type agency," Paul Speer pointed out. (When contacted, the C.I.A. had no knowledge of Speer's disappearance.) Further, it was known that Speer had done work in underwater-mineral research that was often involved with intelligence-gathering operations. The parents even feared that Farlan Speer might have been kidnapped by a foreign power to work on a highly technical project.

Detectives in Oklahoma City had learned that the renter of the post-office box gave as an address a nearby motel. Mrs. Speer called the motel but her son was not registered. The following day, Helen Speer received a long-distance call from a man identifying himself as a "Dr. Martin." The caller explained that "Dr. Farlan" was heading up an entire group of scientists at an undisclosed location. From the information the caller relayed, it was obvious to Mrs. Speer that he had been reading the letters she had sent to her son.

Then investigators were jolted to discover that an Oklahoma driver's license had been issued to Farlan Speer on October 11, 1975. The license had the correct age of the engineer and his exact social security number, but the description of Speer was drastically different from that of the real Farlan. Speer stood six feet, two inches tall and weighed 180 pounds, had blue-green eyes and brown hair. The "new" Speer was five feet, nine inches tall, weighed 158 pounds, and had brown eyes and black hair. Private detectives of the United Research Company, hired by Paul Speer, traced a "Michael Carr Speer" to a house in Norman, Oklahoma.

Pretending to be credit checkers handling a routine auto loan, the detectives interviewed the "new" Speer, a man with dark skin who had parts of two fingers missing. He claimed to be Speer and told the investigators that his parents had died long ago. On July 30, 1976, the detectives returned once more and interviewed the man, telling him that they had been hired by Paul Speer to look into his son's disappearance. The man nervelessly repeated his story but soon fled.

From descriptions of the imposter, detectives pieced together his identity. The man with the dark skin and parts of two fingers missing was none other than Jim Sheker of Centerville, Virginia, the same "Jim" who had lured Speer into the mythical Haiti job while interviewing him in Maryland.

Sheker, from all reports, is an amazingly cunning creature, also an engineer, whose background is awash with bankruptcies, legal actions and fraud in Washington, Florida and Oklahoma. One report had it that Sheker had contacted a friend, Jerry Hargis, an official with the University of Oklahoma in Norman, telling him that he was a C.I.A. agent who had recently been shot on an assignment and was using Speer's name as a cover to confuse foreign agents pursuing him. Hargis reportedly helped Sheker obtain his new Speer identity, thinking he was aiding the government. As Speer, Sheker tried un-successfully to sell large oil companies a new coal-degasification process.

Sheker, at this writing, is a fugitive, wanted for fraud in Washington, D.C. Farlan Speer is still missing. Mrs. Speer rules out the possibility that the brilliant engineer voluntarily absented himself. "He isn't that sort of person," she told a reporter from the *Chicago Sun-Times*. "He loved his friends and family too much. He was warm, kind and religious." And, as events may prove, Farlan Speer was much too trusting.

### Rewards to the Real Missing

True heirs who have been missing and suddenly reappear to claim their fortunes provide the grist of countless happy endings. Their stories are as improbable as these tales of sinister imposters. Andrew Hanford of Wilton, Connecticut, was typical of this breed. He joined the Union Army in 1861 to fight the "Johnny Rebs." He was gone for sixty years. During that period, his father, John T. Hanford, acquired considerable land around Wilton and built up a handsome fortune.

In 1921, at the age of eighty-one, Andrew Hanford returned to Wilton to find his parents and his brothers Moses, Amari and Daniel dead. When claiming his estate, Hanford merely shrugged in response to newsmen asking why he had disappeared. He finally grumbled: "My brothers were always making fun of me. I was the butt of all their jokes. That's why I never came home."

Another Connecticut man, Patrick F. Kelley, returned home to New Britain after reading that he was legally dead. He had suddenly disappeared on August 1, 1902, leaving his wife, children and prosperous painting and decorating business. When he popped up in 1923 to claim his own estate, he refused to say why he had vanished, but he was happy to relate that he had had a wonderful time in Ireland and Mexico. Collecting his fortune, the Irishman winked at reporters and told them he was going to Argentina, reminding them not to list him as dead until it became a substantiated fact. "You can knock the *l* out of Kelley," he said, repeating the old tagline, "but it's hard to kill a good Irishman."

Often irony and tragedy go hand in hand with claimed fortunes, the vanished reappearing too late by days or hours to save themselves from the vacuums they stepped into years before. Mrs. Suzie Powell Nichols, heiress to a $40,000 fortune, received her money in Fort Worth, Texas, in 1941, but by then it did not matter. The elderly woman, long suffering on relief, lived only thirteen days as a rich lady before dying of malnutrition.

It was the same for Gustave Wickstrom, of Superior, Wisconsin, whose father was a court official. Gustave joined the Army and, fighting on the Western front, earned a decoration for valor. He wrote to his father after the war that he would not return home until he had made good on his own. Nothing was heard of him after that time. His father died and left Gustave $30,000. A nationwide search was conducted for the heir. Only hours before dogged investigators caught up with him, Wickstrom finished himself. To quote a report: "Gustave's corpse was found in a freight car on a siding near Toledo, Ohio, his throat slashed from ear to ear, his gnarled right hand clutching a safety razor blade."

Missing heirs are found in the most obscure places and in the most inadvertent ways. Frank Harmon, whose uncle had left him $5,000, was sought, with advertisements about his inheritance appearing in newspapers coast to coast. More than five hundred persons by that name claimed the fortune, but it was months before the real Harmon was found, working as a night watchman in a woolen mill in Rockville, Connecticut.

William R. Snyder, who had vanished from his Detroit home on June 14, 1939, at age twenty-one, was left a $12,000 estate by his grandfather a year later. Snyder was found working as a deck hand on board a 68-foot yacht owned by film actor Barton MacLane. When told the news, Snyder fell into the water and had to be fished out and revived.

Edythe Lippman, a librarian at the North Jersey Training School in Little Falls, had been missing for years after her father and mother were divorced and she was placed with foster parents. Miss Lippman was listening to a radio show dealing with missing heirs in 1940. She heard the announcer state: "This was the case of the unclaimed estate of the late Francis L. Lippman, whose heir is his child and who would be now twenty-six years old, but whose name is unknown."

The young woman sank bewildered into a chair, remarking to her roommate, "Why, that's my father." Days later, Edythe Lippman, librarian, was awarded an estate of $160,000.

The wildest missing-heir case on record involved the estate left by a retired Toronto plumber named William J. Wright, who died in 1938. Wright left his entire fortune, about $13,000, to a "Miss Babe." All that was known about this woman was that she had appeared at the age of five on the stage of a Fort Wayne, Indiana, burlesque house on April 18, 1918, when Wright had seen her. The little girl had sung "Oh You Great Big Beautiful Doll" in such a fashion as to capture Wright's heart (and fortune) forever.

Investigators later learned that "Miss Babe" had been the child of a burlesque couple named Coughlin. In answer to nationwide appeals, more than 240 women, most of them chorus girls who had been in show business since childhood, appeared, all claiming that they were the one and only "Miss Babe." While authorities were trying to sort the hordes of claimants out, Wright's relatives, all cut out of his will, attempted to prove him insane before death, relating that he kept a pistol on the kitchen table while eating and would run his hand over it menacingly if anyone came near him during his meal, and "how he inveigled little boys and girls into believing moth balls were candy."

Insanity, it seemed, prevailed. The fortune was finally split by two women who convinced all concerned that they were entitled to the estate, both being named Wallie "Babe" Coughlin.

Religion is seldom employed as a motivating force in modern-day disappearances. Yet, in the early part of the century communion with Divine Spirit often required, it seemed, a complete break with friends and family before the absentee could come in touch with the Great Holies. Many a religious fanatic had no thought of hurting loved ones; their departures into spiritual limbos had its own peculiar logic, one that seemed perfectly normal to them. If the world at large thought such disappearances the acts of lunatics mouthing magnificent obsessions in order to escape the realities of the day, the absentee merely shrugged indifferently and went without comment or contact on his or her unpredictable pilgrimage or soul-saving crusade. One such dedicated missionary was the Reverend Arthur R. Teal.

### Gone to Glory

The Reverend Mr. Teal had been for many years the pastor of the Katonah Presbyterian Church in White Plains, New York. He was quiet in demeanor, and his sermons were far from the hell-and-damnation diatribes so popular in that high-collar day. A Princeton graduate, the Reverend Mr. Teal spent most of his time with his considerable library, meditating the imponderables. His supportive wife, Jane Babcock Teal, was to discover that her husband, beneath his retiring exterior, burned to travel the highway of the world for salvation's sake.

This noble ambition was displayed for the first and last time in the Teal marriage on the evening of June 7, 1902, when the Reverend Mr. Teal walked quietly into the parish-house kitchen and informed his wife that he was going out to call on some of his parishioners. She smiled and kissed him on the cheek. The Reverend Mr. Teal kissed her back, then trod slowly out the door and out of her life, never to return.

When it became known that the clergyman was missing, police and church societies across the land inaugurated a frantic search. The Reverend Mr. Teal was a well-known cleric whose disappearance touched even President Theodore Roosevelt, who ordered federal agencies to conduct a worldwide search for the missing clergyman. Nothing could be found of the man; one report had it that he "had covered up his tracks."

When the hunt for the Reverend Mr. Teal was at its zenith, Mrs. Teal received a telegram, ostensibly from her departed husband, which read, "Have gone West to preach the gospel."

The search was called off, and Mrs. Teal sat back and waited for her husband's religious ardor to wear thin. Seventeen years rocked away, and no word came. One day in 1919, Mrs. Teal was informed by a United States agent that her husband had been located as a result of his application to work on a federal project. He was working as a common laborer in the shipyard at Newburg, New York, riveting plates onto a government vessel.

Patience and understanding evaporated in Mrs. Teal. She stormed into the New York Supreme Court petitioning for a legal separation against her husband, charging him with horrible abandonment. The deserted woman took a great deal of time to describe to Justice Arthur B. Tompkins the details of her wedding ceremony in Manhattan's Church of the Heavenly Rest before demanding her separation. Tompkins heard out Mrs. Teal and promptly granted her the separation, remarking from the bench: "This is a very unusual case, very unusual." If Tompkins thought the Teal case was unusual, one might have wondered what his notions would be about a downright religious zealot like Elsie Sigel, whose escapades with the spiritual world ran to exotic Chinatown, where all of Elsie's lights burned bright.

### "The Real Yellow Peril"

Early in the summer of 1909, the prestigious Manhattan household of Paul Sigel rustled with upsetting rumors. The servants were lined up, and the master quietly quizzed them as to the whereabouts of his attractive, voluptuous daughter, Elsie. No one had any answers. Much to her strict parents' objections, not to mention the hardheaded disapproval of her aunt, Elsie had gotten into the habit of traveling at whim about the country, usually seeking do-gooder's work. The thirty-three-year-old daughter sought only to serve her own spiritual needs. She never required money; her family was wealthy and endowed with more than a footnote in the pages of American history.

Elsie's grandfather Franz Sigel had gleaned the glory for the family name more than sixty years earlier. Sigel, in 1848, had led four thousand revolutionaries in a bloody but abortive attempt to overthrow the regime in Prussia and to replace it with a constitutional government similar to that of the United States, a country he greatly admired. When the revolution failed, Sigel selected the United States as his new home. Sigel fled Europe with a price on his head, and he settled in St. Louis, where he became a schoolteacher. A violent antislavery man, Franz Sigel is credited with holding the German communities in Missouri faithful to the Union. He organized the Third Missouri Infantry at the outbreak of the war, and he rose rapidly in the military, his battlefield bravery finally earning for him the rank of general.

Following the Civil War, the Sigels relocated to New York, where they became pillars of the community; Sigel entered New York politics and became the state's Collector of Internal Revenue. He began a German-American newspaper that was widely read, and the German residents began erecting monuments to his achievements in the Civil War, the most notable monument being a towering statue of Sigel in battle dress on Riverside Drive. He died in 1902, fully aware that the granddaughter, upon whom he so lavishly doted, had grown into a religious zealot forever seeking to save souls for the Lord. The old general sighed a moment before death, wishing Elsie would get married.

Elsie, however, thought marriage too conventional, too earthbound. Salvation dominated her life. Some days after her last disappearance, Elsie Sigel sent a telegram to her father from Washington, saying that she was accomplishing some wonderful missionary work in the black ghetto there and that she would return in a few days. Almost a week passed before Paul Sigel grew alarmed at her continued absence. He hired private detectives. They turned up nothing. Sigel went to the police and insisted that they put his daughter on the "confidential list," asking them to make discreet inquiries as to her whereabouts. Nothing came of that either, until June 18, 1909.

On that day, a badly decomposed body of a female with a sash cord tied so tight about the neck that it was embedded in the flesh was found in a furnished room above Sun Leung's chop-suey restaurant in New York. The body had been stuffed into a trunk, and the police recorded their find as "unknown, woman, white, about 33 years, five feet, about 130 pounds, dark complexion and hair, partly dressed with white cotton underwear."

The fourth floor, rear-hall room at 728 Eighth Avenue, had been occupied by a Chinese waiter named Leon Ling, who, like Elsie before him, had vanished. Inside the room, police found scores of letters to Leon from Elsie gushing eternal love. Authorities quickly discovered that Elsie, during her missionary work in Chinatown, when she busied herself with distributing Bibles and preaching the Christian word to the heathen Oriental, met and fell in love with Leon.

The waiter, of course, was the prime suspect in the murder. Worse, the slain woman's family was disinclined to claim the body, the circumstances of Elsie's death too repugnant for them to accept. The idea of a white girl from high society consorting with a lowly Oriental waiter in that Edwardian era was too awful for the Sigels to contemplate. Staring at the strangled body in the morgue, Paul Sigel muttered to reporters: "I do not know her." Paul's prim and narrow-minded sister snapped to the press: "My niece was a faithful member of the Audubon Society and would not wear a bird on her hat as this poor creature did. We do not recognize the body in the morgue as Elsie Sigel and will not bury it. We are convinced that she has wandered away in a temporary fit of mental aberration."

Police, however, were convinced that the dead woman was indeed Elsie Sigel, and when officers brought some of the jewelry found in Leon's threadbare room to Elsie's mother to identify, Mrs. Paul Sigel broke down sobbing and admitted the gems belonged to her daughter. Her sister-in-law again called a press conference the following day and told reporters that Elsie's mother had been taken forcibly to an insane asylum in Connecticut. "Mrs. Paul Sigel is a raving lunatic," the protective aunt announced, "and we doubt that she will ever recover."

The shame of the sham was too much for Elsie's father; he cracked wide open three days later and confessed that the dead woman was his daughter. On the heels of Sigel's admission, police unearthed a waiter in Sun Leung's establishment, one Chon Sing, who had disappeared about the same time as Leon Ling. Chon had occupied a room adjoining Ling's and he was quoted by police as stating, "We talk now." His monologue described Leon Ling's infatuation with Elsie. Ling discovered that Miss Sigel was also seeing another Chinese, Chu Gain, who owned a restaurant on Mott Street, and he found a note (which police recovered) from the sexually active Elsie to Chu; it read: "I don't want you to feel too bad because Willie [her nickname for Ling] was here tonight. You know that I love you and you only and always." Chon watched horrified through the open door between his room and Ling's as the waiter went berserk, grabbed a sash cord and quickly looped it about his true love's neck, strangling her to death amidst shrieks and curses.

Elsie Sigel's vanishing act in the name of religion, her affairs with Orientals, and her ugly demise, fascinated newspaper readers for weeks in Manhattan. The *New York World* gave many columns to the story, featuring in one edition a cartoon showing an attractive young white missionary girl about to enter a Chinatown mission and captioning it with "The Real Yellow Peril." Preachers mounted the pulpits in scores of churches, sermonizing against the horrors of miscegenation. One deacon thundered: "The number of mission workers ruined by their pupils would shock the country."

And Leon Ling? He never reemerged from the world of the vanished into which he conveniently slipped after killing Elsie. His last note to the errant missionary, still in police files, ended with: "I hope you do not get mad with me, because all the trouble comes from me. Hope some day the happiness come to us both."

## In India's Sunny Clime

One true martyr who sought to bring the word of his religion to the masses, in this case the most isolated spot on earth, was Sadhu Sundar Singh, a famous Christian Indian mystic and evangelist. Singh's journey from revelation to disappearance was one of Divine enchantment, he said, although his parents and friends took violent issue with such ideas.

God was a Great Perhaps to Singh in his youth; he was nonchalant when it came to any kind of religion. Then, at the age of sixteen,

Singh was later to relate, a miracle occurred. One morning, as he rubbed the sleep from his eyes, Christ appeared to him in a radiant cloud in his room. He informed his parents and teachers of this marvel and was rewarded for his candor by threats, then outward physical violence, as his entire family literally threw him from his home.

The young convert to Christianity, a wholly unpopular religion in India, went undaunted into the world. Singh embarked upon an evangelistic career that saw him tramping by foot across the great lands of India and China with an occasional sojourn into the hostile heart of Japan. He sought no riches and took no donations of money in his crusade for converts. He carried no money or baggage. Singh became world famous and visited London in 1920 as the first Christian missionary from India.

This truly pious preacher was last seen in 1929, when he headed into the far reaches of Tibet to spread the word of Christ to the mountain people. Somewhere in those lofty peaks, Singh undoubtedly perished for want of food, or succumbed to the bitter climate. Rumors filtering back to civilization said he was killed by gurus who considered him a religious threat. Others reported that he had abandoned his faith and decided to dwell in the high mountains. He was never seen again. On April 24, 1933, an Indian court "presumed" Singh dead.

A month later in that same year an American convert to the teachings of the great Mahatma Gandhi, one Nila Cram Cook, created a worldwide sensation by causing the Mahatma so much shame that he went into a twenty-one-day fast to atone for her blatant sins. Miss Cook was a spiritual wonder, if not the zaniest convert to Hinduism India ever witnessed.

Nila Cram Cook was the flamboyant, irrepressible twenty-two-year-old daughter of George Cram Cook, who, more than any other person connected with the Provincetown Players, was responsible for the first plays of Eugene O'Neill being produced. Nila was as impetuous as her poetic father was inspired. She drifted in and out of the theater and art worlds during the early 1930s before traveling to India in 1932, where, moved by the dedication of Mahatma Gandhi, she "received the call," and without hesitation donned a robe and the Hindu religion at the same moment, changing her name

*Nila Cram Cook as a Gandhi zealot in India before her spectacular vanishing act.*

299

to Nagini Devi, which roughly translates into "Blue Serpent Goddess." Nila placed her small son in a school at Ahmedabad and then threw herself into studies of Gandhi's teachings.

Exactly what the ardent and often capricious Nila did to embarrass the great religious leader is uncertain to this day, but it probably had to do with her moral conduct concerning other young male Gandhi converts. Sick as Gandhi was at the time, the frail little man began a twenty-one-day fast inside his cell at Yerovda Jail on May 8, 1933, to atone for the "errors" committed by his American disciple. Nila wrote a letter to Gandhi while he was fasting in prison, and this subsequently appeared inside the pages of *Harijan*, Gandhi's newspaper, which he edited during his prison fastings. In her letter, Nila Cook admitted and apologized for the "impure and extravagant way" in which she had recently conducted herself.

Asked what the confession meant, Gandhi replied that Miss Cook had done "irreparable damage to her adopted faith by injuring the cause of the Untouchables and corrupting the morals of youths who gathered round her." He insisted that those who worked with the Untouchables, as his disciple Nila Cook had done, must maintain the highest purity.

The "Blue Serpent Goddess" was more than contrite for her sins; Nila visited the Mahatma in the Yerovda Jail, telling reporters when she emerged that she had "made a clean confession to him of my past life . . . I now want to lead a new life in accordance with the teachings of Gandhi."

But the quiet pacifism of Gandhi did not go down easy with Nila, who vanished from the Mahatma's *ashram* (retreat) on October 7, 1933. The distraught Gandhi called a rare press conference at Wardah and made a public appeal for Nila's safe return.

Two days later, on October 19, Nila appeared in Muttra, a Hindu pilgrimage center. She stood outside the home of a Dr. Sharma, one of Gandhi's fervent supporters. The "Blue Serpent Goddess," apparently on her last legs, asked that Dr. Sharma take her in, explaining that she was Gandhi's famous American follower. Sharma demanded proof that Nila was a Gandhi supporter before he would give her shelter.

"I can't give you that proof now," Nila stated, "But allow me inside and I will telegraph to Gandhi and you will have your proof."

Sharma, leaning out of a window, repeatedly wiped his brow and explained that it was all too much for him and that he was ill, running a temperature of 104. The doctor told the "Blue Serpent Goddess" to go away.

"No!" yelled Nila defiantly. "I shall lie at the gate of your house until you allow me inside!" With that, she threw herself down into the dust.

The doctor told Nila that he would send for the police. Sharma ordered a servant to run for the constables. With that Nila Cook jumped up, brushed the dirt from her resplendent robe and dashed off down the street to once again disappear. She was missing for another week, but there were reports of her visiting several Hindu shrines and being denied admittance to an American mission house, where she provoked another shouting match.

A massive search was conducted for the missing Nila, but she was nowhere to be found inside India. A month later, to Gandhi's relief, Nila Cram Cook showed up in New Delhi. But she was a much-changed religious zealot. The stern, spartan life of Gandhi and his followers were not for Nila—not any more. She complained to reporters that she had slept without blankets on a bed of bricks for eight months, and the food at the cantonment made meals served in Salvation Army posts epicurean delights. She decided to turn her back on that "rigid" life. "One day," she recalled, "Gandhi stated that he had not put a fence around the cantonment and any girl could leave, so I took the hint and left while the others were busy with their prayers. . . . I am finished with it. I took the seminary vows too seriously. . . . I do not wish to be uncharitable, but I would rather draw the veil on the ashram life and think of realizing my new dreams."

What were Nila's dreams? Well, she explained, she was seriously considering an offer to star in a movie to be made by a Bombay film company. She was not sure about that kind of career for, perhaps, she was still a little under the Mahatma's spell.

Before concluding her conference, Nila Cram Cook turned back to newsmen and pronounced loudly: "I don't care what others say. I want speed! I want to fly! I want to attend orchestra dances!"

A short time later, Nila, borrowing an auto from a European firm, jammed the accelerator of the car almost through the floorboard until she reached speeds in excess of 70 m.p.h. on the rough, ungraded roads outside New Delhi, speeds which caused the car to turn over several times. She received only minor bruises, but it convinced everyone that the "Blue Serpent Goddess" had definitely made up her mind.

Nothing more touching exists in the realms of the missing than family members reunited after long periods of time—lost brothers finding each other, a mother discovering her daughter or son, a father found or a father finding his family. These moments are the emotionally charged highlights of many a lifetime. But often such reunions serve up heartbreak, disillusionment and outright rage.

### Daddy's Little Girl

The first significant disappearance and reunion in this century's family portrait began on April 23, 1900, when thirteen-year-old Adele Boas went shopping with her mother in the better stores along Manhattan's Fifth Avenue. Adele, who attended a fashionable private school, was tall for her age; in fact, she looked like a young woman. As her mother browsed through some jewelry, Adele took the opportunity to slip away. The Boas family—the girl was the niece of Emil L. Boas, general passenger agent of the prestigious Hamburg-American Steamship Company—reacted by calling out police and private investigators, and alerting the press.

Adele's father advertised far and wide for her return, offering huge amounts of money to anyone who could find her. Several years elapsed, but Boas would not give up the hunt for his daughter. A bookbinder, who had read about the rewards posted for Adele, finally led the father to his daughter; she was slinging hash in a Boston diner. The bookbinder collected a $5,000 reward. The Boases were reunited, newsmen taking pictures of Adele as she sobbingly collapsed into her father's arms, the father embracing his daughter, while he too wept openly. Later, Adele confided to classmates that she had left home to strike out on her own. "I was tired of being a mamma's baby," she said.

Like the long-searching Boas, Earl B. Beers, of Newark, New Jersey, had spent years, eighteen in all, searching for his daughter Margaret, whom he had not seen since he divorced his wife when the girl was only twelve months old. Beers spent thousands of dollars utilizing every conceivable method to locate his child, but to no avail. In 1926 he had the idea of using the radio, and he broadcast his appeal over Station WGCP in Newark. The gimmick worked.

Mrs. Bertha Scheideman of Rochester, New York, heard the broadcast and immediately wrote to Beers, telling him that his daughter had married and was living in Detroit as Mrs. Howard J. Bowman. Beers left for Michigan and was soon reunited with his happy, though somewhat startled, daughter.

Nothing could have shocked Dr. Joseph T. Buxton more than hearing that his eighteen-year-old daughter Helen vanished on January 30, 1930, from the exclusive Wood School in Langhorne, Pennsylvania. Dr. Buxton, head of the Elizabeth Buxton Hospital in Newport News, Virginia, caused a six-state alarm to be sent out on his daughter.

It was only a matter of a few days before Helen was found, but it was time enough to badly frighten Miss Buxton's doting father. Helen, using the name Mildred Carlston, had taken a job as a maid in the North Philadelphia home of Mrs. Margaret Kraft. Mrs. Kraft became suspicious of the girl after hearing about the missing Helen Buxton and noticing the initials "H.B." in a pair of her new maid's galoshes, and she immediately informed authorities. Helen was returned home, glad to be back among the living. Domestic work was more demanding than she had expected, although she told reporters: "I wanted to show Dad that I was able to earn my own living in the world."

The daughter of John Lee Johnson, an engineer in the merchant marine, was lost to him in 1947. Johnson, while on board a Japanese vessel, was suddenly paralyzed and sent to a hospital in Japan when the ship docked. While recuperating, the hospital staff lost all his papers including the names and addresses of his family then living in Norfolk, Virginia. Johnson was not aware of his wife's death during his absence, nor the fact that his daughter, ten-year-old Doris Lee, had been sent to live with distant relatives.

When he returned to the United States, Johnson began a search for Doris Lee. In February, 1977, Johnson told his story to a reporter of the *Norfolk Ledger Dispatch*, which ran his lost-daughter tale. Johnson shipped out, but one of Doris' cousins read the article and called Johnson's daughter, who had become Mrs. Doris Lee Jackson, of Gainesville, Florida. Mrs. Jackson later explained to reporters that "since the story gave the name of daddy's boat and the company he worked for, my cousin was able to follow his course along the East Coast and finally get the number of the boat in New York."

When Johnson walked down the gangplank of his ship in New York he was amazed to hear a dockside sailor call out to him: "Your daughter's on the phone." Johnson stepped to the phone, and his most precious dream was realized. Johnson and Doris Lee excitedly made plans to visit each other that night, Mrs. Jackson and her sixteen-year-old son, Thomas, flying from Florida to New York. And that night in the Sheraton Inn at La Guardia Airport, father and daughter raced into each other's arms, crying, hugging and laughing.

Tall, thin, beaming, the fifty-seven-year-old Johnson sat down and rubbed his tear-swollen eyes. "In my fantasies in my search for my daughter," he said in a breaking voice to newsmen, "I wondered when, where and how it would end. . . . I imagined walking up to houses, knocking and asking little kids if their mother's name was Doris Lee." Johnson held onto his daughter. "She was a pretty baby," he said, in a choked voice. Taking her hand, the sailor looked at her. "She's still pretty."

### Seeking Sisters and Brothers

A last-minute decision to postpone a trip not only saved the life of twenty-one-year-old Mary Thompson, but oddly doomed her to the world of the lost for eighteen years. When Miss Thompson decided not to sail on the *Lusitania*, on May 15, 1915, she dashed off a note to her two sisters saying she would be traveling with a British couple as their maid. The note never arrived. Neither did the *Lusitania*, which led Mary's sisters to believe that she had perished on board the great liner after it had been torpedoed off the Irish coast.

Mary traveled for sixteen years with the British couple, sending off letters from remote corners of the world to her sisters. Their addresses, however, had changed, and, for one reason or another, the missives were never delivered. For all those years, Mrs, John L. Brown, of Geneva, New York, and Mrs. Terrance Mooney, of Philadelphia, thought Mary dead.

In 1933, her health failing, Mary Thompson, then thirty-nine, retired from domestic service in Atlantic City, New Jersey. Having nothing but time to squander, Mary began to actively seek her sisters. Some months later she found Mrs. Mooney and Mrs. Brown. "It's as if she had returned from the dead," remarked the joyous Mrs. Brown.

Of the many hundreds of relatives found by various social agencies, one of the most remarkable was the locating of Mrs. Dorta Rafeld, who in 1929 had been living in Riga, Latvia, being separated from her sister, Mrs. Anna Taube, of Tacoma, Washington. The sisters had parted in 1909, but Mrs. Taube had never ceased to search for Dorta. The locating of the lost sisters, accomplished by the Department of Immigrant Aid of the Council of Jewish Women, was instigated in 1929 by none other than Nadejda Constantinovea Krupskaya, wife of Nikolai Lenin, founder of Soviet Russia. Madame Krupskaya became interested in the case after Mrs. Rafeld wrote her a letter asking for help in finding her sister. Lenin's widow quickly contacted the Jewish organization that had also been contacted by Mrs. Taube. This set in motion a joyous reunion between the sisters a short time later.

It took the memory of marks on a tiny body to locate George Burke, who had been stolen by his father and taken to Boston to live with his paternal grandmother in 1903. In 1918, George's mother, Mrs. Margaret Reid, since remarried, read a story of a sixteen-year-old youth named George Burke, who was being held in the New York Tombs prison.

The story related how the boy had been placed in a Catholic orphan asylum following the death of his grandmother and remained there until he was twelve when he was sent to work for a farmer. Several years and beatings later, George ran away. He was arrested for vagrancy in Boston and sent to the Massachusetts Training School at Westborough. He was paroled in 1918 and traveled to New York to obtain a job. There he was arrested for possession of a revolver. How he came to be carrying the revolver, Burke did not say. The boy was described as having a peculiar scar on his forehead.

Mrs. Reid sent for her eldest son, John R. Burke, a warrant officer in the U.S. Navy who was stationed at the Brooklyn Navy Yard. Burke went to the Tombs and asked to see George Burke. He was shown to the boy's cell. John Burke looked down at the thin boy before him, saying nothing for a full minute as he scrutinized his face.

"I thought you might be my brother," he said.

"I never knew I had a brother," stammered George. He put out his hand and John Burke seized it and held onto it.

"My mother read in a paper of your arrest and somehow she got the idea that you were her lost son. She told me that I would know you by a scar and a birthmark. The scar she said was plainly visible at the time you were taken away, when you were seven months old."

George Burke nervously rubbed his hand over the scar on his forehead. John Burke asked him to remove his shirt, saying he should have a pink birthmark on his right shoulder. The boy bared his shoulder. The birthmark was present.

"Can I see my mother before they send me away?" George asked.

"Yes," John Burke said, "if you are my brother . . ." The strapping warrant officer gave a great sigh, and tears welled up in his eyes. He clasped the boy to him. ". . . and I believe you are! And they won't send you away either, kid. . . . No, sir . . . not if there's any way on God's green earth to prevent it."

Mrs. Reid and John Burke met with authorities the next day. George Burke, ex-orphan, was put in custody of the family he had lost fifteen years earlier.

A bitter quarrel between Hippolyte and Russell Van den Berg, father and son, resulted in sixteen-year-old Russell running away in 1913. Though the Van den Berg family, of Elizabeth, New Jersey, searched for the boy, there was no word of him until a telegram arrived from Police Chief Brannon of Albany, Georgia, in 1922, stating that their son Russell was being held on a vagrancy charge. Victor Van den Berg traveled to Georgia, paid the youth's fine and took him home with him to New Jersey.

"Where did you go?" Victor asked his brother on their train ride home.

"I was in China," replied Russell.

"China! How did you get way over there?"

"I was in Japan, too, and a lot of those other strange countries way out East."

"Lordy!"

"I had fun," smiled Russell Van den Berg, "and plenty of it!"

### Mother and Child

There is nothing so persistent in this world as a mother in search of her lost child. She will usually sacrifice everything—love, home, friends, security, peace of mind—to retrieve that bit of flesh and blood that she feels is so exclusively hers. Not even war and famine stood in the way of one mother, a woman named Raymond, who had lost her boy in the dust of the Kaiser's marching legions.

Gabriel Henri Raymond, thirteen years old, was playing in the middle of a street in his home town of Mericourt, in the Department of Pas de Calais, on October 3, 1914, when the street was suddenly filled with German cavalry, a mortal storm of rattling sabers, guttural shouts and threats, trampling, killing hooves of dashing horses that drove all before it. The boy was swept up with more than two thousand other villagers and chased from the area. He ran for his life all the way to distant Lens. There he stayed, an orphan, for months, never being able to contact his mother.

Mrs. Raymond was told by authorities that her son had drowned when a refugee ship en route to England struck a German mine and sank. Still, the woman refused to believe the report. All through the war she wrote hundreds of letters to various government agencies, both German and French, but received no word. Long after the war, Mrs. Raymond continued her letterwriting, even contacting officials in London in hopes that Gabriel had, after all, eventually escaped to England. In 1927, when her belief in her son's existence was almost at an end, the French mother received word that Gabriel was, indeed, alive in London. Mrs. Raymond's thirteen-year vigil was rewarded when her son, who had forgotten everything about his youth except his last name, returned to the village of his birth and the arms of his mother.

There are countless stories similar to that of the Raymonds. Charles F. Killelea, although only sixteen years old, ran away from his Leominster, Massachusetts, home, despite his mother's violent opposition, to join the British Royal Air Force in 1915. He wrote from France many times, but received no reply; his mother had moved. Following the war, Killelea traveled to India, where he became ill. When he emerged from the hospital some months later, Killelea was told that his mother had been informed that he was dead. He then enlisted as an able seaman aboard the *Leviathan*, one of the great luxury liners of the 1920s. In 1926 Killelea's mother found him, after steamship officials checked his name against their employee roster; the woman had haunted every business in New York seeking her son, not believing him dead at all.

The two were reunited in New York, where the mother had moved, when the *Leviathan* docked. Able seaman Killelea was allowed to be the first to walk down the gangplank into the arms of his waiting, weeping mother. Overcome by the shock, the elderly woman collapsed and had to be hospitalized.

Harry Dahl, long thought to have been killed in World War I, suddenly appeared in his mother's house in Jenison Park, Michigan, on Christmas Day, 1920. Without a word, the tearful Mrs. John Dahl motioned her son to sit down in a vacant chair she had kept for six years, *knowing* he would return one day to her.

The return of seventeen-year-old Friddel Mueller of Bayonne, New Jersey, on New Year's Day, 1915, after he had been missing since July 6, 1910, not only cheered his foster mother, but may have saved her from imprisonment. Friddel, who had been placed with Mrs. James Hess when but a youngster, ran away on a lark. The joke boomeranged. Police picked him up several hundred miles away and he was subsequently placed in a boy's school in Poughkeepsie, New York, where he remained for three years. Friddel escaped from the home in 1913 and traveled to Brooklyn, where he got a job.

Police were puzzled until Friddel appeared as if by magic. He explained to astonished police and neighbors that when New Year's Day arrived, he remembered his happy childhood days with his foster mother and, moved by nostalgic longing, decided to visit her. Friddel Mueller, upon hearing of ridiculous charges brought against Mrs. Hess, shouted: "I am dead, huh? Murdered, huh? Well, let's see how they like a corpse living around here." He moved back into his foster mother's house permanently.

Tragedy and joy are equal products of mothers seeking lost children. Mrs. Helen M. Walsh, seventy-eight, sought her son, Frank, for twelve years after he disappeared in 1904, when he was thirty-six. Since Frank was known to have liked the sea, Mrs. Walsh rented rooms along the New York waterfront, plaguing ship's captains for any news of her missing son. She died in 1916 in a dockside rooming house after walking the piers all day in search of her son. Frank P. Walsh never made the long voyage home.

In 1918, E. W. Curtiss stole his nine-year-old daughter, Grace, and deposited her in a spot unknown. He defied the courts to take his child from him and place her with Mrs. Curtiss, who had recently been divorced from him. Cited for contempt, Curtiss imprudently published a volatile pamphlet attacking Lucien F. Burpee, the judge in the case. He was arrested, convicted of criminal libel, and sentenced to jail. Curtiss became so violent during his sentencing that he was ultimately placed in an insane asylum, vowing that he would never reveal where he had sent his daughter.

Mrs. Curtiss conducted a four-year search for her child, but Grace was nowhere to be found. Then, by mind-staggering luck, Mrs. Curtiss was returning to her Connecticut home on July 17, 1922, when she spotted a teen-age girl who looked familiar, in Manhattan's crowded Grand Central Station. Clawing, fighting, elbowing, shoving her way through the mass of people, Mrs. Curtiss managed to overtake the girl. It was her daughter Grace. "Mommy? Is it really you?" the girl said. The mother was too overcome with emotion to respond in any other way than by clutching Grace to her.

### Out of the Wilderness

No greater fear can grip a parent than one who has lost a child in the wilds. Of such dangerous disappearances the threat is two-fold—one entailing the human element, which poses kidnapping or murder; the second, to be left to the fate of starvation, climate and preying beasts. All these were the fierce apprehensions of John and Jeanette Papol one sunny day in late August 1962, when they discovered that their small son had vanished inside New York's vast Heckscher State Park during a Cub Scout outing.

Other families and droves of running little scouts were interrupted while gulping potato salad and hot dogs to hear a loudspeaker suddenly blare: "A small boy has been lost! He is blond, three years old, wearing a plaid shirt and brown shorts. His name is Stephen Papol!"

It was nothing new. Tens of thousands of children on such outings disappear momentarily each summer as their parents conduct a frantic search that ends usually in minutes, the relieved mother and father delivering a finger-wagging lecture or a paddle to the behind. In little Stevie Papol's case it was not a matter of minutes but long grueling hours of agony.

John Papol repeatedly told how Stevie had vanished into the woods while his sister, Victoria, age seven, who was in charge of the little boy, ran to get a sandwich from her grandmother. (Mrs. Papol, age twenty-nine, had her hands full; the mother of nine was watching six of her eight other children.) The family searched deep into the dense woods beyond the picnic clearing for hours. As the sun began to set, Papol took over the loudspeaker himself, desperately pleading with the indifferent crowds: "Hasn't anyone seen him? He's wearing orange socks, one of them is darned with brown thread, I know. I darned it."

Officials were hurried into the search. State Police by the score arrived. Heckscher State Park is no limited forest preserve but a 1,500-acre morass of thick woods and swamps running along the shore of Long Island, New York. By 8 P.M. the Coast Guard had sent out helicopters, which hovered along the shoreline, their searchlights spot-flooding dense parts of the forest. Police, firemen, volunteers, more than a thousand persons, joined in the search. Dozens of bloodhounds were pressed into service. They tramped along through hundreds of acres, shouting the boy's name, crashing through the tangled underbrush and sending wildlife scurrying before them.

At midnight a terrific storm halted the search. The following day, the number of searchers had swelled to more than two thousand people who encompassed the huge park and began moving slowly toward its center from its limits. Another storm came up the second night, and the hunt had to be momentarily abandoned. By this time, Jeanette Papol began to lose hope. "I am beginning to fear that some love-starved woman took him," she nervously blurted.

Many in the search reacted the same way, stating that no three-year-old could survive without food or water, and exposed to two violent storms. The boyhunt plodded on, but as hours slid by, the searchers began to lose their determination. Many of the volunteers gave up and went home.

One person who could not give up was an elderly woman named Mrs. Rosemarie Finger, a grandmother who, with her husband Raymond, had marched through the woods looking for Stevie for two days: "He's in that wooded area near the picnic grounds," she told her husband. "I know it." Following her hunch, the Fingers went back to the site on the morning of the third day. As the grandmother crunched through the bushes, she looked down and saw a pair of orange socks. Sweeping aside a bush with her hands, Mrs. Finger found little Stevie. He was scratched, dehydrated and covered with insect bites. He had taken off his shoes and orange socks and placed them neatly at his side.

Rubbing his eyes, the three-year-old blinked up at Mrs. Finger and said only one word: "Mommy." The grandmother took him in her arms and wept. "I've never known such a feeling," she later said.

Stephen Papol was rushed to a hospital, where he was found to be in good condition, despite his sixty-seven-hour ordeal. While he was eating ice cream and fondling a lollipop, Mrs. Papol rushed into the room. The boy smiled at her with tired eyes and, before she could embrace him, he said: "I looked for you last night but you didn't come."

Kevin Dye wasn't looking for anyone when he disappeared amid the towering cliffs and timbered canyons of Casper Mountain, Wyoming, on July 18, 1971. In fact, the blond, blue-eyed nine-year-old went out of his way to evade discovery, for Kevin was emotionally disturbed, a child who, inside his own disappearance, became like the wild things of the forest.

The Dye family's ordeal began with a pattern identical to the Papol near-tragedy. A picnic of the United Methodist Church was held high up on 8,200-foot Casper Mountain. Philip Dye, the church's thirty-five-year-old treasurer, had noticed his son having difficulty speaking to other boys playing on swings. Kevin had suddenly screeched incoherently, flailed his arms about and badly frightened his companions. The father took his son to the family

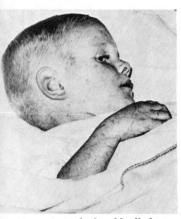

*Scratched and badly bitten but otherwise healthy was little Stephen Papol after his horrendous three-day disappearance in New York's Heckscher State Park in 1962. (UPI)*

car, where he sat for fifteen minutes to calm down. It was not an unusual occurrence for the Dyes. Their son suffered from aphasia, and he was subject to epileptic seizures, for which he was constantly taking special medicine. Dr. Robert Fowler, the family's physician, had pointed out that Kevin was not retarded; he merely had trouble voicing his thoughts, which led to such intense frustration that he would babble, grope, and throw his arms helplessly in the air, and often went into crying jags and tantrums. Fowler called Kevin an "expressive aphasic"—"He's like a little radio set with a damaged speaker. The input is perfect, but the speaker connection doesn't work."

When the church picnic broke up, Philip Dye and his wife Carolyn returned to their car. Kevin was not there. Philip ran to a knot of little boys playing ping-pong. Yes, Kevin had been playing with them, but he had gone off. Maybe he was in a roughhewn treehouse nearby. Philip checked the treehouse, but Kevin was nowhere in sight. Dye rounded up a few of the men still lingering at the picnic and began a search. Two hours of calling through the forbidding woods and climbing the craggy slopes of the mountain produced nothing. Dye drove to a resort restaurant and called Casper Sheriff William Estes. A posse was quickly formed and converged on the camp site.

Carolyn Dye had returned to her nearby home, growing anxious as each hour passed. At sunset a phone call informed her that her son was missing. In the words of writer Edward D. Fales, Jr., "she felt her throat tighten as she looked out her big picture window toward the mountain, a gloomy lump of granite towering over Casper like a great wave about to break." Mrs. Dye jumped into a neighbor's car and sped back up the mountain to join her husband and the sheriff's posse in the search. The party crashed through the almost impenetrable forest on the mountain, falling over rocks and rotting timber. By 3 A.M., finding themselves bruised, cut, and in pitch darkness, the searchers called off the hunt, to resume the search at dawn.

The Casper *Star-Tribune* had banner-lined the story by then. Something strange happened. The town of Casper, labeled dissolute and indifferent to the cares of others, a community where murder, divorce and crime seemed to be the order of the day, came to life,

313

its citizens galvanized into one force by the striking story of the mentally crippled little boy lost on the shooting peaks that loomed above their all too predictable lives.

Sheriff Estes was amazed the next morning to see thousands of cars wending their way up the mountain roads to the camp site as half the town turned out to look for Kevin. Boy Scouts, laborers, cowboys, a contingent of National Guardsmen, plain citizens formed a 4,000-person search party that began to comb Casper Mountain inch by agonizing inch.

As the word went out on the boy's disappearance, volunteers from as far as Chicago, St. Louis and Philadelphia traveled to Casper to look for Kevin. Everyone had a theory, everyone had a plan. Sheriff Estes was told by well-meaning hunters that search teams should be dressed in Santa Claus costumes to entice the boy from the woods since by that time it was known he was purposely avoiding the searchers. Someone else insisted that the bell-ringing song from an ice-cream truck be broadcast through the woods.

The Dyes did employ real inducements, offering in their shouts for their son his favorite sandwich, peanut butter and syrup, loudly singing his favorite song, *I Love Trash*, from the TV program *Sesame Street*. There was no response. The Dyes worried not only about Kevin's survival against nature but against his own body, knowing that he would require his daily medicine to ward off an epileptic attack. Carolyn Dye drove to a cliff overlooking the dangerous Elkhorn Canyon, where the boy was said to have been seen, and, using a police bullhorn, pleaded for her son to come to the sound of her voice. Her pleas echoed hauntingly through the canyon but no answer came.

Days sank into the west, but the searchers were indomitable. Keeping hope alive were the many reports that Kevin had raided garbage cans and empty cabins, stealing food to stay alive as he moved even deeper into the wildest territories, areas incredibly dense with lodgepole pines, blind deep gorges easily stepped into, an angry wilderness acrawl with poisonous rattlesnakes and hungry brown bears.

One report from a cabin couple had it that Kevin passed their place along the Crimson Dawn Trail. He was singing, whistling, and talking to the birds, striking the ping-pong paddle that he had taken from the picnic area against the sides of trees as he went. Some days later a nineteen-year-old youth, who was mentally retarded, approached a group of searchers holding that paddle. It was flecked with blood. Asked where he had found the paddle, the confused youth stammered and shrugged; he could not remember. Now it was thought Kevin might have been a murder victim. But hours later, the pilot of a helicopter chopping over the 12-square-mile area marked off for the search sighted something moving rapidly into a canyon; he caught a fleeting look at a small boy dressed in loafers, shorts and a blue T-shirt. He was obviously frightened by the copter and was hiding.

The Dyes drove their small car to that area. They had filled it with Kevin's favorite toys. Carolyn Dye placed a toy clock from Kevin's school room on the car and a large sign reading: "Kevin the clockwatcher says it's time to go home. Wait here for Mama." The Dyes moved off into hiding, thinking not to scare their son away. The car sat silent and no one arrived.

Natrona County Sheriff Estes, as the days elapsed, tried to be optimistic with newsmen; he told them, "We know where he is. . . . We just can't find him." Deputy Sheriff Roy Street was less enthusiastic; he grumbled, "I don't think they're ever going to catch him—if he doesn't want to be caught."

Countered Carolyn Dye: "He's become a small animal pursued by big animals and he's frightened."

Crack rescue teams, trained in finding lost people high in the mountains, arrived from Boulder and Evergreen, Colorado. An official lectured them: "This boy has become an animal. He doesn't think like any of us. If you see him, grab hold of him. And it might take two or three, because he'll fight!"

One five-man team of the Rocky Mountain Rescue Group, decided to investigate Middle Fork Canyon, where the bloody paddle had been found, if the sketchy memory of the retarded youth who found it was to be believed. It was the tenth day of the search. Burly, intrepid Mike Murphy of this group followed one stream in the area, thinking the boy would naturally drift toward a fresh-water course. The lone searcher sloshed down the stream, jumping onto rocks, climbing arduously about fallen timber. He kept his eyes on the banks of the stream as he moved slowly along. Suddenly he

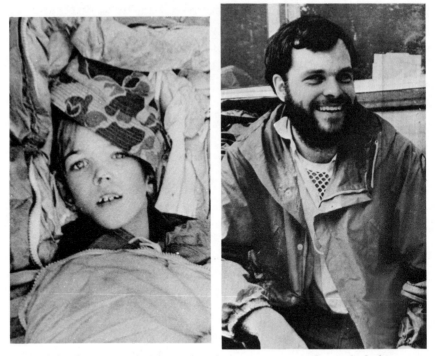

*Exhausted and near starving, Kevin Dye is shown moments after being plucked from the Wyoming wilderness. Rescuer Michael Murphy followed his instincts to find the missing boy. (*UPI *and* WIDE WORLD*)*

froze. There, lying on a soft verdant patch of grass next to the water, his shoes off, was the thin sleeping body of Kevin Dye.

Murphy quietly approached the boy. Another member of the team, Charles Demarest, who had come up the stream, stood off in the distance, watching Murphy creep forward. "There is a mystical moment when you rescue someone whom you've been seeking for a long, long time," Demarest later remembered. "It's reverence. You don't want to approach him—for suddenly you have discovered how wonderful a human life is."

Kneeling beside the sleeping child, Murphy gently ran his hand over Kevin's horribly scratched face, noting the boy's pencil-thin legs. There was no fever. Kevin awoke to the human touch. Murphy smiled wide down at him and softly said: "Hi, Kevin. Do you want to go home?"

The boy's eyes popped open. From his mouth came a long, sighing "ye-e-es." Dehydrated, near starvation, the child was carefully placed upon a stretcher. He had lost twenty-five pounds. Dr. Fowler later stated that one more day in the wilderness would have certainly spelled his death. (The traumatic experience, as was learned months later, somehow helped Kevin enormously to communicate with his peers; he stopped his tantrums and arm-flailing.)

As Mike Murphy and another rescue-team member carried the once lost boy through the wilderness trails, the party became aware of the beauty of life about them, the sun filtering through the high pines, the sweet aroma of wildflowers filling their nostrils, the rustle of animals beneath the leaves, the trills and chatters of birds above them.

"Gee," said Mike Murphy, "what a great day for a hike!"

The Great Unknown has been for centuries the resting place for the strangest, most bizarre disappearances in history, a netherworld where dwell all manner of ghosts and all forms of good and evil in the supernatural. It is in this highly speculative Valhalla of the once-was, the maybe, the perhaps, that the most intriguing mysteries have their answers. At least it is convenient for researchers, historians, and detectives to point in that direction as a way of explaining the inexplicable. But what, in such weird cases of missing persons, one might ask, is the true direction? Which way, for instance, did the 120 inhabitants of Roanoke Island go in 1587? Sleuths are still looking for that wilderness path.

### *"Croatoan" Only Knows*

Roanoke Island, off the coast of Virginia, was discovered for the first time in 1584 by two British captains sponsored by Sir Walter Raleigh. Seven more of Raleigh's British ships arrived in 1587, led by Governor John White. The visitors planned to establish a permanent settlement at Roanoke. The small colony, however, was in deep trouble by late summer; they had less provisions than would be required to endure long winters on the windswept island. White and his ships departed for England on August 27 to replenish supplies. The Governor left behind 120 pioneer souls, including his wife and his daughter Eleanor, wife of Ananias Dare. (Their daughter, Virginia Dare, named after the state of Virginia, was the first Christian child born in the new land on August 18.)

Delayed by more than three years because of England's war with Spain, Governor White was unable to return to Roanoke until 1590. As his ships approached the island he had his trumpeters blare recognition signals. The British seamen loudly sang tunes, their husky voices echoing across the water as they made for the harbor. But no one answered them. As White and his men landed, there was no one to greet them, and, as the relief party worked its way through the forests to the main camp, they became increasingly alarmed at the sights that met them. The fields of crops had been long abandoned, fencing was in disrepair. Not far off the beach they found a large tree, completely stripped of bark and etched deep into its wood the letters CRO, which had no meaning whatever to White and the others.

As they entered the encampment the hearts of the relief party sank. It was completely deserted, the cabins empty, the stockade overrun with creeping underbrush and vines. Frantically White and others searched for a carved sign of the cross, a sign that, on their departure in 1587, they agreed with the colonists to look for if there would have been any trouble, especially with the Hatteras Indians. There was a sign, but it was as arcane as the first one found that day.

White wrote into his journal:

> We passed toward the place where they were left in sundry houses, but we found the houses taken down and the place very strongly enclosed with a high palisado of great trees, with curtains and flankers very fort-like, and one of the chief trees, or posts at the right side of the entrance had the bark taken off, and five feet from the ground in fair capital letters was graven CROATOAN without any cross or sign of distress; this done, we entered the palisado, where we found many bars of iron, two pigs of lead, four iron-fowlers, iron sacker-shot, and such like heavy things thrown here and there, almost overgrown with grass and weeds. From thence, we went along the water side, towards the point of the creek to see if we could find any of their boats or pinnace, but we could perceive no sign of them nor any of the last falcons or small ordinances which were left with them at my departure from them.

The only trace found of what was to be called the "Lost Colony" was a fresh footprint left in the sand near the northern tip of the island. White and his men later construed this to be that of an Indian hunter. The mystery of the mass disappearance of 120 persons remained a mystery. There were many theories that took up the Roanoke Island puzzlement. Some said that raiding Spaniards or hostile Indians had dragged the settlers off and then massacred them. There certainly would have been signs of a struggle and of these there were none, not even a broken crock to bear out the idea.

North Carolina historian Hugh T. Lefler hypothesized: "One of the most plausible theories—though seldom advanced—is that the colonists, finally despairing of relief, sailed for England in a boat which had been left with them by White in 1587 and were lost at sea." This idea is not a savory one; the colonists knew all too well

319

that the small boat left for their convenience would never hold up in an ocean crossing. The boat was strictly for travel between the island and the mainland.

Perhaps the best explanation lies with the Hatteras Indian tribe also known as the Croatoans, a friendly lot who had encouraged the settlement from the start, bringing the colonists food from their neighboring island of Hatteras and even helping to erect the stockade. Most logical is the idea that the settlers, having been attacked or threatened with attack by a hostile, nomadic tribe of Indians, sought safety with their admiring friends the Croatoans.

Advancing this most credible theory was historian John Lawson who wrote in 1709:

> A farther confirmation of this we have from the Hatteras Indians . . . who tell us that several of their ancestors were white people, and could talk in a book, as we do, the truth of which is confirmed by grey eyes [a Caucasian, not an Indian physical feature], being found frequently amongst these Indians, and no others. They value themselves extremely for their affinity to the English and are ready to do them all friendly offices. It is probable that this settlement miscarried for want of timely supplies from England, or through the treachery of the natives, for we may reasonably suppose that the English were forced to cohabit with them for relief and conversation, and in the process of time, they conformed themselves to the manners of their Indian relations.

Ten years after Lawson put forward this concept, and more than a century after the "Lost Colony" vanished, white trappers pushed through the wilderness to what was then called Robinson, North Carolina, about one hundred miles inland from Roanoke Island. Here they found, to their amazement, another tribe of Indians whose skins were almost white, whose eyes were blue or gray, and whose language was English. Census takers in 1790, moving through Robinson County, discovered that 54 of the 95 families names used by the Roanoke settlers were being used by Indian families in this area.

According to author Edwin C. Hill in 1934:

> In Robinson County, N.C., live some 12,000 Indians known as the Robinson County Indians. They are a fine and handsome people. Some have blue eyes. Some have gray eyes. They speak only the

English language. They use phrases of speech that have scarcely been heard since the days of Shakespeare.

Are these, then, the descendants of Roanoke's "Lost Colony," one might ask? Only a 400-year-old history has that answer, history and the person who thoughtfully confused the world by carving that cryptic "CROATOAN" onto a tree.

## Of Counts and Courts

For Count Philipp von Königsmarck, a dashing young Swedish nobleman, there would never be any other woman in his life than the beautiful Sophia Dorothea of Lüneburg. They had been playmates together as children, growing up in the Swedish and German courts, both of them born into the aristocracy. There was one problem, however, that prevented the pair from consummating their fiery love. Princess Sophia was married to her brutish, power-lusting cousin, George Louis, Crown Prince of Hanover, who was to become George I of England when the Hanoverian rulers assumed the British throne. (Sophia's historical position in the line of kings proved to be astounding, for she was to become the direct ancestress of the Hohenzollern and Windsor dynasties, the unhappy progenitor of both Kaiser Wilhelm and King George V.)

The love-starved Sophia returned Philipp's affection and by early 1694, the affair leaked out to intriguers in the Hanover court, not the least of whom was the much-married Countess von Platen. By that time Philipp had been named the Commander of the Palace Guard at Hanover. He lived in a large mansion adjacent to the royal palace, with only a large garden separating him from his true love Sophia. How many times the count and the princess met through the hedgerows is a matter of speculation; it is still highly doubtful that they ever slept together, a not uncommon sexual suppression in that day of chivalrous foppery, when a lady's honor usually meant a man's celibacy.

Going and coming to the royal court, Königsmarck presented himself as the beau ideal of young and noble manhood. He worshiped Sophia from twenty feet beneath her throne, and she lovingly glimpsed him whenever her husband George was busy upbraiding servants and ministers, belching tirades against other royal houses, and gustily living up to his image of being the greatest boor and petty tyrant in Europe.

Always close to the Commander of the Guard was the scheming Countess von Platen, who, though ten years Philipp's senior, lusted after the young man with the passion of a berserk nymph. When she learned of Königsmarck's love affair with Sophia, the countess did her utmost to thwart their meetings and seduce the young count. But the lovers generally outwitted the countess and found ways to maintain their spiritual trysts.

The count's letters to his love princess became more daring. In one missive, anticipating their meeting in the garden, Philipp gushed: "I shall embrace tonight the loveliest of women. I shall kiss her charming mouth. I shall worship her eyes, those eyes that enslave me. I shall hear from her very lips that she loves me. I shall have the joy of embracing her knees; my tears will chase down her incomparable cheeks. I shall hold in my arms the most beautiful body in the world. Verily, Madame, I shall die of joy. But so long as I have time to tell thee that I die thy slave, I care for naught else."

Though Sophia's letters to Philipp were never so grandiloquent, her plans for happiness with the count were much bolder. Only through complete escape could they ever be happy, the princess insisted. "Why should we not fly tonight?" responded Philipp. The couple made elaborate plans to elope. To where they knew not, only that they must flee.

Countess von Platen's court spies intercepted some of the couple's letters. She and her henchmen, it was later claimed, were waiting for the dashing Philipp on the night of July 1, 1694, when he entered the Electoral Palace to steal his princess away. He was seen by many to march up the palace stairs in his handsome Guard's uniform, clutching the hilt of his sword that Sunday night. No one, including his true love Sophia, ever saw Philipp Königsmarck again.

Five days later the princess was informed that Königsmarck was missing. The woman, frantic from waiting in vain from that night of mystery, could learn nothing of his fate. Only rumors were passed on to her by court members, all of them contradictory. The count had been thrown into a dungeon after his elopement plans had been discovered by the love-scorned Countess van Platen, it was said. He had been driven into exile and compelled to live incognito for the rest of his life, came another report.

Königsmarck's relatives, powerful aristocrats all, demanded an explanation from George and his minions. They were answered with vague, evasive replies. When one of the count's relatives, Frederick William von Königsmarck, arrived at the Electoral Palace to conduct an investigation, members of the household guard blocked his path, pressing bayonets to his chest. He was informed by an officer that if he ever showed his face in Hanover again he would be shot on sight. William departed hastily but not before getting from the officer some hazy answers to his questions, answers that led him to believe that Philipp was yet alive.

Another story, one that did not surface for years, had it that Königsmarck, once inside the palace, while walking through the giant, shadowy Knight's Hall, was set upon by assassins in the employ of Countess von Platen, the countess herself being present, and urging, out of her envy, hatred and vengeance, that her hirelings murder the count. It was reported that he put up a terrific battle, dueling four accomplished swordsmen for a half hour, killing two of them before his own cape, which he had discarded in the struggle,

*The possible disastrous end of the missing Count Philipp von Königsmarck.*

323

was hurled about him and entangled his swordarm. By then, the account stated, the countess was at the fringe of the fight, screeching her encouragement to her killers, one of whom bringing down a battle-ax, which split the count's skull and sent him crashing to the stone floor of the palace before the great fireplace. The body was dragged to a vestibule and the smirking von Platen held up a torch to better see the death of the man who would not return her love.

The count's eyes fluttered open and he glared for some seconds up at his murderess. Even to her hired killers, in the flickering light from the torch she held, her face appeared to be horribly grotesque and malignant. Philipp cursed her and with that the countess brought her foot down on his mouth, jamming his head onto the bare floor. The grand lover was dead.

But even this story was pure conjecture to most reliable archivists. The count's body was never discovered; though hundreds of high-placed persons attempted to find a trace of him, Königsmarck had vanished completely. His enigmatic end persists as such to this day, and legend has it that Philipp's ghost haunted the Electoral Palace for centuries, calling out for his beloved Sophia.

The princess had her own haunting to perform—that of her husband, George, who was certainly connected with Philipp's disappearance. On July 17, Countess von Platen, as George's emissary, informed Sophia that Philipp had been killed while resisting arrest. No explanation accompanied this terse announcement. Sophia, for her indiscretions, was exiled to the remote castle of Ahlden in Celle, where she was kept a prisoner. She was allowed to leave the castle only once, to journey to Hanover, where she was officially divorced from George, charged with willful desertion. Königsmarck, though it was obvious he was the corespondent in the divorce, was not mentioned.

Sophia remained a prisoner at Ahlden until her death in 1726. George, by then King of England, returned briefly by coach to Hanover. A small pouch was thrown into his carriage by a mysterious stranger who galloped alongside the coach. Inside the pouch was a letter from his ex-wife. Sophia, in her posthumous missive, spewed forth her loathing for George, telling him that she would see him at Judgment Day and, with her final curse, reminded him of a prophecy made by a Gypsy woman years earlier that he would die immediately following her own demise. The superstitious George did exactly that, perishing some months later, consumed by a frothing fit that ended only in death.

The plotting Countess von Platen fared no better. For years she complained that the ghost of Königsmarck haunted her bedroom and even danced on her "wicked old bed," according to the novelist Thackeray. Before her end came in 1705, the vicious countess first went blind. Then she went mad.

## A Split-Second Vanishment

Few men on record have disappeared so quickly and so mysteriously as the erstwhile Sir Benjamin Bathurst, secret British envoy to the court of the Emperor Francis of Austria. Nothing and no one on this earth could ever precisely explain how this reserved, cautious man evaporated in the middle of a street while surrounded by a half dozen human beings.

Bathurst, born on March 14, 1784, was the third son of Dr. Henry Bathurst, Presbyterian Bishop of Norwich. He had entered diplomatic service early in life, becoming the secretary for various British legations, distinguishing himself at Leghorn. Married to Phillida Call in May 1805, Bathurst was, by then, deeply involved in diplomatic espionage, working with those countries locked in mortal combat with the conquest-mad Napoleon Bonaparte.

Early in 1809, Benjamin Bathurst was sent to Vienna by his relative Earl Bathurst, a ranking official in the British Foreign Department. His mission was to encourage then neutral Austria to join the European federation against Bonaparte. More, Bathurst told the Austrian court, was expected. England promised to invade Spain to combat Napoleon's legions there if Austria would declare war on France. At Bathurst's special urging, Austria did announce hostilities against Napoleon and sent its troops marching into French-occupied territories in Italy, Bohemia and Tyrol. Bathurst, for his efforts, felt that Bonaparte had marked him for death.

The Austrian gambit failed at Wagram, where Napoleon's troops crushed the Austrian army; Bonaparte concluded a swift peace settlement that left great tracts of Austrian lands in his control. Bathurst, who had awaited events at the Austrian court, realized that it was time to flee for England. Napoleon's spies and assassins were everywhere, Bathurst knew, so he selected his escape route carefully. He rejected the route through Trieste and Malta as too dangerous and elected to escape via Berlin, through northern Germany, and then sail for England from Hamburg. By fast coach, Bathurst, traveling under the guise of a merchant named Koch (his secretary took the name Fisher), reached the small town of Perleberg, halfway between Berlin and Hamburg, on November 25, 1809. He was carrying two pistols, both his secretary and valet were also armed, and more arms were kept in the coach in case Napoleon's men should attack.

Stopping at the post-house in Perleberg for fresh horses before dashing on to the next town, Lenzen, Bathurst grew hungry. The secret envoy made no secret that he was a man of wealth, entering the White Swan Inn to order a sumptuous meal while dressed in gray trousers, gray frogged shortcoat, a handsome sable greatcoat lined with violet velvet and a matching fur cap adorning his head. He also wore a beautiful scarf with a large diamond stickpin. Finishing his midday meal, Bathurst demanded to know who commanded the German troops stationed at Perleberg. He was told a Captain Klitzing, who lived in a small house behind the Town Hall, was in charge. Bathurst went to Captain Klitzing, telling the soldier that he was a man named Koch and that he feared that his life was endangered, that mysterious killers were on his trail. He begged for an armed guard. Klitzing laughed at his fears; but, thinking to humor the obviously rich traveler, he assigned two soldiers to stand guard outside the inn while fresh horses were brought to the carriage.

A lady guest at the White Swan saw that Bathurst was in a state of near-collapse, reported *Cornhill Magazine* years later. She "noticed that he seemed profoundly agitated, that he trembled as though ague-stricken, and was unable to raise a cup of tea that was offered him to his lips without spilling it."

It was about 9 P.M. before Bathurst's carriage was ready to depart. He walked outside the inn. He had already dismissed his two-man guard. Bathurst's secretary stood on the inn's stairs paying the innkeeper for services rendered. His valet was at the back of the carriage. A servant from the post-house was adjusting the reins of the lead team in front of the carriage. Though the street was dimly lighted, lanterns hanging nearby shed considerable light on Benjamin Bathurst as he stepped from the inn, walked across the street and walked around the heads of the horses—*and vanished completely and forever.*

The valet came from behind the carriage to talk to his master, but Bathurst was not there. The hostler also stepped to the far side of the coach, and he saw only the bewildered valet. There was nothing on the far side of the coach but an open area where the horses were kept. Looking back to the inn, only the innkeeper and Bathurst's secretary were present. Soldiers at each end of the street never saw the man. The inn was ransacked as soon as the alarm went out. Captain Klitzing ordered every building in Perleberg searched. No one could have spirited the man away, it was certain. Bathurst's carriage was the only one on the entire street when he disappeared.

Many explanations of the Bathurst riddle were put forth over the years. He was murdered by thugs at the inn; he was kidnapped and killed by emissaries of Napoleon; his body was secreted in a dozen distant cities; he committed suicide; he secretly sailed from Königsberg and was lost at sea. None of these was plausible. There was simply no way for the man to escape undetected from the street after he stepped around the horses' heads within view of a half dozen persons. There was no way known to the living of that day or this.

### In Plain View

More than rivaling the amazing disappearance of Benjamin Bathurst was the incredible case of Orion Williamson, who vanished one hot July day in 1854. Williamson, whose farm was just outside Selma, Alabama, was sitting on the porch of his farmhouse with his wife and child, peering across a field to where his horses grazed beneath the sun. Williamson stood up and stretched. "I think I'll bring the animals in," he said to his wife as he started walking

327

across the field to the horses. He picked up a small stick as he went and swished it absent-mindedly against the ankle-deep grass in his path. His family watched him stroll into the field.

A neighboring farmer, Armour Wren, and his son returning from Selma in a buggy were on a road on the other side of the field. They stopped as they saw Williamson approaching. One of them stood up and raised his arm to wave a hello. At that split second, with four sets of human eyes riveted upon him, Williamson seemed to evaporate. A moment earlier, the farmer had been strolling across the wide-open, treeless field. Now he had vanished into thin air, as the saying so knowledgeably goes.

With their mouths agape in disbelief, the Wrens leaped from the buggy and dashed into the field. Mrs. Williamson and her child ran from the opposite end of the field and they met breathlessly at the point where farmer Williamson vanished. There was nothing but bare ground, sparsely covered with grass, at their feet.

"Where? Where?" Mrs. Williamson hysterically cried.

"Impossible," Armour Wren mumbled, on his knees and running his hands over the undisturbed earth. "It's impossible."

For two hours, the Wrens, the wife and the child methodically searched the field. There was no trace of Williamson. Realizing this, Mrs. Williamson, in shock, collapsed and was taken to Selma, where she was hospitalized. More than three hundred men of the town, when the news was frantically spread that afternoon, formed a gigantic search party and proceeded to the field. They formed three hand-to-hand ranks and moved across the field by inches, stopping every foot and kneeling down and threading the ground and the thin grass with their hands. The ranks swept the field in this manner dozens of times until every square inch had been examined, touched, even smelled. When night fell, the operation resumed by torch-lights, with fifty bloodhounds, all given Williamson's scent from old clothing, sniffing back and forth, back and forth across the field.

Weary searchers the next morning were joined by hundreds of the curious from neighboring settlements. A geologist led a team of experts to the middle of the field where Williamson had disappeared and began digging. A few feet beneath the surface was limestone bedrock. There were no cave-ins, crevices, wells, there was nothing but the field.

Williamson's sensational disappearance brought several journalists to the area. One morbidly curious scribe, writing later of this spectacular case in *Can Such Things Be?* was the acerbic Ambrose Bierce, who would himself disappear. In the end, nothing was found of Williamson, not a button or a human hair.

The following spring revealed an odd circle about fifteen feet in diameter. It was the very spot where the farmer had vanished. Within this ring all the grass was dead. This strange looking patch of ground was pointed out to Mrs. Williamson by investigators, but by then the woman was reluctant even to mention her husband's name. Her strange behavior brought forth a barrage of questions. Her voice quavering with fear, the woman finally broke down and told the dogged searchers that for days following the disappearance of her husband she and her child distinctly heard Williamson's voice calling for help from the very spot where he had disappeared. They had run to the spot every time they heard the call but found nothing, groping at land and air in futile gestures. The calling continued for almost two weeks, Williamson's voice becoming weaker and weaker. On the last night of the calling, the family slept just outside the vanishing spot and listened to what they later termed were Williamson's "death whispers."

Writer Bierce did more than merely interview some of the searchers in the Williamson affair. He consulted with a Dr. Maximilian Hern, a Leipzig scientist who specialized in such quirky occurrences and was the author of *Disappearance and Theory Thereof.* Hern minutely went over the disappearance and then stated that Williamson had inadvertently walked into a "void spot of universal ether." Dr. Hern, whose theories provided doubters with thigh-slapping guffaws, went on to explain that such void spots lasted only a few seconds but were capable of destroying any and all material elements that purposely or, by happenstance, ventured into their realms.

More "scientists" stepped forward, each with his own pet theory on the disappearance. One beard-stroking academic explained that the farmer had walked into a periodic "magnetic field" that disintegrated the atomic structure of the victim, sending him, in a different form, into another unknown dimension, that could not be seen by the human eye but could sometimes be heard. This was how, he pointed out, the family was able to hear Williamson calling. His body had been transformed, so to speak, but his spirit, part of it or all of it, was still earthbound.

None of these high-blown theories served to discover the missing Orion Williamson. Ambrose Bierce thought the whole thing farcical and wrote a satire about the odd happening, which is ironic given his own frightening disappearance in the following century.

(This story is now famous, not only for the weird "facts" that it relates, but because it has been altered from its very real site. Over the years, a thorough investigation on the part of the author and his staff revealed, Williamson's name and place of residence have been changed for various reasons by several writers. This began when a wandering salesman named McHatten from Cincinnati was trapped by a snowstorm in 1889 in Gallatin, Tennessee. With nothing to do except drink, McHatten sat in the Sindle House Hotel and rewrote the Williamson story in an attempt to make a bit of extra change by selling it as an original report. He changed Orion Williamson's name to David Lang, the site of his disappearance from Selma, Alabama, to Gallatin, Tennessee, and the date of the occurrence from July 1854 to September 1880. McHatten's story, except for the basic facts of Williamson's disappearance, was a gross fabrication that has been almost universally accepted and rewritten and published in a score of reputable journals and books, not the least of which is the recent *People's Almanac*. No such person as David Lang ever existed in Gallatin, nor did any family named Lang during this period. Orion Williamson was no figment of the imagination but a real, live resident of Selma, Alabama—until, of course, he slipped into eternal mystery.)

## Quick as a Wink

Sir Benjamin Bathurst and Orion Williamson were not the first or last persons to vanish into thin air before the eyes of their friends or relatives. The seven-foot French brigand Jean Petit, after pillaging the town of Mirepoix in 1363 rode off into the Forest of Bélène at the head of his thieving band. Following Petit at breakneck speed, the entire mob of cutthroats, almost a hundred in number, in sudden amazement, pulled their horses up so short that many were thrown from their mounts. One minute their leader, Petit, was there, riding before them; the next second his horse was riderless. He was never found.

When Captain Fritz Alswanger died of apoplexy in 1811, his valet, a cunning fellow named Diderici, thought to improve his fortunes through some dangerous play-acting. The valet impersonated the Prussian officer in order to draw his pay, as well as the attention of several lovely aristocratic ladies. Diderici was exposed and sent to the fortress prison of Weichselmunde, outside Danzig on the Vistula River, where he occupied cell number 80. One day in 1815, while the prisoners were exercising in the yard, which was surrounded by a twenty-foot wall, Diderici vanished, or his physical form, according to fellow inmates, seemed to slowly fade, then become invisible. It happened in seconds, both guards and prisoners told the warden. The valet was ponderously trodding the yard behind several men, with more men behind him, all in single file, and all manacled at hands and feet, and linked by chains to each other. Diderici, before the bulging eyes of everyone, utterly vanished, his chains and manacles left in a clinking metal heap where his form had once been.

A shoemaker named James Burne Worson, who resided in Leamington, Warwickshire, England, had often boasted of his prowess as a long-distance runner, capable of racing from town to town in record time and without loss to lung or limb. Bragging thus on September 3, 1873, to two friends, Worson was challenged outright to run from Leamington to Coventry, a distance of forty miles.

Worson jumped up and happily accepted the dare. He began to trot from the town as his friends Barham Wise, a linen draper, and Hamerson Burns, a photographer, followed behind him in a horse cart. Never was the runner out of their sight; the men in the horsecart kept pace with him and followed only a few yards behind.

Running with ease and even talking to the men behind him, Worson dashed on for several miles. Suddenly, not more than a half dozen yards from his followers, and, with their eyes full on him, right in the middle of the road, Worson appeared to stumble. He fell headlong forward and, as he pitched downward, he gave out an awful cry of terror, and completely disappeared. His body never struck the ground; he vanished in the middle of his fall, never touching the earth. Try as they might, Burns and Wise could not find a shred of the man.

Both men flew back to Leamington in abject fear, tearing into the police station to inform startled constables. They were first arrested as wild drunks, but finding that they were sober, responsible persons (with no motive for foul play), they were released. An exhaustive search of the area where long-distance runner Worson disappeared revealed nothing, absolutely nothing.

On November 9, 1878, Charles Ashmore, whose father's farm was only a few miles outside Quincy, Illinois, vanished forever into the thin winter air. Charles, a level-headed twenty-two-year-old, grabbed a bucket and stepped from the farmhouse at 9 P.M., on his way to the nearby spring for fresh water. When he was gone for more than ten minutes, his father, Christian Ashmore, went to the door and called for him. There was no reply.

Ashmore then took a lantern from the wall, lit it, and walked onto the porch of his house, accompanied by one of his daughters. It had snowed about an hour earlier and Charles Ashmore's footprints were clearly visible in the snow by the light of the lantern. Ashmore and his daughter followed the tracks for about seventy-five yards. Then the tracks, so clear that the impressions from the hobnails on Charles's boots could be clearly seen, came to an abrupt end. The Ashmores called and called for Charles, but no response came. The entire family then searched the area, careful not to disturb the tracks and making a great circle around them. There was nothing to be found.

Christian Ashmore slowly lifted his lantern toward the clear starlit sky and let out a long, low moan of despair.

### Mysteries of the Air

Since the Wright Brothers first climbed agonizingly into the sky, the number of pilots and passengers vanishing without a trace has spiraled into legions. The earliest puzzler of the skies involved two British pilots, Flight Lieutenant W. T. Day and Pilot Officer D. R.

Stewart, who were on a routine reconnaissance flight over the Iraq desert on July 24, 1924. For unexplained reasons, Day and Stewart, landed their plane in the desert and simply walked into oblivion. Rescue parties shortly found the craft without a scratch or malfunction of any kind; the fuel tank was still half full. From one side of the undamaged plane, clearly visible in the sand, were two sets of tracks, the footprints of Day and Stewart. The tracks extended about forty yards from the plane and abruptly, inexplicably, stopped. There were no other tracks about of any kind.

Searching the desert for more than a hundred miles in all directions, rescuers found absolutely nothing, not even one nomadic Arab. Day and Stewart remain today as the first skymasters whose ends became enigmatic. As the years passed and aircraft became more sophisticated, dozens of pilots, planes and passengers disappeared in similar manner. Charles Nungesser and François Coli, French World War I aces, attempted to be the first to fly the Atlantic on an east-west flight on May 8, 1927, only twelve days before Charles Augustus Lindbergh departed on his magnificent solo to Paris. Nungesser and Coli were never heard from again after taking off at dawn from Paris' Le Bourget Field in their Lavasseur biplane.

Andrew Carnegie Whitfield, twenty-eight-year-old nephew of the billionaire Andrew Carnegie, proved to be one of the more unusual in the gallery of missing flyers. Whitfield, a Princeton graduate who had logged 200 hours in the air, 50 hours short of obtaining his commercial license, took off in his small plane from Roosevelt Field, Long Island, at noon on April 17, 1938. His plane had enough fuel for 150 miles, but his destination was Brentwood Airport, a mere twenty-two miles away. He never arrived. Dozens of planes took off only hours later to conduct a massive coastal search. Scores of police and invesigators combed the likely ground areas where Whitfield might have made a forced landing. It was useless. The young pilot was gone. There were numerous, though zany, reported sightings of Whitfield. One account on August 26, 1939, had it that Whitfield, unkempt, dirty and still wearing his tattered flying togs, was seen riding a freight car outside Council Bluffs, Iowa. The report stated that Whitfield made no comment but grinned as the freight rumbled past railroad detectives in a yard and waved five one-hundred-dollar bills in their direction. Such flamboyant stories notwithstanding, the missing Whitfield was declared dead in 1946.

Planes are forever disappearing in that forbidding area known chillingly as the Bermuda Triangle. Most of these, despite oversimplified and illogical theories to explain away these disappearances, remain genuine mysteries to this day. On December 5, 1945, five Grumman TBM-3 Avenger torpedo bombers manned by fourteen crew members soared into nothingness in the Triangle. The radio comunications between the Flight 19's leader, Lieutenant Charles C. Taylor, and ground control at Fort Lauderdale were erratic at best. The pilots suddenly became confused, not even knowing which way was west, despite the most modern direction-finding equipment on board the planes. Taylor's last sputtering words seemed to echo all the fears the terrible Triangle ever posed: "Everything is somehow strange. . . . Direction is unclear. . . . Even the ocean looks different." The contact went dead and the fourteen Navy pilots remained missing; a PBY Flying Boat, with thirteen Marines on board was sent out immediately on a rescue mission, and it too vanished without a trace. An armada of ships in subsequent days failed to discover one piece of floating debris.

Dozens of planes have since been lost over this perplexing area, not the least of which were two passenger planes, the *Star Tiger* in 1948 and the *Star Ariel* in 1949. On December 28, 1948, a chartered DC-3 being flown to Miami by Captain R. Lindquist with thirty-three passengers on board was preparing to drop to a landing altitude and was in contact with ground control. The ground operator could hear the passengers singing Christmas carols before the contact went dead and the plane utterly vanished.

### The Empty Mary Celeste

Other than the unpredictable, overwhelming storms that suddenly boil up in the oceans and claim the ships trapped in the vortex of such storms, there remain myriad mysteries of vanished ships or crews, mysteries that no weatherman can explain. Like the planes lost in the Bermuda Triangle, that area has gulped alive hundreds of vessels since the middle 1550s, when the first recorded sea traffic began. No plausible explanation serves to clarify the disappearance of most of these ships, from the vast Spanish gold fleet of General Angel de Villafane in 1554 to the freighter *Anita* lost without a clue in the Triangle in 1973. (Almost directly opposite the Bermuda Triangle on the earth's circumference is a similar "doom spot" known as the Devil's Sea, off the southeast coast of Japan, where hundreds of vessels have mysteriously disappeared over the decades without a trace.)

The ranking mystery of the sea, however, involves not a missing ship but a missing crew, that of the celebrated brigantine, the *Mary Celeste*. A well-built ship, the *Mary Celeste* (first called the *Amazon* when initially launched in 1861, her name was changed to *Mary Celeste* in 1868) was captained by Benjamin Spooner Briggs, an experienced, reliable and thoroughly trustworthy master, who owned a piece of the ship and all of the cargo it carried. Briggs sailed the *Mary Celeste* from New York bound for Genoa with a load of alcohol valued at $3,400 on November 7, 1872. On board were Briggs, his wife, Sarah Elizabeth, his two-year-old daughter, Sophia

The *Mary Celeste, the most mysterious ship in the annals of the sea.*

Matilda, Albert G. Richardson, the ship's top-notch first mate, plus six long-serving and more-than-capable seamen. (Ironically, the brig *Victoria*, which departed New York for England the moment the *Mary Celeste* got under way, vanished completely with all hands.)

At 10 A.M. on the morning of December 4, 1872, Captain David Reed Morehouse was edging his three-masted Nova Scotian brigantine *Dei Gratia* toward the Azores. One of his crew members suddenly saw a two-masted brig that appeared to be a derelict, listlessly plowing the waves under half sail. Morehouse peered through his binoculars as the two ships closed. There was no one at the wheel of the ship.

Rushing to the deck, the captain grabbed his megaphone and shouted: "Do you need help?" He called several times, but he received no reply. He ordered his first mate, Oliver Deveau, to take two men and board the strange ship. As the apprehensive Deveau rowed alongside the silent ship he saw her name on the bow: *Mary Celeste*. He and his men climbed aboard and slowly began to investigate the vessel.

The ship's boats were gone and not a soul was aboard. Deveau and his men spent hours combing every corner of the *Mary Celeste* for human life. Briggs, his wife and child, and his seven crew members had utterly vanished. A close inspection found that the wheel was not lashed. The binnacle, however, had been knocked over, and the compass had been destroyed. Only the fore-upper-topsail had been blown away, and most of the ship's remaining sails were properly furled. Captain Briggs's unmade bunk had been slept in by a child. There were plenty of provisions aboard, enough for six months, but, contrary to the wild tales later spread about the *Mary Celeste*, there was no food cooking in the galley nor a lukewarm meal untouched on the captain's table.

The ship was in good condition, according to Deveau—"fit to go round the world," he later said. A small amount of water in the hold was quickly pumped out, and the *Dei Gratia*, claiming salvage rights, took the *Mary Celeste* in tow. Eight of the alcohol drums on the ship were empty by the time the ship was towed to Genoa.

News of the "ghost" ship soon created a worldwide sensation and presented a towering mystery that no naval board of inquiry has solved to this day. What happened to Briggs and the nine other humans on the *Mary Celeste?* That they hastily abandoned the ship for one reason or another was obvious to most, because of the missing lifeboats. But why? One theory had it that Briggs and Morehouse were in collusion to swindle insurance companies, that the captain of the *Mary Celeste* and his family and crew hid on board the *Dei Gratia* until salvage and insurance claims were settled on the ship and its cargo. But the fact that Briggs and the others were never again seen dispels this gossip.

Morehouse, Deveau and the others on board the *Dei Gratia* murdered all on board the ship and threw their bodies into the sea in one compulsive, lunatic act of piracy, others claimed. There was never any evidence to support such a theory. The *Celeste's* cargo, for one thing, was not sufficiently worthwhile to spark such a bestial deed, especially in men who were known to be honest, churchgoing sailors. It was noted by Deveau in his original inspection of the ship that heavy fumes from the alcohol drums were escaping into the hold. These fumes may have so alarmed Briggs and his crew that he decided to abandon ship, hastily lowered a boat, and grabbed up the sextant, the chronometer, and the ship's register, all of which were gone when the ship was boarded. In this instance, the crew may have rowed into a minor storm, capsized and drowned. This theory, perhaps the most believable, is shaky when realizing that Captain Briggs was not an impulsive man who would, out of an instant's fear, abandon his ship; he would have corrected any cargo hazard. (With the hatch sealing the ship's hold, the fumes really posed no problem to the crew; this hatch, however, was mysteriously open when Deveau boarded the ship.)

There is no explaining the mystery of the *Mary Celeste*. The missing persons on board that ill-fated ship were set adrift in legend that has them sailing forever in the murky and mythical Sargossa Sea, where all ghost ships were anchored, and rotting unto eternity.

# 14

*Rackets
and
Ruses*

For almost every unfortunate who permanently steps into the ranks of the missing, there have been three or four unsavory individuals who, without morality or ethics, busy themselves with hoodwinking for profit the relatives and friends of those who have disappeared. The swindle has many angles and variations, but it involves essentially the same promise—the location of the living person who has vanished. Some of the unconscionable crooks who have duped well-meaning people in stupefying mazelike schemes for the return of a loved one are motivated by more than money, but these inventive characters are in the minority.

Most of these con artists consider the gray areas of missing persons a racketeer's paradise where the quick dollar is easily gotten for information that is useless and will not incriminate them. Such was the likes of the sleazy Gaston B. Means, a former Bureau of Investigation agent (before the name of the agency was changed to Federal Bureau of Investigation), who fleeced the copper-mine heiress Evalyn Walsh McLean out of $100,000 on the empty promise that he and certain underworld associates could deliver the missing Lindbergh baby.

Robert Netherland, of Brooklyn, had for years—until his capture—made a fortune out of missing persons. His *modus operandi* was simple. Netherland would subscribe to most of the important newspapers in the country and pay careful attention to notices that advertised for the return of those who had disappeared. He would usually offer bogus information on the missing person to the advertiser for a price, anywhere from $50 to $500. Netherland's cold-hearted operation was brought to a halt in 1933, when he went one step further and *became* the missing person.

In November of that year, the con man spotted an ad placed by a Wisconsin woman asking that her husband, who had disappeared two years earlier, return home. Netherland became the husband, writing short notes to the distraught woman, stating that he would come home if she would send money for his travel expenses. The woman sent the money. Netherland needed more; he was ill, he had to purchase medicine. The woman sent the money. She also notified postal officials, who tracked Netherland's letters and arrested him. The thirty-three-year-old did his writing from then on from a prison cell.

Wealthy Baltimore sportsman Dwight Mallory decided to do some duck hunting on November 26, 1915. He called one of his upper-crust friends, M. C. Gill, who shared an exclusive duck blind with Mallory on Chesapeake Bay near the Susquehanna flats. The two arranged to meet there. At noon of that day, Dwight Mallory hopped into his 90-horsepower motorboat carrying several shotguns, ammunition enough for a small war, and a flask of brandy. He roared away from his private Baltimore pier and headed toward his hunting blind.

Gill had already arrived at the duck blind. He waited all through the day for his fellow huntsman to appear. Mallory did not arrive. That night a missing-persons report was filed by Gill and police spread out a six-state dragnet.

Mallory was no easy person to be mislaid. He was not only the crack shot of Maryland, but a director of the Federal League's Baltimore Baseball Club and the son of J. D. Mallory and the nephew of D. D. Mallory, both enormously wealthy machine manufacturers. Married to Lelle Bartlett, whose family too possessed fabulous wealth, Mallory was one of Baltimore's leading citizens and a member of almost every exclusive club along the Atlantic seaboard.

Things looked bleak for Mallory on November 30, when his waterlogged boat was found in the Chesapeake. Inside the boat was found only one of the three life preservers the vessel carried, a shotgun and one oar. Attached to a stick in the boat were two pieces of torn white cloth that Mallory may have used as a distress signal. Officials found one of the missing man's shoes. That night a reward of $500 was posted for information regarding the distinguished sportsman's fate.

The next night at 10 P.M. Charles J. Symington, one of Mallory's closest friends, a socialite and a wealthy man in his own right, picked up the phone in his Short Hills, New Jersey, home.

"Hello, Charley," said a voice. "This is Mallory . . . Dwight Mallory."

Symington almost reeled physically with the shock. "Heavens, man, we thought you were dead a week. We thought you were drowned in the Chesapeake Bay. Where are you?"

"Yes," the voice replied, "I understand all Baltimore is looking for me. But I'm in pretty bad shape. I don't want to see you."

"But where are you?"

"In the Holland House in Newark."

"Well, wait there for me. Don't go away."

"I am ashamed of myself. I can't meet you, I tell you," the caller insisted.

"What's the matter, old man?"

"I'm ashamed, that's all. I don't want to face Mr. Hoffman."

This remark was more than curious to Symington, who was the vice-president of the T. H. Symington Company, of Baltimore and Rochester. The caller was obviously referring to William Hoffman, the treasurer of the firm. Mallory was assistant manager of the firm's Baltimore offices. Later, Symington thought Mallory, if he was the caller, had become temporarily demented; nothing was found wrong with the company's books, and it was the first time Mallory had refused to see him. Symington and Mallory were lifelong friends. Moments after the mysterious caller hung up, Symington collected some of his friends and sped by auto to Newark, but not before Symington had called the Holland House and the Chief of Police in Newark to alert them to what appeared to be an unbalanced Dwight Mallory.

Minutes after Symington put down his receiver, a phone in the Baltimore police station rang. "This is Doctor Smith of Newark," a voice said. "Dwight Mallory is in the Newark Hospital. He was picked up by a tugboat in the Chesapeake Bay last Saturday and brought to Newark. He is in bad shape." The caller refused to say more but did state that his phone number was Market 3559. When police checked, this turned out to be the phone number of the Holland House.

Symington and his friends, plus about a hundred detectives and policemen converged on the Holland House at about the same moment, rushing into the lobby with great displays of agitation, shouting frantically for the missing socialite. The manager, totally nonplussed by the invasion, could tell Symington and Lieutenant of Detectives Frank Brex nothing. There was no Dwight Mallory staying at the Holland House; he had never seen the man. No one at the swank hotel, down to the maids and bellhops, had ever seen Dwight Mallory. It was all very confusing.

Hours later, Mallory's sister and some friends staying with her at the Continental Hotel in Newark, received an odd visitor, a thin, gaunt man named William Rickson. "I'm a detective," he informed them. "I've come to help you get your brother back. In my private detective work I've solved many a missing-person case, and I can solve this one for sure. It's like cutting a piece of cake."

Mallory's sister would have none of it, telling Rickson that the Newark police were at work on the case.

"They are, huh? Well those flatfoots don't know a thing about finding people who have disappeared. That's my game." He scratched his jaw and snarled in true gumshoe tradition, "There's a reward of five hundred dollars for this bird Mallory. I aim to collect it. I'll work with the police and then still get the reward." With a tug on the brim of his hat, William Rickson was gone.

Within a short time, Rickson, the master detective, arrived at police headquarters and volunteered his services to Lieutenant Brex and Detective Daly. When the officers objected to his presence, Rickson tersely informed them that he was in the Mallory family's employ. The policemen reluctantly took the private eye with them as they scoured the city of Newark. Rickson wasted little time attempting to prove his prowess as an investigator, embarrassing Brex and Daly as he shoved, pushed and grabbed average citizens by the lapels when asking blatant questions about the missing Mallory. Brex quickly informed his superiors that Rickson was acting strangely. "This guy is an amateur," Brex complained. "He doesn't know anything about police work. I think he's a phony."

By the time police picked up Rickson for questioning, he was busy telling Mallory's harried friends that he had loaned a quarter to a tall man in a hunting suit, a man he presumed was Mallory, so that he could make his phone calls to Symington and the police.

Lieutenant Brex and his men got an entirely different story from the private eye after he was grilled for several hours. The whole thing was a plot, Rickson finally admitted, a scheme to obtain the $500 reward and, perhaps, more, should the Mallory family hire him as a private detective, a position he had never held in his life. He and an unnamed convict, Rickson blubbered, had cooked up the entire fantastic plot to impersonate the missing man, run his family and friends and police around in circles and collect what they could while Rickson pretended to be working to find Mallory. Rickson could not remember the name of his shadowy accomplice, he said, only that they had once served time together on Blackwell's Island.

Rickson had been in Newark for only a few months, coming from Troy, New York, after serving several terms for theft in the Elmira Reformatory, on Blackwell's Island, and in the Union County, New Jersey, jail. "Go easy," said the deflated con man to police after signing a confession. "I got a wife and two kids."

William Rickson, alias William Whalen, was sentenced to two to ten years' imprisonment for fraud on February 3, 1916. His partner in the impersonation scheme, the clever ex-convict without a name, was never found, if he ever existed beyond the fertile imagination of the energetic Mr. Rickson. Dwight Mallory was never found either; his body was presumed to have been washed out to sea.

### *"Death to the Fourth Milne"*

It was the cool, snow-flurrying night of December 14, 1935, when Caleb Milne IV, heir apparent of the textile empire of C. J. Milne and Sons, of Philadelphia, received a visit from a Dr. Green of Gracie Square. Caleb's grandfather, seventy-four-year-old Caleb Milne, Jr., Dr. Green sorrowfully informed the twenty-four-year-old youth, was failing fast in his Germantown, Pennsylvania, mansion. "You had better come along with me," the doctor was reported later to have said. "I have a car waiting outside." Without hesitation, Caleb threw a coat over his shoulders and hastily left his Manhattan apartment.

At 6 A.M. the following morning, Caleb's eighteen-year-old brother, Frederic, who roomed with him at 157 East Thirty-seventh Street, received a letter postmarked at Poughkeepsie, New York; it said: "We have your brother in the country. Keep in touch with your grandfather in Philadelphia and have a large sum in cash available. We will communicate with you again."

Frederic immediately went to the police with the note. He stated that he had not seen his brother depart with Dr. Green; the landlady had reported Caleb leaving in a hurry, mentioning to her that he was called to his grandfather's home by the good doctor before dashing out into the wintry night.

On the morning of December 17, Caleb Milne, Jr., received at his Germantown estate a letter inside a package that contained a wrist watch the grandfather had given to Caleb IV in 1925. The second and hour hands on the dial of the watch had been broken, a symbol, police undoubtedly felt, that foretold of the youth's murder if Milne failed to comply with the orders of the kidnappers. The orders were in a letter inside the package. The writer demanded $50,000 in small denominations. The money was to be delivered to Frederic Milne in Manhattan. "If you fail," the kidnapper warned, "you will find him dead. Death for the fourth Milne. Take the money to New York to your grandson who is waiting for orders." The package and letter had been mailed from Grand Central Station.

Hearing of the abduction, Mrs. Milne, Caleb's mother, fairly leaped into her limousine and roared away from her country estate at Woodstock, New York, going to the Manhattan apartment shared by her two sons. Caleb Milne III, the kidnapped youth's father, called the F.B.I., and soon agents were swarming throughout New York and Pennsylvania. (A violent argument ensued, with substantial coverage by the press, between N.Y.P.D. Commissioner Valentine and F.B.I. Director J. Edgar Hoover as to who had control of the case. Valentine insisted that it was still a missing-persons case until proved otherwise. The F.B.I. roared that it was a kidnapping.) State police, fanning out in great numbers, searched the most remote areas in New York, many squads converging on the Catskill Mountains area on an anonymous tip that they "would find something interesting." All they found were the beams of their own jiggling flashlights. Police in Manhattan were even less effective in their massive search. When Detective Edward McAuliff, who was in charge of the case, arrived at the apartment shared by the Milne grandsons, he discovered that Mrs. Milne was already there and had given orders that no one could enter. McAuliff's way was barred by a family lawyer and chauffeur. "In all my career as a detective," McAuliff carped to reporters, "this is the first time that I have been on a case where I am on the outside looking in."

*Caleb Milne, IV, whose 1935 disappearance turned into a kidnapping nightmare for his wealthy family.*

That was exactly the position of every law-enforcement officer engaged in looking for the missing Milne. The friction between F.B.I. agents and New York police became intense as they bumped into each other at every turn. Mayor Fiorello La Guardia, who was visiting the Capital at the time, and Director Hoover felt that it was necessary, in the interests of public harmony, to issue a joint statement that the two groups were cooperating with each other.

Before the entire affair turned into a gigantic investigative fiasco, the much-sought Caleb Milne IV was dramatically discovered. Driving to Philadelphia on the night of December 19, on Old York Road near Doylestown, Pennsylvania, S. R. Gerhart saw "a struggling object in a ditch two feet off the highway." The elderly man stopped his car, keeping his headlights on the slightly squirming thing in the distance. Gerhart was fearful to approach the moving object. Another car came along within minutes, and Gerhart stopped it. "Hey you fellows," he croaked to four young men, "I'm glad you came along, because there's something over here I'm afraid to look into."

One of the young men, ironically enough, was Robert Keser, son of an acting inspector in the Philadelphia Police Department. Keser and his friends approached the figure in the ditch. Keser walked forward to see "a man lying there with adhesive tape all over his face, covering his eyes and mouth. His wrists were tied together with rope and lashed to his knees so that he could not move. He seemed to be exhausted, and there were bruises on his face." Keser slowly removed the tape from the man's face. He murmured: "Milne . . . Caleb Milne."

"Say," Keser remarked, astonished, "do you have a grandfather in Germantown?"

Caleb Milne IV nodded and then seemed to collapse. Keser noticed, as he and his friends gently lifted the youth into their car, that Milne wore no socks and only one shoe. The camel-hair coat slung about his shoulders had been oddly torn; the sleeves had been ripped away and then fastened back onto the coat with safety pins. Keser and the others could detect the distinct smell of chloroform or some other potent drug. Milne was rushed to a nearby doctor's offices in Buckingham and then to the Doylestown Hospital. There an F.B.I. agent took one look at Milne's condition and said to members of the press on hand that the youth looked like he had been "rolled out of a moving car."

Worse, a hospital physician found twenty-five marks on Milne's right arm, marks that appeared to be needle punctures; the insidious kidnappers had obviously drugged the young Milne repeatedly with morphine, said the doctor. Coming around, the groggy youth mumbled the story of his ordeal, stating that "Dr. Green" took him into his dark sedan, where three other men were waiting. The sedan "sped through the Holland Tunnel, rushed out over Pulaski Highway and then took a branch road leading toward Easton, Pennsylvania." At this point Milne remembered with dread, "Dr. Green" dropped his fatherly pose and sneered: "You're not going to see your grandpa! This is a kidnap job! You're staying with us and you're going to keep your trap shut!"

Outside Sommerville, Pennsylvania, Milne remembered, he was tied up and adhesive bandages were placed over his eyes and mouth. He was shoved to the floor of the car, where he stayed until the car reached a deserted country spot; Milne was dragged into an empty farmhouse. (Police later determined that the vacant farmhouse was near Wrightstown, Pennsylvania, only a few miles from the Germantown estate of Caleb Milne, Jr., from whom the kidnappers expected to collect the $50,000 ransom. All during this exciting period of time, the crotchety grandfather refused to deny or admit that he had paid the ransom.)

F.B.I. agents began to press the young Milne for more information, especially descriptions of the kidnappers. "I can't tell you!" Milne responded angrily. "I can't. They'll kill me if I do! They said they would."

Some days later Mrs. Milne arrived, scooped up her son into her limousine, and, accompanied by six federal agents, roared to Woodstock nonstop at speeds of 70 m.p.h. Grandfather Milne at this time informed police and F.B.I. agents that he had not paid one dime of the demanded ransom, cryptically commenting: "Now I guess the only thing is to look for the other fellow." Asked what he meant by the statement, Caleb Milne, Jr., only shook his gray-haired head and remained silent. Some days later, while his grandson was recuperating from his abduction in the sweet, soft comforts of his mother's Woodstock estate, grandfather Milne was asked if the four-day disappearance of Milne IV was a hoax.

"Preposterous!" exclaimed Milne, Jr. He did say that he thought his grandson "lived in a dream world." He paused and then said: "I am confident that the Department of Justice will arrest the persons responsible for this kidnapping."

F.B.I. agents remained at the Milne mansion in Woodstock, "watching over the young Caleb." Harold O. Nathan, in charge of the case, told reporters that, by no means, was Milne IV under arrest. "He can go anywhere he wishes."

One of the N.Y.P.D. officers, Inspector M. F. McDermott, who had handled the Milne case as a missing-person matter, arrived at the Woodstock estate to chat with Caleb. McDermott had his suspicions about the case from the beginning; he had marked the original police report of the Milne disappearance with one word: "Publicity."

As he talked with the youth, McDermott had him repeat the story of his abduction. As he described the time of night when the kidnappers arrived at the deserted farmhouse, McDermott casually asked, "How did you know what time it was?"

"I looked at my wrist watch," Milne answered matter-of-factly.

McDermott leaped up and gambled a shout: "You told us the kidnappers had taken your watch from you when they seized you! How could you possibly have had it?"

Caleb Milne IV went to pieces. He became confused. He began to stammer. Then he confessed. He had kidnapped himself! It had all been very clever, he thought, as clever as the detective stories Caleb had written by the score but had been unable to sell. "The whole idea came to me around the fourth or fifth of December," Milne blubbered. He explained how he purchased rubber gloves so as not to leave any fingerprints in his self-abduction. He cut "a whole lot of odd words out of different newspapers and pasted them on a sheet of wrapping paper." These clippings made up the two ransom notes. He explained that on the night of December 14, he made a point of rushing out of his apartment in such a manner as to alert the landlady, Mrs. Tarbell. Caleb made sure that she knew he was leaving with the mythical Dr. Green.

"Previously," Caleb patiently explained, "I made up a package containing my wrist watch and one of the letters. I made this up in my room. I wrapped this in an Albany newspaper and put a little blood on the newspaper from one of my gums . . . I mailed it from the Grand Central Annex. I then waited until 1:40, when an Albany train was to leave. I took the letter [written to] my brother, and put it on the end of a Pullman car as it pulled out of the station." (Caleb figured that the porter on the train would mail the letter near the end of the line, thinking a passenger had forgotten to post the missive. He was correct in his assumption; a porter dropped the letter off in Poughkeepsie, New York, thus giving the kidnapping note the right authenticity of distance and plot, proving, if detectives began to suspect him, that it was not he who had mailed the letter, since he could not have been in two places at the same time.)

Milne IV spent two days in various train and bus terminals. He then took a bus to Trenton, New Jersey, where he spent the entire day hiding behind bookshelves in the free library. That night he took another bus to Lambertville, crossed the Delaware River to New Hope, Pennsylvania, and from there walked on a road toward Philadelphia. Close to Doylestown, Milne threw away his socks and one shoe, sliced away the sleeves of his camel-hair coat and pinned them back on to give subsequent investigators a taste of exotic kidnapping methods and present another inexplicable factor in the case to further confuse things. He doused himself with chloroform and used a pin to make twenty-five punctures in his arm, as if his supposed kidnappers had injected him with drugs.

"I then stopped, taped my eyes and mouth with tape that I had purchased previously and then tied my ankles, knees and hands with slipknots. I rolled down a hill until I felt the roadway underneath me. Within ten minutes on the roadway, a car stopped and picked me up."

But what was the real purpose of the elaborate self-kidnapping, the youth was asked, if not to collect a ransom from his grandfather, a ransom that was never paid. "I am an actor," Milne proudly told Inspector McDermott. "I felt, since I was seeking work on the stage, that if I could get some publicity I would get a job." Any lead role on Broadway would do, he said, and if the motion pictures wanted Caleb Milne IV to star in films, that would be just fine.

Arrested, the youth was brought before a New York grand jury on February 20, 1936, but the jury members failed to indict him. As Lamar Hardy of the Department of Justice pointed out, there was no federal law existing that covered self-abduction. For all of his blustering in the case, coupled to his phalanxes of agents scurrying frantically about the countryside, Caleb Milne IV's impossible self-kidnapping left F.B.I. chief J. Edgar Hoover with the proverbial custard pie dripping from his face. Hoover had stated that before the Bureau entered the Milne case the F.B.I. had solved sixty-three kidnappings.

"It is still sixty-three," grumbled Hoover to newsmen. "This one does not count."

For most of the relatives and friends of the estimated ten million persons who are reported missing—some only for hours—each year in the United States (there are three to four times that many world-wide), including an average of 600,000 teen-age runaways, there is short-lived apprehension. About 95 percent of this staggering number return to the living in a matter of a few days, sometimes hours. The remaining 5 percent are left to be found by federal, state and local agencies, and national social and religious groups and organizations. Every major city in the world has a missing-persons bureau or department on its police force to which relatives can turn. After that, the only avenue open for those seeking the vanished lies in the cloudy regions of the on-and-off private detective agencies.

### The Stare of the Private Eye

Private eyes can be expensive, and the results of their investigations are often inconclusive. The private detective uses essentially the same tools available to the average citizen; he, however, is aware that these tools exist, and that awareness becomes the special knowledge that gives him his professional status. Intuition, moxie, a worldly air, an acting ability to convey the image of an incisive, probing mind in gathering an amplitude of facts about the missing person from a relative invariably make up the balance of a private detective's often exorbitant fee.

Private detectives are most frequently used to track down persons who have voluntarily absented themselves. The detective realizes that most of these persons will cling to their own past somehow, using close variants of their real names, or, at least, clinging desperately to their identity by somehow using their real initials in their "new" life. The private eye will therefore establish a series of possible names and immediately write letters to states in a certain area, requesting copies of driver's licenses which are available to the public. He will send off a small check to cover this fee and await results. Usually they are good because the predictable flight pattern of the missing person generally defines the general area in which the person should be. (It is known that Easterners usually fly to the

West Coast, or escape in the sun-belt, Midwesterners go East or West, Southerners North and to the Midwest.)

If the driver's-license check fails, the gumshoe turns to his master source of information, the credit bureaus and credit-card companies who maintain approximately 130 million files on American citizens, organizations that contain more hard data on the average citizen than do all the police forces in the country combined with the F.B.I.

The F.B.I. regularly contacts certain special sleuths who work exclusively for credit firms to obtain information on missing persons, usually felons. One of these calculating fellows, known to the author, was approached one day by F.B.I. agents from the Bureau's Chicago office. Could he, the agents wanted to know, find a man who had been selling stolen autos? The agents stated that they had gone to the man's home and found him no longer at the address. The sleuth hemmed and hawed. He was finally paid a handsome fee to lend his professional-detective acumen to the case (paid informants are not unknown to F.B.I. bookkeeping). The detective obtained the address of the wanted man within minutes after the agents departed. He then waited several days, however, before informing the F.B.I. as to the man's whereabouts in order that his investigation on behalf of that agency would appear to have been laborious and worth the price. The detective merely looked the man up in a phone book, where his new address was listed.

One of the most effective private detective agencies specializing in missing persons, albeit a record set in the considerable past, was that operated by the indefatigable sleuth William J. Burns. The agency solved thousands of missing-persons cases before Burns became the head of the Bureau of Investigation, the precursor of the F.B.I. In one instance, the Burns agency hunted missing Boston businessman Henry Clarke Coe, Jr., for months, eventually finding him in the wilds of Fairbanks, Alaska, in April 1915.

Burns's good friend, Sir Arthur Conan Doyle, creator of the immortal Sherlock Holmes, was known to have solved several disappearances in England, one in 1909 wherein Doyle tracked down a missing husband-to-be. He was to write later: "In another case, where a girl had become engaged to a young foreigner who suddenly disappeared, I was able by a similar process of deduction to show her clearly both whither he had gone and how unworthy he was of her affections."

Probably the best private detective agency in the East today, at least according to their claimed record of solved cases, is Tracers Company of America, Inc., located in New York City. Midwest sleuths who, like Anthony J. Pellicano and Robert Nemecek, specialize in missing persons also have amazing records of solved cases, according to their own count. Nemecek solved a strange tangled case in 1965 that trailed back through embezzlement and fraud for more than twenty-eight years.

A Chicago ice-cream peddler named Fred F. Beck died in obscure circumstances in 1958, leaving a $15,000 estate. The dead man had no known relatives, and the money was held up in probate court for eight years, until Nemecek solved the court's dilemma. Beck, the detective learned, had no friends, but had mentioned having attended a school called Hillhouse High. Through exhaustive checking, Nemecek finally located the school in New Haven, Connecticut. In his search, the detective showed New Haven police a photo of Beck and he was immediately identified as G. Henry Brethauser, a former Controller of New Haven, who fled the city in 1938, only days before a shortage of $12,647 was discovered in his accounts. Brethauser resurfaced in Chicago and began a twenty-year bogus life as Beck the ice-cream peddler, a role in which he felt comfortable enough to die.

Nemecek did not stop with his identification of Brethauser, but, using his only other clue, a gold watch with an inscription on it left by Beck at his death, found the missing man's widow. The eighty-three-year-old woman told the detective that she had given the watch to her husband at the time of their marriage in 1916. He was fifty-three years old when he vanished, and Mrs. Brethauser never remarried, thinking her husband would some day return. The widow declined her husband's estate, saying that she was financially secure. At her request, the money was turned over to a nephew, Richard Tyner, Jr., of New Haven.

In addition to private detectives, such organizations as the Red Cross and especially the Salvation Army, who have established amazing results in finding missing persons, the three branches of the United States armed services have active departments dealing with

**351**

men listed as AWOL (Absent Without Leave). The British Army has a particularly energetic missing-persons division, one that never rests, it seems, until the last grenadier to vanish has been found. This was clearly demonstrated in 1948.

Walter Campbell, who had deserted his British East Yorkshire Regiment in Jamaica in 1888 and then vanished, was forever being sought by missing-persons specialists of the British Army. The man apparently never had a moment's peace, moving from country to country, from town to town, investigators always a few steps behind. When he felt that they were closing in one day in May 1948, Campbell, who holds the world's record for being AWOL—sixty long years—reported back to his old outfit, confessing his desertion and ready to go to prison. The British Army, methodically looked up the eighty-year-old Campbell's records, and he was officially mustered out, given handsome demobilization pay and a new overcoat. "They also gave me a new conscience," the octogenarian grinned.

### A Citizen Search

The average citizen who is stalled and blocked by official missing-persons agencies—which often happens—and embarks on his own quest to find a lost loved one is certainly facing almost insurmountable odds. These intrepid souls, as Florence Fisher, of New York, painfully discovered, must be prepared to give up great periods of time and endure abuse and ridicule. In Florence Fisher's case, the grand effort was worth more than the pain of the mother who bore her.

Florence Laddin was an adopted child, a fact she did not discover until she was seven years old, when she found a name on a piece of paper—Anna Fisher. It puzzled her. When she was sixteen, Florence came across the paper again, noticing that the name of the obstetrician who delivered her was also on the paper. At the age of twenty-one, following the death of her stepmother, Florence began to search for the doctor and her real parents. She remembered her stepmother's mentioning the name "because she used to speak of 'labor pains,' as if she had actually given birth to me herself!"

In 1951 Florence managed to locate the doctor who delivered her, and she called him on the phone. "This is Anna Fisher," she said, giving her real name and explaining how she was raised by the Laddins.

"Oh, the adopted child," the doctor remembered.

"I'd like to find out who my real parents were," Florence practically begged.

The doctor paused and then shouted, "That's ridiculous!" He hung up.

Florence's search for her parents became dogged, a crusade that would consume almost twenty-four years of her life. She haunted adoption agencies, with no luck. In some instances, the agencies told her to forget about her real missing parents and seek psychiatric help. (It is the standard policy of all legitimate adoption agencies never to reveal the names of parents who turn their children over to them for placement with adoptive parents.)

Finally locating the hospital where she was born, Florence called the administration office and asked for information. This was denied her, but her unflagging persistence was rewarded. After calling the hospital every day *for fifteen years*, a harried clerk answering the phone made the mistake Florence prayed would happen. He merely checked a file and gave Florence the names of her real parents. She then went to the enormous files of the genealogy department of the New York Public Library (one of the few libraries to maintain such a precious reference section) and plodded through the source material. "A mere five years more," Florence stated, "and I found my mother."

The woman first denied being Florence's mother when confronted in 1973. Florence returned day after day. On the fourth day, the woman, weeping, called her and confessed everything. Yes, she was her mother, the woman admitted, but her own family did not even know of Florence's existence. Her marriage, Florence's mother stated, had been quietly annulled by her grandmother. It took another ten months for Florence to find her father, who was thrilled at being reunited with her.

Florence's difficulties with adoption agencies in her quest for real parents have since inspired her to establish a nationwide organization of adopted children who are searching for their natural parents. (As head of the organization, which has its base in New York, Florence uses the pen name of Florence Fisher.) For Anna Fisher, all's well that ends well, after three decades of hunting. For others, the search goes on.

### The Find of a Lady News Hound

The 1952 discovery of Mary Agnes Maroney, who as a two-year-old child had been kidnapped from her Chicago home in 1930, and her jubilant reunion with her family was an all-newspaper affair, prompted and perpetuated by the press, chiefly an extraordinary lady reporter for the *Chicago Daily News,* one quick-stepping marvel named Edan Wright. The auburn-haired Miss Wright, at thirty-four, had attacked her editorial chores with the vitality of a Broadway actress in round-the-clock performances that would give Helen Hayes pause and Katharine Hepburn the jitters.

To get her stories, this human dynamo had portrayed everyone from a prisoner in a woman's jail to a patient in a mental hospital, from a nasty scrubwoman to a wild juvenile delinquent. She even waited on tables in scanty garb in a strip joint to obtain one feature. Perhaps the only thing Edan Wright had not done was to enact the role of a detective. In the case of Mary Maroney, Miss Wright became a detective, of the newspaper variety, giving a skillful performance that made her famous throughout the nation.

The *News* had an abiding interest in the Maroney case from the moment that little Mary Agnes vanished, twenty years earlier. The paper had printed a letter in 1930 from Michael Maroney, who begged for employment, telling Chicago readers that his wife was pregnant and that he was broke. In answer to this letter, a well-dressed young woman appeared at the Maroney household, telling the family that she was a social worker. After depositing two sacks of groceries with the grateful Maroneys, the "social worker" took little Mary Agnes Maroney "around the block" to "buy her some new clothes."

The lady bountiful and Mary Agnes completely vanished, although the Maroneys did receive a strange letter a few weeks later from a woman who did not sign her name. The trusting parents were told that "my cousin, Julia Otis" had taken the child in overwhelming grief over the loss of her own baby. "Julia Otis"—her identity was never discovered—had taken the child to California, but would return her "safe & sound," the letterwriter promised. The Maroneys never heard about their child again, until Edan Wright of the *News* got an idea.

While working on a missing-persons story, Miss Wright scrutinized a photo of the Maroney family, which had blossomed to two boys and five girls after little Mary's abduction. All of the children looked amazingly alike, Miss Wright concluded. The enterprising Edan put the picture on the wire with a question: Would there be a twenty-four-year-old woman anywhere who resembles these children, and who might possibly be the long-lost Mary Agnes?"

The *Oakland Tribune* picked up the wire photo and caption and ran it. A young auto mechanic Everett McClelland, spotted the photo and picked out Anastasia Maroney Miranti, remarking to his wife Mary that she and the girl in the photo looked "like twins." The *News* and the *Tribune* worked in tandem over the next six months to prove that Mary Beck McClelland was, indeed, the lost Maroney baby.

Edan Wright interviewed retired police officers who had handled the 1930 missing-persons case. She collected blood specimens from all members of the Maroney family and Mrs. McClelland and had them compared by analysts. The samples, according to experts, pointed toward a "could-be" relationship. Miss Wright had phrenologists compare physical characteristics of the family and Mrs. McClelland. There were striking similarities. Next came dental comparisons. Bertram Kraus, a specialist in "genetic factors in teeth" at the University of Arizona, studied the Maroneys' dental impressions and then picked Mrs. McClelland's plaster impressions from a group of thirty-four unmarked casts as having "18 points of hereditary similarity" to the Maroneys in one tooth. It was enough evidence to inspire the *News* to finally break the story with a banner headline reading: "22-Year Search for Kidnapped Baby Ends."

Mrs. Catherine Maroney and Mrs. Mary McClelland met for the first time in the executive offices of the *News*. For a moment, the mother of the missing child looked over the twenty-four-year-old California woman. Tears came to her eyes.

*Mrs. Mary McClelland (center), who may or may not have been the long searched for Mary Agnes Maroney of Chicago, shown with a hopeful Catherine and Michael Maroney.*

"You look like her . . ." Mrs. Maroney said through sobs.

Mrs. McClelland, also weeping, stepped forward and embraced the woman she thought to be her mother.

"Mary," Mrs. Maroney said in a near-whisper. "It's been so long."

"It feels right," soothed Mary McClelland.

It was the scoop of the year, a scoop that brought back for a moment the golden newspaper heyday of Victor Lawson, William Randolph Hearst and Colonel Robert McCormick. But there were many things about the case, as subsequent weeks revealed, that did not "feel right," especially to Mary McClelland's foster mother, who claimed she had gotten Mary from a California foundling home two and a half years before the Maroney baby disappeared. Mrs. Beck, however, could not produce records to prove her claim. Dr. E. W. Merrithew, an aging physician from California, insisted that he had delivered Mary Beck to an unwed mother whose name he refused to divulge on November 17, 1927, in Martinez, California. Dr. Merrithew, however, could not prove the birth. Further questions were raised by a Chicago Police report that stated Mary Maroney had undergone an operation for a ruptured navel as an infant; Mary McClelland had no scar.

In the end, Mrs. Maroney was left to battle her doubts. "I would like to believe that this girl is Mary Agnes," she said, "but I just don't know . . . I probably will never know for sure."

And that is as positive as many can ever be in the eternally confusing world of the missing.

The following is a chronology, beginning in 1800, that is designed to include the most distinctive and notorious disappearances—chiefly in the United States, but throughout the world as well—in the annals of the missing. Chapter numbers follow those cases treated extensively in the general narrative.

## 1800

Wiley "Little" Harpe, who, with his brother Micajah "Big" Harpe, had been the scourge of the Wilderness Trail snaking westward from Knoxville, Tennessee, vanishes completely after "Big" Harpe is captured and beheaded by vigilantes.

## 1809

Secret British envoy Benjamin Bathurst vanishes in Perleberg, Germany, in the middle of a street while a half dozen dumbstruck witnesses look on helplessly. (XIII)

*Brigand Wiley "Little" Harpe is depicted firing upon settlers in the Ohio Wilderness before his disappearance.* (NEW-YORK HISTORICAL SOCIETY)

## 1811

Three-year-old Thomas Dellow disappears in November in front of a greengrocer's store on Cannon Street in London. Some months later, Mrs. Dellow discovers her child living with Mrs. Harriet Magnis in Gosport. Mrs. Magnis, tried for kidnapping, explains that she only took the child to pass him off as her own to please her sailor husband who had been at sea for three years; she is acquitted on a technicality.

## 1815

A convict named Diderici at Danzig's Weichselmunde Prison is reported missing from the prison yard while taking his exercise with other prisoners; it is claimed that he evaporated inside his chains. (XIII)

**1819**

The fierce South American pirate Benito Bonito sails away from Cocos Island off the coast of Costa Rica after burying 150 tons of pure gold, never to be seen again. (VII)

**1826**

Russian Tsar Alexander I, who has often stated that he wishes to abdicate, to escape the rigors of the throne, and who has "officially" died on December 1, 1825, is reported to be alive and living the life of a hermit. Some high-ranking officials insist the Tsar substituted the body of a military courier named Maskov for his own when the Tsar's coach turned over in an accident; others stated that the emperor's funeral at St. Petersburg on March 13, is held in secret to hide the fact that his casket is empty and that the Tsar has vanished, later to take up the disguise of the hermit Fyodor Kouzmitch living at the outskirts of Krasnorechensk. The hermit is to die on January 20, 1864, in a house built for him by a rich merchant near Tomsk, many believing that he is, indeed, Alexander I of Russia. Asked on his deathbed to tell his real name, the hermit replies: "God knows my name." He points to a small pouch which he has carried on a cord around his neck for decades and says, "There is my secret!"

Following the hermit's death, the pouch is inspected and a fading document with a coded message is discovered. Some experts later decipher the message as being from Tsar Paul, Alexander's father, to his wife; it reads: "We have discovered a terrible flaw in our son. Count Pahlen informs me of Alexander's participation in the conspiracy. We must hide tonight, wherever it is possible." It is a known fact that Alexander conspired against his father and was responsible for his father's death by strangulation. It is also known that the hermit Fyodor at death is eighty-six-years-old, the same age Alexander I would have been in 1864 he had staged his own death and assumed the role of the hermit, who is an exact look-alike. Tsar Alexander II has his uncle's tomb opened in 1865 to quell the rumors of Alexander's disappearance. Alexander's coffin is reported empty. In recent years the Soviets remove the bodies of the Tsars from the fortress of SS. Peter and Paul; the casket of Alexander II contains a few stones, according to one report . . . A mysterious, wealthy woman, living in a château outside of Hidburghhausen, Germany, completely disappears. She is thought to be the missing Duchesse d'Angouleme.

*The Duchesse D'Angouleme, missing in Germany.*

## 1828

A Nuremberg resident, Georg Weichman, finds a strange youth named Kaspar Hauser wandering at the edge of the city on May 26 and thinks he is either drunk or crazy. The boy, about seventeen years old, will say only, "I want to be a soldier as my father was." He carries a letter from a shoemaker, who addresses the "Captain of the 4th Squadron of the 6th Regiment of Cavalry in Nuremberg" and asks that the boy be looked after, and a note written in Latin by a woman who claims to be the boy's mother and states that she is too poor to take care of him. Hauser proves to be exceptionally brilliant, but ignorant in certain basics, calling all animals "horse" and all humans "boy." He is frightened by thunder, the chiming of clocks, and naïvely thrusts his fingers into the fire of burning candles until painfully burned. He has no sense of color or money. He is adopted by the Englishman Lord Stanhope, who undertakes his formal education. Of his mysterious background, experts can only surmise that he has been a prisoner in a dark, confining cell for most of his life. German criminologists Anselm von Feuerbach and others concluded that Kaspar Hauser is of royal blood, a missing relative of the ducal family of Baden, and that, after several assassination attempts on his life, he is marked for death because of his lofty lineage. The docile Kaspar Hauser will be murdered by an assassin in blackface on December 14, 1833, stating cryptically with his dying gasp: "I didn't do it myself. Many cats are the sure death of a mouse."

*The mystifying Kaspar Hauser, drawn shortly before his death.*

## 1829

Retired New York Supreme Court Judge John Lansing leaves his hotel in New York to mail a letter on the Albany night boat on December 12 and is never seen again. (VI)

**1840**

Ship-captain-turned-pirate Charles Thompson deposits a treasure estimated to be worth more than a hundred million dollars, the entire wealth of Lima, Peru, on mysterious Cocos Island, off the coast of Costa Rica, and vanishes with his ship the *Mary Dier*. Thompson surfaces twenty years later in Newfoundland but disappears again after being unable to convince residents of the treasure's existence. (VII) ... The large French vessel *Rosalie* (often confused with the *Rossini*) is discovered adrift off Nassau in perfect sailing condition on August 27. The ship's entire crew and passengers are gone, the only occupant of the *Rosalie* being a cat, and a half-starved canary in a cage.

**1842**

*Shown hatless and disposing of one of his many victims with an accomplice is John A. Murrel, the notorious killer of the Natchez Trace who vanished in 1842.*

John A. Murrel, known along the blood-soaked Natchez Trace as the "Great Western Land Pirate," who was responsible for the deaths of dozens of travelers he has robbed, is released from a Nashville prison after serving ten years for attempting to lead a black revolution in the South. Murrel promptly and permanently disappears.

**1845**

Sir John Franklin's massive polar expedition vanishes and is last seen six years later on April 6, 1851, a ghost flotilla off Newfoundland. (III)

**1847**

Successful Williasmsburg, Virginia, store owner Thomas O'Grady disappears. He is found in the Sandwich Islands in 1877 after being missing for thirty years; he refuses to return to his home. (II)

Dr. George Parkman of the Massachusetts Medical College is last seen alive as he enters the campus offices of Dr. John White Webster on November 23. A search ensues with college janitor Empraim Littlefield insisting that Parkman and Webster have argued violently —Webster owes Parkman, a professor-turned-loan shark, a great deal of money—in recent weeks and that Dr. Parkman never came out of Webster's offices. Three days later a reward of $3,000 is posted for information leading to the finding of Parkman. Janitor Littlefield suspects Professor Webster and tears down a wall to get to Webster's small laboratory furnace, where he finds the dissected parts of a human body half-burned in the furnace. Professor Webster is arrested for murder and attempts to swallow poison but fails.

*One of 28,000 reward posters issued for Dr. George Parkman.*

1850

Attractive Lydia Atley in Ringstead, Northamptonshire, vanishes on July 22 after taking a moonlight stroll with her married lover, William Weekly Ball, who is arrested on suspicion of murdering her but is acquitted; he is arrested again in 1864 for the same disappearance and again acquitted (V) . . . Following a long trial, Professor John White Webster is convicted of the mutilation slaying of Dr. George Parkman, considered today to be America's "classic murder." Webster is hanged in August.

1854

Heir to one of the greatest fortunes in England, Sir Roger Doughty Tichborne is lost at sea in April on the ship *Bella* sailing from Rio de Janeiro. He will be impersonated by Arthur Orton, known later as The Claimant, in Britain's most spectacular inheritance trials of 1871 and 1874, eventually being sent to prison for fraud. (X) . . . Alabama farmer Orion Williamson simply disintegrates before the eyes of his family and friends in July while walking across a field. (XIII)

**1861**

Connecticut youth Andrew Hanford, joins the Union army, but fails to return home following the Civil War, being listed as dead for 60 years. He suddenly appears in 1921. (X)

**1864**

Convicted murderer James Wilson, sentenced to hang for the 1861 murder of Thomas Terry in Atlanta, is pressed into Confederate service, along with all other prisoners at the Milledgeville, Georgia, prison to help stem the onrushing advance of Union General William Tecumseh Sherman on his famous march to the sea. After brief service at the defense of Atlanta, which falls to Sherman on September 2, murderer Wilson slips away from the shattered Confederate battle lines and is never again seen.

**1866**

The Swedish bark *Lotta* bound for Havana from Göteborg disappears in the Bermuda Triangle north of Haiti.

**1868**

John W. Lee, of New York City, leaves to fight with an insurgent army against the Spanish in Cuba and is never heard from again, although his wealthy sister, Mrs. Sarah E. Cooke, refuses to believe him dead, leaving Lee $11,500 on January 19, 1904, an inheritance that is never claimed. . . . The Reverend Benjamin Speke disappears from his rectory at Somersetshire, England, and is found some months later in the disguise of a cattle drover. (VII) . . . The Spanish merchant ship *Viego* vanishes in the Bermuda Triangle.

New Jersey youth George Miller, while on a business trip to New York in July, vanishes completely; he returns home thirty-five years later with one of the strangest explanations for disappearing on record. (IV) . . . The brig *Victoria*, which sails on the same day from New York as the mysterious *Mary Celeste*, vanishes at sea. The *Mary Celeste* presents itself as the great enigma in the recorded history of the sea by being found on December 4, 1872 a derelict off the Azores, its entire crew vanished. (XIII)

### 1873

An Albany, New York, boy, John Patterson, goes on an errand for his mother, September 1, and is never seen again. (IX) . . . On September 3, James Burne Worson, while running from Leamington to Coventry, England evaporates into thin air before the eyes of his friends. (XIII)

### 1874

Harriet Lane, the sultry mistress of London businessman Henry Wainwright, leaves her lodgings on September 11 and is never seen alive again. Wainwright has been leading a double life, consorting with Harriet under the name of Frieake. When Harriet presses Wainwright for money, he shoots her three times with a revolver and buries the body in the back yard of the home he maintains under his alias on Whitechapel Road. Rumors circulating among workmen who heard the shots fired by Wainwright plague the killer, until, twelve months later, he decides inexplicably to move the corpse to the shop owned by his brother Thomas. Wainwright, to make the transfer more convenient, chops up Harriet Lane's body into pieces, bundles the grisly remains into two packages, and steps from his shop to hail a cab. While stepping into the street to do so,

363

Wainwright incredibly asks a passerby to hold the two bundles. The passerby smells the distinct odor of rotting flesh, yells for a policeman, and Wainwright is arrested. He is later hanged for the murder; his brother Thomas, is sentenced to seven years' penal servitude for collusion in the hiding of Harriet Lane's body.

## 1876

*Investigators inspecting the open and robbed grave of Alexander Stewart.* (NEW YORK PUBLIC LIBRARY)

Frank Parker, assistant sexton at New York's St. Mark's-in-the-Bouwerie church, discovers that the tomb of Alexander T. Stewart has been opened and the remains of Stewart, a department-store tycoon worth thirty million dollars at his death earlier that year, have been stolen. The missing body is finally ransomed for $20,000 in January of the following year, the money collected by a grave robber calling himself "Harry G. Romaine," who also vanishes after receiving the ransom on a dark, lonely road while wearing a mask. He is later identified as New York thug Traveling Mike Grady, but the charge is never proven. . . . Prosperous Brooklyn merchant James B. Wheatley travels to Philadelphia, where he disappears, his $50,000 life-insurance policy being settled on his family the following year.

## 1878

To avoid marrying a girl to whom he had long been engaged, Barent de Klyn Anthony disappears, his hat, cane and pocketbook found near the East River, which leads police to believe the missing lawyer's clerk has been murdered. Police Captain Allaire suspects a hoax and manages to intercept a letter from Anthony to a friend, proving that the young man faked his own death. Allaire explodes: "Anthony placed his hat, cane and book where they were found. A friend was with him when he did it. It was a put-up job, as I said. They intended to create a sensation in order to allow Anthony a chance to fly from this city. The sensation was created. He did. He is now in Topeka, Kansas. He had the ticket for that place in his pocket when he deposited his hat, cane, and book where they were found. His father and mother and friends know where he is. Many of them knew where he was all along ... and allowed the public to be deceived into believing that an outrageous murder had been committed. The man's betrothed actually believed he had been killed, and that belief almost crazed her, and yet these people allowed her to go on with her sorrow without relieving her by giving her any inkling of the truth. It was the meanest thing I ever heard of. Why, believe it or not, there were some of his relatives who really knew where he was and yet came daily to me, sobbing and crying to all appearances as though their hearts would break, asking if I had learned anything about his body. It was an outrage!" ... On November 9, 1878, a twenty-two-year-old Charles Ashmore steps out of his Quincy, Illinois, farmhouse to fetch a pail of water, walks seventy-five yards toward the spring and vanishes. (XIII)

## 1879

Anna Fellows, a married Massachusetts woman, leaves her home and does not return until twenty years later. Staying with her husband for three years, Mrs. Fellows again disappears in 1903. (IX) ... Cattleman John W. Hillmon vanishes and is later alleged to have been shot at a camp site on Crooked Creek near Medicine Lodge, Kansas, on March 17. Insurance firms who have covered Hillmon with large policies challenge the death, stating that the man shot is really Frederick A. Walters. Mrs. Hillmon, after twenty years of court battles with the insurance companies, finally collects a huge settlement. ... On June 23, Patrick Smith, an aged sufferer of malaria, decides that he is a burden upon his Newburg, New York, family and runs into a nearby woods, where he vanishes; he is found wandering only a few miles from his home half-demented and suffering from starvation—reduced from 164 to 90 pounds—on August 28, after consuming almost all the treebark in the forest. ... Well-known manager of lectures, James Redpath, of New York City, disappears on August 27, telling associates that he is going to Europe on "secret business." Redpath is missing for eight weeks, before he contacts the *San Francisco Chronicle* by mail, informing readers who have followed the case from coast to coast that "a carbuncle or tumor" had affected his brain and "my will lost control over my body," compelling him to escape to the Lesser Antilles to seek rest and repose. He denounces all relatives and friends, apologizing to the *Chronicle* "for intruding these strictly personal affairs on your readers, but my business is what the Sea Island Negroes call 'momuxed up' enough already!" . . . Chief clerk at Stein's Drugstore in Manhattan, one Charles E. Resag, vanishes for several days, his employer alerting police and press alike to the disappearance. Resag mails a letter from Wilmington, Delaware, within a week telling all he is "alive and well" and asking his employer that "the past may be forgotten," a reference to his accounts, which were not in order.

### 1880

In August, Henry L. Edward, a passenger on board the *City of Dallas*, disappears before the ship docks in Jacksonville, Florida, and is never seen again. (IX) . . . On November 15 the Reverend John Marsland walks out of his home in Plainfield, Connecticut, and is later seen purchasing a train ticket for Hartford. Marsland absents himself for a month; his wife finally discovers him working as a grain-elevator operator in Binghamton, New York. The wayward clergyman will give no reason for his disappearance.

### 1881

Prosperous London baker Urban Napoleon Stanger steps inside his bakery late on the night of November 12, 1881, and never emerges again. His wife and bakery assistant, Franz Felix Stumm, later arrested and tried for defrauding the Stanger estate, claim that the baker simply returned to his native Germany, but most evidence points to killing. (IX) . . . The British ship *Ellen Austin* encounters a derelict in mid-Atlantic waters; the schooner is completely abandoned but seaworthy. The *Ellen Austin* attempts to tow the schooner to Newfoundland, but the tow lines break in a fog and the ship disappears. . . .

Mary Hortense Smith, of New Orleans, absents herself with a lover and remains in the land of the lost for forty-eight years. (I) . . . Eliza Carter, twelve years old, disappears February 4 from her sister's home in West Ham, England, one of many sinister disappearances in that area during the decade. (IV) . . . In April, Charles Wagner vanishes from West Ham; his body is later found and he is thought to have been another victim of the "West Ham Fiend." (IV)

## 1884

William F. Fegan departs from his Massachusetts home, and is not again identified until his death some fifty years later as a Royal Canadian Mountie; he leaves $7,200 to two sisters, Esther, age ninety, and Gertrude, age seventy-eight, the inheritance bringing the sisters together for the first time in fifty-four years. . . . A wealthy lumberman, Ira Lewis, of Elmira, New York, vanishes mysteriously; he is recognized by an old friend, Senator Dix W. Smith, twenty-six years later in Reno, Nevada, on March 26, 1911, when Lewis, by then an old man down on his luck, tries to beg a dollar from Smith. . . . The Italian schooner *Miramon*, bound for New Orleans, vanishes in the Bermuda Triangle.

## 1887

Following an argument with his brother Leonard over the girl he intends to marry and the attention that she is paying to Leonard, John Kemper leaps from a carriage, cursing Leonard and telling him he will never speak to him again. Kemper disappears and is not heard from again until 1937, when he dies in Jefferson, Texas, where he has discovered oil on his farm only a year before his demise; John Kemper leaves a fabulous fortune to Leonard, the man he swore he would never talk to again. Leonard too, however, in the intervening years has disappeared and never claims his brother's inheritance.

*The discovery of Mary Ann Nichols' body, the first of Jack the Ripper's victims in 1888. The enigmatic mass-murderer vanished as quickly as he had appeared in London's slums.*

Walter Campbell deserts his British regiment in Jamaica and for sixty years is listed as missing before turning himself in and establishing the world's record for being AWOL. (XV) ... The most notorious murderer in history, known only to a horrified world as "Jack the Ripper," begins his slaughter of London prostitutes in the Whitechapel area on Friday, August 31, slitting the throat and then disemboweling streetwalker Mary Ann "Polly" Nichols. Although more than twenty such brutal slayings will be attributed to Jack, only five exhibit the *modus operandi* of his peculiar, most gruesome avocation: Mary Nichols, "Dark" Annie Chapman, slain on September 8, her head almost severed, disemboweled, her uterus carefully cut out and taken by Jack; Elizabeth Stride and Catherine Eddowes on September 30, both with throats slit, Catherine's intestines ripped away and thrown over her right shoulder, Elizabeth dead only by the throat wound, Jack having been interrupted at his work by a pony cart with Louis Diemschutz in it on his way to work; "Black" Mary Jane Kelly, on November 9, throat slit, her entire body dissected with pieces of her anatomy piled meticulously on a nightstand, her uterus stolen by Jack. Here the murders attributable to the Ripper end, and he vanishes. His crimes cause Queen Victoria to demand of Lord Salisbury a special investigation, but the murderer is never caught, even though, over his two-month reign of terror, he taunts London's newspapers, which first dub him "Leather Apron," thinking he is a slaughterhouse worker. Replies Jack to angry editorials: "Dear boss, I keep hearing the police have caught me, but they won't fix me just yet. ... I am down on whores and I shan't quit ripping them till I do get buckled." He predicts his slaying that day of Stride and Eddowes: "You'll hear about Saucy Jack's work tomorrow. Double event this time." He then sends George Lusk, head of the Whitechapel Vigilance Committee a gruesome artifact, a fragment of Catherine Eddowes' kidney: "From Hell, Mr. Lusk, sir, I send you half the Kidney I took from one woman, prasarved it for you, tother piece I fried and ate it; it was very nice." Try as they might, with half of London's police force looking for Jack, he is never apprehended, although many claimants for his bloody identity come forward and are dismissed as insane, like the mad butcher. Suspects over the years abound. Arthur Conan Doyle puts forward the theory that Jack is a deranged midwife, because of the killer's particular knowledge of anatomy and his (or her) skill in dissecting the victims. Other suspects include the sexually berserk Thomas Cutbush, the outrageous poisoner George Chapman, the mass killer Thomas Neill Cream, even a mad Russian doctor named Michael Ostrog. In later years, suspicion reaches toward the most high-born of England, one loosely threaded supposition having Edward, Duke of Clarence and grandson of Queen Victoria as the real Ripper; another expert proposes Edward's tutor, Cambridge-educated J. K. Stephen, as the likely killer. None of these suspects is ever remotely proven to be that most awful practitioner in world crime. Why Jack the Ripper vanished remains as inexplicable today as his first exercise in gory horror.

### 1889

Austrian Crown Prince Rudolf and his mistress Baroness Maria Vetsera disappear and are found later in the Royal Hunting Lodge at Mayerling, seventeen miles distant from Vienna, both apparent suicides. Rudolf, a married man, shoots Maria, who insists upon dying with him when he announces his intention to kill himself over their impossible love affair. Rudolf lingers until dawn and then sends a bullet into his own brain.

### 1890

Adventurer John Nepomuk disappears on sailboat trip around the world after departing from Hamburg, Germany. He is officially declared dead by the Austrian government in 1911, but many acquaintances claim to have seen him in various parts of the globe many years later. A man in Denver claims to have Nepomuk's skeleton. . . . Another West Ham, England, victim, fifteen-year-old Amelia Jeffs, vanishes and is later found brutally murdered. (IV) . . . Brilliant inventor Louis Aimé Augustin Le Prince, who is the uncredited father of the motion picture, disappears in September after boarding a train to Paris. (VI)

In February, Lewis Redwine, the young assistant cashier of the Gate City National Bank in Atlanta, Georgia, vanishes with $66,000 missing from his account; he is discovered in hiding some days later and is sent to jail for embezzlement. (V) ... President Grover Cleveland's secretary lets out the story that the Chief Executive will retire for most of the summer to his retreat at Buzzard's Bay. But, on June 30, President Cleveland actually disappears with a few trusted aides and several doctors, boarding the yacht *Oneida* loaned by Commodore Elias C. Benedict to undergo a secret cancer operation of the mouth. The main salon has been fitted into a surgery room with all the modern medical equipment available, and Dr. Joseph Byrant and Dr. William W. Keen operate on Cleveland, cutting a large lethal sarcoma from the roof of the President's mouth and filling the hole in the mouth with a hard-rubber plug. The President endures incredible pain as he slowly recovers, remaining hidden in his cabin on board the *Oneida* until August 5, the ship inconspicuously sailing back and forth on Long Island Sound. By August 7, President Cleveland is in Washington to deliver a speech at a special session of Congress. Cleveland lives until 1908, dying of a heart condition but without a trace of cancer. Outside of the few on board the *Oneida* at the time of the operation, no one ever knows of the life-and-death operation or the fact that President Grover Cleveland had virtually vanished for more than a month.

*The yacht* Oneida *where President Grover Cleveland sequestered himself with doctors for a secret operation.*
(UPI)

**1894**

Scourge of New Mexico and Arizona, the notorious Apache Kid, killer of a half dozen persons, including two law men, vanishes outside of Tucson.

*The notorious Southwest bandit, the Apache Kid, among the missing since 1894.* (ARIZONA HISTORICAL SOCIETY LIBRARY)

**1895**

On October 21, 1895, convicted murderer William J. Myers escapes the Fulton County Jail in Atlanta and is never seen again. (V) ... Common laborer Edward Rush, of Lynn, Massachusetts, vanishes and then reappears thirty-five years later, and like a modern Count of Monte Cristo, lavishes enormous wealth upon his family who have lived in poverty all through the decades of his absence. (VII)

**1896**

Joseph Grosjean leaves Omaha ostensibly to work on a ranch in Montana. His sister Josephine leaves Grosjean a hefty inheritance in 1936 and the missing man steps forward—a hermit living in a Missoula, Montana, pine cabin—to collect the money forty years later at age seventy-two. ... The British bark *Bankholme* with nineteen crew members, four of them boy apprentices, vanishes within sight off Martin Vaz, Peru; there is no wreckage and no survivors.

**1897**

Willie Guldensuppe, a rubber in a New York City Turkish bath, disappears for a week before police fish parts of a human body from the rivers about Manhattan; there is no head, but Willie is identified from the corpse's torso on the chest of which is a risqué tattoo of a naked woman, a tattoo Willie is known to have had. Police finally track down the murdered man's landlady, Mrs. Augusta Nack, and her star tenant, Martin George Thorn, who is Mrs. Nack's lover. The two are charged with murder, and Thorn

*The ill-fated Willie Gulden-suppe was eventually found —in pieces.* ( NEW-YORK HISTORICAL SOCIETY )

confesses. Willie, as one of the sex-crazed Mrs. Nack's many discarded lovers, had proved such a nuisance that Thorn obligingly shot, stabbed and dissected him and dropped him piece by piece into the Hudson and East rivers. Thorn is sent to the electric chair murmuring, "I am positive God will forgive me." Mrs. Nack goes to prison for twenty years, is pardoned in ten years, and then disappears much more thoroughly than did her onetime star boarder Willie. . . . Asbury Gentry, one of Atlanta's infamous moonshiners, escapes from the Fulton County Jail and is never seen again. . . . New York lawyer and cultural leader Luther Maynard Jones travels to England and is not seen again for eleven years, until a friend spots him on a London street; he vanishes once more until discovered in 1912. (II)

### 1898

George A. Himmel, a bank cashier, disappears for eight years. He is later discovered to be an inmate of Auburn Prison, serving time for forgery under the name of White. Himmel remembers nothing of his former life, recollecting only that he must have suffered amnesia after being beaten by thugs on the day of his disappearance. . . . Grace Marian Perkins vanishes from her New England home, and is identified as a corpse. During funeral services, the lost woman bursts in on her own burial ceremonies. (I) . . . John O'Brien of Brooklyn goes to his neighborhood bar one night and is never again seen alive. (III)

### 1899

Marian Clark, a small child, is stolen from her New Jersey home and is not recovered for several years; her kidnappers are caught and imprisoned. (IV)

### 1900

Wealthy Philadelphia businessman Henry C. Koehnemann, considered a "skeptic" and a "cynic" by friends, vanishes completely, leaving a wife and two sons; he is found as Henry C. Schwenck, paralyzed by a stroke and never explaining his disappearance. . . . Fred Strow, missing for years, dies a recluse in Greenwich Village, leaving a small fortune in tin cans. (IX) . . . Rich girl Adele Boas vanishes on a New York street and is found years later slinging hash in Boston. (XII) . . . On March 3, schoolteacher Carrie T. Selvage absents herself from her Indianapolis hospital room and is discovered twenty years later under mysterious circumstances. (IX) . . . Edward J. Cudahy, Jr., millionaire's son, is kidnapped in Omaha, Nebraska. (IV)

## 1901

Boston sailor James Howard vanishes with his ship the *Horatio* and is not found until October 1921, marooned and close to death on a South Sea island. (III)

## 1902

William A. Goodnew disappears from his South Sodus, New York, home; he surfaces eighteen years later, after being legally declared dead, to claim his uncle's inheritance of $200,000, contesting the will against the wife and son he has abandoned. . . . Patrick F. Kelley closes his painting shop in Hartford, Connecticut, and does not return for twenty years, when he learns that he is about to be declared legally dead. He refuses to explain why he absented himself. (X) . . . Dr. William Horatio Bates vanishes from his New York offices, an apparent amnesia victim. (II) . . . After $26,000 are discovered missing, County Treasurer William O. Garrison, of Bridgeton, New Jersey, absents himself, and his whereabouts are not known until April 1921, when officials learn that he has lived incognito in Australia and has died; his body is secretly shipped back to Bridgeton and buried outside the city. . . . Frederick Tisher walks away from his LaPorte, Indiana, home and does not return for twenty years. (III) . . . Fortune-seeker Fred Jaques leaves England, abandoning his child after his wife dies in childbirth, then spends the next fifty-one years searching for his lost son. (VII) . . . Absenting himself to spread the word of the Lord the Reverend Arthur R. Teal, of White Plains, New York, abandons his wife, who patiently waits seventeen years before locating the wayward preacher. (XI) ... The German bark *Freya* and all hands are lost on October 21 while the ship is en route to Punta Arenas from Manzanillo, Mexico.

### 1903

Stolen as an infant, George Burke, of New York, enters a life of crime at an early age before he is miraculously discovered by his family. (XII)... Theatrical mogul Edward Burke Scott strangely vanishes; his onetime wife and operatic star Kate Condon finds him in 1927. (V)

### 1904

Seaman Frank Walsh disappears, prompting his mother to conduct an agonizing twelve-year-long search ending in tragedy. (XII)

### 1905

Yonkers, New York, businessman Charles E. Austin completely disappears from his home. (IX) ... Robert C. Davidson, former mayor of Baltimore, disappears without a trace.

### 1906

Unable to bear the death of his twin brother, George, John Kennedy, of Springfield, Massachusetts, vanishes at funeral and is never heard from again.... Consulting engineer William U. McKeekin of Red Bank, New Jersey, disappears on his wedding day, July 4, telling his wife that he is going to find a carriage "to take you riding in" and is never seen alive again; Mrs. McKeekin conducts a nationwide search for her one-hour husband but gives up the hunt in

1923 and asks court to grant her an annulment. . . . Typhoid breaks out in the Oyster Bay, Long Island, home of New York banker Henry Warren on August 27; medical investigators tirelessly track down the source of the contagion to Mary Mallon, the Warren cook, who will be known to the world as "Typhoid Mary." She disappears. (Almost 23,000 persons die of typhoid in this year alone.) Mary, moving as a domestic helper and cook from one wealthy household to another through many years, is a chronic carrier of typhoid of classic proportions, infecting fifty-three persons with the disease and being responsible for three deaths. After many years of confinement in hospitals (where the medical staffs are infected by her), she dies on November 11, 1938.

## 1907

New England girl Mary Clay disappears from her home, setting herself up as a member of European royalty; she remains in this disguise for several years, bilking suitors. (VII) . . . Lawyer Lex Brame, Jr., vanishes in Vicksburg while reading a book on a bank of the Mississippi. (VI) . . . Harvard student Albion Davis Pike totally vanishes on March 15. (IX) . . . Cincinnati banker Seward Heidelbach loses his memory in New York City and finds himself months later in Europe. (II)

## 1908

Margaret Beers, is lost to her father; for eighteen years Earl Beers searches for his missing child, finally discovering her in Detroit through radio. (XII) . . . Although reports have it that western out-law "Butch" Cassidy (Robert Leroy Parker) is killed in San Vincente, Bolivia, by soldiers in an attempted mine holdup, many later accounts insist that Cassidy survives and lives in obscurity under an alias until 1937, dying in Johnie, Nevada, where some claim his grave can be located. . . . Belle Gunness, mass-murderer of lovelorn suitors—fourteen in all—vanishes from LaPorte, Indiana, following the burning of her home. . . . Apprentice artist Adolf

*Bandit Butch Cassidy, who some say survived his reported death and vanished into obscurity for 30 years before actually dying in Nevada.* (WYOMING STATE ARCHIVES AND HISTORICAL DEPARTMENT)

Hitler disappears from his hovel in Stumper Alley, losing himself in the underworld cesspools of Vienna, Austria, living like a nameless tramp for two years, begging in the streets, occasionally seen in long queues waiting to be fed by soup-kitchen charities. He is to write of this time that he "shuddered in horror" of his lost identity. He grumbles and curses under his breath the handouts he takes from the Sisters of Mercy at the convent in Gumpendorf Strasse. He sneers at a Hungarian Jew named Neumann, an old-clothes dealer, who pities him and gives him a worn overcoat. A drunken rich man almost beats him to death with his cane when he begs the man for money. He eats horse sausage, when he is fortunate enough to find it, and drifts ever deeper into the worst section of the city, Brigtittennau, which Hitler will always remember because of its "miserable holes where people lived, the lodgings and tenements, those repulsive expanses of garbage, disgusting filth and worse." Adolf Hitler does not emerge from the world of the missing until 1910. "To that period," he will recall, "I owe it that I grew hard." . . . Oil heir John K. Van Arsdale, Jr., vanishes. (IX) . . . Thomas Sullivan, Jr., is abandoned by his father, who runs off to seek fortune in South America; the father finds his son twelve years later in Wellsville, Pennsylvania, where the boy is working as a farmhand.

## 1909

*Captain Joshua Slocum, considered to be the world's greatest sailor, is shown sitting on the deck of his boat* Spray *on the day he sailed from Martha's Vineyard into the Bermuda Triangle and oblivion.* (WIDE WORLD)

Walter D. Stymus of Port Chester, New York, walks away from his home and is never seen again; his brother Thomas becomes one of the most distinguished decorators in the United States, working on the homes of the Vanderbilts and the Carnegies, and designing the interiors of many great ocean vessels. He leaves $200,000 to his lost brother thirty-five years later on the proviso that Walter is found. He is not located. . . . Dorta Rafeld is separated from her sister Anna in Riga, Latvia; the sisters remain lost to each other for twenty years. (XII) . . . Willie Whitla is kidnapped from his Sharon, Ohio, school. (IV) . . . Elsie Sigel, daughter of one of New York's most distinguished families, vanishes and is later found murdered. (II) . . . Captain Joshua Slocum, considered to be the world's greatest and most experienced sailor, vanishes with his yawl, *Spray*, in the Bermuda Triangle after leaving Martha's Vineyard on November 14.

Jacob Bowers steps outside his Brooklyn home for a cigar and completely disappears. (IX) ... Farm boy Albert L. Kenney leaves his Butler County, Nebraska, home to seek work in Lincoln and never returns, even though his father leaves him a fortune. ... Mrs. Harvey Crippen (Cora Turner, née Belle Elmore) vanishes from her London home on January 31 in one of the most sensational murder mysteries in Britain's history. (V) ... Friddel Mueller runs away from his Bayonne, New Jersey, home on July 6 and returns five years later, just in time to save his stepmother from possible murder charges. (XII) ... Bronx, New York, policeman James J. Judge evaporates around a corner. (IX) ... Manhattan heiress Dorothy Harriet Camille Arnold disappears while shopping on December 12 and causes one of the greatest manhunts and mysteries in America. (I) ... William Frederick Tisher leaves home and remains missing for twenty years. A victim of wanderlust, Tisher is found swinging on the front porch of his home in LaPorte, Indiana, in 1930. "My wanderings have taken me to every corner of the globe," is his terse explanation before calmly walking inside to sit down to dinner.

## 1911

Rich man's son Ira Lewis disappears and is found twenty-six years later. ... Wealthy expatriate Henry Lawrence Wolfe vanishes in Rome without a clue. ... William Hurley, brother of future General Patrick J. Hurley, is thought to have been killed by a raiding party of Mexican bandits in El Paso, Texas. Surfacing briefly in 1926, Hurley learns that he has been officially declared deceased and decides to remain "dead," again disappearing. He is not found again until 1948, when his brother, General Hurley, discovers William living in Marysville, California.

## 1912

Small-town manufacturer Sherwood Anderson walks out of his Elyria, Ohio, office, apparently an amnesia victim, and is gone for days; he later becomes one of the most celebrated writers in America. (II)

**1913**

Sir Francis Barrow, a noted English baronet who serves in the Colonial Office vanishes mysteriously and is never found again.... William Whitehall, of Brooklyn, disappears and is not seen again until his wife Charlotte asks court to annul her marriage. (IX) ... Youth Russell Van den Berg runs away from his Elizabeth, New Jersey, home and is not found until nine years later. (XII) ... Manhattan streetsweeper John McHugh vanishes in August. (IX)

**1914**

James Regan boards the German liner *Prinz Heinrich,* on January 28, leaving Marseilles for Naples. Regan is seen strolling on deck during the voyage and then suddenly disappears. His luggage, oddly enough, vanishes with him in mid-voyage.... Leonard Douglas, of New York, is reported missing and presumed dead, only to return home without explanation ten months later (one report has it that Douglas had been "playing cards with gangsters").... Albert Daniel Rounds disappears from his Sioux Falls, South Dakota, home. (IX) ... The brother of future TV personality Steve Allen is placed in a foster home; Allen spends years looking for his brother Edwin without success, learning only that he probably resides, if alive, somewhere in Alabama, perhaps under the name Johnston, Johnson, Powell, Rudolph, or Smith. Edwin would be sixty-six years old at the time of this writing.... Mamie Nagle, of New York, is abducted only to be dramatically rescued months later. (IV) ... Yetta Levinthal is kidnapped from her New York school. (IV) ... John Kasler of Wallington, New Jersey, vanishes and is found a year later by his daughter, Mrs. Anne Casper, as he lies dying in a Passaic, New Jersey, hospital; the seventy-three-year-old Kasler, an amnesia victim, does not remember his daughter.... Harry Dahl is thought to have been killed in World War I but miraculously reappears six years later. (XII) ... Henri Desiré Landru ("Bluebeard") begins his wholesale abduction and murder of Parisian women in order to obtain their money and valuables; the murders of at least ten missing women are attributed to Landru five years later when he is apprehended. (V)

*Television star Steve Allen with Young M. Smith (seated, right), whom he thought to be his brother Edwin, lost since 1914.* (WIDE WORLD)

... Writer Ambrose Bierce vanishes mysteriously in revolution-torn Mexico. (III) ... Philadelphia boy Warren McCarrick disappears on March 12, his body found three months later. (IX) ... Anna Standroup is enticed into prostitution while walking in Central Park in April; she is missing for several months. (IV) ... New York broker Thaddeus Stone disappears with his company's money. (V) ... Bronx teenager Katherine Larkin vanishes on August 7 and is later discovered abducted and horribly abused. (IV) ... Gabriel Henri Raymond, while playing in the streets of Mericourt, is caught up in the headlong advance of the German armies on October 3 and is swept into oblivion, remaining among the missing for thirteen years. (XII)

## 1915

Chicago pianist Grace Stewart Potter walks away from home, her memory obliterated. (II) ... Charles F. Killelea vanishes from his home in Massachusetts and is thought killed in World War I; he is traumatically reunited with his mother eleven years later. (XII) ... Mrs. Mamie McCann Foley and her son leave their home and do not surface until 1927. (IX) ... Missing for months, Boston businessman Henry Clarke Coe, Jr., is tracked down in Alaska in April. (XV) ... Manhattan millionaire Gustave Stern loses his mind and vanishes in May. (II) ... Mary Thompson disappears; she is mistakenly thought to have been drowned when the *Lusitania* sank on May 15. (XII) ... Dr. Edward E. Rowell, Jr., of Stamford, Connecticut, is stricken with amnesia and is listed missing on May 25. (II) ... Bank official Harry S. Bradley disappears from his New York firm with $100,000 on August 18. He is indicted for theft but is never found. ... Reverend Thornton R. Sampson vanishes while climbing a mountain in Colorado on September 2. (III) ... Leopold Godowsky, celebrated Polish composer and pianist vanishes on September 3 from his Avon, New Jersey, home, causing thousands of police to search for him along the Eastern seaboard. He appears a week later telling all that he has been at a remote cabin, finishing a composition. (The note he left to inform his wife of his departure had been opened by a snooping servant and, fearful of losing her job, the maid

The missing composer Leopold Godowsky (left) with Albert Einstein and Arnold Schönberg. (WIDE WORLD)

hid the letter. She is fired when Godowsky returns home.) . . . Baltimore playboy Dwight Mallory vanishes on a hunting expedition on November 26, his disappearance used to establish a colossal fraud. (XIV)

### 1916

John Francis Langan argues with his father and leaves his family's Topeka, Kansas home, vowing never to return or talk to the elder Langan again. Despite John Langan senior's seventeen-year search for his son and the $10,000 he leaves to the absentee at his death in 1933, the younger Langan is never seen again. . . . Gustaf Duner is wounded on the Western Front, becoming an amnesia victim, his real identity is clouded for years. (II)

### 1917

Harry Miller, of Salt Lake City, is attacked on his way to an Army induction center by a gang of ruffians who are after his money and receives a blow on the head that results in devastating amnesia. (III) . . . Jerry Tarbot, a World War I veteran, becomes an international celebrity as "the classic amnesiac." (II) . . . Boston scholar Dr. John L. Brand loses his memory and vanishes for three years. (II) . . . Wounded in the head during trench fighting, British soldier C. H. Peachey wanders lost for ten years. (II) . . . With a $700,000 deficiency in his accounts, New York financier William Lustgarten fakes his own suicide and absents himself on August 16, detectives following doggedly in an epic manhunt. (V)

### 1918

New York businessman John J. Ragan vanishes during a party; his wife waits until 1927 to apply for his insurance, but is refused payment until she can prove his death, which she never does. . . . Fred Ackerly, of White Plains, New York, disappears; his body—head

*Another victim of the Bermuda Triangle, the U.S. Navy supply ship* Cyclops *vanished en route to Baltimore.* (WIDE WORLD)

sticking downward into the mud of a quarry in Tuckahoe, New York —is found three years later, Ackerly's end theorized by police to be that of a Black Hand killing. . . . The U.S.S. *Cyclops*, a 19,600-ton Navy collier, sails from Barbados, West Indies, on March 4, with 307 crew members and passengers, bound for Norfolk, Virginia. The 542-foot ship, one of the largest afloat, never arrives and is presumed by most responsible experts over the years to have been lost in the Bermuda Triangle. . . . Wallie "Miss Babe" Coughlin appears as a child performer in Fort Wayne, Indiana, on April 18 and will be the subject of a nationwide search twenty years later. (X) . . . Tsar Nicholas II and all members of his family are reportedly executed on July 16 at Ekaterinburg, Russia, but doubts from that very day, arising from conflicting accounts, point to the survival of the Romanovs, who are secretly, either with Lenin's tacit approval or through the initiative of low-ranking Soviets, smuggled into Poland. The British High Commissioner present in Ekaterinburg reports that the Tsarina and her daughters leave the city on a sealed train one day *after* the alleged massacre. Other reports have it that the Tsar and his family escape to Poland, where they head the anti-Communist underground, the Empress dying peacefully in 1924, the Tsar as late as 1952. Colonel Michael Goleniewski, a mysterious Polish officer working with the C.I.A. in the late 1950s, who is responsible for exposing scores of Soviet agents in the West, including the notorious Kim Philby, defects to the United States in 1960, later claiming that he is none other than Grand Duke Alexis, only son of Tsar Nicholas II. Goleniewski bears physical characteristics almost identical with Alexis; he suffers from hemophilia as did Alexis, and his fingerprints and dental work almost match that of the Grand Duke. Goleniewski, is supported by onetime C.I.A. Research Director Herman Kimsey,

*Tsar Nicholas II with the royal family. Many experts argue that the Romanov family was not assassinated but escaped into obscurity in 1918.* (WIDE WORLD)

381

who believes him to be the legitimate heir to the Romanov throne and the inheritor of four hundred million dollars deposited by the Tsar in Western banks and waiting to be claimed. Goleniewski, alive at this writing and living under an alias in Long Island, New York, is not officially recognized, nor is New York resident Mrs. Eugenia Smith, who claims to be the living Anastasia, youngest daughter of the Tsar. Anna Anderson, a German citizen, also claims to be Anastasia, and her claim is supported by many experts and researchers. . . . Nine-year-old Grace Curtiss is abducted by her father after a divorce action and secreted away. Her mother conducts a four-year search that ends in her accidental discovery. (XII)

### 1919

Baroness F. C. Von Cottendorf disappears forever from her estate in The Hague, Holland. . . . Colorado student Harold Frank vanishes. (IX) . . . Onetime judge and leading New York Republican Robert W. Scott, disillusioned over his failing political career, absents himself and is discovered penniless and dead in Chicago in 1931. . . . Donald A. Dodge, of New Britain, Connecticut, slips into the ranks of the missing and is not found until American Legionnaires, at the request of Dodge's brother, track him down in a fleabag Yonkers hotel twelve years later. . . . Arthur Phillip Wentz, a seven-week-old baby, is abducted from a New York street on July 29; he is never found. (IV) . . . In October Dr. Charles F. Hastings, of Pittsburgh, completely vanishes. He remains absent for six years, until he surfaces in Erie, Pennsylvania, where he has operated a toy shop and changed his name to John Hugh. "My real name was too fancy," he comments to the press after returning to claim a $50,000 inheritance. . . . Canadian theatrical tycoon Ambrose J. Small mysteriously disappears on December 2. (IX) . . . Staten Island inventor Paul Gesner vanishes on December 2 and is gone for two years. (VII)

### 1920

Henrietta Bulte, fifteen-year-old, disappears on April 12 from her New York home. Although ransom notes from alleged kidnappers arrive, Louis Bulte finds his daughter in Los Angeles about a month later, after advertising nationwide for her; Henrietta has used the name "Vivien Vianini" in her abortive attempts to become a movie star.... Victor Grayson, an esteemed British politician and onetime Parliament member, disappears in July, telling friends he is going to Ireland and cryptically commenting, "It will be the last journey I shall make." Although family and friends search for years for Grayson—he is spotted often up to World War II walking about London—the politician is never found.... The Reverend Cornelius Densel, of Passaic, New Jersey, runs away with his prettiest parishioner on November 12, leaving his church and family in hysteria. (I)... St. Louis editor Jacques Villard is abducted from his Chicago hotel room. (IV)... In December Frank L. Birdsong, Postmaster of Homeville, Virginia, fakes his suicide and vanishes, only to be tracked down by a dogged insurance investigator. (V)... Robert Burns, an unemployed World War I veteran burglarizes a store of $5.29 and is sent to a Georgia chain gang. He escapes and is missing several years until discovered in Chicago, where he works as a $20,000-a-year magazine editor. Georgia authorities, tipped off by his first wife, claim Burns who returns to the chain gang on the promise of receiving a quick pardon. He is not pardoned, and his brother, a prominent New Jersey minister, makes a national issue of the case. Before a hearing can be held by the governor, Burns, fearing that he will be kept on the chain gang, escapes in 1930 and again disappears. He is eventually located in New Jersey, where he runs an antique shop. He is to write a series of articles, later compiled into a book entitled *I Am a Fugitive from a Chain Gang*, which is produced as a powerful motion picture in 1931 with Paul Muni in the feature role. The motion picture enrages Georgia officials who demand that the modern Jean Valjean be turned over to them. A hearing in New Jersey is a sensation, with Clarence Darrow acting as Burns's defense counsel. Many state governors support the wanted man, and hundreds of thousand of petitions begging that he be pardoned are introduced. The Georgia penal system is exposed for all its medieval brutality, the "sweat boxes"—small barrels with iron staves on top into which "insolent" prisoners are inhumanly crammed are exhibited. New Jersey refuses to turn Burns over to Georgia. When Eugene Talmadge becomes governor of Georgia in 1941 he tries

*Robert Elliott Burns (right), with his mother and brother, Vincent J. Burns, shortly after the publication of his book,* I Am a Fugitive From a Chain Gang. (WIDE WORLD)

383

once more to obtain the missing prisoner. New Jersey's Governor Edison refuses to allow Burns to be returned. By this time, Burns has remarried, is the father of two children and the secretary of a New Jersey association. He is shocked at Georgia's persistence to reclaim him as a prisoner, crying out to the press: "How long will they keep this up? Will I never have peace?" Fugitive Burns has his peace in 1955 when he dies.

### 1921

The five-masted schooner *Carroll A. Deering* vanishes in the Bermuda Triangle after sailing from Barbados in January. The ship is later found a derelict off Diamond Shoals, her crew completely disappeared.... Amnesia victim James H. Epworth, of Nutley, New Jersey, vanishes. (II) ... William Daniel, of Brooklyn, leaves home and his mother conducts a sixteen-year search for him; he is discovered on the West Coast, explaining that he departed because a play he had written had not been produced.... Mount Vernon, New York, socialite Mrs. Ella Berentsen crawls out of her four-poster bed on January 19 and disappears. (IX) ... New York preacher's daughter Juanita McHargue disappears in April and remains missing for four years. (IX) ... On August 21, Mary Romer, of Brooklyn, runs away. (IX) ... Madame Eve Delbreuve, a wealthy patron of the arts in Paris, disappears in September. She had, the police learn, supported an engineer named M. Comte, who is suspected of murdering Madam Delbreuve for her money and hiding the body. When gendarmes arrive at his door, Comte swallows prussic acid and dies. Comte's first wife, authorities later reveal, had died under mysterious circumstances a year earlier, probably murdered by her husband.... Chicago heir to millions Gordon Duffield vanishes from his New Jersey private school on October 14. (III) ... Thomas O'Connor, known in Chicago as "Terrible Tommy," escapes the Cook County Jail in December, only days before he is scheduled to be hanged for the murder of a Chicago policeman. The wily robber eludes a massive dragnet and is never found, thought to have returned to his native Ireland, where he may have been killed in the Civil War in 1922. By court order, the gallows upon which O'Connor is scheduled to hang—the last man to be so executed in the state of Illinois, which thereafter employed the electric chair—are preserved until the gangster can be found or his death confirmed. At this writing, the gallows are stored in the basement of Chicago's Criminal Courts building.

## 1922

Rice Institute student Ben Kimble vanishes. (IX) . . . Seven-year-old Anna Gallow disappears in a New York subway, her body is found weeks later; officials state that she "had died of fright.". . . William Lebert argues with his wife and abruptly leaves his Port Huron, Michigan, home. A nationwide search for Lebert is conducted, his wife seeking reconciliation, but he is not found. On July 28, 1925, a ragged stranger commits suicide by leaping into the furnace stack of the Imperial Oil Company plant at Sarnia, Ontario, and before the body can be recovered it is all but cremated. A coroner's jury then concludes that the burned body is that of the missing Lebert and he is officially declared dead; his widow Adelaide is awarded $10,000 in life-insurance money. With this, Adelaide builds an apartment house, which she names after her husband, and remarries, wedding a seventy-five-year-old Civil War veteran named William Manley. In 1925, Lebert magically returns alive without explaining his absence and promptly sues his wife, Manley, and every member of the coroner's jury who has declared him dead. . . . On April 6, Mrs. Jenny Becker is reported by her husband, Abraham, to be missing from her Bronx home. Months later it is proved that Abraham Becker, aided by his friend Reuben Norkin, has murdered Jenny Becker, who was beaten unconscious and then buried alive in an ashpit. Both men are sent to the electric chair at Sing Sing in 1924. . . . Mrs. Oscar Hammerstein, widow of the operatic impresario, leaves a despondent note in her Manhattan apartment and vanishes, having remarked earlier to her maid that no one should "be surprised if I am found dead some night on Oscar's grave." She is located a few days later in a 115th Street rooming house, living under the name of Mrs. Ellsworth. A month later, without explaining her disappearance, Mrs. Hammerstein begins a cabaret act in Atlantic City, interpreting "ancient Inca music" played by Peruvian musician Carlos Valderramma.

**1923**

Mary Woodson, daughter of a prominent Washington family, runs away and is found by her mother, socialite Mrs. A. B. Woodson, two years later in New York, married to one John Spargo, of Brooklyn, who, it is discovered, is really one Jack Seldow (Seldowitz), an ex-convict wanted for parole violations; it is later proven that Seldow is a bigamist who has deserted an earlier wife, Augusta Redenbach, in May 1918. Seldow is sent to prison while eighteen-year-old Mary Woodson is granted an annulment. . . . Sydney Denning absents himself from his Queens Borough, New York City, home. He returns three years later to find his wife under arrest for identifying the wrong corpse to collect his insurance. (IX) . . . Wilbur Clark, treasurer of a Long Island school district, disappears after embezzling $1,500 from school funds. He is found in April 1926 in Dayton Ohio, living with a seventeen-year-old flapper who gives her name as Dollas Doxsee. . . . Mrs. John Kearns receives a telegram from her sailor husband telling her to meet him in Grand Central Station. He never arrives, but, after a nine-year absence, and being legally declared dead, Kearns appears in his Toronto home, saying only: "I think my status is uncertain."

**1924**

Bogus reporter, James J. Bailey, is arrested after his missing-persons racket is exposed. Bailey has, for a number of years, extorted money from relatives on the promise that he will reveal the whereabouts of their lost loved ones. . . . New Jersey youth Irving Schiff vanishes and is later found as a member of a jazz band. (IX) . . . Brooklyn baker Benjamin Levy disappears, an apparent kidnap victim of bootleggers; he is later discovered sweeping out a hallway in midtown Manhattan, his memory a blank. (II) . . . Elsie Dunlevy, of Manchester, Iowa, is held a prisoner by her uncle in Chicago for two years. (IV) . . . Amnesia victim Robert S. Henderson wanders away from his Rolla, North Dakota, home and remains missing for twenty-two years. Found on July 22, 1956, in Buffalo, New York, Henderson tells police, "I don't know who I am, but I suppose I should." He is

*Missing for twenty-four years, Robert S. Henderson, amnesia victim, is reunited with his mother.*

reunited with his mother in Modesto, California. . . . John Edgar
Davis fakes his own suicide in Pittsburgh and is declared dead; he is
found in Pasadena, California, fourteen years later. (V) . . . Nathan
F. Leopold and Richard Loeb abduct and murder fourteen-year-old
Bobbie Franks on May 21. (IV) . . . Britain's ace mountain climber,
George Leigh-Mallory, vanishes with A. C. Irvine close to the summit of Mount Everest. (III) . . . Pilots W. T. Day and D. R. Stewart
vanish in the middle of the Iraq desert, presenting searchers with
one of the great mysteries of the twentieth century. (XIII) . . . Loan
shark Aaron Graff disappears in New York on August 8 and is later
found murdered and dissected in the basement of a client. (VI) . . .
May and Nina Martin, ages twelve and eight, vanish from their Los
Angeles home on August 23. The bodies of the girls, both obviously
murdered, are later found in a shallow brush-pile grave the following February. Their slayer is never apprehended.

## 1925

Carl Henry Proehl absents himself from his Minneapolis home and
is not discovered until ten years later in Long Beach, California,
where he is a coffee-shop operator. Meanwhile, his mother has died
and left him $45,000. . . . Reverend Thornton Wilson leaves his wife
and congregation in Uvalde, Texas, to attend a Presbyterian enclave
in Brownsville and never returns. Wilson is thought either dead or a
victim of amnesia and remains missing for two years until he inexplicably writes to his wife that he is living in California. . . . Mrs.
John Torrance disappears on a vacation in La Jolla, California, and
she is found dead on February 11. (IX) . . . Raimonde von Maluski
vanishes on March 29 from his Manhattan home. Mrs. Mary Jones
is later accused of kidnapping the three-year-old child and murdering him. Although the boy's corpse is never found, Mrs. Jones is
convicted on the testimony of witnesses and sentenced on June 25,
to twenty-five to forty years in prison. Before being removed to
Auburn Prison, Mrs. Jones, wearing a cynical smile, hears Judge
Collins thunder: "I believe you killed that child!" Comments the
forty-one-year-old Mrs. Jones as she is led in handcuffs to prison:
"That is the end of it." . . . The Japanese steamer *Raifuku Maru*,

sailing in April from Boston for Hamburg is caught in an apparent storm and is sent into the Bermuda Triangle after being sighted by the White Star liner *Homeric*. Its radio operator reportedly shouts "It's like a dagger! Come quick! Please come! We cannot escape!" The vessel and its forty-eight crew members are never seen again. . . . Two six-year-olds, Virginia Arnold and Janet Campbell, wander away from their Manhattan home and explore a deserted apartment building. They are trapped in a closet, locked from the outside and are posted missing. Virginia compels Janet to lie on the floor and breathe air through the crack beneath the door to avoid suffocation; they are found alive two days later. . . . The great explorer Colonel Percy Harrison Fawcett vanishes on April 20 with his son Jack and Raleigh Rimmel after plunging into the vast jungles of Brazil's Matto Grosso, to create one of the longest-standing mysteries in modern times. (III) . . . Isabel Bennett, daughter of New York socialites, absents herself on November 13. (IX) . . . Rochester real-estate broker Charles A. Lee, a married man with three children, fakes his own suicide on November 26 and runs away with another woman. Lee is found two months later in Los Angeles and charged with defrauding insurance companies out of $22,000. . . . The cargo ship *Cotopaxi* disappears with all hands on December 11 as it sails into the Bermuda Triangle en route from Charleston to Havana.

## 1926

The freighter *Suduffco*, sailing from New Jersey, disappears inside the Bermuda Triangle on March 13. . . . The most controversial evangelist in modern times, Sister Aimee Semple McPherson, vanishes while swimming off Venice, California, on May 18, a disappearance that will be talked about for decades. (I) . . . Mystery writer Agatha Christie, an apparent amnesia victim, disappears in the manner of her own haunting fiction and creates England's greatest missing-persons hunt. (II) . . . Mrs. Gladys Houck, wife of a distinguished Washington, D.C., doctor, disappears on December 15. Her body is found the following March 23, fully clothed and without any mark of violence, floating in the Potomac. . . . Amnesia victim Alice Breen vanishes on a New York street. (II)

## 1927

Marion Parker, twelve-year-old daughter of wealthy Los Angeles banker Percy H. Parker, is kidnapped by the deranged William Edward Hickman, who ransoms her and delivers her corpse. (IV) . . . Billy Gaffney, four years old, vanishes on February 11, and his fate is not determined until madman murderer and cannibal Albert Fish is arrested and executed in 1936. (IV) . . . French pilots Charles Nungesser and François Coli are lost while attempting to fly the Atlantic on May 8. (XIII) . . . Tom Scott Goolsby, the twenty-two-year-old son of Dr. R. C. Goolsby, of Forsyth, Georgia, disappears on July 1 and is not discovered until December 23, 1927, in Tyler, Texas, by his searching father. He is found living under the name J. C. Morrison and remembers nothing of his former life, his memory a total blank. Goolsby cannot even recall attending Emory University or any of his friends and relatives. Returning to Georgia, Goolsby comments, "Kind of funny—everybody knows me and I don't know anybody." . . . James Kelly, of Dallas, Texas, vanishes completely. (IX) . . . Long Island rooming-house owner Eugenia Cedarholm suddenly and mysteriously vanishes in November; one of her boarders, Edward Lawrence Hall, is charged with her murder. Although Miss Cedarholm's corpse is never recovered, Hall is sentenced to twenty years' imprisonment in Sing Sing. (VI)

## 1928

The 7,000-ton steamer *Asiatic Prince* vanishes completely with its crew of forty-eight after sailing from Los Angeles for Yokohama on March 16. . . . Wealthy Manhattan businessman Sam Abrams fakes his own suicide and disappears. (V) . . . Grace Budd, twelve-year-old New York girl, vanishes and is later discovered to be the brutal murder victim of lunatic killer Albert Fish. (IV) . . . David Courtois, a Quebec trapper, takes his sons René, nineteen, and Michel,

389

thirteen, into the bush country on a hunting expedition. He leaves his boys for a side hunting trip, but when he returns to the camp site, the boys are missing. Search parties scour the desolate area for a year before finding Michel, who explains that he and his brother wandered away from the camp site and had gotten lost. They survive for months on berries, roots and fishbones before René dies. Michel stays with his brother's body for two months, keeping a fire burning in a pail with his only two matches. When rescuers approach the boy with a plate of food, he screams: "Take away that food! I'll faint—maybe I'll die!" Michel survives. . . . Two children—a girl, six, and a boy, twelve, it is estimated—die in a horrible train wreck outside Cotswold Village, Charfield, Gloucestershire England, along with fourteen other passengers on October 13, when a passenger train crashes at 50 m.p.h. into a stationary freight train. The resulting fire consumes one wooden coach and kills all inside. Fourteen of the bodies are identified. Other remains indicate the remains of two children. Ticket collector Henry Haines is positive that he saw two children on board the train. The remains are buried in the village cemetery after no one responds to a nationwide appeal for their parents to claim the bodies. An explanation for the mystery of the unwanted children might be that the charred body fragments really were the remains of Philip Jenkins, a twenty-two-year-old electrical engineer who is thought by many to have gotten aboard the train at Derby, whose corpse is not recovered, and who remains missing to this day. The two children, however, have been given a kind of immortality—the tombstone above the grave containing the unrecognizable remnants is marked "Two Unknowns." . . . Wealthy Dr. Charles Brancati, a secretive figure whose associations link him to Arnold Rothstein and other underworld characters, vanishes from his Long Island mansion on November 19, and is never seen again, and his vast holdings also begin to disappear. (V) . . . The training vessel *København*, sailing for Melbourne from the River Plate with a crew of seventy-five on board, is last heard from via radio, giving its position on December 22 as nine hundred miles off the island of Tristan da Cunha. The ship and its entire crew are never seen again. . . . Fordham University student Robert Emmet Boyle disappears while on Christmas vacation and is not found until April 1, 1930, when a private detective, hired by his wealthy physician-father, tracks him down in Vicksburg, Mississippi, where he is driving a cab. "Hell," says Boyle, "I just wanted to make my own way ... but seeking a fortune is a tough job."

## 1929

Christian missionary Sadhu Sundar Singh disappears while preaching the Gospel in Tibet. (XI) ... Prospector Harry Bell Lasseter vanishes while searching for gold in the Australian bush country; he returns with nuggets and claims to have found an entire mountain of gold. Lasseter again vanishes on a return trip to his glittering reef. (VII) ... John Kachnycz vanishes in Pittsburgh, is declared dead, murdered in a brawl; he returns years later very much alive. (IX) ... Robert Romero, on board the Chilean steamer *Huasco* en route to Paita from Salaverry, utterly disappears. He is known to be carrying about $60,000. Crew men break into Romero's locked cabin and find only his traveling case. A heavy-set man, Romero could not have squeezed through his cabin's tiny porthole. ... Dr. Ernest Watzl, of Cleveland, leaves his wife and children with lover Mrs. Mary Horvath MacGranahan, fakes his suicide and embarks on a tour of the world while being tracked by detectives. (I)

## 1930

Helen Buxton, daughter of wealthy Virginia doctor Joseph T. Buxton, disappears from her exclusive Pennsylvania finishing school on January 30. (XII) ... Judge Joseph Force Crater vanishes on a Manhattan street on August 6, creating the greatest missing-persons mystery in New York on record. (VI) ... Electrical wizard Philip T. Van Biber disappears on September 18 on a Newark, New Jersey, street. (IX) ... Mary Agnes Maroney is abducted from her home in Chicago and will later be the subject of a massive search and identification by the nation's press. (XV) ... Anna Fisher is placed in a foster home in New York as Florence Laddin and takes thirty-five years to discover her true identity. (XV).

*1931*

New York jeweler Henry Levy vanishes; his body is found five months later in the East River. (VI) . . . Prostitute Queen Vivien Gordon disappears on the eve of talking to investigators probing the corrupt Jimmy Walker regime. (V) . . . Starr Faithfull, a twenty-five-year-old New York showgirl, vanishes on June 4, her body is discovered sometime later floating off Long Island. It is claimed that Starr either was pushed or jumped from the liner *Mauretania* while trying to stow away for England to meet with Cunard Line ship surgeon Dr. George Jameson-Carr, of the *Franconia*. Despite the exhaustive work of scores of detectives, murder is never proven. . . . Wealthy Japanese merchant and leading silk importer in the United States, Hisashi Fujimura, disappears on August 14 while on the liner *Belgenland* as the vessel nears Fire Island. It is concluded that Fujimura, who has been blackmailed for $200,000, has been pushed from the ship, murdered by unknown assassins. . . . Edgar F. Hazelton, Jr., sixteen-year-old son of Judge Hazelton of Queens, vanishes on Long Island Sound on August 20. He is first thought to be kidnapped, but Hazelton returns after being discovered in Harrisburg, Pennsylvania. The youth explains that he "wanted to see the country." . . . Heir to millions Thomas Craighead Buntin of Nashville, Tennessee, disappears in September as does his former secretary Betty McCuddy. (1) . . . Following the derailment of the Vienna

*Mad train bomber Sylvester Matuska (center) escaped from prison and vanished.* (UPI)

Express while crossing the Bia Torbagy, sixteen miles west of Budapest, killing scores of passengers, authorities arrest one Sylvester Matuska. Officials learn that Matuska is responsible for blowing up several trains in recent months. He confesses that he has derailed several trains in order to emphasize the feasibility of a new train safety device he has invented! Matuska is sentenced to life imprisonment, but escapes in 1945 when the Russians overrun Hungary and is never seen again. . . . The Norwegian ship *Stavanger* vanishes with forty-three on board in the Bermuda Triangle in October.

## 1932

Senhora Josina do Amaral, whose Brazilian estate is worth many millions of dollars, vanishes from her São Paulo mansion. She is found a year later locked in a closet of the home of her son Mario, who has been attempting to take over her fortune. Mario's twenty-year-old son Paulo, direct heir to the Amaral estate, is also discovered missing at the same time; he is not found for two years, until a relative spots him wandering the streets of São Paulo "famished, clad in rags, and suffering from amnesia." . . . Charles A. Lindbergh, Jr., vanishes on March 1, from his Hopewell, New Jersey, home. (IV) . . . On April 19 the two-masted schooner *John and Mary*, which has sailed the previous month from New York en route to Venezuela, is found a derelict near Bermuda, its entire crew missing. . . . Vitriolic crusader against alcohol Colonel Raymond Robins suffers an amnesia attack and vanishes on September 3, 1932. (II) . . . Department-store executive Lee Schlesinger, of Portland, Oregon, is thought dead when his car is found in the Columbia River off a Vancouver dock. He is found two years later living in South America under a different name.

## 1933

William A. Hamm, Jr., heir to the Minneapolis brewing fortune, is kidnapped on June 14. (IV) . . . Millionaire oilman Charles F. Urschel is abducted in July in Oklahoma City. (IV) . . . On July 1 shadowy

*Jake "The Barber" Factor whose 1933 kidnapping by the Roger Touhy gang would later be proved a hoax.*

businessman Jake "The Barber" Factor is allegedly kidnapped by the Roger Touhy gang of Chicago; years later the kidnapping will be proven a hoax and Touhy an innocent victim sent to prison for life. . . . Dexter Case, postmater of Sound View, Connecticut, suffers from amnesia and wanders away from home; he is gone for more than two years, located in a lumber camp in Greenville, Maine. . . . Religious zealot Nila Cram Cook vanishes in India. (XI) . . . San Jose heir Brooke Hart is abducted on November 9. (IV) . . . Robert Netherland, operator of a missing-persons racket, is captured by police in early November. (XIV) . . . Well-to-do Agnes Tufverson, of New York, vanishes on December 20. She is thought to have been murdered by her zany lover-husband Captain Ivan Poderjay. (VI)

### 1934

Thomas H. Robinson, Jr., is kidnapped. (IV) . . . Minneapolis banker Edward G. Bremer is abducted by the Barber-Karpis gang on January 17. (IV) . . . Mrs. Florence Neacy Paul of Flushing, New York, disappears in a taxicab while on her way to a maternity ward with policeman Frank L. Schultz. Mrs. Paul's disappearance on May 31 is not reported for seven months. Officer Schultz, suspected of committing foul play, is suspended from the police force, but Mrs. Paul is never discovered. . . . Super bank robber John Herbert Dillinger is reportedly gunned down outside a Chicago theater on July 22. Discrepancies of the dead man listed in the official autopsy— the dead man lacks Dillinger's known scars and wounds; he is heavier, shorter than Dillinger; his eyes are brown, whereas Dillingers' are blue; he has a rheumatic heart condition, whereas Dillinger has none—point to Dillinger's permanent escape and disappearance. . . . On September 28, Harold Dutcher of Newark, New Jersey, absents himself, telling his wife, Mary, in a note that he is "leaving forever." He returns eleven years later, penniless, explaining that he has wandered all over the world. By that time Mary Dutcher has had her husband legally declared dead. He arrives one hour before the mailman is to deliver a check for his life insurance. . . . Director of Boston's Massachusetts General Hospital George H. Bigelow wanders from his office on December 3, an amnesia victim. (II)

*Bankrobber John Dillinger who, records apparently proved, did not die outside a Chicago theater in 1934 but escaped.*

William F. Ferry suffers a collapse when his young wife dies in New York in late January. He visits her grave every day for a month in the Gates of Heaven Cemetery at Valhalla, placing fresh flowers on her tombstone. He is last seen by caretakers arriving at and departing from the cemetery on February 5. According to one report, Ferry hopped into his blue sedan and "drove out through the cemetery gate and into the fourth dimension . . . not only that, but he took the blue sedan with him." . . . Oxford, Massachusetts, student Etta Reil vanishes. (IX) . . . Mrs. Gladys Lawson of Mechanics Grove, Pennsylvania, disappears; she is later found to be the victim of a butchering abortionist. (V) . . . Heir to millions, Caleb Milne IV, is the apparent kidnap victim in a bizarre plot on December 14. (XIV)

1936

Enid, Oklahoma, businessman John R. Crosswhite vanishes; he surfaces thirty-seven years later in a Joplin, Missouri, hospital, an amnesia victim. (II) . . . Oscar Weber Leberg, a Mississippi dock worker missing for three decades, dies on the floor of Father Dempsey's Hotel for unfortunate itinerants in St. Louis, telling a priest to give his bankbook to his brother August. The brother is never found. . . . Private Edward Deal, stationed in Hawaii, vanishes from his camp on May 29 and remains lost on the slopes of Mauna Loa for a week before being rescued by Territorial Forester Leslie W. Bryan. Says Bryan to astonished newsmen, he "was led to the place where Private Deal was wandering at the edge of a forest by a dream he had last night. Before daylight he arose and started for the spot where, in the dream, he had seen the soldier. To his amazement he found him at exactly that place." Said Private Deal, hungry but in good condition: "That experience was worse than hell!" . . . Fred Brochwel Lloyd, an international financier, who is staying in New York's Savoy-Plaza Hotel with his wife, has lunch with a friend at the Bankers Club. He then travels by cab to Times Square, where the friend gets out. Lloyd goes uptown in the taxi and is never seen again. Until her death in 1945 Mrs. Lloyd waits for her husband to return. In her New York suite, investigators find $545,000 in securities, $50,000 in unclipped coupons, along with great quantities of jewelry and three uncashed insurance policies on her missing husband's life.

## 1937

*American dancer Jean de Koven disappeared in Paris in 1937; she was later found murdered. Eugene Weidmann, her killer, stands wounded in a Paris police station.* (UPI)

Greeting-card tycoon Charles S. Ross is abducted in Chicago. (IV) . . . Would-be Communist spy Juliet Stuart Poyntz vanishes from her New York apartment in June and is thought to be liquidated by Soviets. (VIII) . . . Heiress Mrs. Alice W. Parsons disappears from her Stony Brook, New York, estate on June 9. She is first thought to be kidnapped when her husband receives a ransom note demanding $25,000 for her return, but the F.B.I., after conducting a fruitless ten-month search for the woman, concludes the millionairess has been murdered and gives up the hunt. Mrs. Parsons is never found and is declared dead in 1946. . . . Lady pilot and explorer Amelia Mary Earhart disappears on a mysterious Pacific flight on July 1. (VIII) . . . Jean de Koven, a twenty-two-year-old American dancer visiting Paris is suddenly discovered missing from her hotel on August 7. Though a ransom note demanding $500 for the girl's safe return is received by an aunt, Mrs. Ida Sackheim, who had been traveling with her niece, Miss de Koven remains missing. The dancer's abductor, Eugene Weidmann, a German living in Paris to avoid military induction, is tracked down at his villa at Celle-Saint-Cloud. Investigators are wounded by Weidmann as they take him into custody. He admits murdering the de Koven girl for her traveler's checks, and slaying several others. Police dig up the girl's body from beneath the front porch of the villa. Weidmann is executed for the murders. . . . The 4,000-ton steamer *Haida* (built in 1909 and originally called *Burgeo Star*) sails for Seattle from Hong Kong on October 24 and is never heard from again. . . . Mr. and Mrs. Donald Robinson (alias Rubens), of New York, disappear in Moscow on December 2 in what will become a mazelike spy yarn. (VIII)

G. Henry Brethauser, Controller of New Haven, Connecticut, absents himself with more than $12,000 of city funds. He is not found until his death in Chicago twenty years later. (XV) ... The *Anglo-Australian,* a 5,500-ton freighter, vanishes in the North Atlantic with its entire crew of thirty-eight after sailing on March 8 from Cardiff. ... Andrew Carnegie Whitfield, the nephew of tycoon Andrew Carnegie, disappears in his small plane on April 17 after leaving Roosevelt Field on Long Island on a routine flight. (XIII) ... Roy Selwyn Buckles of Broken Arrow, Oklahoma, disappears and is found two years later as a dishwasher in Fort Worth, Texas, where he is informed that his mother has died and left him $12,000.

*1939*

Miss Ada Constance Kent, of Whalebone Corner, England, a wealthy spinster, vanishes from her cottage. Over the years, the deserted cottage is searched three times. In 1949, a constable, at the request of a bank in which Miss Kent has mysteriously placed funds, again searches the cottage and finds the fully clothed skeleton of Miss Kent seated at a table and beside it a tray laden with fresh food. The grisly mystery is never explained. ... American adventurer Richard Halliburton vanishes with a crew of thirteen after sailing his specially equipped Chinese junk from Hong Kong on March 23 en route to San Francisco. (III) ... Heir to a fortune, William R. Snyder disappears from his Detroit home on June 14. (X) ... James Sarsfield of Normal, Illinois, travels to the World's Fair in New York and vanishes. (IX)

*1940*

The schooner *Gloria Colita* sails on January 21 from Mobile, Alabama, and is found abandoned in the Gulf of Mexico on

February 5, its captain and crew missing. . . . Missing for years, Edythe Lippman is discovered to be a librarian in Little Falls, New Jersey, an heiress to $160,000. (X) . . . One of the most intensive searches ever conducted for a disappearing heir involves one Francis Smith, of Westmoreland, Kansas, who has been missing several years. He is reported a derelict drifting in and out of hobo jungle camps along the route of the New York, Ontario and Western Railway. Investigators often miss Smith by days, once by hours. He is finally found in Steubenville, Ohio, a ragged, bearded, impoverished man. Told he has inherited $6,500, Smith attempts to punch the investigator for "pulling my leg." Finally accepting the report as truthful, Smith goes into a wild jig and then collapses. . . . Mrs. R. Levi, refusing to believe that he has been killed with all hands on a British warship, begins a search for her nineteen-year-old son. She travels the world over and finally finds her boy in a mental asylum in Cape Town, South Africa. According to one report, "he is a human wreck and could only mutter '*shalom, shalom*'—the Hebrew word for 'peace.'" Mrs. Levi takes one look at her lost son and drops dead. . . . Amnesia victim Emily Kobylansky wanders away from her Braddock, Pennsylvania home; she regains her memory in 1949; by then she is the wife of John Norton in New Rochelle, New York, a mother of two young children.

### 1941

Mrs. Suzie Powell Nichols, heir to a large fortune, is found close to death, after being missing for several years, in Fort Worth, Texas. (X) . . . U.S.S. *Proteus*, in November, and U.S.S. *Nereus*, in December, both sailing from St. Thomas and bound for Atlantic seaports, are lost with all hands in the Bermuda Triangle.

### 1943

George Wallace, of the Royal Air Force, is found shell-shocked and wandering aimlessly through the Libyan desert. He identifies himself as John Crisp, and not until 1948 does the memory of his true identity return. By then he is operating a window-cleaning business in Birmingham, England, and refuses to return to his wife and child in Leeds.... Rose Brancato, twenty-eight-year-old reporter for the New Haven *Journal-Courier*, disappears from her West Haven, Connecticut, home on July 5 and is sought from coast to coast as a possible amnesia victim. Authorities learn the following year that Walter Law, thirty-nine-year-old superintendent of New Haven's Woolworth Building, has lured the girl reporter into the basement of his building, strangled her, and burned her fully clothed in a boiler. Law pleads drunkenness and is sentenced to life imprisonment on second-degree murder.... Mr. and Mrs. Andrew Toth utterly vanish without a clue while shopping in New York. (IX)

### 1944

Swing-era bandleader Glenn Miller disappears on board a U.S. Army plane lost in a fog. The wreckage of Miller's Norseman plane is reported in 1972 to be two hundred feet under water twelve miles southeast of Dymchurch, England, on the English Channel.... On October 22, 1944, the Cuban cargo ship *Rubicon* is spotted as a derelict off the coast of Florida. All hands are missing, although the ship is in seaworthy condition and the personal effects of the crew members are still on board.

*Bandleader Glenn Miller, gone since 1944.*

### 1945

One of the most celebrated missing servicemen of World War II, known only as "Charles Jameson," is delivered wounded to a Boston hospital. (II) ... Martin Bormann, Hitler's private secretary and one of the ranking powers in Nazi Germany, escapes the *Führerbunker* on May 1 in Berlin as Russian troops close in and is never again seen. Based upon extensive investigations by several experts it is widely believed, at the time of this writing that Bormann, who has given up on neo-Nazism, is living comfortably in Argentina.... Coast Guard Yeoman Philip C. Ford, of New York City, returns from India in October and, after visiting his Coast Guard district office a

*Hitler's deputy, Martin Bormann, who vanished from the ruins of Berlin in 1945.*

month later, vanishes. His stepfather, Edwin Booth, offers a $5,000 reward for information leading to his discovery. His mother purchases a $1,800 church bell for the Village Presbyterian Church in New York, stating that she is not making the gift in her son's memory, but "rather in the thought that he will hear a church bell ringing somewhere and remember who he is." Ford's badly decomposed body is found alongside the Farm-to-Market Road outside Bedford, New York, on December 21, 1947; Ford apparently has died on his way to his family's nearby summer place. . . . Five Grumman TBM-3 Avenger torpedo bombers with fourteen crew members vanish in the ominous Bermuda Triangle on December 5. (XIII)

### 1946

Six-year-old Suzanne Degnan is kidnapped in Chicago on January 7. (IV) . . . Paula Weldon, a Bennington sophomore, vanishes on December 1. Carl W. Rockel is arrested in Cambridge, Massachusetts, two years later as a suspect in the Weldon case, newspaper clippings about the missing girl stuffed in his pockets. Rockel is originally arrested for slashing Ernest R. Varney, Jr., fifty-four times in order to steal fifty-nine cents. Rockel is never connected with the Weldon disappearance.

### 1947

Seaman John Lee Johnson begins a thirty-year search for his lost ten-year-old daughter Doris Lee. (XII) . . . Chicagoan Harry N. Lanning disappears and is doggedly hunted down by his wife in New York two years later. (IX)

### 1948

On January 30, the *Star Tiger*, a Tudor IV plane operated by British South American Airways, en route from London to Havana, vanishes in the Bermuda Triangle with all on board. (XIII) . . . Interna-

*Jockey Al Snider, shown aboard Citation after winning the Flamingo Stakes at Hialeah in 1948. Six days later he was gone forever in the Bermuda Triangle. (UPI)*

tionally celebrated jockey Al Snider, who has ridden the racehorse Citation to victory, and two friends vanish while fishing during a storm inside the Bermuda Triangle on March 6.... Socially prominent Orja Glenwood Corns, Jr., of Winnetka, Illinois, with his wife and child out of town on vacation, whiles away the night of July 2 at Chicago's Parody Club on North Clark Street, mixing with B-girls, strippers, touts and shady characters and then disappears. Corns, allegedly carrying about $150, is thought to have been murdered for his money, but a gas-station owner later swears that he has seen Corns on July 6 while driving his 1947 green Oldsmobile. Corns and his car are never seen again.... British freighter *Hope Star* disappears with her crew in the North Atlantic while en route to Philadelphia, her last message sent on November 14.... The former Liberty ship *Samkey* vanishes off the Azores with its entire crew of forty-three men.... A chartered DC-3 disappears in the Bermuda Triangle with thirty-three on board. (XIII)

## 1949

On a clear-weather morning flight to Jamaica, the *Star Ariel*, a British South American Airways plane, taking off from Kindley Field, Bermuda, with seven crew members and thirteen passengers, vanishes completely in the Triangle on January 17. (XIII)

**1950**

West Point Cadet Richard Colvin Cox disappears on the grounds of the Academy on January 14, becoming one of the most celebrated missing students in American history. (IX) . . . A U.S. Air Force Globemaster with fifty-three persons on board crashes and disappears on March 23 in the North Atlantic while on a flight from Ireland to the United States. . . . Philadelphia housewife Mrs. Dorothy Forstein, spouse of Judge Jules Forstein, vanishes from her home in a bizarre abduction mystery. (IV) . . . Embezzler William Henry Waldon, Jr., absents himself from his Huntington, Virginia, home; he is found sixteen years later in Florida, where, under a different name, he is under indictment for murder. (V)

**1951**

*Guy Burgess (above) and Donald Maclean, British diplomats who were listed as missing in 1951 but later turned up as proud defectors in Russia.* (WIDE WORLD)

Guy Burgess and Donald Maclean, British diplomats, disappear on May 25. Rumors of the diplomats being dead, homosexual runaways, or drunkards abound, but nothing is found of the two men. On September 11, 1953, Donald Maclean's American-born wife, Melinda, and her three children also disappear. Both diplomats finally emerge at a press conference in Moscow on February 11, 1956, under Soviet sponsorship. Both men, it is learned, have been spies for the Communists and have defected when their "covers" began to crack under probes by Western agents.

**1952**

Scientist Albert Clark Reed, an apparent amnesia victim, vanishes from his California home on July 7; he is found two years later working as a race-track groom. (II) . . . In December William and Martha Burton of Long Island, New York, vanish together. Burton, a former prosecutor of leaders of organized crime, has received many threats for years and his home has been bombed in 1946. The couple disappear on a trip to Florida, leaving an estate of $90,000.

Says one investigator: "I think it has to be assumed that they met foul play. No trace of them was ever found." The Burtons are pronounced dead by the courts twenty-four years later in October 1976.

## 1953

A British York Transport with thirty-nine persons on board, flying from the Azores to Gander vanishes on February 2. . . . Mrs. Lyde Marland, of Ponca City, Oklahoma, absents herself in February. The wife and adopted daughter of the onetime oil baron and governor Ernest Whitworth Marland, who has scandalized Oklahoma through his excesses, Mrs. Marland drives away from her family estate with $10,000 in her handbag and paintings worth about $3,000. Always an eccentric, Lyde later stays in a motel outside Independence, Missouri, dressed in a tacky squaw's outfit and working with the proprietors in making up beds to keep busy. She hides whenever a car with Oklahoma license plates arrives. Authorities search for Mrs. Marland for years but discover nothing, except that in 1956 she has placed a long-distance phone call to Knoedler's Gallery in New York to ask if her painting "The Buffalo Hunt," by Alfred Miller, has been sold. The courts declare her dead in 1960. . . . James A. Schultz of Richmond, California, absents himself and technically "abducts" his two sons, Craig and Brent, on June 19, when he learns that the boys are to be put in his wife's custody following her remarriage. For nine years, the mother of the boys searches for them, finally discovering her ex-husband in Hollywood, Florida, where he is living and teaching under the name of Charles V. Howell. . . . Father Henry Borynski, a Roman Catholic priest serving a Polish community in Little Horton, England, mysteriously disappears on July 13, many think as a Communist captive. (VIII) . . . The interisland 240-ton French steamer *Monique*, with 120 persons on board, vanishes without a trace on August 1 in the South Pacific while en route from Mare, in the Loyalty Islands, to Noumea, New Caledonia. . . . Two American flyers, Alexander I. Rorke, Jr., and Geoffrey Sullivan disappear on a Caribbean flight on September 24. They are thought to be victims of Cuban antiaircraft. . . . Six-year-old Bobby Greenlease, Jr., is abducted in Kansas City. (IV)

## 1954

British tennis star Joan Ross-Dilley wanders lost with amnesia in Vermont. (II) ... Gold-seeker Jaroslav Renza vanishes in the Australian bush country. (III) ... Millard Good, a trusty prisoner in the West Virginia Penitentiary, disappears while working outside the walls. He remains missing for twenty years before turning himself in to authorities. Good has worked for an Ohio farmer for nineteen years as Delbert Shamblin, living in a single room above a cellar, only a hundred miles away from his wife and children. He is given probation by Governor Arch A. Moore, Jr., and is reunited with his family in 1974. ... Argentine steamer *General San Martin*, a 9,589-ton ship with a crew of fifty-four, disappears completely on September 12 off the coast of Chile. ... Four-year-old Lavern Enget vanishes from his North Dakota farm in October. (IX) ... A U.S. Navy Super-Constellation disappears October 30 during a trans-Atlantic flight from New Jersey to the Azores. The plane and its forty-two passengers, despite a massive air and sea armada of searchers, are never found. ... The 3,337-tone freighter *Southern Districts* vanishes off the Gulf of Mexico on December 7; although the wreckage of the vessel is found two weeks later off Sand Key, Florida, the crew of twenty-four are missing.

## 1955

Rufus K. Dryer, a prominent Rochester, New York, businessman, absents himself on February 8, leaving his wife and children. Dryer, an apparent amnesia victim, is found in April in Pensacola, Florida, working as a circus clown. ... Scientist Carl Vernon Holmberg walks out of his Syracuse University office on May 11 and is not seen again until six years later, when he is discovered in Rockford, Illinois, under a different name and working as a day laborer. (II) ... Florida Judge C. E. Chillingworth and his wife vanish from their beachside home; they are later discovered to be murder victims. (VI) ... Three-year-old Steven Damman disappears while his mother is shopping in a Long Island store. (IX) ... The motor yacht *Connemara IV* is found abandoned in the Bermuda Triangle on September 26 by the tanker *Olympic Cloud;* the crew is never found.... The twin-screw cabin crusier *Joyita*, once the private yacht of screen star Mary Pickford, vanishes in October with twenty-five persons on board; the vessel is found off the Fiji Island on November 13 with all hands missing. The mystery is never solved.

## 1956

Long Island businessman Lewis H. Hanno absents himself on January 16. (IX) ... Volatile anti-Trujillo teeacher Dr. Jesus de Galindez vanishes on March 12 in New York City; it is later determined that Galindez is the victim of a bizarre kidnapping. (VIII) ... British adventurer and frogman Lionel Kenneth Phillip Crabb disappears while on a secret underwater mission to inspect two Russian vessels visiting Portsmouth, England. (VIII) ... Peter Weinberger is kidnapped from his Long Island home on July 4. (IV) ... Ionel Grigoriu, a Rumanian language instructor at Fort Ord, California, mysteriously disappears from his Pacific Grove home on October 5; bloodhounds trail the instructor's scent to the ocean, where his abandoned car is found. He is thought to be a suicide and is declared dead two years later.... A Navy patrol bomber with ten men on board is completely lost on November 10 just north of the Bermuda Triangle. Not one piece of debris is found, despite massive searches.

## 1957

Lawrence Joseph Bader disappears from his Akron, Ohio, home on May 15; he is discovered eight years later to be one of the leading personalities of Omaha, Nebraska, one John Francis "Fritz" Johnson, suffering one of the classic amnesia attacks on record. (II)

## 1958

Millionaire publisher of *Yachting* and *Aviation Age*, Harvey Conover, considered to be one of the best sailors in the world, vanishes

*Wealthy publisher Harvey Conover, who vanished in the Bermuda Triangle in 1958, is shown presenting an award four years earlier to Vice President Richard M. Nixon while Mrs. Nixon looks on, and taking the helm (arrow) of his 45-foot yawl* Revonoc *on which he sailed into oblivion. (UPI)*

with three others in the sleek 45-foot yawl *Revonoc* inside the Bermuda Triangle on January 7.

### 1959

*Onetime assistant Navy secretary Edward B. Germain drove out of a Buffalo, New York parking lot in 1959 and was found dead four years later.*

Bruce Nelson Campbell disappears in bright-green monogrammed pajamas from the Sandman Motel in Jacksonville, Illinois, on April 14. Campbell and his wife, Mabelite, have been visiting their son after a long trip from Massachusetts, where Campbell is an investment counselor. Confused and disoriented after the long drive to Illinois, Campbell takes a few pills and is missing when his wife awakes in the motel room. His money, keys, car, and all his belongings remain. Campbell is never found and in 1967 is declared dead. . . . Edward G. Germain a wealthy banker and former Assistant Secretary of the Navy drives out of a Buffalo, New York, parking lot on June 11; Germain's badly decomposed corpse, with identifying papers in the pockets of trousers, is found four years later in the waters off Squaw Island, New York. His car, which had apparently gone off the road and into the water, was later pulled from the lake. . . . New York executive James Laurence Barber leaves a suicide note for his wife and then, after registering in several eastern seaboard hotels, takes a motor boat into the Atlantic, where he vanishes on September 24.

## 1960

On February 10 the abandoned bloodstained station wagon of beer tycoon Adolph Coors III is discovered in a remote spot near Denver, Colorado. Police later find that he was kidnapped and murdered by a Joseph Corbett, Jr. (IV) . . . Loy D. Clark goes AWOL from the Marine Corps and gives himself up sixteen years later in Forest Park, Illinois. . . . On July 17 Norman H. Briggs, of Troy, New York, has disappeared and is thought to have drowned. He is found on a Newcastle, Wyoming, cattle ranch in March 1965. His wife, who has collected his life-insurance money, is forced to return it.

*Insurance man turned cowboy Norman Briggs, who brought about his own disappearance, is returned to Troy, New York in handcuffs.* ( WIDE WORLD )

## 1961

Michael Clark Rockefeller, son of Nelson Rockefeller, begins to explore the rugged, wild coasts of New Guinea. His small boat is swamped and Rockefeller disappears as he attempts to swim to shore. (III) . . . William C. Waters, a Kentucky camper on vacation, is lost in June in the wilds of northern Alaska; he is found near death three months later. (III) . . . While skin-diving near the Statue of Liberty in New York Harbor on July 28, Jersey City doctor Larry L. Feder vanishes. Massive air and sea searches are made to recover his body, but all fails. Investigators then realize that Feder has absented himself. He has fired his nurse two weeks before his alleged drowning, given up his post-office box, and rented an apartment by mail in Amarillo, Texas. A note from Feder to his wife is delivered. It reads: "I ran away to start a new decision in life to get out of the old dying rut."

## 1962

A U.S. Air Force KB50 aerial tanker with nine crew members on board, leaves Langley Air Force Base, Virginia, for the Azores on January 8 and vanishes in the Atlantic, the last position given by Major Robert Tawney is 250 miles east of Cape Charles. . . . In

August, three-year-old Stephen Papol strays from a picnic spot in New York's Hecksher State Park; thousands search for the boy for three days. (XII)

## 1963

The 520-ton tanker *Marine Sulphur Queen* with its entire crew of thirty-nine vanishes on February 4 in the Bermuda Triangle while en route from Beaumont, Texas, to Norfolk, Virginia. Small debris of the ship is later discovered. . . . The 63-foot charter fishing boat *Sno' Boy*, with fifty-five persons on board, disappears inside the Bermuda Triangle on July 4. Some wreckage found later is said to be that of the fishing vessel. . . . Two giant KC-135 U.S. Air Force tankers on a classified mission over the Atlantic disappear on August 28 with eleven crew members in the Bermuda Triangle. . . . John T. Symes, vice-president of the Farmers and Mechanics Savings Bank, in Lockport, New York, absents himself on September 15, leaving a note for his wife—"I have to get away for a while. I love you and the family. John." He does not return.

## 1964

Las Vegas businessman George F. Knoop fakes his own death in an insurance-money swindle in which his wife participates. (V) . . . California matron Mrs. Gertrude Jones steps from her home on May 10 and disappears forever. (IX) . . . Dr. Bernard M. Bueche, after constructing a bizarre building in Spotswood, New Jersey, vanishes completely on July 14. (IX)

## 1965

A U.S. Air Force C-119 Flying Boxcar, with ten persons on board, vanishes in the Bermuda Triangle on June 4.

## 1966

George Gilbert and his wife are thought to have been killed when their boat explodes off the Massachusetts coast. Gilbert is found alive in Las Vegas three years later after being mugged and robbed. Gilbert, who claims amnesia, is charged with the murder of his wife.... Charles Keith Beth, a forty-one-year-old salesman from Tucson, Arizona, utterly disappears at the Mexican border; Beth's car is found locked and parked near the U.S. Immigration complex at Nogales.

*George Gilbert was thought to have been blown up when his boat exploded in 1966; he was located three years later and charged with the murder of his wife.*

## 1967

A Chase YC-122 converted World War II glider disappears en route to Bimini with four persons on board on January 11. This disappearance marks the beginning of what some will call "Black Week" inside the Bermuda Triangle.... A Beechcraft Bonanza, with four persons on board, vanishes on January 14 in the Triangle after taking off from Miami International Airport.... A Piper Apache plane and its four occupants disappear in the Triangle on January 17. No debris from any of the planes is ever seen, although a huge rescue search is made.... After radioing the mysterious fact that it has struck a strange submerged object, the 23-foot cabin cruiser *Witchcraft*, lying off Miami in the Triangle, vanishes with two men on board on December 24.

## 1968

On May 21, the 3,075-ton nuclear-powered American submarine *Scorpion* disappears with ninety-three crew members in the Atlantic, southwest of the Azores. The vessel is located in November at 10,000 feet below the surface.... Barbara Jane Mackle, the twenty-year-old daughter of Florida land development tycoon Robert Mackle, is kidnapped on December 17 and is held in an underground box for eighty-three hours near Norcross, Georgia, before kidnapper Gary Steven Krist informs the F.B.I. as to her whereabouts. Krist receives close to a half million in $20 bills (all recorded) but is soon captured in Florida and sent to prison for life. His associate, Ruth Eisemann-Schier, is sentenced to seven years' imprisonment.

## 1969

Political professor and intriguer Thomas Riha, whose background and associates are fraught with mystery and possible espionage, vanishes from Boulder, Colorado, on March 15. (VIII) . . . Peter Wallin, of Stockholm, sailing alone in his 20-foot yacht *Vagabond*, vanishes in mid-Atlantic; his abandoned vessel is found on July 2. . . . On July 10 the 41-foot three-hulled yacht *Teignmouth Electron* is found abandoned in mid-Atlantic. Its one-man crew, Donald Crowhurst, the most prominent sailor in an around-the-world race, remains missing.

## 1970

In one of the most spectacular husband-and-wife disappearances on record, Mr. and Mrs. Edward P. Andrews, of Arlington Heights, Illinois, vanish after a Chicago cocktail party on the night of May 15. (IX)

## 1971

Chicago Alderman Fred D. Hubbard disappears with $110,000 of federal funds. (V) . . . Nine-year-old Kevin Dye vanishes in the Casper Mountain range of Wyoming on July 18; the boy, a sufferer of epilepsy and aphasia, sparks one of the greatest manhunts in recent Western history. (XII) . . . The Dominican Republic ship *El Caribe*, a 338-foot freighter, vanishes with thirty crew members on the night of October 15 while making its way through the Bermuda Triangle.

The *V. A. Fogg*, a 572-foot American freighter, vanishes off Galveston on February 2. The vessel is later found by divers in ninety feet of water. Only the bodies of the captain and two crew members are recovered, thirty-six others are completely missing. . . . Student Steven Chait walks out of his dormitory at Columbia University on March 13 and is never heard from again, despite the prolonged efforts of his parents to find him. They write to more than five hundred newspapers begging that their story be published. Chait remains missing. . . . Nineteen-year-old Robin Lee Reade, of Lake Forest, Illinois, disappears on March 27 while on a trip to California and Hawaii. Her parents hire two detectives, who turn up nothing. The Reades then employ mystic Peter Hurkos, who takes them on a tour of Oklahoma, Buenos Aires, Argentina and Honolulu. Though Hurkos points out several buildings to the Reades, stating that their daughter is buried somewhere inside, nothing is uncovered. Chicago private detective Anthony J. Pellicano, who specializes in missing persons cases, is employed by the Reades in March 1977. Within one month he finds Robin Reade's grave on the side of a mountain outside Honolulu.

*Private investigator Anthony J. Pellicano, who specializes in missing-persons cases, explains how he solved the Robin Reade case in 1972.*

## 1973

Gregorio Florencio Cordova-MacArthur, grandson of billionaire John D. MacArthur (brother of playwright Charles), and reputedly America's richest man, vanishes while on a hitch-hiking trip from Mexico to San Francisco in April. Gregorio is thought to have been murdered on the road. MacArthur refuses to lend his financial support to the hunt, stating that he cannot recall his grandson's first name. . . . Eugene Paul Getty II, the sixteen-year-old grandson of the "world's richest man," J. Paul Getty, and a spoiled "Jet-set-brat" who is called "the golden hippie," is kidnapped on June 10 and held for a ransom of $2.9 million, which his grandfather pays only after boy's right ear is cut off and delivered as proof of the abduction. When Eugene Getty is released on December 15, he calls to thank his grandfather for paying the ransom. The richest man in the world

*Eugene Paul Getty II after his ordeal by kidnapping in 1973.* (WIDE WORLD)

refuses to talk to his grandson, fearing the call is part of the kidnapping plot, but through an aide, wishes his grandson "good luck." ... On May 22, the Norwegian freighter *Anita* disappears with all hands off the coast of New Jersey. No SOS is sent by the ship.

## 1974

Harold Goldberg of Sedalia, Missouri, disappears in January. His wife, on the basis of a scar, a bent finger and missing teeth, identifies a decomposed corpse as that of Goldberg; he is declared dead, and his corpse is buried. Three years later, on November 7, 1976, Goldberg calls his wife to tell her he is alive, working as a restaurant operator in the Ozarks, and that he has had amnesia; the body in the Missouri grave is never explained.... Lisa Anne Berry, of Oakland, California, goes to a bank to cash a thirty-dollar check for baby-sitting and never returns. Three months after the fifteen-year-old girl disappears, her grandmother dies and leaves her $200,000.... Reg Murphy, editor of the *Atlanta Constitution*, is kidnapped and ransomed for $700,000; he is freed on February 2. Murphy's abductors, Mrs. Betty Ruth Williams and William Halm Williams are quickly apprehended.... Newspaper heiress Patricia Campbell Hearst is allegedly kidnapped by the terrorist group S.L.A. on February 4.... Balloonist Thomas Gatch vanishes on a flight across the Atlantic on February 18. (III) ... John Stonehouse, British Member of Parliament and financier, disappears from Miami Beach on November 20; he is later arrested in Australia, explaining that he absented himself because of financial difficulties.

## 1975

An unnamed Chicago policeman who shoots and kills 18-year-old Michael Gilmore as the youth stands innocently on a street corner on February 11 is never found.... James Riddle Hoffa, vitriolic union leader, vanishes from the parking lot of the Machus Red Fox Restaurant, in Bloomfield Township, outside Detroit, on July 30.

*Lisa Anne Berry of Oakland, California, who vanished in 1974; a $200,000 inheritance still awaits her.* (UPI)

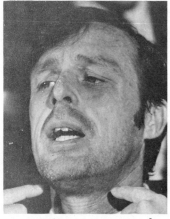

*Atlanta Constitution editor Reg Murphy was kidnapped in 1974.* (WIDE WORLD)

*Heiress Patricia Hearst, who disappeared into violence in 1974.* (UPI)

Though his body is never found, many experts believe he is the murder victim of organized crime. . . . Raymond Yablum, a rare-coin dealer in Chicago, vanishes on August 17; his body is found the following year at Yosemite National Park, California, and three men are charged with his murder. . . . Engineering genius Michael Carr Speer, of Evanston, Illinois, disappears on November 17, an apparent murder victim. (X)

*Jimmy Hoffa shortly before he was lost from sight in 1975.* (UPI)

## 1976

A number of children begin to disappear in February in and about Detroit suburbs; their bodies are later discovered along the highways. (IV) . . . Kay Johnson, of St. Paul, is found wandering about aimlessly in a Milwaukee, Wisconsin, bus station; an amnesia victim, her true identity is discovered through the help of the press. (II) . . . Foreign service officer William Bradford Bishop, Jr., disappears on March 1; his wife, three sons and mother are found bludgeoned to death in their Maryland home. (V) . . . Twelve-year-old Abby Drover, of Port Moody, Canada, vanishes on March 10; she is found six months later, a prisoner in a neighbor's private dungeon. (IV) . . . On July 6, Herve de Vathaire, Jean Kay, and his girl friend Daniele Marquet vanish in Paris after Vahaire embezzles $1.6 million from his employer, Marcel Dassault, the French airplane manufacturer. All are tried in absentia and sentenced to long prison terms.

*French embezzler Herve de Vathaire escaped with more than $1 million and remains among the missing.* (WIDE WORLD)

## 1977

As a result of the strong-arm methods employed by the military junta headed by General Pinochet in Chile, more than 1,500 persons, mostly political dissidents, are listed as missing. . . . Helen Vorhees Brach, of Glenview, Illinois, heiress to an enormous candy fortune, disappears on February 17, after she is dropped off at O'Hare Airport in Chicago, supposedly to leave on vacation for Florida. The airlines have no record of reservations or ticket charges for Mrs. Brach. At this writing, several suspects are being investigated by

413

police and private detectives, all pursuing an unknown murderer. . . . Union leader Al Bramlet vanishes in Nevada on February 24; his body is found in remote Mountain Springs, and two men are subsequently charged with his murder. (V) . . . Taweeyos Sirikul, of Chicago, disappears on March 4 after showing a stranger his car, which is for sale; his body is later found in a storage locker. (V) . . . Mrs. Betty Bronson Williams, fifty-eight, of Ketchum, Idaho, a member of a wealthy Pennsylvania manufacturer, vanishes on board the luxury liner *Monterey*. She is last seen leaving the table of Captain Sven Rogenes at 10 P.M. on March 14, when the ship is still two days west of Honolulu. Mrs. Williams' diary later reveals that she is in love with Captain Rogenes. The skipper of the 14,799-ton vessel laughs off the suggestion, stating that such shipboard crushes are typical. Michael Burton, Mrs. Williams' son, rules out suicide. Wallace Shrimplin, a Pacific Far East Lines official, states that the wealthy woman could not have accidentally fallen from the ship, which was constantly in serene waters. "Those railings are four feet high," he emphasizes. "I defy anyone to fall off, unless a person climbs up on the railing and jumps." According to one comment, "that leaves only one conclusion: murder."

*Mrs. Betty Bronson Williams (extreme right) is shown dining at the captain's table on board the liner* Monterey; *she left her seat minutes later never to return.* (UPI)

The research for this book was done in libraries throughout the United States and Europe, city archives, and a plethora of departments handling court records, especially documents involving probate. Many interviews were conducted with police (particularly missing-persons bureaus and departments), along with postal inspectors, private detectives and onetime missing persons themselves. What follows are some of the most helpful published sources.

*Bibliography*

**BOOKS**

Adler, Polly, *A House is Not a Home.* New York: Rinehart, 1950.

Allen, Edward, J., *Merchants of Menace—The Mafia.* Springfield, Ill.: Charles C Thomas, 1962.

Allen, Frederick Lewis, *Only Yesterday, An Informal History of the Nineteen Twenties.* New York: Harper, 1931.

Almedingen, E. M., *The Emperor Alexander I.* London: Bodley Head, 1964.

Altavilla, Enrico, *The Art of Spying.* Englewood Cliffs, N.J.: Prentice-Hall, 1967.

Anderson, Sherwood, *Dark Laughter.* New York: Boni & Liveright, 1925.

———, *A Story Teller's Story.* New York: Grove Press, 1958.

Anonymous, *American vs. Italian Brigandage.* Philadelphia: Barclay, 1875.

———, *Legends and Traditional Stories.* London: n.p., 1843.

———, *Mysterious Disappearances.* London: n.p., 1868.

Ashe, Samuel A'Court, *History of North Carolina.* Greensboro, N.C.: E. M. Uzzell, 1908.

Ayers, John H., and Bird, Carol, *Missing Men, The Story of The Missing Persons Bureau of the New York Police Department.* New York: Putnam, 1932.

Baker, General L. C., *History of the United States Secret Service.* Philadelphia: J. E. Potter, 1899.

Bales, William A., *A Tiger in the Streets.* New York: Dodd, Mead, 1962.

Barker, Ralph, *Great Mysteries of the Air.* London: Chatto and Windus, 1966.

Barnes, T. S., *Memoir of Thurlow Weed.* Boston: Houghton Mifflin, 1884.

Bemis, George, *Report of the Case of John W. Webster.* Boston: Little, Brown, 1850.

Berger, Meyer, *The Eighty Million.* New York: Simon and Schuster, 1942.

Berlitz, Charles, with J. Manson Valentine, *The Bermuda Triangle.* Garden City, N.Y.: Doubleday, 1974.

Bigelow, W. E., *The Boston Tragedy: An Exposé of the Parkman Murder.* Boston: n.p., 1850.

Bishop, Jim, *The Murder of Judge Peel*. New York: Simon and Schuster, 1962.

Blythe, L., *Marshal Ney, A Dual Life*. New York: Stackpole, 1937.

Botkin, Benjamin A., *The Treasury of American Folklore*. New York: Crown Publishers, 1944.

Botkin, Gleb, *The Real Romanovs*. New York: Putnam, 1931.

Boucher, Anthony, ed., *The Quality of Murder*. New York: E. P. Dutton, 1962.

Brace, Charles Loving, *The Dangerous Classes of New York*. New York: Wynkoop & Hallenbeck, 1880.

Brenton, Myron, *The Privacy Invaders*. New York: Coward-McCann, 1964.

Briand, Paul, Jr., *Daughter of the Sky*. New York: Duell, Sloan and Pearce, 1960.

Brooks, Van Wyck. *Our Literary Heritage*. New York: Dutton, 1956.

Brown, F. Yeats, ed., *Escape*. New York: Macmillan, 1933.

Bruce, M., *Lavalette Bruce and His Adventures*. London: Marshall, Morgan & Sweet, 1953.

Brynes, Thomas, *Professional Criminals in America*. New York: Chelsea House, 1969.

Buchanan, Sir George, *My Mission to Moscow*. New York: Little, Brown, 1923.

Burgess, Robert F., *Sinkings, Salvages and Shipwrecks*. New York: American Heritage Press, 1970.

Butterfield, Roger, *The American Past*. New York: Simon and Schuster, 1947.

Bykov, P. M., *The Last Days of Tsar Nicholas*. New York: International Publishers, 1934.


Caesar, Gene, *Incredible Detective: The Biography of William J. Burns*. Englewood Cliffs, N.J.: Prentice-Hall, 1968.

Carr, John Dickson, *The Life of Sir Arthur Conan Doyle*. New York: Harper, 1949.

Casey, Robert J., *Chicago, Medium Rare*. Indianapolis: Bobbs-Merrill, 1949.

Ceram, C. W., *Archaeology of the Cinema*. New York: Harcourt, Brace & World, 1975.

Chambers, Walter, *Samuel Seabury*. New York: Century, 1932.

Charroux, Robert, *Forgotten Worlds*. New York: Walker, 1973.

Churchill, Allen, *They Never Came Back*. Garden City, N.Y.: Doubleday, 1960.

———, *A Pictorial History of American Crime*. New York: Holt, Rinehart and Winston, 1964.

Churchward, Robert, *Explorer Lost; the Story of Colonel Fawcett*. London: Routledge, 1936.

Clapp, Jane, *Vanishing Point*. New York: Scarecrow Press, 1961.

Clarke, Donald Henderson, *In the Reign of Rothstein*. New York: Vanguard Press, 1929.

Clarkson, Jesse D., *A History of Russia*. New York: Random House, 1961.

Cleveland, Catherine, Duchess of, *The True Story of Kaspar Hauser*. New York: Macmillan, 1893.

Congdon, Don, ed., *The Thirties*. New York: Simon and Schuster, 1962.

Connable, Alfred, and Silberfarb, Edward, *Tigers of Tammany Hall*. New York: Holt & Winston, 1967.

Costello, A. E., *Our Police Protectors, A History of the New York Police*. New York: C. F. Roper, 1885.

Crater, Stella Force, with Fraley, Oscar, *The Empty Robe*. Garden City, N.Y.: Doubleday, 1961.

Crichton, Robert, *The Great Impostor*. New York: Random House, 1959.


Dedman, Emmett, *Fabulous Chicago*. New York: Random House, 1963.

Duke, Captain Thomas S., *Celebrated Criminal Cases of America*. San Francisco: James H. Barry, 1910.

Dulles, Allen, *The Craft of Intelligence*. New York: Harper & Row, 1963.

Dulles, Eleanor L., *Depression and Reconstruction*. Philadelphia: University of Pennsylvania Press, 1937.

Dumas, Alexandre, *Celebrated Crimes*, translator: Jacques Wagrez. Philadelphia: Rittenhouse Press, 1895.

Duncan, Lee, *Over the Wall*. New York: Dutton, 1936.

Earhart, Amelia, *Last Flight*. New York: Harcourt, Brace, 1937.

Edwards, Frank, *Stranger Than Science*. New York: Lyle Stuart, 1959.

Eisenberg, Daniel M., as told to Beffel, John Nicholas, *I Find the Missing*. New York: Farrar & Rinehart, 1938.

Ellen, Mary, Murphy, Mark, and Weld, Ralph Foster, *A Treasury of Brooklyn*. New York: Sloane Associates, 1949.

Evans, Mrs. Elizabeth Edson (Gibson), *The Story of Kaspar Hauser from Authentic Records*. London: Swan and Sonnenschein, 1892.


Farley, Philip, *Criminals of America; or Tales of the Lives of Thieves*. New York: Philip Farley, 1876.

Fatout, Paul, *Ambrose Bierce, The Devil's Lexicographer*. Norman, Okla.: University of Oklahoma Press, 1951.

Fay, Charles Edey, *Mary Celeste, The Odyssey of an Abandoned Ship*. Salem, Mass.: Peabody Museum, 1942.

Feuerbach, Paul J. Anselm, Ritter von, *Caspar Houser*. London: Lindberg, 1834.

*Bibliography*

Finn, John T., *History of the Chicago Police from the Settlement of the Community to the Present Time.* Chicago: Police Book Fund, 1887.

Fleming, Peter, *Brazilian Adventure.* New York: Scribner's, 1934.

Fort, Charles, *Lo!* New York: C. Kendall, 1931.

Fosdick, Raymond B., *American Police Systems.* New York: Century, 1920.

Fraenkel, Franz, *Missing Persons.* Dobbs Ferry, N.Y.: Oceana Publications, 1950.

Freeborn, Richard, *A Short History of Modern Russia.* New York: Hodder & Stoughton, 1966.

Freuchen, Peter, *Peter Freuchen's Book of the Seven Seas.* New York: Julian Messner, 1957.

Furlong, Thomas, *Fifty Years A Detective.* St. Louis: C. E. Barnett, 1912.

Furneaux, Rupert, *The World's Most Intriguing True Mysteries.* New York: Arlo Publishing, 1965.


Gaddis, Vincent H., *Invisible Horizons.* Philadelphia: Chilton Books, 1965.

Gallagher, Robert S., *If I Had It to Do Over Again.* New York: Dutton, 1969.

Gavshon, Arthur L., *The Mysterious Death of Dag Hammerskjöld.* New York: Walker, 1962.

Gilbert, Paul Thomas, and Bryson, Charles Lee, *Chicago and Its Makers.* Chicago: University of Chicago Press, 1929.

Godwin, John, *This Baffling World.* New York: Hart, 1968.

Goerner, Fred, *The Search for Amelia Earhart.* Garden City, N.Y.: Doubleday & Company, 1966.

Goldfader, Ed, *Tracer!* Los Angeles, Calif.: Nash Publishing, 1970.

Gould, Rupert T., *Enigmas.* New York: University Books, 1965.

Grahame, Stephen, *New York Nights.* New York: Doran, 1927.

Greene, Laurence, *The Era of Wonderful Nonsense.* Indianapolis, Ind.: Bobbs-Merrill, 1939.

Grenander, M. E., *Ambrose Bierce.* New York: Twain Publishers, 1971.

Gribble, Francis H., *Emperor and Mystic: The Life of Alexander I of Russia.* London: Nash & Grayson, 1931.

Griffin, Bulkeys, *Offbeat History.* New York: World Publishing, 1967.


Halliburton, Richard, *The Royal Road to Romance.* Garden City, N.Y.: Garden City Publishing Company, 1925.

———, *The Famous Adventures of Richard Halliburton.* Indianapolis, Ind.: Bobbs-Merrill, 1932.

———, *The Romantic World of Richard Halliburton.* Indianapolis, Ind.: Bobbs-Merrill, 1961.

Hanser, Richard, *Putsch!* New York: Pyramid Books, 1971.

Hart, Smith, *The New Yorkers*. New York: Sheridan House, 1938.

Hawks, Francis L., *History of North Carolina*. Fayetteville, N.C.: E. J. Hale, 1857.

Hawthorne, Nathaniel, *Twice-Told Tales*. Boston: Ticknor, Reed and Fields, 1851.

Hazeltine, Rachel C., *Aimee Semple McPherson's Kidnapping*. New York: Carlton Press, 1965.

Hecht, Ben, *A Child of the Century*. New York: Simon and Schuster, 1954.

Heiden, Konrad, *Der Fuehrer*. Boston: Houghton Mifflin, 1944.

Hill, Edwin C., *The American Scene*. New York: Witmark & Sons, 1933.

Hocking, Charles, *Dictionary of Disasters at Sea During the Age of Steam*. London: Lloyd's Register of Shipping, 1969.

Hoehling, Adolph, *They Sailed into Oblivion*. New York: Thomas Yoseloff, 1959.

Hoover, J. Edgar, *Persons in Hiding*. Boston: Little, Brown, 1938.

Horan, James D., *The Desperate Years*. New York: Crown Publishers, 1962.

———, *The Pinkertons, The Detective Dynasty That Made History*. New York: Crown Publishers, 1967.

Hort, Major, *The Rock*. London: n.p., 1839.

House, Brant, *Crimes That Shocked America*. New York: Ace Books, 1961.

Howe, Irving, *Sherwood Anderson*. New York: Sloane Associates, 1951.

Hutton, J. Bernard, *Frogman Spy: The Incredible Case of Commander Crabb*. New York: McDowell, Obolensky, 1960.

Hynd, Alan, *Murder, Mayhem and Mystery*. New York: Barnes, 1958.

Irving, Henry Brodribb, *A Book of Remarkable Criminals*. New York: Doran, 1918.

———, *The Trial of the Wainwrights*. Edinburgh and London: William Hodge, 1926.

Jeffrey, Adi-Kent Thomas, *The Bermuda Triangle*. New York: Warner Paperback Library, 1975.

Jessup, Morris K., *The Case for the UFO*. New York: Citadel, 1955.

Johnson, Hugh. *The Blue Eagle from Egg to Earth*. New York: Doubleday, Doran, 1935.

Katcher, Leo, *The Big Bankroll, The Life and Times of Arnold Rothstein*. New York: Harper, 1959.

Keyhoe, Donald E., *The Flying Saucer Conspiracy*. London: Hutchinson, 1957.

Kingston, Charles, *Remarkable Rogues*. New York: John Lane, 1921.

Klein, Alexander, ed., *Grand Deception*. New York: Lippincott, 1955.

Knox, Thomas W., *Underground, or Life Below the Surface*. Hartford, Conn.: Burr, Hyde, 1873.

LaCroix, Robert de, *Mysteries of the Sea*. New York: John Day, 1956.

Landsburg, Alan and Sally. *In Search of Ancient Mysteries*. New York: Bantam, 1974.

Lang, Andrew, *Historical Mysteries*. London: Smith, Elder, 1904.

Lavigne, Frank C., *Crimes, Criminals and Detectives*. Helena, Mont.: State Publishing, 1921.

Lavine, Sigmund, *Allan Pinkerton, America's First Private Eye*. New York: Dodd, Mead, 1963.

Lefler, Hugh T., *North Carolina History Told by Contemporaries*. Chapel Hill, N.C.: University of North Carolina Press, 1934.

Leighton, Isabel, ed., *The Aspirin Age, 1919–1941*. New York: Simon and Schuster, 1949.

Leonard, Jonathan N., *Three Years Down*. New York: Carrick and Evans, 1939.

Livingston, Armstrong, and Stein, Captain John G., *The Murdered and the Missing*. New York: Stephen-Paul Publishers, 1947.

Lloyd, H. E., *Alexander I*. London: Treuttel & Wurtz, 1826.

Logan, Guy B. H., *Rope, Knife and Chair*. London: S. Paul & Co., 1930.

Lonsdale, Gordon, *Spy*. New York: Hawthorne Books, 1965.

Lord, Walter, *The Good Years*. New York: Harper, 1960.

Ludlow, Fitzhugh, *The Heart of the Continent*. New York: Hurd and Houghton, 1870.

Lynch, Denis Tilden, *Criminals and Politicians*. New York: Macmillan, 1932.

MacGregor, Geddes, *The Tichborne Impostor*. Philadelphia: Lippincott, 1957.

Mackaye, Milton, *The Tin Box Parade*. New York: McBride, 1934.

Maine, C. E., *The World's Strangest Crimes*. New York: Hart Publishing, 1967.

Malone, Dumas, *Dictionary of American Biography*. New York: Scribner's, 1933.

McAdoo, William G., *Guarding a Great City*. New York: Harper, 1906.

McClement, Fred, *The Strange Case of Ambrose Small*. Toronto: McClelland and Stewart, 1974.

McCurdy, Harold G., with Follett, Helen Thomas, *Barbara: The Unconscious Autobiography of a Child Genius*. Chapel Hill, N.C.: University of North Carolina Press, 1966.

McMaster, John Bach, *History of the People of the United States*. New York: D. Appleton, 1891.

McWatters, George S., *Knots Untied*. Hartford: Burr & Hyde, 1871.

McWilliams, Carey, *Ambrose Bierce, A Biography*. New York: A. & C. Boni, 1929.

Messick, Hank, and Goldblatt, Burt, *Kidnapping*. New York: Dial Press, 1974.

Millard, Mara, *Hail to Yesterday*. New York: Farrar & Rinehart, 1941.

Minehan, Thomas, *Boy and Girl Tramps of America*. New York: Farrar, 1934.

Mitchell, Broadus, *Depression Decade: From the New Era through the New Deal*. New York: Rinehart, 1947.

Mitgang, Herbert, *The Man Who Rode the Tiger: The Life and Times of Judge Samuel Seabury*. Philadelphia: Lippincott, 1963.

Monat, Pawel, with Dille, John, *Spy in the U.S.* New York: Harper & Row, 1961.

Myers, Gustavus, *History of Tammany Hall*. New York: Boni & Liveright, 1917.


Nash, Jay Robert, *Citizen Hoover, A Critical Study of J. Edgar Hoover and His FBI*. Chicago: Nelson-Hall Publishers, 1972.

————, *Bloodletters and Badmen, A Narrative Encyclopedia of American Criminals from the Pilgrims to the Present*. New York: M. Evans, 1973.

————, *Hustlers and Con Men, An Anecdotal History of the Confidence Man and His Games*. New York: M. Evans, 1976.

————, *Darkest Hours, A Narrative Encyclopedia of Worldwide Disasters from Ancient Times to the Present*. Chicago: Nelson-Hall, 1976.

Neale, Walter, *The Life of Ambrose Bierce*. New York: W. Neale, 1929.

Norden, Pierre, *Conan Doyle, A Biography*. New York: Holt, Rinehart & Winston, 1967.

Northrup, William B., and Northrup, John B., *The Insolence of Office*. New York: Putnam's, 1932.

Noyes, Arthur, and Kalb, Lawrence, *Modern Clinical Psychiatry*. Philadelphia: Saunders, 1958.


O'Connor, Richard, *Hell's Kitchen*. Philadelphia: Lippincott, 1958.

O'Donnell, Elliott, *Strange Disappearances*. New Hyde Park, N.Y.: University Books, 1972.

O'Sullivan, F. Dalton, *Crime Detection*. Chicago: O'Sullivan Publishing House, 1928.


Packard, Vance, *The Naked City*. New York: David McKay, 1964.

Paine, Ralph D., *Lost Ships and Lonely Seas*. New York: Century, 1922.

Paleologue, Maurice, *The Enigmatic Czar*. London: Harper & Brothers, 1938.

Pares, Sir Bernard, *History of Russia*. New York: Knopf, 1953.

Pearson, Edmund, *Masterpieces at Murder*. Boston: Little, Brown, 1924.

Pies, Herman, *Kaspar Hauser*. Stuttgart: Lutz, 1926.

Pinkerton, Allan. *Criminal Reminiscences and Detective Sketches*. New York: G. W. Dillingham, 1878.

Pinkerton, Matthew Worth, *Murder in All Ages*. New York: A. E. Pinkerton & Co., 1898.

Platnick, Kenneth B., *Great Mysteries of History*. Harrisburg, Pa.: Stackpole, 1971.

Porter, Garnett Clay, *Strange and Mysterious Crimes*. New York: McFadden Publications, 1929.

Price, H., *The Most Haunted House in England*. New York: Longmans, Green, 1940.

Pugh, Marshall, *Frogman, Commander Crabb's Story*. New York: Scribner's, 1956.

Putnam, George Palmer, *Soaring Wings, A Biography of Amelia Earhart*. New York: Harcourt, Brace, 1939.

Quinn, David B., *Raleigh and the British Empire*. London: Hodder & Stoughton, 1947.

Rathlef-Keilmann, Harriet von. *Anastasia, Survivor of Ekaterinberg*. New York: Putnam, 1928.

Reid, Ed, *Mafia*. New York: Random House, 1952.

Richards, Guy, *The Hunt for the Czar*. Garden City, N.Y.: Doubleday, 1971.

Riess, Curt, ed., *There They Were*. Putnam, 1944.

Riess, Lawrence. *She Who Was Helena Cass*. New York: Doran, 1920.

Robbins, Blackwell P., *The North Carolina Guide*. Chapel Hill, N.C.: University of North Carolina Press, 1955.

Rogers, Agnes, and Allen, Frederick Lewis, *I Remember Distinctly*. New York: Harper, 1947.

Root, Jonathan, *Halliburton, The Magnificent Myth*. New York: Coward-McCann, 1965.

Ross, Christian K., *The Father's Story of Charley Ross, the Kidnapped Child*. Philadelphia: Potter, 1876.

Rowan, Richard Wilmer, with Deindorfer, Robert G., *Secret Service, 33 Centuries of Espionage*. New York: Hawthorn Books, 1967.

——, *The Pinkertons, A Detective Dynasty*. Boston: Little, Brown, 1931.

Runyon, Damon, *Trials and Tribulations*. New York: Lippincott, 1926.

Ryan, Cornelius, *The Last Battle*. New York: Simon and Schuster, 1966.

Sanger, Joan, *The Case of the Missing Corpse*. New York: Green Circle Books, 1936.

Sann, Paul, *The Lawless Decade*. New York: Crown Publishers, 1960.

Seth, Ronald, *Unmasked: The Story of Soviet Espionage*. New York: Hawthorn Books, 1965.

Shannon, David A., ed., *The Great Impostor*. New York: Prentice-Hall, 1960.

Shirer, William L., *End of a Berlin Diary*. New York: Knopf, 1947.

Sinclair, Andrew, *Era of Excess*. New York: Harper & Row, 1964.

Singer, Kurt, ed., *My Strangest Cases*. Garden City, N.Y.: Doubleday, 1958.

Singh, Rev. J. A. L., and Zingg, Robert M., *Wolf-Children and Feral Man*. New York: Harper & Row, 1942.

Slocum, Victor, *Captain Joshua Slocum*. New York: Sheridan House, 1950.

Smith, Edward H., *Mysteries of the Missing*. New York: Dial Press, 1927.

———, *You Can Escape*. New York: Macmillan, 1929.

Snow, Edward Rowe, *Great Gales and Dire Disasters*. New York: Dodd, Mead, 1952.

———, *Mysteries and Adventures Along the Atlantic Coast*. New York: Dodd, Mead, 1948.

———, *Mysterious Tales of the New England Coast*. New York: Dodd, Mead, 1961.

———, *Unsolved Mysteries of Sea and Shore*. New York: Dodd, Mead, 1963.

Spencer, John Wallace, *Limbo of the Lost*. Westfield, Mass.: Phillips, 1969.

———, *No Earthly Explanation*. Westfield, Mass.: Phillips, 1974.

Stewart, Oliver, *Danger in the Air*. New York: Philosophical Library, 1958.

Stick, David, *The Outer Banks of North Carolina*. Chapel Hill, N.C.: University of North Carolina Press, 1958.

Stoker, Bram, *Famous Impostors*. New York: Sturgis & Walton, 1910.

Strakhovsky, L. I., *Alexander I of Russia*. New York: Norton, 1947.

Stuart, William H., *The 20 Incredible Years*. Chicago: Donohue, 1935.

Sullivan, Mark, *Our Times*. New York: Scribner's, 1926.

Sullivan, Robert, *The Disappearance of Dr. Parkman*. New York: Prentice-Hall, 1960.

Sutherland, Edwin H., *White Collar Crime*. New York: Holt, Rinehart & Winston, 1949.

Tannenbaum, Frank, *Crime and the Community*. New York: Columbia University Press, 1938.

Tanner, Louise, *All the Things We Were*. Garden City, N.Y.: Doubleday, 1968.

Teller, Walter, *Joshua Slocum*. New York: Sheridan House, 1950.

Thomas, Lately, *The Vanishing Evangelist*. New York: Viking Press, 1959.

———, *Storming Heaven*. New York: Morrow, 1970.

Thomas, Lowell, *Book of the High Mountains*. New York: Julian Messner, 1964.

Titler, Dale, *Wings of Mystery*. New York: Dodd, Mead, 1966.

Toland, John, *The Last Days*. New York: Random House, 1966.

Tomalin, Nicholas, and Hall, Ron, *The Strange Last Voyage of Donald Crowhurst*. New York: Stein and Day, 1970.

Tredgold, A. F., *Mental Deficiency*. New York: William Wood and Co., 1920.

Trevor-Roper, H. R., *The Last Days of Hitler*. New York: Crowell-Collier, 1962.

Tully, Andrew, *Era of Elegance*. New York: Funk & Wagnalls, 1947.

Villiers, Alan, *Posted Missing*. New York: Scribner's, 1956.

Vorres, Ivan, *The Last Grand Duchess*. New York: Scribner, 1964.

Vyrubeva, Anna, *Memories of the Russian Court*. New York: Macmillan, 1933.

Walker, Stanley, *The Night Club Era*. New York: Stokes, 1933.

Walling, George, *Recollections of a New York Chief of Police*. New York: Caxton Books, 1887.

Waters, James F., *The Court of Missing Heirs*. New York: Modern Age Books, 1941.

Waters, R., *Undiscovered Crimes*. London: n.p., 1862.

Wecter, Dixon, *The Age of the Great Depression: 1929–1941*. New York: Macmillan, 1941.

Wellman, Manly Wade, *Dead and Gone*. Chapel Hill, N.C.: University of North Carolina Press, 1934.

Weston, J. A., *Historic Doubts as to the Execution of Ney*. New York: T. Whittaker, 1895.

Weyer, Edward, Jr., *Jungle Quest*. New York: Harper, 1955.

White, Ray Lewis, ed., *Sherwood Anderson's Memoirs: A Critical Edition*. Chapel Hill, N.C.: University of North Carolina Press, 1969.

Wilkins, Harold T., *Strange Mysteries of Time and Space*. New York: Citadel Press, 1959.

Wilkins, W. H., *Love of an Uncrowned Queen*. London: Longmans, Green, 1900.

Winter, Lumen, and Degner, Glenn, *Minute Epics of Flight*. New York: Grosset & Dunlap, 1933.

Wise, David, and Ross, Thomas B., *The Invisible Government*. New York: Random House, 1967.

————, *The Espionage Establishment*. New York: Random House, 1967.

Woodruff, Douglas, *The Tichborne Claimant*. London: Hullis & Charter, 1967.

Woollcott, Alexander, *While Rome Burns*. New York: Grosset & Dunlap, 1934.

Wraxall, Lascelles, *Remarkable Adventure and Unrevealed Mysteries,* Vols. I, II. London: W. H. Allen, 1865.

Wren, Melvin C., *The Course of Russian History.* New York: Macmillan, 1963.

Young, Filson, ed., *The Trial of Hawley Harvey Crippen.* Edinburgh and London: William Hodge, 1926.

Zierold, Norman, *Little Charley Ross.* Boston: Little, Brown, 1967.

**PERIODICALS**

Adlerstein, F. R., "How Europe's Lost Are Found," *American Mercury,* October 1945.

Alexander, Jack, "What Happened to Judge Crater?" *Saturday Evening Post,* September 10, 1960.

"The American Cheka," *Freeman,* February 28, 1923.

"Amnesia: Genuine or Faked?" *Science Digest,* May 1950.

"Amnesia Often Faked!" *Science Digest,* February 1952.

"Amnesia Victims Recover Easily," *Science Digest,* November 1957.

Anderson, Robert T., "From Mafia to Cosa Nostra," *American Journal of Sociology,* November 1965.

Asimov, Isaac, "That Odd Chemical Complex, The Human Mind," *New York Times Magazine,* July 3, 1966.

Austin, Mary, "George Sterling at Carmel," *The American Mercury,* May 1927.

Bariatinsky, V., "Mysterious Hermit," *Fortnightly Review,* May 1913.

Bell, Daniel, "Crime as an American Way of Life," *Antioch Review,* June 1953.

Blair, Lorne, "Is This the Man Who Ate Michael Rockefeller?" *Oui Magazine,* April 1977.

"Blaming the Giant Octopus for the 'Cyclops' Mystery," *Literary Digest,* March 8, 1919.

Bloom, Murray Teigh, "Is It Judge Crater's Body?" *Harper's Magazine,* November 1959.

Bolitho, William, "The Natural History of Graft," *The Survey,* April 1931.

Bourke, Charles Francis, "Pinkerton's National Detective Agency," *Strand Magazine,* November 1905.

Brean, Herbert, and Conant, Luther, "The Mystery of the Missing Cadet," *Life,* April 14, 1952.

———, "The Mystery of the Frogman's Dive for the Red Secrets," *Life,* May 28, 1956.

Briand, Paul, Jr., "Was She on a Secret Mission?" *Ms. Magazine,* September 1976.

"Brother of the Pilot Spreads the Word," *Life,* March 12, 1965.

Browning, Norma Lee, "The Truth About Amnesia," *Science Digest,* May 1959.

Burns, William J., "Disappearance of Edna Kent," *Woman's Home Companion,* December 1915.

Call, George Cotsford, "The Search for the Lost Mr. Bathurst," *Westminster Review,* October 1890.

Carlson, Eric T., "The Unfortunate Dr. Parkman," *American Journal of Psychiatry,* December 1966.

Carson, Charles, "One Underworld," *Author and Journalist,* November 1945.

"A Child Is Lost—and Found," *Time,* August, 9, 1971.

"Colonel Fawcett's Expedition in Matto Grosso," *Geographical Journal,* February 1928.

Cusack Michael, "The Deadly Mystery of the Devil's Triangle," *Science World,* September 20, 1973.

"Dead for 22 Years," *Life,* December 7, 1953.

"Dead or Alive?" *Newsweek,* February 22, 1965.

Deindorfer, Robert G., "Agatha Christie at 84, Still Getting Away With Murder," *Parade,* December 8, 1974.

"Detective Burns and His Psychological Method," *Current Literature,* June 1911.

"Disappearance of Bathurst, The," *Cornhill Magazine,* January 1887.

"Disappearance of the Cyclops, Another Mystery of the Deep," *Literary Digest,* June 8, 1918.

Doyle, Arthur Conan, "J. Habakuk Jephson's Statement," *Cornhill Magazine,* January 1884.

Eckert, Allen W., "The Mystery of the Lost Patrol," *American Legion Magazine,* April 1962.

Edelberg, Jerome, "The Mystery of the West Point Cadet," *Coronet,* November 1954.

Eisenberg, Daniel M., "I Bring Them Back," *Scribner's Commentator,* February 1941.

Elliott, Lawrence, "What Happened to Dorothy Arnold?" *Coronet,* November 1953.

————, "The Mystery of Amelia Earhart's Last Flight," *Reader's Digest,* July 1957.

Fales, Edward D., Jr., "Lost Boy on Casper Mountain," *Reader's Digest,* January 1972.

"The Fate of Colonel Fawcett," *Geographical Journal,* July 1936.

"Father and Son," *Newsweek,* December 4, 1961.

Fawcett, P. H., "The Lost City of My Quest," *Blackwood's Magazine,* January 1933.

Fluegel, Edna R., "The Burgess-Maclean Case." *American Mercury,* February 1957.

Follett, Wilson, "To a Daughter One Year Lost," *Atlantic,* May 1941.

"Footloose, But Not Fancy-Free," *Time,* August 22, 1969.

Gaddis, Vincent H., "The Deadly Bermuda Triangle," *Argosy,* February 1964.

Gatlin, Dana, "Tracking Anonymous Letter Writers," *McClure's,* April 1911.

Grahame, Arthur, "Missing! How Strange Diseases Accounts for Army of Lost Persons," *Popular Science Monthly,* August 1933.

Hamill, Pete, "The Cult of Amelia Earhart," *Ms. Magazine,* September 1976.

"Has Mount Everest Been Conquered?" *Current Opinion,* September 1924.

"He Has Orange Socks," *Newsweek,* September 3, 1962.

"Hell to Purgatory," *Newsweek,* September 11, 1961.

Hicks, Albert C., "Blood in the Streets," *New York Times Magazine,* December 15, 1957.

Hindman, William P., Jr., "The Presumption Against Suicide in Disappearance Cases," *The Insurance Law Journal,* November 1965.

Hirshberg, Al, "The Long Search of Laurie Van Buren," *Good Housekeeping,* July 1967.

"History of William J. Burns," *The Nation,* November 23, 1927.

Hodges, Mary Jane, "Where Is Mrs. Forstein?" *Coronet,* September 1954.

Hogan, Don, "Who Is the Living 'Unknown Soldier'?" *Collier's,* October 12, 1956.

"Human Chain Hunts Lost Boy," *Life,* November 1, 1954.

Hynd, Alan, "America's Front Page Detective," *True,* March 1951.

"It Seems Silly Now," *Newsweek,* December 7, 1953.

Jacobs, Stanley S., "Who Am I?" *Todays Health,* July 1959.

Jarintzoff, N., "Legend of Alexander I and the Hermit Theodor Kowzmitch." *Contemporary Review,* June 1912.

Jarman, Rufus, "The Pinkerton Story," *Saturday Evening Post,* May 15, 22, June 5, 1948.

"Journey's End," *Time,* November 23, 1953.

Kobler, John, "Where Is Lyde Marland?" *Saturday Evening Post,* November 22, 1958.

"Lapses of Memory." *Literary Digest,* December 24, 1932.

"A Last, Long Look for Danny Dawson," *Life,* October 8, 1965.

"Law and Order," *Illustrated London Times,* January–February 1868.

Lessing, Lawrence, "Inside the Molecules of the Mind," *Fortune,* July 1966.

Liebler, Leslie, "Limbo of Lost Ships," *This Week,* August 4, 1968.

"Lost, Strayed, Stolen," *Holiday,* May 1949.

Lyons, D. L., "Steve Allen's Search for His Lost Brother," *Ladies Home Journal,* December 1974.

Mallory, George Leigh, "The Assault on Mount Everest," *Living Age,* November 11, 1922

———, "Everest Unvanquished," *Asia Magazine,* September 1923.

Manning, Gordon, "The Most Tantalizing Disappearance of Our Time," *Collier's,* July 29, 1950.

"Martin Guerre," *All Year Round, A Weekly Journal Conducted by Charles Dickens,* June 29, 1867.

Martin, John Bartlow, "Have You Seen Orja Corns?" *Saturday Evening Post,* March 4, 1950.

Martin, John Stuart, "When the President Disappeared," *American Heritage,* October 1957.

McDonell, Michael, "Lost Patrol," *Naval Aviation News,* June 1973.

McMorrow, Thomas, "Skip Tracers," *The Saturday Evening Post,* September 18, 1943.

McWilliams, Carey, "The Mystery of Ambrose Bierce," *The American Mercury,* March 1931.

Mencken, H. L., "George Sterling Poet," *Literary Digest,* December 11, 1926.

———, "The Ambrose Bierce Mystery," *The American Mercury,* September 1929.

Miller, J. Earle, "Mysteries of the Sea," *Popular Mechanics,* July 1926.

Mills, James, "The Detective," *Life,* December 12, 1965.

"Missile Age Mystery." *Newsweek,* October 1, 1962.

"The Missing Judge." *Newsweek,* August 29, 1959.

"Mount Everest Kills and Conquers." *Literary Digest,* July 12, 1924.

Murphy, T. E. "Amnesia—Civilian Shell Shock." *Liberty Magazine,* January 23, 1943.

"Mystery of the Cyclops, The," *Scientific American,* May 1934.

"Mystery of the Kidnapped Baby." *Life,* September 22, 1952.

"Mysterious Disappearance at Turkey Creek." *Life Magazine,* February 22, 1960.

Nash, Jay Robert, "Terrible Tommy and the Waiting Gallows," *Chicago Land Magazine,* March 1968.

Nobile, Philip, "The Strange Search for Martin Bormann," *Midwest Magazine* (*Chicago Sun-Times*), November 24, 1974.

O'Higgins, Harvey J., "The Amateur Detectives," *McClure's,* November 1911.

Palmer, John Williamson, "The Pinkertons," *Century Magazine,* February 1892.
Parkhurst, Genevieve, "Missing," *Good Housekeeping,* March 1921.
Pitman, Jack, "Amelia Earhart's Last Flight," *Coronet,* February 1956.
Porter, Charles O., "The Butcher of the Caribbean," *Coronet,* June 1957.

"Reconciliation." *World's Work,* July 1908.
Rinehart, John C., "Tracing People—Lost, Stolen and Strayed Away," *The American City,* October 1929.
Robinson, Ted, Jr., "How to Disappear," *Harper's Magazine,* March 1952.
"Runaway Boy and Girl Problem, The," *Literary Digest,* May 10, 1924.

Sand, George X., "Sea Mystery at Our Back Door." *Fate,* October 1952.
Sanderson, Ivan T., "The Spreading Mystery of the Bermuda Triangle," *Argosy,* August 1968.
Scott, E. Kilburn, "Career of L. A. A. LePrince," *Journal of SMPE,* July 1931.
"Search for Michael." *Time,* December 1, 1961.
"The Search for Missing Men," *The Literary Digest,* November 19, 1932.
"Search for the Lost Mr. Bathurst," *Westminster Review,* Vol. CXXXIV.
Shockwill, George Archie, "Wolf-children," *Lippincott's Monthly Magazine,* January–June, 1898.
"Silent Mystery," *Time,* December 12, 1955.
Sitwell, Sir Osbert, "New York in the Twenties," *Atlantic,* February 1962.
Smith, Marshall, "The Devil's Triangle," *Cosmopolitan,* September 1973.
"Speaking of Pictures," *Time,* December 12, 1955.
"Star of the Secret Service," *Overland Monthly,* January 1908.
Sterling, George, "The Shadow Maker," *The American Mercury,* September 1925.
Stolley, Richard B., "So Bad Even the Bloody Trees Can't Stand Up," *Life,* December 1, 1961.
Sufrin, Mark, "The Case of the Disappearing Cook," *American Heritage,* August 1970.

Tazelaar, Marguerite. "The Harbor-Master at the Port of Missing Men," *The Literary Digest,* September 8, 1934.
Thistlewayte, M., "Memoirs and Correspondence of Dr. Henry Bathurst," *Cornhill Magazine,* January–June 1887.

429

Thomas, Frank P., "The Mystery of the Missing Persons," *Reader's Digest* May 1961.

"Tom Cat and the Colonel," *Time*, February 9, 1970.

"Travelers Who Never Return," *The Literary Digest*, December 29, 1923.


"Undiscovered Daughter," *Newsweek*, September 15, 1952.

"U.S. Special Project Linked to UFOs," *U.F.O. Investigator*, June–September 1963.


"Vanishing Americans." *Newsweek*, February 24, 1964.

Varney, Harold Lord, "What Is Behind the Galindez Case?" *American Mercury*, June 1957.

"Visitors in Limbo," *Time*, December 7, 1953.


"Weird Clue in the Crater Mystery," *Life*, November 16, 1959.

Welles, Chris, "Man with Two Wives—Amnesia or Hoax?" *Life*, March 5, 1965.

Wells, W. Calvin, Jr., "When the Insured Disappears," *Mississippi Law Journal*, Vol. 35.

"When a Man Imagines He Is Someone Else," *Literary Digest*, December 10, 1932.

"Where Is Steven Damman?" *Life*, April 17, 1956.

"The Wild Child," *Newsweek*, September 9, 1971.

"William J. Burns," *McClure's*, February 1911.

Wilson, Edmund, "Ambrose Bierce on the Owl Creek Bridge," *The New Yorker*, December 8, 1951.

Winchester, James, "Port of Missing Seaman," *Senior Scholastic*, February 1956.

Winer, Richard, "Bermuda Triangle—UFO Twilight Zone," *Saga*, August–September 1972.

Winkler, John K., "Where Are They Now?" *Collier's*, November 21, 1925.

Wisehart, M. K., "The Trail of Missing Persons," *Saturday Evening Post*, May 3, 1924.


DOCUMENTS, PAMPHLETS AND REPORTS

"Bermuda Triangle Adds to Baffling Sea Lore," *National Geographic News Bulletin*, December 22, 1967.

Board of Investigation into five missing TBM airplanes and one PBM airplane converted by Naval Air Advanced Training Command, NAS Jacksonville, Florida, December 7, 1945, and related correspondence, Washington, D.C., U.S. Navy, 1946.

"Collier Cyclops Mystery Still Causes Speculation," *Proceedings*, September 1923, U.S. Naval Institute.

Dewey, John, *New York and the Seabury Investigations.* New York: City Affairs Commission, 1933.

*Documents A/5069 and Add 1,* United Nations Study, New York, April 1962.

Nervig, Conrad A., "The Cyclops Mystery," *Proceedings,* July 1969, U.S. Naval Institute.

*Report,* Bureau of the Budget, Washington, D.C., July 1966.

*Report of the Court Investigation of the Accident to the Tudor IV Aircraft "Star Tiger" G-AHNP, on the 30th January, 1948* (Cmd. 7517). London: His Majesty's Stationery Office, 1948 (Ministry of Civil Aviation).

*Report* (on Borley Rectory), Society for Psychical Research, 1954.

*Report on the Loss of Tudor IVb Star Ariel G-AGRE Which Disappeared on a Flight Between Bermuda and Kingston (Jamaica) on 17th January, 1949* (M.C.A.P. 78). London: His Majesty's Stationery Office (Ministry of Civil Aviation).

Seabury, Samuel, *Final Report of Investigation of the Magistrate's Courts in the First Judicial Departments.* New York, March 1932.

*Social Aspects of the Depression.* New York: Social Science Research Council, 1937.

"United States Asks Dominican Republic to Reopen Gerald Murphy Case," *United States Department of State Bulletin,* April 15, 1957.

**NEWSPAPERS**

The following newspapers were used extensively in researching this book. Many—such as *The New York Times* and *The Times* of London—at one time or another specialized in missing-persons cases. All herein apply to disappearances receiving major profiles; however, dates of use are too numerous to cite here.

*Akron Beacon-Journal*
*Anchorage* (Alas.) *Daily News*
*Arizona Republic*
*Asbury Park* (N.J.) *Press*
*Atlanta Constitution*
*Baltimore Sun*
*Boston Evening Post*
*Boston Globe*
*Brooklyn Daily Eagle*
*Casper* (Wyo.) *Star-Tribune*
*Charlotte* (N.C.) *News*
*Chicago Daily News*
*Chicago Sun-Times*

*Chicago Today*
*Chicago Tribune*
*Christian Science Monitor*
*Cincinnati Enquirer*
*Cleveland Leader*
*Cleveland Plain Dealer*
*Columbia Missourian*
*Daily Hampshire Gazette* (Northampton Mass.)
*Denver Daily News*
*Denver Post*
*Denver Rocky Mountain News*
*DetroitFree Press*
*Detroit News*
*Eagle-Tribune* (Lawrence, Mass.)
*Elkart* (Indiana) *Daily Truth*
*Elyria Chronicle-Telegram*
*Gadsden* (Ala.) *Times*
*Germantown Courier*
*Germantown Telegraph*
*Hartford Courant*
*Houston Post*
*Indianapolis News*
*Indianapolis Star*
*Jacksonville* (Ill.) *Journal*
*Jersey Journal*
*Kansas City Times*
*Kansas City Star*
*Lockport* (N.Y.) *Union Sun & Journal*
*London Daily Graphic*
*London Daily News*
*London Daily Mail*
*London Evening Post*
*London Gazette*
*London Globe*
*Los Angeles Examiner*
*Los Angeles Times*
*Miami Herald*
*Milwaukee Journal*
*Milwaukee Sentinel*
*Minneapolis Tribune*
*Monterey* (Calif.) *Peninsula Herald*
*Montreal Star*
*Newark Daily Advertiser*

*Newark Evening News*
*Newark* (N.J.) *Star Ledger*
*New Haven Register*
*New Orleans Picayune*
*New Orleans Times-Democrat*
*News Journal* (Mansfield, Ohio)
*News of the World*
*New York Daily News*
*New York Herald Tribune*
*New York Journal*
*New York Mirror*
*New York Post*
*New York Sun*
*New York Times*
*New York Tribune*
*New York World*
*New York World Journal Tribune*
*New York World-Telegram*
*Norfolk Star-Ledger*
*Oakland* (Calif.) *Tribune*
*O Fornal* (Rio de Janeiro)
*Omaha Sun*
*Omaha World-Herald*
*The Oregonian*
*Paris* (France) *Herald*
*Penny Illustrated Newspaper* (London, England)
*Pittsburgh Post-Gazette*
*Pittsburgh Press*
*Philadelphia Evening Bulletin*
*Philadelphia Evening Star*
*Philadelphia Illustrated New Age*
*Philadelphia Inquirer*
*Philadelphia North American*
*Philadelphia Record*
*Philadelphia Public Ledger*
*Philadelphia Times*
*Point Pleasant* (N.J.) *Leader*
*Providence Journal*
*Salt Lake City Times*
*San Francisco Chronicle*
*San Francisco Examiner*
*San Jose Mercury*
*San Jose Mercury News*

433

*Bibliography*

*South Carolina Gazette*
*St. Louis Globe-Democrat*
*St. Louis Post-Dispatch*
*St. Petersburg (Fla.) Times*
*Syracuse Herald-Journal*
*Syracuse Post-Standard*
*Toronto Star*
*Trenton (N.J.) Record*
*Troy (N.Y.) Record*
*Tucson Citizen*
*Tucson Star*
*The Wall Street Journal*
*Washington Post*
*Washington Star*
*Wilmington Star News*

Cox, Richard Colvin, 261–65, 403
Crabb, Lionel Kenneth Philip, 235–239, 405
Craig, Charles L., 188
Crain, District Attorney Thomas C. T., 185
Crater, Douglas, 173
Crater, Frank, 173
Crater, J. F. "Pa," 173
Crater, Judge Joseph Force, 163, 173–89, 391
Crater, Lelia Montague, 173
Crater, Margaret, 173
Crater, Montague, 173
Crater, Stella Mance (Wheeler), 173, 174, 176, 177, 179, 182, 183, 185, 186, 187, 188
Cream, Thomas Neil, 369
Crillon Hotel, 201
Criminal Courts Building (Chicago), 385
Crippen, Cora Turner (Kunigunde Mackamotzki), 134–39, 377
Crippen, Hawley Harvey ("John Philip Robinson"), 134–39
Croiset, Gerary, 188
Crooked Creek (Medicine Lodge, Kansas), 365
Crosswhite, John R. ("John R. Cross"), 56, 395
Crowe, Pat, 106
Crowley, Forrest Lee, 144–46
Crowley, Seaborn, 144, 145
Cudahy, Edward A., Sr., 105, 106
Cudahy, Edward A., Jr., 105–06, 373
Culinary and Bartender's Union, 143–44
Cummings, John, 162
Current Opinion, 84
Curtiss, E. W., 310
Curtiss, Grace, 310, 382
Curtiss, Mrs. E. W., 310
Curtiss School of Aviation, 213
Cutbush, Thomas, 369
Cutty Sark, 70
Cyclops, 381

Daguerre, Louis, 158
Dahl, Harry, 309, 378
Dahl, Mrs. John, 309
Dalton, J. Frank ("Jesse James"), 277
Daly, Det., 341
Damman, Mrs. Marilyn, 260
Damman, Steven, 260–61, 404
Dancing Partner (musical), 178, 181, 182
Daniel, William, 385
Daniels, Frank, 130
Dare, Ananias, 318
Dare, Mrs. Eleanor, 318
Dare, Virginia, 318
Darrow, Clarence, 109, 383
Dassault, Marcel, 413
Davidson, Robertson C., 374

Davis, Edward, 190–91
Davis, John Edgar, 387
Day, Lt. W. T., 332–33, 387
Deal, Pvt. Edward, 395
Degnan, Suzanne, 110, 400
DeHaven, Mrs. Hugh, 68
Dei Gratia, 336, 337
de la Croix, Robert, 77
de la Maza, Octavio, 231
Delaware River, 259
Delbreuve, Madame Eva, 384
Dellow, Thomas, 357
Dellow, Mrs. Thomas, 357
Delmar, Abbé, 157–58
Demarest, Charles, 316
Denning, Sydney, 254–55, 386
Densel, Rev. Cornelius, 23–25, 383
Denver Art Museum, 242
Denver Post, 243, 244
Department of Justice, 346
The Desperate Years (Horan), 141
Detroit Free Press, 203
Deveau, Oliver, 336, 337
Devil's Sea, 335
Dew, Chief Inspector Walter, 136–138
Dias-Moreya, Melchior (Moribeca), 87
Dickens, Charles, 276
Diderici ("Captain Fritz Alswanger"), 331, 357
Diemschutz, Louis, 368
Dillinger, John Herbert, 394
Dillingham, Charles B., 130
Disappearance and Theory Thereof (Hern), 329
Dodge, Donald A., 382
Dominican Minimum Wage Committee, 230
Dominion Bank (Toronto), 268, 269
Donkersloot, Mrs. William, 23
Donnellan, Judge George L., 165
Doughty, Edward, 283
Doughty, John ("Charles B. Cooper"), 268, 269
Doughty, Katherine, 283, 287
Douglas, Leonard, 378
Douglass, Joseph, 104
Doyle, Arthur Conan, 270, 350, 369
Doylestown Hospital (Pa.), 344
Dracula (Stoker), 284
Dreyfus, Capt. Alfred, 281
Drover, Abby, 113–14, 413
Duffield, Gordon, 384
Duner, Gustav ("Capt. de Montalt"), 65–66, 380
Dunlevy, Elsie, 112–13, 386
Dunlevy, John, 113
Dupré, M., 155
Dutcher, Harold, 394
Dutcher, Mary, 394
Dye, Carolyn, 313, 314, 315
Dye, Kevin, 312–17, 420
Dye, Philip, 312, 313, 314, 315
Dyott, Commander George, 91

Earhart, Amelia Mary, 210–27, 396
Earhart, Edwin Stanton, 211, 213, 214
Earhart, Mrs. Edwin Stanton, 211, 213, 214, 225
Earhart, Muriel Grace, 211, 212, 214
East River (New York), 104
Eddowes, Catherine, 368
Eden, Anthony, 238–39
Edison, Gov., 384
Edison, Thomas, 158
Edward, Duke of Clarence, 369
Edward, Henry L., 245–46, 367
Egbert, Mrs. Barbara, 242–43
Eiffel Tower, 201
El Caribe, 410
Electoral Palace (Hanover), 322, 323, 324
Elizabeth Buxton Hospital (Newport News, Va.), 304
Ellen Austin, 366
Ellis, Emil K., 187, 188
Elson, Albert, 269
Elyria Chronicle-Telegram, 73
Empire Trust Company (New York), 180
Empress of China, 31
Empress of Ireland, 138
The End of Her Honeymoon (Belloc-Lowndes), 203
Engaged Girl's Sketches, An (Blake), 26
Enget, LaVern, 260, 404
Enoch Arden, 123
Epes, Horace, 94
Epworth, James H., 48–49, 384
The Era of Trujillo (Galindez), 230, 234–35
Erebus, 77
Erie Railroad, 24
Ernst, Morris, 233
Espaillat, Arturo, 232
Estes, Sheriff William, 313, 314, 315
Evans, William, 253
Everest Committee, 82
Ewald, Judge George F., 177, 178, 188

Factor, Jake "The Barber," 393
Faithfull, Starr, 392
Fales, Edward D., Jr., 313
Famous Impostors (Stoker), 284–285
Father Dempsey's Hotel (St. Louis), 395
Fawcett, Jack, 88, 91, 93
Fawcett, Col. Percy Harrison, 77, 86–93, 96, 388
Fawn Press, 210
Fay, Lorraine, 180, 181

Hazelton, Judge, 393
Hazelton, Edgar F., 392
Heady, Bonnie B., 110
Healy, Martin J., 177, 178
Hearst, Patricia Campbell, 412
Hearst, William Randolph, 80, 356
Heaton, Ed, 63
Heaton, Rita ("Kay Johnson"), 62–63
Hecht, Ben, 72
Heckscher State Park, 310, 311
Heidelbach, Ickelheimer & Company, 47
Heidelbach, Seward, 47, 375
Heirens, Williams, 110
Hemingway, Ernest, 170
Henderson, Loy W., 207
Henderson, Robert S., 386
Henry, O. (William Sydney Porter), 53
Henry, Thomas R., 53
Hepburn, Katharine, 354
Hern, Dr. Maximilian, 329
Hess, Mrs. James, 309
Hickman, Edward, 110
Hill, Edwin C., 320–21
Hill, John, 132
Hill, L. T., 127, 128
Hillary, Edmund, 83
Hillhouse High (New Haven, Conn.), 351
Hillmon, John W., 364
Hillmon, Mrs. John W., 364
Himmel, George A., 372
*Hinemoa*, 70
Hitchcock, Alfred, 204
Hitler, Adolf, 256, 375–76
Hoffa, James Riddle, 412–13
Hoffman, William, 340
Hogan, Don, 70
Hogarth, Dr., 89
Hohenzollern (dynasty), 321
Holland House (Newark, N.J.), 340
Holland Tunnel (New York), 345
Hollywood Park Race Track, 54
Holmberg, Professor Carl Vernon ("Verne Hansen"), 55–56, 405
Holmes, John Maurice, 116
Holmes, Sherlock (fictional character), 270, 350
Holzapfel, Floyd Albert ("Lucky"), 170, 171, 172, 173
*Homeric*, 388
Hoover, President Herbert, 50, 51, 53, 174
Hoover, J. Edgar, 244, 343, 344, 348
*Hope Star*, 401
Horan, James D., 141
*Horatio*, 373
Hospital College (Cleveland), 134
Hotel Sacher (Vienna), 18
Hotel Thayer (West Point, New York), 264
Houck, Mrs. Gladys, 388–89

*A House Is Not a Home* (Adler), 140
Howard, Fred R., 254
Howard, James, 373
Howard, Minnie, 254
Howard-Burg, Col. C. K., 83
*Huasco*, 391
Hubbard, Fred D., 131–32, 410
Hudson's Bay Company, 118
Huerta, Victoriano, 81
Hughes, Howard, 289
Hughes, Rupert, 66
Hurkos, Peter, 411
Hurley, Gen. Patrick J., 377
Hurley, William, 377
Huron Road Hospital (Cleveland), 72
Hutton, J. Bernard, 239
Hyde Park High School (Chicago), 211
Hydro Harrogate resort (Yorkshire, England), 75

*I Am a Fugitive from a Chain Gang* (Burns), 383
Iguassu Ximary River, 91
Ingwerson, Gustav F., 242, 243
Irvine, Andrew C., 82, 84
Irwin, May, 130
*Itasca*, U.S.S., 221, 222, 223, 224

Jack the Ripper, 252, 368–69
Jackson, Donald, 233
Jaediker, Kermit, 187
"Jameson, Charles A.," 69–71
Jameson-Carr, Dr. George, 392
Jansen, Eibrink, 100
Jaques, Fred, 199, 200, 373
Jaques, John Charles, 199, 200
Jefferson, Thomas, 167
Jeffs, Amelia, 102, 369
Jenkins, Phillip, 390
*John and Mary*, 393
Johnson, Doris Lee, 304–05
Johnson, Frederick A., 181
Johnson, John Lee, 304–05, 400
Jones, Mrs. Gertrude, 251–52, 408
Jones, Luther Maynard, 44–45, 372
Jones, Mrs. Mary, 387
Jones, Rev. Levi, 44
*Joyita*, 405
Judge, James J., 253, 377
*Jungle Quest* (Weyer), 93
*Jungle, The* (Sinclair), 106

Kachnyez, John, 247–48, 391
Kahler, Fred, 176, 182–83
Kalapalo Indian tribe, 91, 93
Kasler, John, 378
KBON-Radio (Omaha), 58
Kay, Jean, 413
Kearns, John, 386
Kearns, Mrs. John, 386
Keen, Dr. William W., 370
Keith, John S., 29–30
Kelley, Patrick F., 291–92, 373

Kelly, Dr. Arthur G., 117
Kelly, "Black" Mary Jane, 368
Kelly, George "Machine-Gun," 115
Kelly, James, 247, 389
Kelly, Police Capt. James A., 120, 121, 122
Kemper, John, 367
Kemper, Leonard, 367
Kendall, Capt. Henry, 138
Kenny, Albert L., 377
Kennedy, George, 374
Kennedy, John, 374
Kennedy, Minnie ("Ma"), 31, 34, 35, 37, 40
Kent, Ada Constance, 397
Kentucky Military Institute, 78
Kenward, Deputy Chief Constable, 75
Keppel's Head Hotel (Portsmouth, England), 238
Kerby, Henry, 229
Keser, Robert, 344
KETV-TV (Omaha), 58, 59
Keyes, District Attorney Asa, 38, 40, 41
Khrushchev, Nikita, 236
Killelea, Charles F., 308–09, 379
Kimble, Abe, 261
Kimble, Ben W., 261, 385
Kimsey, Herman, 381
Kindley Field (Bermuda), 401
King, Gladys, 26
King, Timothy, 115
Kinner, William, 214
Kirschner, Leo, 108
Klass, Joseph, 225
Klein, William, 182
Klitzing, Captain, 326, 327
Knight's Hall (Hanover Palace), 323
Knipschild, William, 108
Knoop, George F. ("John L. Deviland"), 125–27, 408
Knoop, Janice, 125, 126, 127
*Kobenhaven*, 390
Kobylansky, Emily, 398
Koehnemann, Henry C. ("Henry C. Schwenck"), 372–73
Kokish, John, 243
Königsmarck, Count Philippe von, 321–25
Königsmarck, Frederick William von, 323
Konuzmitch, Fyodor, 358
Kotor, Adm. V. F., 238
Koven, Jean de, 396
Kraft, Mrs. Margaret, 304
Kraus, Bertram, 355
Krist, Gary Steven, 409
Krowick, Louis, 111
Krupskaya, Nadezhda, 307

**443**

JAY ROBERT NASH writes a syndicated column on crime and contributes frequently on the subject for magazines. He was formerly a reporter and a magazine editor and publisher. Nash is the author of numerous books, including *Dillinger: Dead or Alive?; Citizen Hoover; Bloodletters and Badmen; Hustlers and Con Men;* and *Darkest Hours*. He has one of the most extensive private libraries on crime, including more than fifty thousand books, and untold resources consisting of photographs, clippings, and personal letters. He lives in Chicago.

*About the Author*